Michael Wadle

LAW, CUSTOM AND SOCIAL ORDER

AFRICAN STUDIES SERIES 45

BOOKS IN THIS SERIES

LAW, CUSTOM AND SOCIAL ORDER

The Colonial Experience in
Malawi and Zambia

MARTIN CHANOCK

Senior Lecturer in Legal Studies
La Trobe University, Melbourne

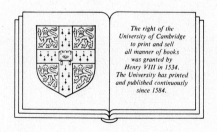

*The right of the
University of Cambridge
to print and sell
all manner of books
was granted by
Henry VIII in 1534.
The University has printed
and published continuously
since 1584.*

CAMBRIDGE UNIVERSITY PRESS

CAMBRIDGE

LONDON   NEW YORK   NEW ROCHELLE

MELBOURNE   SYDNEY

Published by the Press Syndicate of the University of Cambridge
The Pitt Building, Trumpington Street, Cambridge CB2 1RP
32 East 57th Street, New York, NY10022, USA
10 Stamford Road, Oakleigh, Melbourne 3166, Australia

First published 1985

Printed in Great Britain at the University Press, Cambridge

Library of Congress catalogue card number: 84-23207

British Library Cataloguing in Publication Data

Chanock, Martin
Law, custom and social order: the colonial
experience in Malawi and Zambia. – (African
studies series; no. 45)
1. Customary Law – Malawi – History
2. Customary law – Zambia – History
I. Title   II. Series
340.5'2'6897   [LAW]

ISBN 0 521 30137 8

CE

FOR KATE

Contents

Preface

Any historical study depends on its sources and it is therefore appropriate to introduce this book with some comments on the materials on which it is based. The book developed from, and later came to dominate, an interest in the social and economic history of the colonial period. My original concern in using the colonial archives was simply to see what could be learnt about this history by using the surviving records of the local courts, and the files of the Legal and Judicial departments, which were usually passed over by researchers in favour of the more general Secretariat files and District reports. It was only after leaving Central Africa in 1973 that I began to think seriously of using my materials for the more specific purpose of legal history. I began also with the intention of concentrating on the Eastern districts of Zambia and the neighbouring areas of Malawi across the colonial border. For Malawi many of the local records for the period prior to 1920 had been destroyed by fire so I had to fall back on central administration records, though I was able to use both local and central rcords for the period 1920 to 1931, the date up to which the Malawi archives were open at the time of my access to them. In the absence of full local records for my chosen area I broadened the study to include the protectorate as a whole, though elements of the original focus remained. For Zambia the pattern of archival use was different. Local records were available and these were supplemented by central administration files prior to the 1930s. In addition I was able to extend the Zambian side of the study to the late 1940s by having work on specific topics done for me in the Zambian archives. I tried to provide a counterpart to this on the Malawian side, by reading, in the Public Record Office in London, the reports submitted for these years to the Colonial Office. In rounding off developments towards the end of the high colonial period I have mined, as a primary source, the published works of the researchers of the Rhodes–Livingstone Institute.

These preliminary comments raise a major point deserving of comment. The records I have used have been those of the colonisers' instruments of government, and the observations of auxiliaries ranging from missionaries to anthropologists. This means that the work substantially concerns those aspects of African law, life and dispute-processing which come within the ambit of colonial institutions. But the history of the colonial period must be written as a study of interaction, and this is quintessentially such a study. The rulers' misunderstandings of African life are, in this context, not misinformation, but the primary material out of which the history was created. This is an area of colonial rule in which Africans played an important part, having to participate within the forms of colonial institutions and having to express their meanings in the language of the coloniser. The problems and limitations involved in construing meanings and concepts expressed in English, and in confining one's considerations to activities within colonial institutions, are plain. Yet they do not, I think, seriously affect an understanding of the customary law, precisely because it develops within this interaction of ruler and ruled.

There are other major directions which a book about law during the colonial period in Africa might have attempted. One, which the nature of the sources excludes, is a study of dispute-processing and normative concepts beyond the reach of government. But there are enormous problems confronting this sort of study in all societies, and it may be fanciful to try to recapture a history, as opposed to a mythology, of this level of African social processes for much of the colonial period. It becomes plain, nonetheless, as one reaches more recent times, that the model of a dual legal system – of British law, and African customary law – is inadequate. Beyond the customary law recognised in this model is another level, the development of which may well be taking place in opposition to both levels of the state's law. But this would be the subject of another book.

I have also not attempted to describe systematically the content of the colonial legal system, on either its 'customary' or its statutory side. For the former it is because the formal contents are without meaning and only become comprehensible as ideas about, and instruments of, social power when considered as 'law in action'. For the latter a full-scale study of the contents of the colonial statute book, with its multifarious regulation of local life, its inbuilt racial discrimination, and its legal expression of the exploitative economics of colonialism, particularly in the areas of land and labour law, would again be another book.

Acknowledgements

While I have worked on this book I have received many expressions of interest and encouragement, and words of advice. I shall not list names here, but those who are being hereby most gratefully thanked will know it. Special mention should be made of Professor James Read, for initial inspiration and subsequent practical assistance, of Janette Gosstray for her work and patience in the preparation of the manuscript, and of Peter James for his acute editing.

I am grateful also to the Governments of Malawi and Zambia for permission to use their National Archives, to the staff of those institutions, and to the University of Malawi and La Trobe University for financial support. While working on the book I had the support of a fellowship from the Inter-University Council, and academic hospitality from the University of Sussex, the University of Texas at Austin, and the School of Oriental and African Studies. In the way of further acknowledgements, one is to my students at the University of Malawi, through whom I became interested in Central African history. A second is to Robin Palmer and Landeg White, who sent me materials from the National Archives of Zambia which transformed the nature of my study and to whom most special thanks are due. A third is to Kate Neale, and my gratitude for her understanding of African history and her critical faculties is expressed through the dedication.

Part I

Law, anthropology and history

1

Social and legal history in Central Africa

This book is an attempt to understand the historical formation of that part of African law known as customary law.[1] A book about customary law is not simply a book about law, but it is about ways of conceiving the past and, therefore, the present. The way in which a society conceives its traditions is fundamental to its understanding of itself. Traditions symbolise continuity, cultural identity and orderly existence, though the nature of that order may be fiercely disputed. Images of tradition compete and change, and different views are consequently taken of social continuity and the sources of authority. These are political phenomena.[2] In recent African history continuity has been radically disrupted, cultural identity assaulted and social order transformed. I will be trying to examine ways in which, in these circumstances, traditions are maintained, manufactured and presented.

Anglo-Saxon common lawyers, as Maitland once pointed out, are not attuned to the idea of historical change.[3] The common law is theoretically ancient and immutable, and judges search for what the law 'really is' by studying precedents. In this paradigm legal history is an interest in the practical questions of what the pedigree and authority of rules are and whether they are still applicable, or an interest in the evolution of legal doctrine. Custom, to be recognisable by the courts, must be ancient and unchanging. This legal view of the past is specifically unhistorical and it also excludes the general context within which legal change takes place. An added unhistorical ingredient is the wish of lawyers to forge 'new mythic traditions' from the past to use in current argument.[4]

The unhistorical conception of the common law and of custom held by English lawyers has been compounded by the tendency of British functionalist anthropology to present 'traditional' legal systems as extant and functioning in the ethnographic present and to play down the elements of conflict and division which were involved in claims about what the law really was. To this must be added the neo-traditionalism of African legal writing, which is not only affected by the common lawyers' view of legal history, but

3

which has important reasons for finding it attractive, because this view makes it possible to claim a surviving African customary law as a crucial ingredient in cultural nationalism. The value of the African legal heritage has been discovered without its history having been written. In the face of this triple-tiered historicism, I am seeking to occupy this terrain for historical study, and to reunite the subject of law with the economic, social and political history of colonialism in Malawi and Zambia.

The law was the cutting edge of colonialism, an instrument of the power of an alien state and part of the process of coercion. And it also came to be a new way of conceptualising relationships and powers and a weapon within African communities which were undergoing basic economic changes, many of which were interpreted and fought over by those involved in moral terms. The customary law, far from being a survival, was created by these changes and conflicts. It cannot be understood outside of the impact of the new economy on African communities. Nor can it be understood outside of the peculiar institutional setting in which its creation takes place. African legal conceptions, strategies and tactics are formed both by the impact of capitalism and by the interaction of the communities thus affected with the concepts, strategies and power of British colonial legal institutions.

When Kwame Nkrumah opened the University of Ghana Law School in 1962 he said that Ghana was 'reviving part of our African culture and heritage interrupted by the colonial period'.[5] Even the more prosaic lawyers have tended to look upon the customary law – that part of the law applied by the courts in colonial and post-colonial Africa, yet not embodied in local statutes nor a part of English law – as the indigenous African element in the dual legal situation. Thus lawyers adopting this Africanist view have approached the dual system with the aim of legal unification and a desire to strengthen what is seen as the indigenous African element. But if we look at how the customary law came into being, resting an Africanising strategy upon it can look a little odd. It is not simply that customary law has changed in both content and form during the colonial period. It is that the circumstances of its development made it a part of an idealisation of the past developed as an attempt to cope with social dislocation. It was defensive in spirit, defensive not only against British rulers but against those Africans whose growing involvement in wage labour and market agriculture was leading them towards different interpretations of obligations and proprieties. In stressing that customary law is not customary I cannot claim to have made a particularly startling discovery. What remains is to show what it was, how it developed, and how it was used. In attempting this I hope to show that it was part of a process of legalisation, of a transformation in African institutions rather than a continuity. This has been a most important transformation: one, it might be said, of the hidden effects of colonialism, and one which continues to develop in the post-colonial era. Yet the nature of this transformation tends to be hidden behind the ideological screen of continuity implied in the notion of a customary law.

4

Other myths have arisen from the legal colonisation of Africa. There is that of the colonisers, perhaps their last surviving myth, that the legacy of legality, the rule of law, and equal and uncorrupt justice was an important benefit conferred by colonisation. One of the ubiquitous themes of the British imperial experience has been that of the British as lawgivers and many have luxuriated in comparisons with the Roman imperial achievement.[6] It was in the government of India, in particular, that the mission of legal reform came to the fore.[7] In many ways British administration in Africa was a feeble reflex of the Indian experience. The determination to replace communal tenure with individual landholding, which was at the root of British legal reform in India, had been abandoned for all practical purposes by the time British administration was created in Africa, and major codifications no longer appeared to be an obvious panacea. But other intentions lived on. One was that the law should define, defend and enforce individual rights, introduce a certain, predictable and incorruptible machinery of justice, yet at the same time provide a personal and paternal law which would not offend the colonised. There was also a clear commitment to the idea that to hold and exercise ultimate judicial power was a vital part of political domination.

In reviewing the imperial achievement in India there was a general British belief that the establishment of the rule of law and an uncorrupt system of justice had been successfully achieved.[8] The most important elements of the legal inheritance of the African colonial period detailed by Sir Kenneth Roberts-Wray, formerly legal adviser to the Colonial and Commonwealth Office, were the rule of law, the writ of *habeas corpus* and the independence of the judiciary.[9] The legacy of justice bequeathed is one of the most stubborn fantasies about British colonialism, partly because it derives from one of the most stubborn of fantasies about British life itself.

Few people who read this book will be surprised or chagrined to find that its descriptions of the workings of the legal processes show them to have little in common with the ideological representations, though we should not discard these representations entirely because they are an important part of the way in which British judicial officials understood their own actions. Yet there is also an important African counter-myth, developed as much by white anthropologists as by Africans, about the nature of African justice. The distinctive picture of African dispute-settlement that has gradually emerged from this is typified by Maquet. 'Compromise is a key word in Africanity. It is a way of settling personal disputes and conflicts of interest by trying to find a solution acceptable to both parties .... the antithesis of settlement by compromise is settlement by reference to abstract principles. The application of such principles often results in an extreme solution: one of the parties has to be right and the other has nothing.' This was 'distasteful' to Africans who knew that 'reconciliation' was better. Basil Davidson found the governing principle of African law to be the duty to conserve the 'ideal equilibrium', and the emphasis on compensation. Legal writers have also

5

contributed to this view. Nekam, for example, tells us that African law was 'a system of keeping the balance ... geared ... not to decisions imposed but to acceptable solutions'. In the 'traditional African community' there was 'no polarisation of needs, of taste, or of values', and once the facts were established 'the same solutions will appeal to all and ways to achieve them will seem obvious . . . . the feeling of balance will be something spontaneous and self evident.'[10]

Many African lawyers have adopted these images.[11] Customary law, the principles of which guided the processes of reconciliation, expressed, in this view, the immanent egalitarianism of pre-colonial societies.[12] These views have a similar descriptive value to those depicting the British as bringers of the rule of law but, like those descriptions, ideas about restoring the balance do clearly have a part to play in understanding African actions.

The contradictions between African ideology and practice may be illustrated by turning to Marwick's sensitive account of the Chewa: 'the function of Chewa judicial institutions', he wrote, 'is the removal of hatred from human hearts by patient examination and persuasion in terms of a community accepted code.' A more perfect statement of the idealist position would be hard to find, yet it occurs in a book devoted to the bitterest of disputes. On the one hand he describes a village meeting at which the rancour between disputants is 'removed by patient examination'. On the other he writes that over the past century Chewa 'prestige and self respect have been assaulted and, on balance, diminished.' The Chewa recalled the days before the British and Ngoni conquests, when they were the owners of the country and

> when their way of life, especially in its moral aspects, was uncontaminated by the evils of the present . . . . traditional morality they memorialise by depicting the 'good old days' when harsh punishment kept sorcery, theft, adultery and disobedience at a minimum . . . .
> Their golden age serves as a reference point for their present degradation. And it is when they are assessing their decline and accounting for it that their attitudes are forcibly expressed.

The Chewa, he wrote, held the Europeans responsible for the moral decline, for forbidding the poison ordeal, the execution of sorcerers and adulterers, the selling into slavery and the mutilation of thieves and the disobedient: 'the Chewa betray what appears to be a contradiction in values; for the brutality of the punishments they hark back to is in sharp contrast to their veneration of the meek in heart.'[13]

Recent trends in African historical writing have broken with an earlier tendency to present a pre-colonial Merrie Africa, and slavery, elders' power, male power and varying forms of class power are now being more closely analysed. Of the image of kingship embodying unity and mystical symbolism which was presented by Fortes and Evans-Pritchard in their classical work on African political systems, Strickland has written, 'The picture conjured up is one of peoples all of a mind, thrown into moral

disarray, if ever, by the machinations of slavers and missionaries ....
Naturally people do experience feelings of solidarity ... yet this is a double
edged affair. The manifestations of solidarity may also mask intense fears
and resentment.' The picture of African social systems that emerges from his
studies is one of 'political dominance along with the ideology of social
solidarity'.[14] The paradigm of consensual dispute-settlement must adjust to
these shifts in emphasis. If harmony is no longer perceived in pre-colonial
societies, a new view is needed of what the essence of 'restoring the
equilibrium' was. Canter has recently observed after fieldwork among the
Lenje in 1970 that too much should not be made of the difference between
courts which judge, and family groups which mediate, because the threat of
banishment was the implied threat in a mediated decision. As for the family
moot, which mediated cases by 'discussion', he writes, 'the neutrality of the
term belies the forcefulness with which families attempt to settle disputes by
this means.'[15] What is necessary, as has been pointed out, is to consider the
differences in power, status and class between disputants, and to be aware of
those unequal relationships which have conflict of interest structured into
them – hirer and hired, master and slave, man and wife. In this context
compromise, a restoring of the equilibrium, means a 'return to the previous
balance of power, or *status quo*.' Maintaining harmony (with 'forcefulness')
loses its patina of egalitarian warmth.[16] Much of the anger is, as Marwick
indicates, an anger at impotence, at a lack of ability to control or to react
effectively to disruptive changes. One of the results of taking criminal
jurisdiction out of African hands, for example, was to produce a demand for
others to act, a call for the recognition of the seriousness of wrongdoing from
rulers who seemed to condone it. And those outraged could find themselves
up against the immense flippancy of some of the colonial administration of
justice. Harry Franklin recalls witnessing his first witchcraft case. A '"very
complicated case"', said the officer who was presiding. '" You might be
interested in having a look at the evidence". On the indictment attached ...
and a foolscap sheet there were a few scattered notes and drawings of an
elephant with calf, a baboon, a bicycle and a silhouette of the interpreter.'[17]

It is not surprising that the colonial rulers all over Africa have depicted
pre-colonial law in terms of savage punishments, but it is surprising, on the
face of it, that this view should be so widely and enthusiastically accepted by
Central Africans.[18] It should not be thought, of course, that Africans alone
are to be held responsible for the peculiar sin of irrational neo-traditionalism. In recent years in Western Europe and America, where the mobilisation of female labour has transformed the structure of the family, and
where recession and economic dislocation have added to a sense of rising
disorder, there has been a marked reaction, and ubiquitous calls for a return
to a more 'traditional' sexual morality, tougher punishments and more
hangings. It is easy to demonstrate that in the good old days sexual
behaviour was nothing like that represented by the moral purists, that law
and order prevailed to a far lesser degree than imagined and that there was a

greater chance of being a victim of an act of violence, but one might do this in vain. For the perceptions of the traditional order arise from current concerns and are necessary to current actions. Problems like these become particularly important when considering the nature of the evidence about customary law. It might seem for example that oral evidence would have a special validity as a means of gathering from essentially African sources materials on precisely the kind of African cultural history that has been both denigrated and distorted by outside observers. But there are great difficulties which arise partly from neo-traditionalist perceptions of the past and partly from the very nature of the claim to legitimation by custom. When the claim of a law to be (or to have been) a law rests upon it having been changeless, the way in which things have always been done, its authority derives from the 'fact' of its changeless regularity. Yet this is, of course, not an historical fact. The claim to changeless regularity, then, is fortified by both the mode of legitimation and the important values which people bring to statements about law. There is great difficulty in separating, in discussion of moral behaviour, 'is' from 'ought' or, in the case of the past, 'was' from 'ought to have been'. Marc Bloch has remarked on the historicity of the customary law in Europe and the changes which it underwent behind a façade of changelessness. 'The strange thing is', he wrote, 'that this law, in whose eyes any change seemed an evil, was in fact one of the most flexible ever known.'[19] 'Remembered truth', wrote Kern, 'was . . . flexible and up to date . . . . There was no conflict between past and present, between ancient precedents and present practice. Customary law quietly passes over obsolete laws, which sink into oblivion . . . but the law itself remains young, always in the belief that it is old.'[20] In an illiterate society, as Clanchy writes, precedents are soon transformed and the 'sanction of immemorial time can be given to relatively new rules'. The purpose of a remembrancer is different from that of an historian. 'The Good Old Law . . . which he recalls will be adapted to the requirements of his hearers rather than historically objective.' Or as Bloch put it, 'Jurisprudence . . . was the expression of needs rather than knowledge.'[21] It is in this 'needs rather than knowledge' that the essential clue to the nature of African evidence about customary law is to be found. For the statements which were (and are still) made about it are not so much statements about what the law was in the past, as claims about what it ought to have been in the past and what it ought to be in the present. The question which faces us is not 'Are these statements true about the period of which they were being made?' but 'Why is there a need to present the past in this way?' Evidence about customary law, then, is primarily evidence about the people giving it, about the circumstances and changes with which they are grappling. Clanchy suggests that customary law is to be linked with genealogies and folk tales, 'all equally myth', meaningful, rather than an objective record. Like myth, as Kern says, the law is timeless: when 'law is called "old", it is rather a description of its high quality than a strict determination of its age.'[22]

Only after the establishment of written forms did the English courts of the middle ages begin to insist that custom be provable in a real historical sense. Literary forms drove the creativity and contemporaneity of custom out of English law, and literacy and the system of precedent were eventually to do the same in the formal courts of Africa, in spite of a professed desire on the part of administrators and judges that this should not happen. 'Fear of ossification resulting from written records', writes Read, pervaded discussion on this matter, and was the main reason for objections to codification.[23] But in a sense the crystallisation is what the absence of codification produced. For claims about customary law, presented in a time of social upheaval to colonial courts which demanded that they be 'historically true', could not appear to be at all mutable. The whole concept of a 'tribe' upon which the system of indirect rule came to rest depended upon the idea of a discrete group with an established system of customary law if not peculiar to itself then at least accepted by all its members. 'Custom' came to be a crucial index of group identity. The extent to which customs were not kept, did not become law, and were not enforceable by the courts was a measure by which identity was lost. And, as different groups became increasingly linked together in the colonial society and economy under a single administration which forced them to settle many of their disputes in its courts and according to its forms, claims about custom became more rigid. As people took a stand on their own customs in 'inter-tribal' cases, so the claims they made about them became more competitive and more explicit. And these explicit claims about custom were being made about a period of great upheaval and disruption. Goody and Watt have remarked on the importance of forgetting in the social memory of non-literate societies, and of how the development of writing means that tradition can no longer be discarded, absorbed or translated.[24] Literacy changes the mutability of custom, but not automatically. Not all customs become fixed: there is competition about what will become part of the immutable tradition. The theory on which the British courts worked was that the pre-conquest period was the time during which the customs, being put forward in the colonial courts, were in being. But the nineteenth century in this region saw several waves of conquest prior to that of the British, as well as a huge acceleration in the slave trade. Political power, punishments, ranks and statuses, marriage and inheritance, land and labour, all underwent far-reaching changes and were all the subject of competing claims and moralities. There was no established normality when the British took over but much conflict which carried over into the colonial courts as different groups of people began to learn to use these courts to their advantage by establishing their claims as custom.

It has become an historiographical reflex to divide the African past into pre-colonial and colonial periods and, indeed, this is a book which is premised upon the importance of that division. But the danger lies in thinking about the pre-colonial period as the established African past, in which African societies existed and African institutions functioned, prior to the 'impact' upon them of foreign conquest, foreign economy and foreign ideologies. This has been a kind of historical version of the anthropologists' 'ethnographic present'. It thus becomes possible, particularly when dealing with matters cultural, to conceive of a reassertion of pre-colonial African-ness, a carrying on after the interruption of the colonial episode. It is particularly important for this study to make an effort to depart from this kind of periodisation, one which would see latter-day versions of custom as reflecting and having essential continuity with working African institutions of the nineteenth century. For not only are the latter-day versions of custom, as I have already argued, the products of the colonial period, but the nineteenth century, which they purport to reflect, was, in Central Africa, a time of violent and rapid change and a succession of conquest states, anything but a traditional world in which custom reigned. We do not have a 'traditional' world as an identifiable baseline and it is important to grasp this because it has been identified as such by many Africans when thinking about the nature of custom, and also by historians and social scientists who, anxious to write about twentieth-century changes, often content themselves with an idealised starting-point. I think that, when dealing with a subject like the customary law, when we simply cannot know how things really worked, the damage done by setting up an ideal typical social-scientist's model as a kicking-off point, or starting with a cultural nationalist idealisation, is so great that a different strategy must be tried. To an extent, therefore, I beg the question of what 'law' was in pre-colonial times, but I do this deliberately. My approach is to let the people 'hit the ground running', in all the disarray of conflict, rather than to begin with them in the stylised formations of the parade ground.

In the second half of the nineteenth century the pattern of dramatic changes in the locus of authority at the centre of political systems was widely felt, as new demands and exactions were made. Political authorities were increasingly involved in the trade in slaves and the newly dominant groups pursued the so-called policies of 'assimilation', which meant taking control of the defeated and turning them into subordinates and dependents. With the declining authority of local rulers, the growing mixture of communities, and the increase in slaving, sorcery accusations and the transfer of persons multiplied. The overlay of the conquest and slaving states took place, it must be realised, very shortly before the British conquest; in some places two generations, in many places but one, had experienced the new normality. The missionary presence began to make itself felt in the 1870s, and by the 1890s the conquest was seriously under way. Very little in the way of political authority, systems of marriage, statuses or 'law' can be regarded as having been established in these circumstances; all were matters of the most intense conflict.

PEASANTS AND MIGRANTS: TRANSFORMATIONS IN RURAL LIFE

We must also be aware that we are by no means looking, after the British conquest, at a smooth process of transition to a *pax Britannica*. Soon after conquest came the unprecedented upheavals of the Great War with its huge drafts of food and labour. Even under the best of circumstances the pickings from the colonial capitalist economy which were available to the rural areas were meagre, and this was made worse not only by the continuing vagaries of the markets for minerals and cash crops but by the Great Depression. This came at a crucial time as it coincided with the institutional devolution so vital to the formulation of the customary law. The depression was a bruising experience for many[25] and one which created circumstances in which whatever optimism there might have been about the new political and economic order was easily replaced by nostalgia for the past. Neo-traditionalism flourished in this climate. In Zambia the effect was primarily felt on jobs. By 1930 over a third of the young males in Zambia were estimated to be in wage-earning employment inside and outside the territory. For many the depression meant the sudden cessation of work, which in turn meant, among other things, that kinship obligations were left unfulfilled and the potential for dispute multiplied.[26] While employment picked up again towards the end of the 1930s, an atmosphere of insecurity about income, social relationships and increased governmental harassment remained. One might recall the long and important hangover in western societies following the experience of these years. In Malawi in particular the depression affected the newly emerging cash-crop farmers as well, and their experiences of the treacheries of the colonial market, which were combined with the impact of increasingly oppressive interference with the conditions of production, produced a widespread and sharply disillusioned reaction. The many-stranded crisis of loss of jobs, collapse of markets and tightening of controls dominated the period in which the customary law of the 'family' became increasingly crystallised. Not only were relationships now to be conducted in an insecure and increasingly commoditised environment but there was a growing experience of state regulation (which will be illustrated later), which limited, denied, controlled and punished. Townships, mine compounds and work places were highly structured by regulation, and this could not be escaped from in the rural 'home' environment where seemingly innumerable rules affected the possible ways in which people secured their livelihoods. The squeeze on both labourers and farmers, which dried the flow of money to the rural areas, slowed down the emergence of paid labour and made unpaid labour more important in growing both food and cash crops. A renewed emphasis on rights to services, particularly of women, and therefore the making of intensified claims based on an 'intensified' custom, were one consequence of depression.

I will be describing the workings of the 'legal' institutions of the colonial state and the African attempts to limit and control these, but of course 'legal' behaviour cannot be separated from the rest of social life, nor yet placed 'in context' because it is a part of the 'context'. The legal history is a part of the transforming of the societies of Central Africa by colonial capitalism and is comprehensible only as a part of that process. In part this area served as an enormous labour reserve for the settler economies to the South, and it was also one in which there was a significant growth of a peasantry producing for the market. The increasing involvement in markets for agricultural products and for labour and the new subordination to the state which this leads to are clearly at the heart of the transformation of 'customary' legal relations in African societies. Thinking about law in terms of legal classifications tends to obscure what is involved in this. Lawyers conceptually shrink the major area of 'customary law' into a category thought of as the law of the family, which does not adequately encompass what family law was about. The control of reproduction and of work and the appropriation of the surplus were all inextricably tied into what administrators and lawyers innocently conceived of as marriage. The disruptive effects of capitalist relations were also, to a large extent, combated by Africans on this conceptual territory. In one real sense marriage and morals appeared to be the issue and it must also be said that the field of customary law was one of the few on which Africans were allowed to play with a winning chance. Yet, of course, the arguments about marriage and morality must also be comprehended on another level.[27] What might be grasped from this 'legal history' is how people worked to exercise both actual and moral control over the processes that were reshaping their world. It must also become clear that it is only by failing to integrate the study of customary law with the huge transformation in the relations of production in colonial Africa that one can possibly continue to hold notions of its survival and continuity.

The two major changes in economic activity, the production of cash crops for sale and the increasing involvement of men in a system of migrant labour, both had powerfully disruptive consequences, and these, particularly the effects of migrancy, have been dwelt upon and described by what one might call the disaster school of Central African historiography.[28] This is by no means a new response and this interpretation of events might be traced back to those concerned liberals and conservatives who began in the 1930s to bemoan the collapse of wholesome African village life and the corruption of African morals in the mining centres.[29] The effects on the rural areas of the mass absence of young males were a constant theme of the district reports and government commissions. Sir Herbert Stanley, when Governor of Northern Rhodesia, wrote in a vein which exemplifies the government's perception of the effects of migrancy: 'the women and children whom they [the migrant workers] should be looking after are left behind to their moral and physical deterioration. In numerous villages there are no people save the elderly, the women, and children, and the whole fabric of native life, *with tribal control for bond and the village for focus*, is in peril of collapse.'[30] In this book the focus is on how people continued to run their lives as these new experiences unfolded. While historians may perceive the 'destruction' of peasantries and the process of proletarianisation, it is far from easy for people affected to understand the nature of the broad processes which are changing their lives, and far easier for these changes to be understood in

12

terms of their nearest and most obvious manifestations. Both subjectively and objectively people found themselves engaged in conflict not with economic forces, not just with white colonial government, *but with each other*. This should be too obvious to need stressing but I think it needs doing because the uncaring brutality of the enforced transformation of these societies has so much forced itself upon the attentions of recent historians that it seems as if the distresses of and consequent divisions within them were in some way unnatural events intruding into a previously largely unified and egalitarian universe. Even if this is not made explicit it is often implied by default in accounts which *begin* with the disruptive penetration of colonial capitalism.

Divisions and struggles within African societies were not new. What was new was the kind of division. The latter part of the pre-colonial period must be understood as a world in which hierarchical differences were usually marked. Those on the economic margins, with few stock or poor land, became clients, pawns and slaves of the wealthy and powerful. The penetration of capitalist relations meant not the creation of classes in an innocent world but the changing of the bases of inequality and power, and the challenging and disturbing of hierarchies. These pre-colonial hierarchies had had their justifications in the ideologies of kinship and custom, and the controls imposed by beliefs in sorcery. Under colonial pressures these were thrown into prominence as the ideological (and, in the case of customary law, also the practical) lines of defence. The challengers were slow to develop their own ideological and symbolic systems. An elite few found those offered by the sacred and secular arms of colonialism to be appropriate but many, struggling for a sense of meaning, had to fall back upon the ideological representations of a society which they themselves were changing. Labour migrants, for example, who used cash to pay their bridewealth, or who transmuted labour service into cash payments, were consciously acting within a traditional system but at the same time changing it. They understood and represented their actions as customary at the same time as they undermined the continuation of custom. The ideologies of custom could be preserved while the material practices were drastically altered. The apparent continuity of custom exists not in spite of, but because of, the destructive transformations in social relations, a neo-traditionalist representation being for many the only appropriate way to accommodate an understanding of these changes and to try to control them.[31]

It was not only migrant labour which had disruptive consequences. As I have argued[32] one alternative strategy in the colonial economy was to grow cash crops for the market and this also involved considerable change and struggle at the level of production. Over most of the area and period with which I deal in this book the availability of land for expanded agricultural production was not a crucial issue, though after the second world war there were signs that it was beginning to become one. The central issue was, therefore, the use and control of labour in the new venture. One of the ways in which the customary law must be understood is as a product of the struggle for control of labour in the changing conditions of the rural economy. The loss of control over the labour of slaves, the potential competition for male labour with the mining sector, and the gradual replacing of kinship obligations by cash payments, all meant that the mobilisation of labour resources for cash-crop farming was taking place in an unfavourable environment (though of course not all these factors were contemporaneously present in all areas). Family head producers could not respond to the market by intensifying their exploitation of slaves, and it was now far harder to manipulate 'traditional' labour obligations to the increased disadvantage of younger men.

Iliffe has suggested that in cash-cropping areas of dense population wage labour was the least developed and the pre-capitalist 'lineage mode of production' was 'revitalised'.[33] But revitalisation, though it is partly explanatory of the accompanying emphasis on 'traditional' obligations, may not sufficiently describe the processes. Cash cropping develops over time, new demands are being made and the mobilisation of kin and household labour comes to take a new form as labour has a new potential value.[34] In the early stages cash-crop farming, kept by administrative policies to limited areas of land and low returns, was heavily reliant on a squeeze of kin and household labour for market purposes, and traditional obligations, especially of household labour, were thrust into prominence. But the logic of the market pushed people towards contractual relationships. People producing cash crops for the market required labour additional to normal household resources for the preparation of the extra ground, weeding, harvesting and preparation for sale, work which clashed with that which was also necessary on food crops. Commercially oriented farmers needed both to cut themselves off from the larger kin group in order to maximise their own control of capital, production and profit, and at the same time mobilise labour from among their close kin for necessary work. By the end of our period Long observes that when commercial farmers 'did utilise ... kinship or affinal ties to acquire extra hands ... they tried to avoid the buildup of a series of potentially burdensome reciprocal obligations by treating them as ties of a strictly contractual nature.'[35] Likewise Poewe observes that people 'prefer to hire "free" labour than to co-operate with matrikin who, when they do not demand undeservedly high pay, can demand indeterminate amounts and kinds of other material awards'.[36] Yet squeezing household labour was in many ways a more convenient strategy than finding scarce and comparatively expensive labour outside of the household. This meant first that the labour of wives became vital: its withdrawal at crucial times, as Long points out, could ruin an entire crop. Wives' work could be secured by an emphasis on marital ties. Secondly it meant that a man striving to become a commercial farmer would be engaged in a struggle to maintain control over the labour of his offspring, and consequently that conflict within marriage was aggravated by quarrels over rights to children and the product of their labour.[37]

14

The spread of slavery as a social institution was a feature of the immediate pre-colonial years. Such a development could not simply be abolished when the new political order, that of British colonialism, ceased to give legal recognition to slave statuses. For patterns of residence, and patterns of dependence and control, were slow in changing. And even while they are changing they remain a habitual and meaningful way in which people conceive and conduct relationships. In writing about the first part of the colonial period there has been a general 'roots' orientation which has sought to trace the early foundations and formulations of new economic behaviour, new relationships and new ideas. As a result people are written about as if they faced forward into a world of money, employment, individualism and nationalism. But this was a world about which they did not know. Even if they were being drawn towards it they moved facing backwards, interpreting and dealing with new exigencies as they arose in terms of relationships and ideas they had already known. The world of controlled dependent relationships, a wide range of which were legitimised by the idiom of kinship, overhangs our period and does, I think, influence it more than the roots of a new social world do. Slavery casts a long shadow into the colonial period and when adjustments in relationships must be made they are made within the weakened idiom of the known world, just as the relationships of the slave period had been accommodated within the idiom of the pre-existing kinship system.

The most widespread interpretation of the effect of migrant labour on the economies of rural Central Africa has been to see its impact as enormously destructive. The absence of the majority of the male population from many areas is, in the mainstream historiography of Central Africa, the major factor in the collapse of indigenous institutions. I choose to focus here not simply on collapse and disintegration, because the process cannot simply be seen as an increase in the net sum of disadvantage for everyone. We are looking at a process of redistributing power in social life, a change in relationships between generations and between sexes. Lancaster has shown how the substitution of cash payments, earned by labour migrants, for uxorilocal service-marriage led to a considerable improvement in the position of husbands/fathers in relation to wives, in-laws and children.[38] Colson too found that the trend towards virilocal residence altered the balance between the sexes in favour of men.[39] Through service-marriage older men had controlled not only access to wives but also the labour of younger men. By the 1930s, however, labour migration meant that in areas such as Bembaland there was a shortage of labour and elders could not find men to do brideservice. This challenge to the political economy run by the elders was intensified when young women started to follow the men to the towns. The rural economy could continue with the presence of daughters augmented by cash payments and occasional labour from men who otherwise worked in towns. But if men could marry women who left for the towns without this tribute to their elders, there was a loss to them of the labour

15

power of both sexes, of money and of control of a working agricultural economy. These circumstances posed the basic challenge to the structure of power and production in the rural areas, which produced the neo-traditional reaction which I detail below.[40]

The issue was fought over in terms of morality, of rights and wrongs, of duty, of proprieties for the young girls, of the correctness of marriages and the moral health of the whole community, but we must be clear that we are dealing not simply with a question of morals, kinship and family law, but with the control of labour, with rights to land and the transformation of a system of production. Audrey Richards observed of Bemba society in 1939 that '*All relationships between an inferior and his superior involve the former in giving some kind of labour.*' It was this that gave substance to the respect which we shall see was so jealously guarded by elders and chiefs. 'Roughly speaking', Richards wrote, 'the aim of every Bemba was to secure rights over the services of others, whether slaves, relatives, fellow villagers of subjects'. Yet this 'dominant factor' in Bemba life was the logic of a system which was passing. The increasing circulation of money provided new ways to acquire the services of others and to give meaning to authority. Richards describes the way in which young Bemba husbands shirked their labour obligations to the annoyance of their fathers-in-law.[41] Bemba fathers-in-law tolerated this because it was possible for the young husbands to render service to the elders by means of migrant labour and the remittance of payments and gifts rather than the performance of manual labour in residence. Furthermore, the monetary demands made by the elders increased with the young men's earnings.[42] Thus there were ways in which the elders could turn the monetisation of bridewealth to their advantage. And as more of the young than the elders became involved in the commercial economy, so the balance of expectations between the generations was changing. Instead of the young men looking to their elders for benefits, the elders sought to share in the rising fortunes of their children. This produced extra tensions and emphases on rights in the relationships involved, as the interests of fathers in the control of their sons as well as of their daughters increased, and men's interest in the maintenance of marital ties was underlined.

STRUCTURES, CUSTOMS AND IDEOLOGIES

We can more easily understand these developments once we leave behind the conceptual world of matrilineal and patrilineal systems operating in different societies according to different sets of principles, to reach into a lived-in world where different possibilities and advantages were competed for, justified ideologically, or put up with. There is now a clear tendency towards an agnostic view of structures.[43] In the West African context McCaskie has written how Fortes reified the kinship structures of the Asante: 'The result was a set of ur-norms founded in jural principles or rules – unity, amity, consensus etc.' This, as he correctly remarks, is an ideology.

The level of truth upon which the jural norms of African societies has been stated is very often both too general and too ideological. Generalisations about marital systems, authority structures and the like can be compared, to use McCaskie's example, to the statement that the 'United Kingdom is a Christian country ruled by a monarchy.' It is necessary, as he says, to try to make the quantum jump from the bald assertion of kinship rules to the level of understanding required for social history.[44] Comaroff has written that past accounts which gave the impression that the conjugal process was orderly and regular were the result of 'methodological orientation, not ethnographic fact'.[45]

Lancaster observed of Goba marriage that 'both matrilineal and patrilineal principles of descent seem to be operating at once.' The Shona, he writes, had traditionally followed a patrilineal ideology but had, in the absence of bridewealth capital, operated under matrilineal principles, 'sometimes referred to by the younger men who must endure it as "slave" marriage because it is considered fit only for poor men or slaves'.[46] The confusion of 'systems' and their ineffectiveness as conceptual tools has also been pointed to by the recent work of Canter, who observes of Lenje inheritance that property may be transferred from father to son but that 'each case is described as unique. Culturally people profess matrilineal inheritance. One gets the strong impression that the Lenje carry in their minds a matrilineal model that is scarcely affected by actual cases of bilateral inheritance.' Lenje claimed to be matrilocal, but few were. The Lenje, he concludes are 'matrilineal in terms of belief and bilateral in terms of behaviour'. The very flexibility 'allows continuity in belief'.[47] There is not, of course, any necessary congruence between the ideology of social systems and what people living in them find it possible to do and this is a basic point to bear in mind when it comes to comprehending the presentation of a set of principles as customary. Claimed custom is sometimes simply ideological, but it is often pragmatic, a claim put forward in a form in which it is likely to be successful. In circumstances of conflict and change where there is an unbridgeable gap between social ideals and the actual ways in which life can be lived, custom, or customary law, cannot be a rule which emerges from, is descriptive of and which governs practice or social system. In this changing world claims about custom were competitive rather than descriptive.

'The villagers of Serenje are not wedded to pre-industrial values. They live in industrial society. There is much coming and going .... But ... *these values and customs are among the armoury of arguments* to be deployed when fighting over the distribution of [the] meagre spoils of industry.'[48] Malinowski's notion that a customary law is to be found in what people 'do', that is in their working relationships, is not really so useful in circumstances of change, conflict and imposition. Where people are trying to make others change what they do, law is a weapon. It describes not regular behaviour, but what some people want others to do.

People experienced these as uneasy times. Lonsdale has referred to 'the

17

African sense of acute social disorder', in a time in which old authorities were weakening and new statuses were still insecure. He writes that 'men cannot so easily detach themselves from old identities and associations in so uncertain a world nor cease to be troubled by the problem of evil . . . . they were . . . tugged at every step by all the cultural symbols with which their elders had taken such pains to endow them.'[49] While neo-traditionalism was in part an ideological response to insecurity, it was more an aggressive response than a resigned one. Van Binsbergen writes of the Nkoya that 'their misery is set off against delusions of past grandeur' and that their ethnicity was based not on primordial attachment to a way of life, culture and language but 'on a collective sense of deprivation in the course of a shared recent history'. Nonetheless this sense of a past and of ethnicity had a purpose. In the process of retribalisation people manipulated the customs and values of cultural tradition to articulate a political organisation to struggle against others. And, in addition to this, there was a need for 'legitimation of kin-based claims of assistance, through which people peripherally participating in a capitalist order seek shelter in non-capitalist relations of production'. Neo-traditionalism is part of the struggle to keep the non-capitalist modes intact.[50] Because neo-traditionalism had a positive political purpose it resulted in a strengthening of 'tribal' authority to an extent which might have surpassed the dreams of those who made the policy of indirect rule. Canter observes, 'Rapid social and economic change throughout this century has reinforced the power potential of traditional roles and offices.'[51]

In the light of these remarks we must now begin to unpack the colonial package of tribe, chief, custom and judgement. Birmingham, surveying the period 1790–1870, the immediate pre-colonial period of this area, sees it as being characterised by 'the rising tide of violence'.[52] Likewise Roberts considers a 'general rise in violence' to be a feature of the late nineteenth century. That most eloquent of contemporary witnesses, David Livingstone, described the area as 'the open sore of the world'. This was also a relatively under-populated area, much of which was exploited by a system of agriculture that required a shifting population with the frequent moving of villages and the breaking away of groups. In this context it seems that too much reality has been given to the presence of functioning mini-state-like institutions. Roberts writes of the growth of the institutions of chieftainship as the characteristic political development of Zambia in the eighteenth and nineteenth centuries. The chief, assisted by his senior subjects, 'was responsible for seeing that law and custom were upheld; that the guilty were punished'.[53] This is an understandable reaction to the black despot view of African political life, but essentially it is premised on a constitutional fiction produced by British political life and descriptive of neither Britain nor Africa. I think that in this context we must try to think of political power and judicial authority as separable and in most cases separate. Roberts' description of Kazembe's state where the governors' 'main task was the collection of tribute' might serve to indicate a better model of the state, while over most of the area of Central Africa it might be more appropriate to emphasise not state building and proto-modern institutions with law and judging as an essential feature, but localism, parochialism, lack of government, arbitrary alterations of statuses, violence between and within communities, as well as bargaining and local consensual arbitration. It is in this context that we must situate our understanding of the nature of power in local chiefdoms. Neither the heterogeneous conquest and slaving states, nor the relatively homogeneous communities which resisted incorporation by the retreat into stockaded villages, were communities governed by custom in the sense of principles underlying a social structure which found their expression and application in everyday life, nor was their political organisation one which included a regular application of judicial authority. I do not mean to imply that people lived with a daily normless anarchy but to sketch a model in which the custom of habit was not legitimated and which understands order in this period as being frequently newly created and constantly challenged. The jurisdiction of chieftaincies was ill defined and intermittently effective; it was British administration which defined and regularised its application. Norman Long has written of the position of headmen prior to British rule: 'one can only present an idealised picture, but it is nevertheless an essential one for understanding the contemporary situation, for it is largely in terms of such a model that the people themselves evaluate the changes that have occurred.'[54] But if historians accept the model as real, as the people do, they will not be able to understand the processes of the creation of a traditional past and will continue to confuse ideology with custom.

Early observers of African societies who saw things in an evolutionary perspective interpreted their institutions as being an early form of something which other societies had already become and which the observed societies might also become. Functionalist anthropology, in reaction against this, insisted that African institutions were not early growths, but could be understood as equivalent and fully formed, as anything else implied an inequality of value and esteem. But they still retained part of a value-laden evolutionism, which appears particularly in discussions of law and judicial institutions, in that there was a tendency to be reluctant to see something as fully formed, and yet still really different from western forms. There has thus been a transposition of western models onto African institutions. Under the influence of a not fully acknowledged evolutionism, functional similarity and actual similarity in form were sometimes confused. It is, of course, the case that some African polities were more hierarchically organised than others, and that *dicta* about, say, the lakeside Tonga will not be applicable to the political organisation of the Lozi. Nonetheless what I am trying to argue is that the model basic to much of the literature has a core which sees Central African societies in terms of state-type organisation, part of which included judging by public tribunals according to rules of law, and to which 'stateless' societies are peripheral. This needs to be replaced by an understanding which reverses the relative importance given to states and stateless, and

19

more importantly separates pre-colonial judicial activity from 'states' and chiefs. Only by such a conscious reversal will it be possible fully to appreciate the spread of public and authoritative judicial procedures as a process. In this view the package of tribe, chief, custom and judgement was largely of colonial creation. Iliffe stresses that the colonial government's search for tribes in Tanganyika conceived of tribes as cultural units with a common language, social system and 'an established system of customary law'.[55] Customary law was thus seen to be an important 'given', its existence was an integral part of the definition of the basic unit of colonial policy, a conception which was both attractive and advantageous to African rulers as well. Prins, however, notes how the Lozi changed the presentation of their past to fit in with European requirements. A constitution was invented once Lewanika had discovered 'what things impressed Europeans in general and colonial officials in particular. These things were age, systematic organisation and size' He argues that Gluckman's image of a well-ordered, highly centralised and hierarchical state apparatus must be replaced by one which is 'much more fluid, with much less formalised bureaucratic structure than has hitherto been thought'. The creation of the Lozi constitution was, as I will try to show of the customary law in general, the result of the interaction of British and Lozi requirements. The British needed suitable indigenous forms through which to rule, and where these did not exist 'they might be imagined into existence.' The Lozi helped. Once the British needs were grasped, 'appropriate forms . . . became visible.' In the 'Bulozi account of state structure were types of traditions invented for particular purposes at particular times'.[56] The apparent insubstantiality of 'tribes' at the beginning of colonial rule is by no means a discovery by latter-day historians. It was noticed at the outset by the administrators of Malawi. The Nyasaland Handbook records the 'unusual difficulties' which had beset the early administration. These were 'the mixture of tribes; the scarcity of important chiefs; the necessity of deposing many of the most powerful; the decline of tribal authority, due to natives in many cases being ruled by conquerors whose arbitrary powers ceased when the Protectorate was declared'.[57] The realities of pre-colonial political life, of conquest, of 'mixture' of weak authorities, were perceived to be an unusual departure from a normality which had once reigned in a fantasy past conceived of in terms of models of tribal political organisation which would now be restored, albeit in modified form. As diagnosed by the Nyasaland administration in 1904, in 'proper' pre-colonial times 'a chief had unlimited powers of life and death and was able to keep his people in order. He did so not by kindness, but through fear.'[58] The restoration of the authoritative and authoritarian tribally pure-mini-monarchies, some formed out of the small communities into which the nineteenth-century conquest states had broken down, some made up by amalgamating those who had remained independent, created the new 'tribes', with a new kind of judicial authority and a new kind of enforceable custom. It has often been observed that the growth and crystallisation of

20

'tribes' has been one of the most important factors of recent African history, and that tribalisation has been a way of mobilising to deal with a new world. My intention here is to draw attention to the connections between tribalism as a form of political mobilisation, neo-traditionalism as an ideology, and the growth of the customary law.

The tribe was not the only apparently traditional basic institution in which the customary law was seen to be embedded. We must consider too the historicity of that other important constituent customary community, the village. We know that the rising tide of violence in the latter part of nineteenth century forced many people who had lived in smaller, scattered communities to group together in stockaded villages for protection. Following the establishment of British rule larger villages began to break up, patterns of settlement became less concentrated and better suited to agricultural practices. But the British authorities in both territories were quick to react to this scattering, and people were instructed, in the words of the Serenje district notebook, to 'build proper villages under their chiefs'.[59] For the convenience of tax collection and general control through government-appointed chiefs and headmen, colonial administration required and created compact villages. Vail writes of Eastern Zambia that for administrative reasons 'a fundamentally abnormal settlement pattern' obliged people 'to dwell in villages in numbers excessive for harmonious social life and efficient production'.[60] I am not sure what a normal settlement pattern was or when it could be said to have existed but it is clear that the village cannot be seen to be a 'given' unit any more than the tribe can. Both prior to the British conquest and afterwards patterns of organisation and conflicts which were far from 'customary' must have developed in the enlarged communities, and tensions given rise to increased accusations of sorcery. Like tribes, in our period the villages were created by the colonial political process and people were learning to live in them, not living traditionally. They were also trying to get out of them, and in fact the amalgamation of villages was progressively abandoned. So the nature of the basic customary law community was a contested one, and customary law a weapon in this contest.

We are no longer naive enough to hope to separate a government of laws from a government of men. The contents of law and the forms of institutions may appear to retain uniformities over long periods but it is the feelings, ideas, interests and ambitions of those who administer them which give them their real meaning and shape their working. It is for this reason that I stress the prevailing ideologies, even more important where the laws were unwritten and the institutional framework uncertain. I will be describing the emergence of a picture of a golden age in which women had been submissive, divorce rare, and adultery heavily punished. It was the counterpart to the picture of virtue maintained by terrible punishments which the colonial generation held of the pre-colonial criminal law. The abolition of ordeal trial made the control of wrongdoing problematic. The abolition of slavery disrupted a basic way of controlling people. The customary law

21

emerged in part as a new defensive weapon for the collapsing slave-owning women-taking hierarchies which had developed in the nineteenth century. Indeed in the undermining of these systems of power and their struggle to re-establish themselves in a new form one can see another possible clue to the ambiguous visions of the pre-colonial past, of terrible punishments and egalitarian reconciliations, in that they are reflections of two levels of pre-colonial 'law', the power of the conquest states and slave-owners, and the customs of the local communities.

The establishing of the Native Authority Courts led to the creation and the beginnings of a crystallisation of an African customary law in a particular historical context by a particular group of men whose outlook had been formed in the process of the history of the early colonial period. The conflicts in and around specific institutions which I shall discuss are a part of the economic revolution experienced by African colonial societies. The disputes with which colonial courts and village courts found themselves dealing were in increasing numbers new conflicts caused by new demands being made of old relationships, or caused by the formation of new relationships which people tried to regulate with concepts and claims appropriate to a passing social formation. New tensions developed which could not be resolved by ordeal trial, and new demands for labour which could not be encompassed by slavery. This was a time not only of disintegrative impact and structural change but also one of attempted restoration and rebuilding. People grappled with the present not in terms of ideas about the future, about which they knew nothing, but in terms of ideas about the past, recast in the heat of present experiences. The forms which this social reaction took could only now be legitimised through British colonial legal policies and institutions. Through them the relevant interests and values were turned into law.

Many of the themes which I will be discussing may be illustrated from Richards' recounting of the life of Bwembya.[61] Bwembya begins by asserting his rank. 'I am Bwembya. I am a great chief. I am not just a headman as you white people think . . . . That is why people give me such respect.' Yet Richards points in contrast to his real material poverty, particularly in contrast to the young wage-earners in his village, which gives rise to this emphasis. His claims to status and respect, which have no apparent justification in terms of the present, must be sustained by an appropriate view of the past. Richards noted his deeply rooted belief in the power and importance of the Bemba chiefs and his 'glorification of war and conquest'. This goes with the images of authority, as exercised in past judicial hearings, as contrasted with the weakness of the unsatisfactory present. 'Everything was done silently and in order' said Bwembya.

> All the children would be sent away. It was not like the courts of the present day, where sometimes you see a chief hearing a case with no-one to listen except the court clerk, a young man. Why, even the Chitimikulu allows a crowd of young children to tumble about all over the place. Nowadays in fact the elders often stay away because the chief no longer respects them, nor

honours them with gifts. He has nothing to give them now since he has no longer ivory or cloth or tribute from his people. Besides, he is always trying to do what the Government wants, and therefore he listens to his clerk instead of his councillors. He thinks 'That young man understands the way of the white men. He will teach me best.' It was quite different in the old days.

Bwembya turns from the pitifully reduced chief, judging amidst children and under the influence of an uppity youth, to a description of the past. Both sides would state their case, the councillors would give their views, 'Then suddenly he [the chief] would stop all talking and give his judgement and everyone would shout to the litigants, "Salute the chief. Salute to the ground both of you. You have received justice! . . ." The men of both families would roll on the ground before him, and the women would kneel and clap and cry their salutations.' The starkness of the contrast reminds us that images of the past are made in the present and for the present. Bwembya's version must be understood in the context of his difficult and changed circumstances. For he found himself in authority in a very different sort of community, one without organic bonds, associating on a new basis. 'They gave me a village', said Bwembya, 'made of all the people who were working for them, messengers, mailmen, carpenters and bricklayers. It was not like an ordinary village for the people were not kinsmen, but they were all living together because they wanted to get money from the white man.' This captures in microcosm the grand transformation which was taking place over this period. In his new community 'many of the women have had bad hearts'; there was constant trouble, 'the men are very unruly.' Men and women 'are always making trouble in my village so that it is constantly splitting up and there is always noise and no respect for elders'.[62]

If neo-traditionalism sums up the world view of those who were losing authority, what about those men and women who were always making trouble and noise, and lacked respect for their elders? Clearly an account of the development of customary law must also encompass their position. We shall see that the revival of authority under indirect rule was both resented and resisted by many and that gaps do open up between what is customarily done and what the Native Courts applied as customary law. The general thrust of nationalist legal politics in Central Africa in the years before independence was one of great hostility to the control of the Native Courts by the traditional authorities and of a desire to get rid of the dual legal system. The ultimate goal of nationalist leaders was a professionalisation of the legal sphere with a trained legal bureaucracy administering a single national legal system. The course which post-independence politics took in Malawi, however, led to a closing of the gap between the surviving nationalist leadership and the traditional leaders and this had its effect in the legal sphere where the traditional authorities were to be confirmed in their role.[63] In Zambia after independence, on the other hand, the nationalist elite continued to voice a dissatisfaction with the colonial legal legacy with a different emphasis from that in Malawi. The Lower Courts Bill, introduced in 1966, was the occasion for a debate on the transfer of judicial powers from the chiefs to a modernised legal bureaucracy. The chiefs were attacked for corruption and their courts for being part of a colonialist strategy of divide and rule.[64] But the customary law, which the chiefs had allegedly been administering, was not rejected. Rather it was to be co-opted by the new legal cadres. Parliament was promised that a written customary law would be produced, that new magistrates would be trained to use it, and that lawyers would be allowed to use the courts which administered it.[65] Customary law was to be fashioned to meet the needs of the new legal bureaucracy. This co-option of customary law was far more typical of the rest of British Africa than was the Malawian strategy of strengthening the chiefs' courts. But both rested partly on the same illusion, that of the essential continuing Africanness of the customary law as opposed to the innovating foreignness of English law. This has clearly been an important part of nationalist ideology in Africa. Gulliver observed of Arusha norms that 'In their modern opposition to outside influences, and their desire and attempt to preserve their distinct way of life, they have in fact come to emphasise these norms.' But the norms were not used as the African lawyers would seek to use them: there was a wide gap 'between the details of an agreed settlement and the declared norms'.

In the chapters which follow I have sought first to give an account of the ways in which African law has been written about by historians, lawyers and anthropologists. I have done this in part to provide a guide to these literatures in a convenient form and to suggest a critique of them. Part II deals with legal administration in general and the 'criminal' law, and Part III with the very wide range of matters encompassed in what the administration thought of as 'family law'. In both of these parts I look at the intentions and preconceptions of the British, for these create the dominant part of the colonial legal environment and by so doing shape African possibilities and the nature of the African response. Then I consider specifically the major ideological and institutional assault in each area: in that of social control generally it was the attack on ordeal trial, and in that of the 'family', the abolition of slavery. Each of these assaults had a major effect on the nature of legal administration, which is described in the third chapter of both parts where I try to show how the colonial courts actually went about their daily business. In the fourth chapter of both parts I describe the African responses to both British intentions and their experience of British practices, and the consequent formulation of what came to be known as the customary law.

24

2

African law and anthropologists

This chapter will provide a commentary on, though not exhaustively survey,[1] anthropological writing related to African law. The first section will look at early major works, which, though few and far between, helped to create a context without which it is hard to understand the directions taken by the 'Rhodes–Livingstone anthropologists' in their later work on Central Africa. Their rich legacy of classical monographs will be considered for the light they throw on social history in the second section, while the third will look at three 'exemplary' approaches, a combination of which is attempted in this book as a whole.

EVOLUTIONISM, FUNCTIONALISM AND THE ANTHROPOLOGY OF LAW

The main tradition of African legal anthropology is associated with the era of indirect rule. The context in which it was written was very different from that of the earlier conquest era with its picture of savage anarchy restrained by black despots, marriage by purchase, slavery and witchcraft. In the inter-war years the investigation of African law assumed importance in the context of the framing of Native Jurisdiction Ordinances, Native Tribunals, and other paraphernalia of colonial policy. In the idiom of this era, the culture and thought of Africa was not simply to be regarded as an obstacle in the way of progress, but as adaptable and usable.

The first of the major African monographs, Rattray's *Ashanti Law and Constitution*, was based upon a strange amalgam of Austinian jurisprudence and Mainean evolutionism.[2] He distinguished sharply between the law of the sovereign state, backed by sanction, and the religious taboos of primitive law in Ashanti. Rattray's view of Ashanti law placed it in the context of a long-term evolution, and a universal legal development. Rather than looking closely at the law as a means by which people in the present were constantly adapting and finding ways to deal with current problems, his focus was distant and his time-scale long. We shall see that this kind of approach, removed from mundane day-to-day observations, was oddly, yet comprehensibly in view of the intellectual context, the one adopted by most of the officials in the colonial service.

After the women's riots in Iboland in 1929, C. K. Meek, the Nigerian government anthropologist, set out to study the causes of this spectacular malfunctioning in the machinery of indirect rule. Because a major cause of the riots had been the imposition on Eastern Nigeria of the warrant chiefs and their courts, judicial institutions of a type which had no roots in local society, Meek was to produce one of the rare studies of law in action during the colonial period.[3] Though Meek had a rather more rationalist view of 'primitives' than Rattray he emphasised nonetheless that when the British used the word law it carried with it the 'definite implications of state authority, judges and magistrates, codes and courts, police and prisons', while religion and magico-religious ideas filled African minds when they thought about law. Colonial rule, wrote Meek, had resulted in the 'weakening of legal sanctions which were basically of a magico-religious order, the declining respect for elders, and the growth of individualism'.[4] The general *leitmotif* of the book was that of the degeneration of authority. When a primitive people meet a modern state, Meek wrote in his conclusion, if great care were not taken their 'political and social organisation is likely to break up and what was before a well-ordered community . . . may become nothing but a disorganised rabble of self seeking individualists.' This anxiety, and the development of ways to deal with it, was a pervasive theme of the indirect-rule years. Nowadays, wrote Meek, the Ibo themselves are complaining about the loosening of social bonds, about the leniency of the British courts and the increase in wrongdoing. Meek's work stressed the importance of the 'kinship grouping', as the 'fundamental unit of law and authority'. In family organisation was 'the cradle of morality . . . and the mainstay of the good ordering' of the community.[5] Meek advocated the restoration of legal business to the community not, as he said, so that the old ways would continue unchanged, but so that they would develop in the hands and under the control of kin heads and village groups.

Meek's approach reflects the line which legal policy-making was to take in the 1930s. The emphasis was neither on the substitution of British law for African nor on the defining of a viable African law. Rather it tended to treat African law as an amorphous batch of mutable equitable principles which were more or less suited to African social conditions. These customs were, it was hoped, in a process of evolutionary modernisation which should not be stifled or arrested by being forced into western legal forms. The important thing seemed to be not to get the law right but to get the politics of court creation right. The proper development of the law and the arresting of social dissolution appeared to depend on the creation of judicial institutions properly founded in the traditional community, which would themselves develop the law. The result was that far from giving legal certainty and the 'rule of law' British rule in the indirect-rule period meant just the opposite. Indirect rule became, with anthropological blessing, essentially a retreat

26

from the reformation of African law, which was deliberately left to be uncertain, unwritten and evolving. It also opened up an area of conflict between the African elite, with its increasingly strong component of western-trained lawyers, and the supporters and rulers of the Native Courts. The latter developed the law in a way which reflected the interests of their age and generation while the former campaigned for a legalised customary law and professionally controlled courts.

In 1934 Driberg, working from a background of both administrative and anthropological experience, published his conceptualisation of African law. The civil/criminal distinction was meaningless, the aim of the law was the maintenance of equilibrium, and it was based on 'collectivist organisation' and not, like western law, on 'an individualistic assumption'. Because the law sought to restore the balance, judgements were 'constructive and palliative' and not penal.[6] Driberg perceived African law to have a rationale all of its own which was different from the individualistic and command-orientated western version rather than simply being a highly defective version of it. Though his analysis retained some evolutionary overtones it summed up a quarter of a century of conceptual retreat and fitted well into the philosophy of indirect rule. (Though he did point out that this policy was not leaving African law alone and that courts were being pushed into an enforcement role instead of their traditional equilibrist one.) The emphasis on the notions of the primitive, taboo and magic was replaced by an attempt to understand the logic of how dispute-settlement might work in smaller-scale societies. In its departure from evolutionism it was very different from the discourse still being used by the legal writers in their discussions of African law, and it helped to create the equilibrist paradigm which was to dominate, with mixed blessings, in the future anthropological writing. One thing was quite clear and that was that an analysis which emphasised reconciliation rather than the enforcement of rules, while it might accord well with the philosophical aura of indirect rule, was not of much use to its practitioners in the field. Both the coexisting fashions of the inter-war years – the older evolutionism and the newly emerging relativism – overlapped in general agreement that where possible it was best for Africans to 'develop' their own law and that this, rather than imposition and codification, was the healthiest course. Neither was therefore of much use to the district officers who had to oversee the workings of the local Native Courts, or to the judges who, very occasionally, had to pronounce on rules of African law. They needed not evolutionary history nor ideas about equilibrium but a knowledge of enforceable rules. There thus developed a third type of African legal literature, the books of rules of customary laws which were supposedly certain and enforceable by courts, and which were usually collected from the older men before they were 'forgotten'.[7] All three kinds of writing essentially neglected the study of short-term legal change: of what was going on around them. The rule-oriented writing was interested only in rules legitimated by supposed long usage, that is, in custom in the English legal sense.

27

The great depth of focus of the evolutionary writing blurred the foreground of recent and current changes, and the relativists were gradually losing interest in what rules were being enforced.

The early anthropologists, and the early legal writers, had been part of a tradition which collected African legal materials as part of a universal history of law and which therefore saw African institutions as forerunners of modern ones and as comparable with the early institutions of other legal systems. They were interested nonetheless in studying African law as law, a focus which was to be abandoned in later writings. The consolidation of functionalism meant that legal norms and rules were no longer studied in isolation but as part of a broader system of social control. This tendency was consolidated by the rise of the realist school of American jurisprudence, which found its way into anthropology of law through the publication of the *Cheyenne Way*.[8] The focus was henceforth not on the question 'what is the law?' but 'where is the court?' and 'how is the dispute settled?' While both anthropologists and administrators had discovered the importance of the courts rather than the rules, their interest was very different and administrators found no way to apply the knowledge gained from Llewellyn and Hoebel's trouble case method. As Sack has written, the prime aim of legal investigation from the colonial point of view was to discover 'the rules of primitive law'.

> Primitive law was to colonial lawyers and administrators neither a system of social control nor what was done in case of trouble. On the contrary, they had come to establish 'Law and Order' . . . . The Colonial Administration and the Colonial Courts were there to make sure that the natives did from now on what they ought to do according to their traditional laws. The white man's machinery of law enforcement was set up to enforce the black man's substantive law.[9]

The African's modes of 'enforcement', which is what the anthropologists focused on, had no place in this scheme of things.

The interest in indigenous ways of dispute-settlement rather than in the application of indigenous law was basic to the development of the consensual paradigm, which I outlined in the first chapter. When the legal writing began finally to draw upon the anthropology of disputing it often reacted to the domination of the African legal world by British laws and British procedures by conjuring up a distinctive essence of customary law based upon an idealisation of the conciliatory features of dispute-settlement. Once this became a given within the legal writing it meant that where the customary law in action in its extant form fell short of this vision it had to be because of its impurity. Nekam, for example, perceived a 'traditional core' around which there were 'all kinds of heterogeneous elements' which had been western-inspired. The 'greatest problem' was 'to find out what customary law in its original, pre-westernised form might have been; to reconstruct it if it is possible, at least to separate it from what later infiltrations in hundreds of ways may have added to it'. In his view the decomposition of the customary law was being hastened by the very persons who appeared to speak in its name. African magistrates were exposed to new values and approaches. 'Such subversion . . . can hardly be detected . . . the form will still seem the same.' Nekam was of course correct in perceiving the way in which the myriad changes in the customary law were subsumed under its traditional mask but misled in thinking of a pure core with a foreign clothing, for there was little purity about custom, which had always been open to many influences. But once change was seen as degeneration rather than continuing legitimate adaption there was no place for a history of the customary law in the colonial period. Study was turned instead towards its original essence and to the revival of a spirit from an era uncorrupted by colonialism, rather than towards an awareness of the making of customary law as an historical process.[10]

Evolutionism, consensuality, and also legal comparability, are all mixed into Gluckman's seminal work *The Judicial Process Among the Barotse*.[11] It not only provided an account of a functioning African legal system during the colonial period but also ushered in modern African studies of legal anthropology. Of all the works by the Rhodes–Livingstone school it was by far the most influential book in the field of law, though not, I think, the most illuminating. It is of some significance that both by the lawyers and by Gluckman the book was seen as an illustration of the proof of the legalness of African law. There was an element of surprise in the introduction to the book by the jurist, A. L. Goodhart, at Gluckman's success in demonstrating that Africans reasoned rationally and had judicial thinking just like other folk. Yet Goodhart fitted this into an evolutionary framework: the book, in his view, was a case book of early law in which one could watch a primitive legal system in action, not an account of the working legal system of a modern people. Gluckman himself felt the need, correctly, to dispose of the irrational black despot myth and to stress that the judicial process was 'in essence similar to that process in western law'.[12] Gluckman continued to adhere to the view that there were 'certain conceptions and principles of law . . . shared by all legal systems'.[13] Like Goodhart he was an evolutionist in his approach to history. African customary law corresponded to early European law, and an historical approach, therefore, was one which used knowledge of early European developments and applied it to the African situation. Neither the emphasis on similarity nor the long-term evolutionary time-scale was likely to make him stress the continuing contemporaneous processes of transformation.

The basic framework of Gluckman's analysis was that people in what he termed multiplex relationships required disputing mechanisms which were conciliatory and which worked to prevent any 'irremediable breaking of relationships'. Lozi judges, he thought, bore in mind the total relationship between litigants and not simply the case before them when giving judgement.[14] Yet he still insisted that this did not lead to their sacrificing essentially legal rules, processes and forms. Other anthropologists differed

29

completely from his insistence on the strict comparability of African and western legal processes. Bohannan rejected both legal evolutionism and the notion that there was such a thing as a corpus of Tiv law.[15] Gulliver also attacked overtly legalistic studies. While Gluckman's work in a way tended towards closing the gap between lawyers and anthropologists by purporting to show that some African institutions and concepts could be understood in western jurisprudential terms, Gulliver's work, like Bohannan's, stressed the differences. Beginning with an exaggeratedly Austinian view of British law and procedure, Gulliver presented a picture of dispute-resolution among the Arusha as one achieved not by the judgements of neutral courts, but by a process of bargaining and negotiations between disputants and their supporters.[16]

Gluckman could not really avoid being aware that the newly emphasised norms were usable not simply as expressions of resistance to outside impositions, but also as weapons in internal social struggles. Moral judgement clearly forms a major part of judicial decision-making anywhere but must be especially prominent in situations of change where the dominant morality is being challenged from below and where written precedents do not impede or embarrass the sway of judicial pontification. Large parts of the judgements of the Lozi courts read like sermons, as flouted ethical norms are being turned into customary law. As Gluckman wrote: 'the judges cite not past court decisions but actual instances of upright behaviour .... law ... is instantly exhibited in the conformity of upright people to norms.' In this way customs which could not have been said to be rules became 'indirectly enforceable at law. The *Kuta* [court] ... pounces on all unorthodox behaviour to find against the defendant.' This has even more point when put together with his observations that the Lozi law was dominated by status, not by equality, and that 'natural justice aims to maintain the established system of social positions and the ideas that justify that system'. Male ideas of how women should behave 'influence judicial reasoning, which thus applies and even develops existent morality in defence of the structure of male–female relations'. Thus 'the application of Lozi law ... defends not only the legal superiority of men, but also existing hierarchy.' Gluckman observed not only the dominance of moralising judgement and the defence of existing hierarchy but also the process by which the judges conferred antiquity on comparatively recent innovations. In the absence of writing, he wrote, 'the Lozi treat fairly recent innovations as ancient custom.'[17] Barnes was to make a similar point about precedent in the absence of writing. Ngoni courts did not quote specific precedents and 'in this undocumented environment' new decisions 'became part of what has always been custom since time immemorial'.[18] These observations about the Lozi legal process, though they were a sideline to the main thrust of Gluckman's book which was his discovery of rationality and comparability in Lozi legal processes, seem to me to be of far greater interest and value for understanding the development of the customary law in its historical specificity.

This view of the customary law in its historical specificity was more central and more pointed in Fallers' *Law Without Precedent*.[19] 'Customary law', he wrote, 'is not so much a kind of law as a kind of legal situation which develops in imperial or quasi-imperial contexts in which dominant legal systems recognise and support the local law of politically subordinate communities.' To add to the realisation that the customary law was a product of the colonial situation there was his sensitivity to the interaction between this product and the rest of the ideas in society. In the absence of writing, he wrote, 'Legal subculture and general common culture interact in the thoughts and acts of amateur judges and of the general adult population.' 'All parties come to court equipped with both popular moral ideas and the legal subculture and interaction between them is continuous'. (This is true, of course, of written systems, though to a different degree.) The resultant Soga system had, he observed, absorbed in addition to its own material of a legal and more general nature both British and Bugandan materials, becoming in the process a 'neo-traditional' one. While he made no attempt to show in any detail how the neo-traditional system evolved, he noted the difficulty of reconstructing the pre-colonial system from memory data, the very sense of continuity being the obstacle. The Soga, he wrote, 'think about their pre-colonial political and legal order as little different from their present one and their memory of the former is heavily contaminated by their experience of the latter'. The pre-colonial material was 'filtered through a screen of present day experience'.[20] Thus finally we emerge beyond an evolutionary anthropology of African law to the understanding that it can be better comprehended within the context of the African social history.

THE 'RHODES–LIVINGSTONE SCHOOL' AS SOCIAL HISTORY

The work of the anthropologists attached to the Rhodes–Livingstone Institute has left to Malawi and Zambia a particularly rich legacy of classical anthropological monographs which are at the same time records of acute observations of the late colonial period. My aim in discussing these books here is not to assess them as works of anthropological fieldwork or theory, nor even to provide a full assessment of the contribution that they have made to the development of the anthropology of law. What I will try to do is to give a general indication of the picture of the customary law that emerges from a reading of the Rhodes–Livingstone anthropology and to consider why this picture is like it is. The period in which the fieldwork for these books was done is the conclusion of the historical period which this book covers and it will be seen that the observations which the anthropologists made then do illustrate the development of the themes of the previous half-century which I will be describing from the archival sources.

There is an important sense in which structural–functional studies, the paradigm within which the earlier Rhodes–Livingstone works were written, necessitated a belief that there had to be a customary law, because they were premised upon regularity of behaviour. Rules constituted the social order which could not exist without or beyond them. As van Velsen wrote of British structuralism, it presented a social system as a unit of parts and processes 'linked to one another by a limited number of principles of wide validity'; its basic assumptions were of homogeneity and stability and of regularity of actions consistent with rules. In addition these regularities perceived in the social structure were seen in the light of analyses of function which, in ingenious demonstrations of functional correspondences, had a tendency to ignore specific differences. Thus Gluckman, comparing functions, could write that Lozi judges performed the same function as judges in all societies – righting wrongs, adjusting claims, defending norms and achieving reconciliations – and make the functional similarities the heart of his analysis rather than the huge differences in the actual processes. Yet a strict structural–functional paradigm could not permanently survive the immersion of researchers in the actual social processes of Central African societies. Both van Velsen and Turner were to provide specific departures from the presentation of behaviour in terms of rule and regularity. As Mitchell was to write, the problem became 'to show how exceptions and variations ignored in the process of delineating a structure are accommodated within it in reality'.[21] Ideal rules, van Velsen demonstrated, did not represent actual practice. Gluckman himself conceded that the search for system in tribal societies, which had demonstrated 'that there is a systematic structure in one field of tribal life after another', had been done at the cost of discarding 'much of the living reality about which we had collected information'.[22]

As the basic model of tribal societies came under examination many of the organising concepts and certainties appeared to disintegrate. Van Velsen found that a 'lack of definition is a general feature of Tonga institutions . . . [with regard to] headmanship, landrights, the matrilineage, and, indeed, with marriage itself'. And, as he wrote with regard to matrilineal and patrilineal descent, there were 'many discrepancies between formal values and actual practice'. Marriage was 'very difficult to define in practice, although not in theory'.[23] Although van Velsen was writing specifically about the Tonga, who have defied many attempts to understand them, models of things like matrilineality, chieftaincy and law with which administrators and anthropologists tried to understand Central African societies presented an image of definedness which was not to be found in real life. This is true of social-scientific analyses of western society also, but in the African case the misrepresentation was exacerbated because of the transposition of western constructs to explain areas of unknown behaviour. And it was false definitiveness, as both van Velsen and MacGaffey[24] were to show, which was then used by the colonial authorities to cut down the range of indigenous choices and variations, in the name of applying customary law.

The importance of the influence of conceptual regularity and certainty can

32

be seen in the area of ideas about African polities, politics and chiefs. Fortes' and Evans-Pritchard's typology of African political systems[25] divided them into kinship societies, where kin group and political group were cotermi- nous; so-called stateless societies where power was exercised by descent groups; and states, with an organised government, with power divided into administrative, political and judicial parts. This last model, because it fitted the categories with which government was analysed in the minds of British anthropologists and administrators, had an enormous magnetic power over all of the models, and even the ways in which power could be exercised in stateless societies came to be understood in its terms. The model of the chief or headman, exercising power, regardless of the scale of the polity, came to dominate the understanding of African politics, with obvious implications for the misunderstanding of law and judicial authority. Watson wrote of the Mambwe that each chief had 'lived in his own village state, with his own administrative officers – executive officers, captains, junior judges etc. The Chief exercised judicial, administrative and legislative authority over his people.'[26] The chief is identified with government, and the kind of authority exercised by government must be divisible into these categories. Of course in some places authority was more organised than in others, but a model of the prevailing type of political organisation in pre-colonial Central Africa which explicitly or implicitly is based on the classical European division of powers is, as I have argued in the first chapter, misleading. It has had its currency, and its appeal, however, not simply because it coincided with European categories of understanding, but also because it came to reflect African desires. Watson wrote that 'The cruelty of the chiefs is a byword among the Mambwe; they emphasise the power and authority that the chief held over their lives and property in the past . . . . his power to take a man's life was his most significant characteristic.'[27] This, along with an insistence on past sexual purity, is, as we will see, a dominant note in African ideology in colonial Central Africa. The importance of this concept of the traditional among the colonial Tonga was observed by van Velsen. Tonga talked about

> the old, traditional law or custom. This phrase is often used with the impli- cation: before the interference of the Boma, for instance in the treatment of sorcerers . . . or adulterers, or before the Boma and the Europeans in general encouraged people to ignore or even despise their headman and chiefs . . . . The headmen maintain they are not accorded the respect which headmen used to receive in the old days.

Yet the Tonga had never had centralised political institutions with powerful chiefs. Van Velsen remarks, 'the Tonga ideal of a "traditional" political structure has in fact inseparably absorbed the values and support of the Administrative system'.[28] The European model gave far more regular authority to chiefs than they had had and for this reason many Africans took to the model. Both sides were pulled for different reasons towards a misrepresentation of the past, which provided the basis for the misunder- standing of African law. The desire for certainty, purity, power and control was vicariously projected back into the past by those who felt the lack of control in the changing and uncertain present under alien rule and unpredictable economic conditions. The idealisation of those polities with skull-bedecked stockades and the generalising of these into a representative political model was the result of a conjuncture of both European and African ideological needs.[29]

The enormous multiplication of minuscule African monarchies, which created the setting for customary courts, customary judges and customary law, was more a feature of the colonial period than a continuation of pre-colonial life. This is not to say that it was a creation of the British. What they had done was unknowingly to create opportunities which were seized upon by some Africans. Turner wrote of the Ndembu that the 'formal structure' of the political system of the colonial period as defined by the Native Authorities Ordinance and the Native Courts Ordinance 'presents a rigid hierarchical appearance quite foreign to the indigenous structure'. Among the pre-colonial Ndembu the authority of the chief was confined to his immediate area, and even then authorities were 'respected rather than obeyed'. In an unstable and mobile society a chief 'could not enforce his rule on senior headmen and the latter could not exact obedience from villagers in their areas.' In these circumstances there were no 'centralised judicial institutions' and force and self-help were resorted to by villagers. A chief might, on application, preside over an ordeal, but in general cases were settled locally without resort to headmen or chiefs.[30] To van Velsen it was clear that in pre-colonial times 'jurisdiction in a certain area, or over a certain group of people was not the exclusive and constitutional right of any one person or headman.' There was no automatic jurisdiction. When people wanted or needed an arbitrator they looked for and found one.[31] Turner and van Velsen are writing about areas with relatively unstructured political institutions, but nonetheless I would stress again that if we are to generalise about political and judicial institutions it is better to do so from this model than from one of a bureaucratic constitutionalism retroactively transposed. Over most of Central Africa the exercise of formal judicial authority by tribal courts was created by the circumstances and the administrative machinery of colonial rule, rather than continuing through it. Marwick observed how the chiefs' courts were gradually encroaching on the terrain of lineage members and elders as the chiefs claimed a judicial authority over the handling of divorce.[32] Colson made similar observations. 'The creation of courts, whose major work is settling domestic disputes, brings family life directly into the ambit of the Native Authority.'[33] Epstein observed of the pre-colonial Lunda that 'neither divorce nor marriage were the concern of the State.'[34]

Marwick's Chewa informants told him that long ago 'practically all' cases were settled by a village meeting, in which the headman's role had been 'to formulate the collective opinion of the participants'. Marwick observes that 'it would not be accurate to describe this as a village headman's court'. But he wrote, 'Informants assured me that there was an increasing tendency to take to the Chief what would formerly have been settled at a village meeting' and that chiefs were becoming more and more involved in the minutiae of village life.[35] This apparently uniform tendency was welcomed more in some circumstances than in others. Colson records a Tonga headman hearing a case and stating his view of the correct procedure thus: 'The wife is also in the wrong. When she found her husband acting thus, she should have gone to her father or to her matrilineal relatives to report before she came to court.'[36] Yet the British administration considered the chief or headman to be the repository of judicial authority and therefore the correct person to be judging cases. Headmen and chiefs who were not active in court were seen as ignoring a vital part of their work and this was one of the surest ways of attracting censure from the Boma. This compulsory expectation that chiefs and headmen attend courts and take part in the delivery of judgements altered their role across much of Central Africa. The judicial processes provided an important avenue for those who were seeking political authority, little enough of which was otherwise available to Africans under British rule. Barnes wrote that:

> All those who work in the courts have in fact an interest in increasing the power of the court system, which the poeple as a whole have not. Disputants will settle out of court if they can, for it is not so far to walk and the whole process is not so disruptive of social ties, but members of a court will sometimes challenge the right of independent arbitrators, village headmen and the like, to come to any binding decisions.[37]

Nyakyusa informed Monica Wilson that 'they have been told to "bring all cases to Court and write them in a book"' by the administration and Wilson recorded the comment of a district officer fining a man for hearing a case out of court: '"I am afraid that arbitration is a common offence."'[38]

The growth in the judicial power and activity of chiefs and the formalising of their activities within a hierarchical state structure is closely connected to changes in the role of kin and lineage, and to the emergence of the individual as the basic jural unit. Colson writes that before the imposition of British colonial rule no state organisation ensured the security of life and property among the Tonga and each person depended on his kin to protect life and property. Thus 'To deny the obligations of kinship was ... in a sense to outlaw oneself, since legal protection was dependent upon the support of the matrilineal group. In such circumstances the rights of ownership vested in the individual sink into the background.' And an individual could not protect himself against his kin as there was 'no outside authority to which he could turn'.[39] Public judicial activity was not contested between individual and state, or individual and kin group, but between kin groups. Van Velsen writes that the lakeside Tonga 'never had a system of impersonal authority to guarantee the individual's full enjoyment of his legal rights. This guarantee had to come from a person's kinsman who would support him.'[40] Marwick's Chewa informants underlined the still-prevailing attitudes of their courts, telling him that 'If you try to take legal action against your sibling, the court people . . . just laugh at you, and you have to go home and settle your quarrel there.' And, in the few instances in which people approached the chief's court alone, 'ridicule' was showered on them as a 'forcible reminder that it is considered proper that judicial contests should mobilise the matrilineages of the contestants'.[41]

Yet the strength with which these norms might be held did not hold against the current towards the individualisation of judicial activity and its incorporation by the state. It was not simply the new institutions of the colonial state which were responsible for the changes. The development of new forms of property and the possibility of individual accumulation had, in Turner's words, a 'corrosive' or 'solvent' effect on corporate kinship bonds.[42] New property was not in itself sufficient: the rights of an individual to new property could only exist through the new institutions. The state and its courts 'not only freed a man from the need to rely on his matrilineal group but also opened the way for him to sue his kinsmen and force them to restore his property or to pay him damages'.[43] And people perceived that the new court institutions were particularly appropriate venues within which to pursue their new claims. Watson wrote, 'if the case is important, involving damages, or cattle or money in any quantity', it would be taken to the new chief's court.[44] The new wealth which made it possible for people to raise 'their own standard of living instead of ploughing back their income into established relationships' was often at the heart of the new disputes. The new quarrels which arose about the social obligations attaching to new property could often not be resolved by the usual ways of settling disputes and therefore often led to sorcery. Marwick describes the typical circumstances of the migrant labourer who remitted his earnings home to his mother's brother, who invested them in the purchase of cattle. Whether the cattle 'belong to the individual whose earnings bought them or to their matrilineages is an ever present tension producing problem.'[45] The replacement of kin by courts as the body which would rule on this question made it possible for the cattle to belong to the younger man alone. The new institutions and the new property were together making it possible for there to be new 'rights' as opposed to the moral obligations of kinship. Colson records a case in 1948 in which a young government clerk brought suit against his mother's brother for using the clerk's cattle to pay compensation in an adultery case. The councillors admitted the 'legal right' of the nephew but also pointed to his 'moral obligation' to help his uncle, and they refused to decide the case.[46] This was not a distinction which could have been made before the emergence of the new legal institutions and their ways of defining property, and it illustrates how the Tonga councillors were trapped in the legalisation process, unable to enforce old obligations, yet unwilling to enforce new rights. The cash economy, as Turner wrote, enabled people to escape from their obligations towards kin. A person who wanted capital for personal expenditure on higher living standards and to invest in business must 'break away from his circle of village kin towards whom he has higher obligations. Everywhere, we see the spectacle of corporate groups disintegrating, and the emergence of smaller residential units based on the elementary family.' Some returning migrant labourers used their cash to enhance their prestige in 'traditional' ways, but other migrants and cash croppers were becoming petty capitalists, embarrassed by the demands of kin for cash and kind. 'If the making of money tends to supplant, as a major aim in life, the acquisition of a following, people try to accumulate money . . . a large following then tends to become an embarrassment rather than an asset.'[47] Economic individualising and jural individuation went hand in hand.

Changing attitudes towards property can also be seen in disputes about inheritance. Formerly the descent group had provided bridewealth as a group and met compensation payments as a group. But in the new economy young men were no longer dependent on elders for subsistence or bridewealth, and no longer had to perform labour service to obtain a wife. Ties of dependence weakened, groups of coresident kin became smaller. Colson points out that what had once been inherited was the 'household', i.e. wives, children and dependents who were assets as followers and labourers, rather than material goods attaching. But by the 1940s the household was more frequently refusing to be inherited, which it could now do as that refusal would be supported by the Boma courts, and the accumulated goods were coming to be seen as the important part of the inheritance. Both the growth of property and the increasing pressure, in some areas, on basic resources made questions of the definition of ownership more important. The 'lack of precision' in property matters looked back to a time when households accumulated little property.[48] But they were increasingly capable of producing surplus wealth which, Colson writes of the Plateau Tonga, the matrilineal group of the husband considered to be its own, and much resentment was caused if the husband spent it on, or consumed it with, his wife and children. Wives and children saw the household goods as being the fruit of their own labours and resented their going to their husband's or father's kin. Similarly men opposed women sharing their goods with their matrikin. 'Men have beaten their wives . . . in furious rage because they have handed on to their kinswomen items of clothing received from the husband.' In one sorcery case recorded by Colson the diviner found that the death of a headman had been brought about by the hatred and anger of his matrikin who resented his buying sugar and maize for his wife and children only and refusing to share it more widely. As the informant said, 'Because of the hatred which they had for his wife who shared these good things, they decided to kill him. So he died because of his property.' A son spoke to her of the hatred which his father's kin had for him: 'They may use sorcery against me to prevent my gaining from my father's wealth.'[49]

In these circumstances of bitter competition for family property between core family and matrikin we can see encapsulated the 'corrosive' effect of the new property, the dissolution of the kin groups which had been the building blocks of the 'customary' legal system, and, in the increasingly common cases of disputed inheritance, a kind of dispute suited to the new set of legal institutions. Yet the corporate lineages *could* not fall apart (which made feelings within them all the more complex) as long as land was not seen as disposable private property, and access to it was still largely dependent on lineage membership. Group membership, and therefore marriage, thus remained of primary importance and developments in marriage must be set against the background of individuation of rights in property, and the growth of the state at the expense of the lineage as a validator of rights. A marked inequality between the sexes was one of the major features of life during the colonial period, and one which was portrayed, in all its manifestations, by the men as 'customary'. We must expect claims about rights in and over persons to have been affected by the changing basis of property relations. One of Henry Maine's better-known *dicta* was that 'The separation of the Law of Persons and the Law of Things has no meaning in the infancy of law.'[50] As Gluckman, basing himself on Maine, wrote, 'property in Lozi law does not consist of rights over things themselves for use, but of claims on persons in respect of things': 'things are nuclei for all kinship and political relationships since the measure of fulfilment of obligatory feelings is inevitably made in material goods.'[51] As it becomes more desirable to be explicit about property so we might expect to find the legalisation (in the sense of growing precision) of matrimonial relationships, especially within and under the influence of the colonial courts, where the new strains on marriages manifested themselves in increasing litigation. We will see in Part III that this is the case.

It must also be remembered that when Turner writes of the cash economy driving many to reduce their dependents and kin obligations it is the wider kin relations which are suffering attrition, not those of the household. Within the household the tendency was in the opposite direction. For many, economic conditions made the need to control labour for household production more and more acute. Labour service marriage was being replaced by cash payments, made possible by the money earned from migrant labour. Control over the labour of young men who looked after the herds until of marriageable age was likewise being undermined by labour migrancy. Colson refers to the intense 'struggle for herd boys' and they escaped from this form of exploitation to that of white farms and towns.[52] And while unpaid labour became scarcer and harder to control, 'nucleation' of production continued. Colson observed that 'Despite the difficulties faced by the immediate family group in coping with the labour involved in agricultural production, the upkeep of the homestead, and the management of the cattle herd, the breakup into individual family groups continues.' Colson also points out the importance of polygamy to men trying to cultivate larger acreages: 'Labour is extremely hard to obtain, particularly permanent labour which will work for more than a few days at a time.' Wives and children alone could fill this need. As one man told her, 'I am seeking a second wife for no other reason than that I need additional labour for my fields. I am trying to get on in business and I need help.'[53]

At the same time as control over household labour is becoming more necessary, property, as we have seen, is coming to be perceived as a household asset. Conflict between husband and wife over ownership and control of household property became more bitter. Colson reported that husbands were increasing their control over wives' shares. 'Here you work hard and the man can take it all,' one woman told her.[54] Matrimonial disputes, therefore, were taking place within a changed context, and their solution can hardly be 'customary'. There was a movement towards definition of rights in and over women which was a strong current counter to the colonial administration's token efforts at emancipation. Women were presented as unequals. 'According to the Yao', Mitchell wrote, 'women are quite helpless in their relationships with others, in illness or in any court cases, and must always have a man to look after them. They are seen to be as dependent on him as children are on their parents.'[55] In courts, Colson observed, women were 'perpetual minors . . . there is always an "owner of the woman", whether it be the father, or mother's brother, or husband.'[56] Gluckman found that women among the Lozi were at all times in 'legal tutelage'. The 'application of Lozi law, even when it is argued in equitable terms or stated in terms of natural justice depends . . . [on] the legal superiority of men.'[57] The Chewa concept of a good woman, wrote Marwick, was of 'obedience and a willingness to be of service'.[58] As I will show below, these attitudes were soon reinforced by the administration. As Barnes experienced it, 'Women listen to court meetings, but rarely if ever speak, for the Administration works very largely through men and it is men who discuss the kinds of things in which the Administration is interested.'[59]

The expanding range of activity of the new public judicial institutions made relationships between men and women directly a public matter. And, because the public sphere was administered by men, the law which they handed down was more severe on women than on men. Colson writes that while before the formalisation of judicial and legal activities men might have beaten women for sexual transgressions, now penal fines were invoked in 'an attempt to combat general licentiousness as far as women are concerned . . . . Such fines . . . have come only with the courts and presumably reflect the influence of European officials and their morality.'[60] Presumptions about the attitudes towards women, Gluckman observed, 'influence judicial reasoning, which thus applies and *even develops* existent morality in defence of the structure of male–female relations.'[61] The addition of courts to lineages as judicial authorities could make women's causes not easier but more difficult. A wife, Colson wrote, 'now has to convince the court as well as her own relatives that she is entitled to a divorce, and this is not always easy'.[62] Courts, under the influence of British forms of procedures, now assumed that one party must always be in the wrong. The party who sought a divorce was blamed and fined. As men never sought divorce, not needing it to marry again, women were always the petitioners and the practice of fining them for coming to court became established. Epstein found after listening to a number of cases that 'one was forced to the conclusion that one brought a suit for divorce "at one's peril".' Lunda courts gave divorces to complaining women but ordered heavy compensation payments against them, arguing that 'since it was the woman who insisted in divorce, it was she who was really responsible for breaking the marriage . . . What does stand out . . . is the way in which the scales are tipped against the woman, supported though she may be by members of her kin group.' A heavy price had been paid by women for the jural equality insisted on by the British. It was 'the development by the courts of a punitive element in the divorce law'. This was aggravated by the growth of migrant labour and the courts' desire to protect the rights of absent migrants, and was a 'reflection of the concern felt by leaders of the community at the growing instability of Lunda marriage'.[63]

The British influence on the way in which judicial procedures were developing meant that vague claims and dissatisfactions, and political claims between lineages, could not be handled by the new courts. When disputes of this sort, which might once have been settled by private arbitration, arose, they had now to be formulated as legal disputes about specific legal rights. Van Velsen records a bridewealth case that really arose out of a political claim regarding the seniority of a lineage. Within a few minutes it became clear from the claimant's opening statement that the political claim was crucial. However, he writes, 'It is the duty of the court clerk to prepare, for possible inspection by the District Commissioner, a neat record of the case, clearly exposing argument and counter argument. At one stage he interrupted and asked: "Now what are you after – the bridewealth or what? You cannot come here to have your dispute discussed in general – you must bring a specific point." '[64] The plaintiff was forced to opt for the bridewealth claim as his other complaints were not, in terms of what was recognised by the new forum, 'sufficiently concrete'. Formalised legal claims, which might not otherwise have been made, were therefore increased by the new institutional processes, while claims of other kinds were not being adequately resolved.

Gluckman wrote of the Lozi: 'In the process of social control every breach of custom is significant, since it distorts the flow of social life: in courts of law almost all customs are sanctioned, indirectly if not directly.' Epstein observed similarly of the Urban Courts on the Copperbelt that 'customs, beliefs and presumptions, none of which would be legally enforceable in themselves, are constantly being channelled into the judicial process.' Cases were settled by reference to these values and 'involve no reference to any particular system of tribal law'.[65] What is occuring here is a process by which one kind of control was becoming another. Customs are no longer persuasive instances but become grounds for decisions. In the new courts custom became law, indeed it had to if it was to be invoked, and the new law was legitimated in terms of its being custom. Barnes observed further that:

There is no recorded corpus of Native Law and Custom which Native Courts are empowered to enforce and, therefore, to say that a new decision is merely a revival of an established usage satisfies the requirements of the Administration ... it enables the court members to legislate without referring the matter to a meeting of the whole tribe ... at which anyone would be free to speak his mind. Thus the group of persons who are in power in the court further entrench their position.[66]

Epstein, like Gluckman, emphasised fundamental likenesses between African and western legal processes. In his work not only is the 'court' similar, but there was also a 'body of law' known as 'Native law and custom'. While there can be no correct definition it is as well to be clear, as I have said above, about the consequences of choosing one definitional approach rather than another. 'For the Court members', Epstein wrote, 'Native Law and Custom consists of rules and standards which already exist and which can readily be applied to any set of circumstances, however novel.' And he quotes a court member referring to a principle as 'no law of the Europeans, it is our African law, which is common to all tribes.'[67] One consequence of a definitional approach like this, however, is that it can obscure understanding of all that the African court members meant when they referred to law. One is left with the assumption that they are referring to the same kind of rules as, say, English rules of law. A different kind of definition would leave one more open to the possibility that their understanding was not like this at all. The reaffirmation of an African customary law did not necessarily refer primarily to rules either lived or enforced. One clue can be derived from the court member's juxta-position of European and African law, a consciousness of an opposition which was crucial to the idea of customary law, conceived not so much as a body of rules as a marker of identity, to be preserved under challenge. Another clue can be gleaned from the Bemba court member who said, 'At home when I arrive at the men's shelter someone will rise and offer me a seat. But here [in town] it is very different – why even a young man with whom you are talking will continue smoking. Why? It is because there is no genuine law.' Thus law is both identity affirmed and authority idealised. Rules are not reaffirmed but created; not that this creation necessarily involves new norms or standards of behaviour, but rather, new ideas about regularity and enforcement. It is for this reason, rather than because, as Epstein says, 'court members see the body of tribal law as known and certain,' that they were so eager to have it codified.[68] Codification would endow the new law and processes of enforce-ment with a new authority. And it would also meet the frequent and significant objections by litigants that courts were not applying the law.

ECONOMY, INSTITUTIONS AND SYMBOLS: SOME EXEMPLARY
APPROACHES

I have considered in this chapter the development of a tradition of anthropo-logical studies of African law which failed to come to grips with historical questions, and I have shown how, in spite of a limiting framework of enquiry, the materials contained in the works on Central Africa are a prime source of social history. In the last section I will discuss three works which embody differing approaches to the study of African law and custom, each of which I believe to be valuable and a combination of which I think is necessary in the writing of legal history.

In the first of these Snyder focuses on the changes wrought on legal form by the subsumption of pre-capitalist societies into the world capitalist economy.[69] In terms of this the heart of the account of the development of customary law must be in the transformation of pre-colonial systems of agricultural production as they are drawn into the capitalist world order, the legal form changing to reflect a world of commodity relations. In this context Snyder considers that there was in Senegal where his study is set a 'fragmentation of patrifilial groups in conjunction with the transformation of labour power into commodity form', and a consequent erosion of 'customary' marriage. While the legal appearance of marriage had only partially been altered, its substantial nature had been radically changed. Marriage had formally involved the circulation of female labour and the allocation of land, and had been the basis of the production of food and the reproduction of labour, but it was transformed by the development of migrant labour in the colonial capitalist framework. In the new economy both labour power and goods could be sold as commodities. Household heads therefore encouraged dependent men and women to labour in varying ways for money. As a result rural households became increasingly dependent on commodity relations and caught up in a struggle for control of labour power between generations.

The production of commodities, which enabled dependents to have access to cash independently of elders, had 'two simultaneous effects. They accentuated patrifiliation as the ideological form through which elders extracted surplus labour from dependents. In addition they resulted in the fragmentation of patrifilial groups and households.' The accentuation of 'custom', therefore, is a response to fragmentation, part of the battle against the economic independence of dependents and the nucleation of households. As can be seen from Snyder's account, as this battle is lost, so ideology shifts to emphasise a new form of male power.[70] As patrifilial groups fragmented so settlement patterns changed and unrelated household heads came to be settled close to each other. This collapse in the community of larger households and villages made up of kin was linked directly to the collapse of the village moot and the increasing referral of cases to the chief's court. And as social relations were altered so the ways in which they were conceptualised changed. The ideological presentations of the past became inappropriate. 'The term *bacam*', writes Snyder, 'which formerly connoted compensation, reimbursement, or equivalent, has lost its association with wider, continuing social relations and now refers almost exclusively to payment, price or wage.'

To emphasise the importance of institutional processes I will turn to work by Howell, who was a student of Evans-Pritchard and an administrative officer over the Nuer. Howell puts himself outside the mainstream by basing his approach on Evans-Pritchard's dictum that 'strictly speaking the Nuer have no law.' Adding to this notorious premise his own experience of working with the courts introduced into Nuer land by British colonial government, he is able to illustrate the 'development of custom into law'.[71] He sees the indeterminate 'rules' of pre-colonial Nuer society being transformed by the new institutional processes introduced by an outside authority and 'applied with . . . consistency and organised force'. Howell was very aware of the problems which Nuer claims about past 'law' presented. Though Nuer gave accounts of instances in the past when blood feuds had been settled, and compensation for wrongs paid, that did not mean 'that every case, or even a majority of cases, was settled'. While Nuer quoted with some consistency the scales for past compensation for homicide or injuries, these were, he wrote, 'essentially idealised and therefore only a basis on which a suitable compromise could be reached', and were an 'indication neither of rigidity of custom nor of constant application'. If disputants were to come together and negotiate there had to be an opening point for discussion and 'an opening was made by reference to traditional scales of compensation which existed largely for that purpose.' In recent times the formulae for compromise 'have acquired a greater rigidity both in amount and in consistency of application because they are now enforced by the courts'.[72] Howell's perspective from the position of administrator was one of Nuer dispute-settlement being transformed by colonial courts because there was 'force behind the decisions of the courts, and this means that in the majority of cases recognition by the defendant of the justice of the other party's cause is not so necessary for settlement, and there is also coercion in that a defendant would be compelled to attend when otherwise he might not bother to answer the request of the plaintiff to take the matter before a mediator at all.'[73]

The reaction to the establishment of government courts noted by Howell follows the pattern which I will be describing in Central Africa. After the military conquest of the Nuer the district officers took judicial powers into their hands and acted directly and personally as givers of justice. Then, once the new pattern of coercive judging had been established, it was handed over to newly created Native Courts based on territorial grouping. Their authority was backed in the first instance by ' "Chiefs' police", some of whom were armed with an outmoded pattern of rifle . . . Since then the Nuer courts have . . . developed in efficiency, power and formality of procedure.' The new arrangements begged the question of what constituted the community for which the law existed, as territorial grouping was clearly not the 'traditional' measure. With territory and group membership changing there were problems in defining law in terms of community even in homogeneous areas. The colonial constitution and definition of the community to which the customary law applied was an innovation, creating and regularising new social boundaries within which duties were said to be owed.

The courts were being used not simply by individuals to enforce specific rights and obligations, but were becoming the instruments of defence of a social order. In courts dealing with criminal matters 'it is not usually the offence itself which is treated as a criminal action but the offender's action in disobeying the orders of the local authorities or the court. The punishment is inflicted for the defiance of authority by the offender rather than for the offence he had originally committed.'[74] The courts were becoming not just instruments of individual legal judgements but 'more and more the sole mechanism through which the social system is maintained . . . . the Nuer are pressing . . . claims for the fulfilment of obligations which were not in the past normally the subjects of dispute at all,' and were creating a situation in which 'obligations of social existence are more and more maintained only by direct action through the courts.' This process of defence through legalisation is brought out in Howell's description of Nuer marriage disputes. Out of the mist of a complex indeterminate series of transactions there gradually emerge the legal landmarks of criteria of validity, enforceable payments, and grounds for divorce. The emerging clarity of definition accompanies a rapid rise in divorce cases, said by the Nuer to have been rare in the old days but now brought to court in considerable and increasing numbers. As Howell noted this was a reflection 'of the wider process of social disintegration which is taking place in Nuerland', and this disintegration expressed itself through the legalisation process.[75] The rise in the legal institutionalisation of divorce came, it should be stressed, not because the Nuer approved of it: 'every effort is made by the court members to prevent it. There is intense feeling on this subject.' But defined legal rights and duties, enforceable through institutions, replaced ongoing relationships containing their own sanctions. The general sharpening of rights and sanctions were a result of 'disintegration' expressing itself through institutional change. 'Rights' were replacing both physical force and compromise.

To an awareness of the processes of economic transformation and of legalisation and their effects we must add an understanding of the place of custom in connection with images of government and authority. For custom is not simply either practice or a collection of rules for enforcement or guidance but is the language of legitimation. What is accepted as customary or traditional depends on the total image of the 'customary' society, on the image or model of political authority which prevailed, of the model of relationships between the sexes and between different classes of people. And we will find that in each case we are dealing with not one set of models, but several. European colonisers had their own models of African societies, of what chiefs were and did, of what primitive marriage meant, of how rights to use land could be conceptualised. The colonised had their models of chiefly authority and of the nature of traditional rights in and over persons and land. The importance of the interplay of these models to the expression and use of custom is brought out in MacGaffey's study of *Custom and Government in the Lower Congo*. 'In the evolution of tradition', he writes, 'the touchstone of merit was very often the presiding judge's concept of customary society, derived ultimately from two sources: the model put forward by the indigenous experts, and a lingering European image of the African kingdom of Prester John.' MacGaffey notes the idea of the perfect kingdom of the past: 'a place of prosperity where each clan, therefore each individual, has its honoured role, and where a benevolent king protects his subjects from all evil and settles all disputes.' This idealisation of the perfect polity and the protective omnipotence of the ruler has its obvious appeal to those under oppressive foreign rule and the uncertainty and insecurity brought about by the exactions and impositions of colonialism. Yet there was often more to the image of the past than this. MacGaffey writes, 'In the imagination of the modern BaKongo, what clearly distinguished the old chiefs as a category was the power to alter both the personal status of others and the boundaries of groups. They killed and burned and enslaved . . . they put down evil and maintained order . . . The idea of such power horrifies and fascinates the people of today'. While it is the case that the second half of the nineteenth century was in Central Africa as a whole a time of concentration of power and increasing stratification and hierarchisation, we are not dealing simply with an historical picture. So we must enquire instead about the function of this ideal authority. Why was the search for security under a powerful man, comprehensible as a feature of the slaving era and the time of colonial conquest, so enduring a feature of the ideology of later Central African politics?[76] The development of the centralised chieftaincies involved great contrasts within the societies themselves. The violence of the chiefs, 'symbolised by the heads impaled around their enclosures, con-trasted sharply with the pacific character of the population at large,' wrote one white witness in 1880. But the violent, rather than the pacific, image became the dominant one, supported by the ideology of both Africans and colonial rulers.

In the setting up of indirect rule, as MacGaffey writes, 'No non-hierarchical system was envisaged, and the emphasis lay on identifying the true chief so as not to upset the local hierarchy.' Once a chief had been 'found' and his court established they were set to 'administering customary law on the assumption that this practice gave official sanction to an indigenous institution'. The assumption was part of the accepted view of the chief, who was supposed to arbitrate disputes among his followers. Respect for custom and respect for the authority of the chief was conflated. But as MacGaffey observes, there is a process at work which lies beyond the confused administrative practices. It is that the analyses of African societies and their traditional practices which were put into practice by indirect-rule policies were part of a broader authoritarian tradition in the social sciences. 'The pervasive theme is social constraint . . . the basic assumption is authoritarian: Individuals must be constrained by specific institutions, if anarchy is not to result. The clan, it is agreed, is an anachronism rapidly disappearing . . . the question is, what shall take its place?' Both analyses and proposed

45

remedies were based 'on the idea of social structure as the primary force constraining the individual in the interests of order'.[77]

The force of structural model-making in combination with administrative practice is nowhere more evident than with regard to the family. 'Anthropology invented *le matriarcat*,' MacGaffey writes, 'and colonial policy was directed towards this ideal construct rather than toward contemporary historical reality.' On top of the constructed model, authoritarian and systemic, came the attitudes of the colonisers towards marriage and the family. As MacGaffey writes, 'The Government was prepared to recognise and sanction unions that corresponded approximately to the European idea of a family.' Thus there came into being a 'Customary marriage [which] could and should be registered by the government and would be sanctioned by the courts'. The formal wedding, with money payment, became the only type which the government would register. Registration meant that the government 'knows' the union, and 'To those who live in the village, the government's knowledge of a marriage means that the courts must constrain an errant partner.' And it was also important for those who lived in the towns where identity papers were necessary, to marry in a way the government recognised, and have dependents entered on their papers.[78]

The making of a colonial customary law of marriage applied from above had little to do with past conceptualisations of the kinds of rights involved. Little agreement remained as to the names and nature of 'the various institutional forms of marriage and slavery in which principles of transfer, as applied to persons, were formerly embodied'. This vagueness resulted from the transformation of the political system by the abolition of warfare and slave-trading. 'The statements of informants, the records of tradition, and a survey of the ethnography suggest that the varieties of slavery and marriage are merely permutations of a simple set of variables.' The 'abolition' of slavery, that is the placing of it beyond jural recognition by colonial courts, broke the continuum of rights in and over persons, separating and legalising those transfers which the colonisers would recognise as a customary marriage from the others. But, as MacGaffey writes, 'No land title, none of the parallel series of personal statuses on a scale ranging from chief to slave, can be unequivocally distinguished from the one next to it in the series. All is disputable, *and tradition is the language of dispute*.'[79] Thus tradition is not something which defines but is a weapon in conflict with which disputants seek to validate claims. The most important affairs which caused conflicts had to do with 'primary social status ... that is, they concern lineage affiliation. Concretely they are landownership and slavery.' Because in the past one acquired access to land through status, it was far more important to define status than land boundaries, which were relatively vague. Much conflict was about the definition of status because it was through these definitions that one might reach security, and they were vital to disputes about land, which depended on accounts of how the rights claims had originated and on what relationships they had been based. Status questions were therefore a vital part of the idiom in which material interests in land were disputed. This is all very far from the idea of a customary land law in the English common law sense of rules handed down and observed over long periods of time.[80]

The weight of the authoritarian model of African society, espoused by both colonisers and colonised, and the institutions of colonial government which activated it, changed the nature and the use of custom. It could no longer be primarily a political resource in a continuing re-negotiation of statuses and access to resources. Legalisation led to a freezing of rural status and stratification, henceforth defined and not negotiated. Custom became a resource of the instruments of government, rather than a resource of the people. Instead of being something that was popular and beyond government, it was gradually incorporated by it. Colonial and post-colonial governments made the same use of custom, both favouring the monarchist model of authority in society. As long as customary courts were left in the hands of the local elders, and custom was uncodified, it could 'be modified and controlled only to a limited extent'. Governments and lawyers gradually sought to control it and make it part of the hierarchic order of government: 'official interest in custom springs from its authoritarian possibilities.' Thus custom was transformed from a way of representing and manipulating the world into a set of government rules: 'under indirect rule the indigenous code of symbolism, rhetoric and magic was made to serve as an administrative code subject to judicial enforcement.'[81]

The general rigidification of defining rules to which all this contributed was augmented by the difficulties and pressures of a new world in which known ways of establishing and conducting relationships were breaking up under the influence of the spread of market relations. The monetisation of relationships placed great strains on interaction between kin, and also created the possibility of ties where no customary basis for them existed. On the conduct of both sets of strained circumstances MacGaffey's comment is apposite: 'The rules and procedures of polite behaviour mark the existence of civilisation, of an ordered community. These criteria of conduct let people in that community know where they stand .... When no polite relationship can be established, a man is frightened .... *Insistence on extreme formality helps to reduce tension.*'[82] Much has been written on the way in which Native Courts under indirect rule spent their time enforcing 'mere' rules of etiquette instead of rules of law, and the need to put an end to this was sometimes advanced as a cogent reason for codification. But standards of respect, politeness, of proper behaviour took priority often in the Native Courts because they were part of a defence of a known social order against a threatening disintegration.

3

African law and lawyers

I have already considered the approach of British jurisprudence to primitive law and the development of the anthropology of law in part as a reaction to the racist and evolutionist premises of the legal thinkers. Yet the functionalism of British African anthropology, while it established itself as dominant in its own academic field, did not become the paradigm in terms of which British lawyers and administrators approached African legal problems. As I will show in the next section they remained firmly evolutionist in their intellectual approach to African institutions. It must also be stressed that their thinking developed within the context of the practical problems, first of the exercise of power in the colonial situation, and later in coming to grips with the devolution and resignation of that power. I will try to show first, by giving a brief historical account of the main themes of this official view, how the development of colonial institutions generated a particular kind of debate which framed particular questions and answers and ignored others. In the last section I will show how contemporary academic writing, freed from the constraints of colonial governance, has developed different conceptualisations. My aim, as in the previous chapter, is not to give a total account of existing scholarship but to show how and why its development, which focused on some questions at the expense of others, produced a particular view of the past.

THROUGH A GLASS DARKLY: THE ADMINISTRATORS' VIEW

In the first period of colonial rule, when the preoccupation of the conquerors was with the establishing of unchallenged power, the new governments had little hesitation in seizing control over as much of the local judicial and disputing processes as they could. British law was introduced, African custom, subject to the repugnancy test, was deemed to continue, but the power of making dispositions, according to whatever rules were deemed to apply, lay with the British courts, from the Boma in the bush to the High Court in the capital. Yet there was such a wide gap between this conception of how things ought to be working and the realities of administrative life that a new formulation had to be developed to justify the widespread use of African agencies. The Lugardian gospel of indirect rule began to spread from West to East and Central Africa after the first world war. And in Lugard's view it was not simply administrative exigency which justified the use of African agencies, but something more fundamental. Why, he asked, make use of a 'crude tribunal . . . of primitive pagans, who . . . have but a limited control over a few families . . .?' Because only in this way was it possible to create a sense of law and order and 'evolve among a primitive community some sense of discipline and respect for authority'. The authority to be respected was the authority of the new state. Judging was to be removed from the private to the public sphere. The object of creating the lowest grade of native courts in primitive communities, Lugard wrote, was to transfer the *patria potestas*, of head of family or council of elders, to recognised judicial tribunals with a wider field of jurisdiction. The way had been opened for the prolonged confrontation between the administrators, supporting the use of African agencies supervised by administrative officers for both the purpose of convenience and the fostering of state authority, and the legal professionals, defending the original imperial promise of a transplanted British law in the interests of a wider imperial mythology. This promise now seemed to have been abandoned. 'The separation of judicial and administrative powers', wrote Lugard, 'would seem unnatural to the primitive African since they are combined in his own rulers . . . . Moreover, in a country recently brought under administration, and in times of political difficulty, occasions may arise when the strictly legal aspect must give way to expediency.'[1]

By the 1930s the orthodoxies of indirect rule were supported by the prescriptions of an immature yet confident anthropology, and policy, in theory, was permeated by a willingness to give weight to African ways of administering justice. Both administrators and anthropologists were conceptually ill equipped to realise that by then the African legal conceptions that appeared to be current had been formed out of forty years of conflict with colonial government, by the economic and social transformations resulting from the colonial economy and by new divisions in African societies. And while much of the rhetoric was about whether African laws or British ones should be fostered as paramount, real life was not about this at all. As we will see, whatever was said on this subject, the British criminal 'codes', the battery of colonial administrative statutes and the current prejudices of headmen and district officers dominated the day-to-day application of the law.

The battle between lawyers and administrators was also fought largely between different ideas about courts and procedures, a battle which tended to obscure the question of what kind of law, if any, was being used. The lawyers were quick to see that the administration of justice fell dismally short of the standards that it professed to uphold. They were also deeply critical of all the favourite administrative tenets. In the early 1930s this criticism came to a head with the appointment of the Royal Commission of Enquiry into the Administration of Justice in Kenya, Uganda, and Tanganyika Territory in Criminal Matters, chaired by H.G. Bushe, the Colonial Office legal adviser. Its report was massively hostile to the administrative approach to law-giving. The notions that district officers should rest their prestige on their powers to judge and punish, and should base their judicial function not on legal training and strict application of the laws of evidence but on their general knowledge of African life, was, the commission said, 'fundamentally unsound'. Courts without technicalities administering a sort of African equity were bound to be anathema to lawyers. Of the administrators' new urging that African ideas be taken into account in the criminal law the commission said, 'It is the duty of Government to civilise and to maintain peace and good order, and this can only be done by the introduction of British concepts of wrong doing.' They quoted with approval a Tanganyikan government memorandum which said that the sanctions of imprisonment and fine were 'the sanctions which all civilised nations accept as permissible' and that these were 'in substitution for the barbarous sanctions of their own law'.[2] The administrators, while in the main continuing to give obeisance to these premises, were doubtful of their immediate application. As the governor of Uganda put it, Britain had imposed an 'alien system of justice. Our object in doing so was ... to inculcate more satisfactory ideas of right and wrong; to teach the native that crime is, in the main, to be regarded as an offence against society, not as an offence against the individual.'

But, he thought, experience had shown that such a transplant could not quickly take place. The administrators stood for simple and speedy justice, if necessary through the use of African agencies, the lawyers for the transplanting of the technicalities of English criminal law and procedures. The debate centred upon the procedures for applying criminal law and in it neither side took a relativist stance regarding the substantive law to be applied. As one governor summed up, even if some of the British procedures were questionable when transplanted to colonial Africa, there was no question about 'the exclusive sacrosanctity of British ideas of right and wrong.[3]

In the event criminal law and court procedures generally were Anglicised (though with obvious rough edges as concessions to administrative reality and, in East and Central Africa, the virtual absence of lawyers). African ideas about conciliation, restitution and compensation were given no official procedural place, nor were African ideas about which offences were most seriously punishable. The result was that colonial courts were, in African eyes, unsatisfactory and alien not simply because they punished severely, which they often did, but because they only punished, when punishment was not seen as the only or the best way of proceeding, and because they treated lightly things which were deeply offensive in African eyes. These confusions on the 'criminal' side had their effect on the 'civil' side. For throughout the discussions it had been taken for granted that African agencies would continue to administer customary law in that area which British lawyers thought of as a civil law – family, succession and land tenure. It did not occur to them that the failure on the 'criminal' side would have repercussions for the way in which African agencies behaved, and on the type of customary law they administered. The role of developing and administering African ideas of right and wrong, of imposing a public morality, which had been excluded from the 'criminal' process, now fell to the 'civil' side of the customary law.

To a large extent liberal opinion supported the lawyers' antipathy to the Africanising of justice. Leonard Barnes, for example, who was one of the most progressive writers on African and colonial questions, took the side of the lawyers and Grattan Bushe, when he attacked the Native Courts system in 1939. These courts, Barnes wrote, heard thousands of cases, had wide powers of punishment, and were 'free to disregard every elementary principle of justice'.[4] The African elite was also on the side of the lawyers and of liberal opinion. They wanted first to 'legalise' the administration of justice, which meant, until the very end of the colonial period, to Anglicise it further. The district officers, traditional leaders and conservative opinion generally wanted the law to be less 'legal' and less technical; and were able to claim that at the same time this made it more African.

This position is typified in the arguments of Melland and Cullen Young, whose administrative and missionary experience was in Malawi and North Eastern Zambia, who argued that the recommendations and ideals of the Bushe Commission, if accepted (which they were not), would mean the end of indirect rule. They supported, which was rare for the time, recognition not just of an area set apart for customary law, but a more widespread fostering of African juristic ideas. Partly they had a positive reason for this in their concept of a compensatory and restitutive African form of justice with deep roots in African society, and partly they felt that a return to a communally minded justice might halt the disruptive growth of individualism and 'self-assertion'.[5] It was this latter note that was to sound again and again in discussions of support for African agencies.

Hailey's Olympian survey of legal problems in his *African Survey* demonstrated that while indirect rule might be seen as a necessary policy, the relativist and non-evolutionary stance of functionalist anthropology had not replaced evolutionism as the basic view of lawyers and administrators. Africa today, Hailey wrote, 'is in one of the states which at different times *must* have marked the development of law elsewhere'.[6] He saw the diffusion of British law in Africa in the light of a grandiose historical analogy with the Roman and British Indian empires. The main tasks for the imperial lawgiver in Africa were 'the provision of a law of crimes, of rules of judicial procedure, and a simple form of procedure regulating commercial transactions, for it is common ground that at the outset anything beyond this must continue to be regulated by custom'. Custom was seen to 'continue', in isolation from new state punishments, new courts and procedures, and a

51

new law of contract. African law, Hailey thought, had an 'apparent deficiency on the penal or deterrent side' (a 'familiar stage in the history of law'), as it represented not the 'act of a sovereign but the belief and practice of a community', backed by magico-religious sanctions. This law he saw as being faced with rapid change imposed upon it from outside. It was a passive, though at times stubbornly reactionary, victim, rather than an active player. 'The strength with which new forces from many angles are playing on African social institutions', Hailey wrote, 'can have no parallel in history.' In this view evolution was taking place in African institutions but it was a disturbed and disrupted evolution, proceeding faster than its 'natural' pace. The British lawgiver's task was to control and regulate this process, to overcome unnecessary resistances in family, land and contractual law and to ensure a 'gradual advance towards individualisation of property in land which may lead to improvement in production'. Certainty in or systematisation of the law was not necessary because 'the procedure of judicial administration is a more important factor in earning respect for the law than the substance of the law itself.'[7]

The next landmark state paper on the administration of justice in Colonial East Africa was the Phillips *Report on Native Tribunals*.[8] Phillips was also an evolutionist. Following Hailey he thought that African legal development was enacting the same stages as the Babylonians and the Greeks and that while 'Africa has been late getting off the mark [it] is now heading in the same direction as its forerunners.' The gloom that was building up about the pace of change is strongly evident in the Phillips report. In Africa, he wrote, Christianity seemed to have supported the westernisation of the family, and he referred as a warning to the writings of H.J. Simons in South Africa on the emergence of the monogamous individual family and the consequent emancipation of youth. Like Hailey, Phillips thought that 'the magnitude of the effects of culture contact can hardly be exaggerated,' and that externally imposed change was interfering with the normal process of evolution. As a result there were great pressures from many Africans to free themselves from the restrictions of the old law, and he quoted Margery Perham's opinion that Nigerian town-dwellers were 'intensely critical of the judicial aspect of paternal government and almost fanatically determined to have all they can of British courts and British law'.[9] That, by the 1940s, customary law was a contentious battleground in African society was certainly true but it is the fear expressed in Hailey's and Phillips' conception that I want to draw attention to now – a conception of premature dissolution, of essential familial and societal ties tearing under the strain of individualism. Early administrators had looked forward to a change in this direction but it was now seen as a change that was happening far too quickly.

There is a little more awareness in the Phillips Report than in Hailey that Africans played an active part in these processes and there are very clear insights into the kinds of changes which I will later discuss. The native law, Phillips wrote, was based on collectivist social relationships, and consisted, not of formal codes, but of the 'principles' which govern these relationships and ensure their conformity with tradition. In the olden days the law was not an objective standard which guaranteed 'rights' but was what the elders, constrained by custom, decided. He noted that while Malinowski had apparently exploded the notion that all savage custom was law, and had taught that a distinction was made between the two, African tribunals in Kenya were not Malinowskian. There was a tendency among them, for example, to administer all rules concerning respect as if they were law. Phillips urged that modern conditions and new judicial bodies now 'necessitated the crystallisation of native law into a set code of rules, involving a clear distinction between law and non-enforceable custom'. The bullet of codification, in other words, would have to be bitten if the tribunals were not simply to function as a weapon for the elders.

East African administrators had begun to feel a need for a clearer body of 'native law', rather than a loose fluid body of social rules, and this was a feeling which was gaining ground elsewhere. There were, however, many confusions involved. In the Phillips report it was felt that the elders of the time were less learned in what really was customary law than their predecessors, which was the reason for wanting it written down.[10] Sir A. Pim, in his report on the Bechuanaland Protectorate in 1933, had spoken of the 'urgency' of compiling African law because the old chiefs were gone and 'new Chiefs and their new advisers have not the same knowledge of the traditions of the past.' This new apprehension was coupled with the realisation that little was known about what African law actually was. Hailey's view that it was not important to know this was overshadowed by new concerns. Writing in 1943 Lewin noted that the Native Courts of British Africa had failed to give rise to a known body of law; that there were no codes or records, and that nothing more was known about African law than before the courts had been set up. 'Has British policy in the past', he asked, 'not shown too much concern for Native Courts and too little for Native Law?'[11]

The idea that the *real* customary law was in the minds of the oldest men (or even of the dead) and that the new elders did not know it properly, seemed to coexist with the idea that the elders were behaving in too traditional a manner and were administering 'social' obligations and not law and should be put on the path of distinguishing between the two and evolving the law in a more modern way. The original premise had been that customary law was innovative and evolving and should be left alone to do this. Now there was a swing towards the historic view of customary law as administrators reacted to the pace of evolution and the way in which the African courts made law. This seemed to highlight the need for a clearer statement of the *rules of law* even at the price of the rigidification of the evolutionary process, and colonial governments now supported the writing of rule books. In 1938, for example, the government of the Bechuanaland Protectorate commissioned Schapera's *Handbook of Tswana Law and Custom*, the precursor of many books of African legal rules. The swing towards rule-recording came at a time when both African elders and British administrators from their differing perspectives perceived a crisis of social dissolution. As new circumstances widened the possible range of apparently legitimate behaviour, so the African courts were pushing old obligations to the fore. This coincided with (and partially caused) the British perception that it was now becoming necessary to write down the rules which African courts thought ought to be obeyed.

To some extent the gap between the lawyers and administrators had been closed. On the subject of customary law, once the administrators were no longer content to leave everything to haphazard and uncontrolled development at the hands of 'Native Courts', there was less insistence on the distinctions between primitive and advanced law and much more on the comparability of African concepts. (Just at this time the opposite tendency was appearing in some of the anthropological literature.) The emphasis on comparability and compatibility of African and western law was helped along enormously by the institutional changes during the 1950s which were a part of the preparation for African independence. African political and cultural nationalism were both reflected in the flowering of African legal nationalism which could not possibly countenance the division of legal systems into two parts with a separate and subordinate African sector in the largely uncontrolled hands of a traditional leadership. African nationalist leadership espoused the lawyers' view. They wanted 'proper' courts, 'proper' procedures, known laws and a separation of the powers. They also wanted an end to the patchwork of customary 'systems' which made up the subordinate part of the law in each British territory. To the state-makers and nation-builders of the 1950s and 1960s the building of national legal systems by integrating the British and customary parts, and by unifying the varied bodies of custom, was the overriding concern, and this contributed pointedly to the development of a particular view of the customary law. For legal nationalism now endorsed customary law as the essentially African part of the colonial legal system upon which the new African law was to be built. This made it impossible to see the customary law as having been created by colonialism. In 1963 the African Conference on Local Courts and Customary Law set out the framework of this understanding: that in the early colonial period 'existing African legal institutions continued to function much the same as they had in the past.' And the coming of indirect rule 'left the composition of the courts unaltered, made few changes in the law administered and the manner of administration except for a few restrictions'.[12]

CONTINUITY, COMPARABILITY AND CULTURAL NATIONALISM: THE LAWYERS' VIEW

The ideal of the survival and continuity of an essentially unchanged customary law was to be the basis of modern lawyers' interpretations, both practical

54

and academic. The pretence of continuity had always been important both in legitimating the control of the colonial state – the idea that the law was really historic and African played a part in its acceptability to Africans – and in legitimating the innovations which some Africans were able to press upon the colonial state. It was an important fiction which now developed new uses. Underlying the drive for legal integration and unification was the drive to indigenise the law, to create the basis of an African common law to replace foreign legal colonisation. The prime need, in Nekam's words, was to 'save the African roots of law in Africa'.[13] It was a necessity, therefore, that the legal plant be a native and not an exotic. Where the focus was on African versus foreign law as it was in the drive for integration, it is not surprising that there was not too much interest in the nature and make-up of the African side of the conflict; rather the emphasis was on its legal parity and comparability and its special suitability to African life. Where the focus was on the unification of customary legal systems the emphasis was on the search for the distinct principles which African law throughout the continent was supposed to share. Both these focuses were valid but they did take attention away from the processes by which Africans had made the customary law during the colonial period – that customary law which was now being portrayed as the basic, continuing, indigenous verity upon which the new national legal systems could base themselves.

Colonial and African lawyers were in conflict as to how far the indigenous law could be used, not as to how it came into being nor as to the validity of its indigenous credentials. English legal planning for the new Africa was that customary law should be limited to the fields of family law, succession and customary land tenure, where it was perceived to have 'continued' to rule. African nationalist lawyers worked on trying to show that African law could be extended to, and was viable in, the field of law as a whole. Legal writers began to work on putting local concepts into recognised juristic forms. Slavery became 'defective capacity'; the ordeal an essentially peripheral problem in the law of evidence.[14] Legal evolutionism was not confronted, it was merely retorted that the customary law had already evolved. The notion that a fully evolved law made a clear distinction between crime and tort was not challenged but accepted, and an effort was made to demonstrate that customary legal systems had done just this. In the colonial writing the presence of a system based on retributive punishment had been taken to show that people had evolved law, while its absence meant that they had not yet developed it. While many of the more idealist anthropologists had by the 1960s rejected this view and were stressing instead the positive nature of African ideas about restitution, a lot of African legal writing, seeing this as colonial stereotyping, was reluctant to follow. Where the old evolutionists had claimed that the distinguishing mark of a real legal system was that murder and other forms of homicide were treated differently, the new legal writing devoted itself to demonstrating that African law lived up to this; that it had had an adequate notion of *mens rea* and had distinguished between murder and homicide; that it was as capable as western law of exacting the death penalty for wrongful killing and did not merely require compensatory payments. Operating under the influence of a reviving African cultural nationalism the lawyers had a hard task. They had to emphasise not only comparability, so that an indigenous law could assert itself in the new law of independent Africa, but also the distinctive ways of an African jurisprudence, in order to demonstrate the need for, and to justify the considerable effort that was going to be needed to create, a new African common law. But the main perceived necessity was expressed by Elias in 1954 when he wrote of the need to see African law 'within the wider framework of a general jurisprudence' and to establish the general thesis 'that African law ... forms part and parcel of law in general'.[15]

African legal nationalists, therefore, following hard on the heels of the new conservatism and rule-orientation of the British administrators, supported the 'restatement' strategy, which sought to put together comprehensive compilations of legal rules gathered from elders, court assessors, chiefs and other repositories of custom in the name of demonstrating the certainty, viability for use, and national unifiability of customary law. How this law got to be what it was, was in this context not a relevant or useful question. The abolition of the Native Courts and the integration of court systems was also seen as a part of the Africanising of the legal system by giving full status to customary law and litigants and setting the stage for a national legal system. The kind of knowledge which was being created by the functional and trouble case studies of law done by the anthropologists was, again, not useful in this context, and the gap between legal and anthropological studies consequently widened. In 1960 the London Conference on the Future of Law in Africa recommended that moves should be made 'to stabilise' customary law. This was an implied acknowledgement that customary law was innovative rather than historic, but, in contrast to the inter-war period when codification had been forsworn for precisely this reason, it seemed that the time had now come to freeze the development of the customary law and to turn it into a body of certain and applicable rules.

It seemed to Schiller, writing in 1965, that it was these problems, arising from the integration of the interacting indigenous and imported legal systems, which had 'prime place' in African legal studies. He defined the indigenous law in historic terms as 'unwritten law tracing back to the habits and usages of the people', and emphasised that there were distinctive features characterising African law: the role of the court in promoting reconciliation and educating public opinion and the parties in legal norms; the evocation of the supernatural; and the involvement of the community in connection with individual rights and duties. But his aim was to emphasise that these distinctive differences did not bring into doubt the status of legalness of customary law.[16]

At the 1960 conference it was pointed out that customary law courts 'may merely reflect the opinion of a powerful section of the community. At the present moment ... it is partly a fiction that African courts are applying "customary" law.' But this was levelled almost as an accusation of aberration, as if there was something wrong because the real customary law was there to apply and properly integrated and regulated courts would do just that.

As an apt example of the way in which the misconstructed past of the administrators and lawyers has affected understanding of Central Africa I will turn to an account which applied it to the law of Zambia.[17] In the early years, the authors write, 'Tribal chiefs continued to administer the customary law .... The British were primarily occupied in suppressing the Portuguese and Arab slave trade and in bringing warring tribes under control.' That chiefs administered customary law like British magistrates administered British law is apparently unproblematic, and there is no hint, for example, that slavery was an institution of this law or that there were any implications for customary law as a result of its suppression. They discuss the establishment of the British courts, the application of the repugnancy clause, and the development of legal dualism, and maintain that 'So long as African litigants were willing to accept the decisions of tribal courts, contacts and conflicts between the two judicial systems would remain at a minimum.' Thus the customary law is not only 'continuing', but is doing so in isolation from the British law: 'the tribal courts continued to administer justice with relatively little interference from the British.' Rubin and Cotran also refer to 'an almost complete isolation of African Courts and customary law in the colonial period'.[18] As I will show, this separation did not in fact exist and both British and African agencies interacted as part of one legal world. But the conceptual separation of the two appears to be a necessary precondition of (and a result of) the idea of the continuing customary law which represents the African side of the law in modern Africa. It is not until the authors consider urbanisation that they think about change in the customary law. And then the problem is seen as that of the adaptation of an unchanged customary law that was 'there' in the 'rural tribal setting' to a new urban environment. In the new urban courts, they write, 'A body of law was being created which was neither customary nor British.' This view was also that of the Chief Justice of Zambia in 1936 whom they quote as saying, 'It is now seriously suggested that the Government should allow to grow up in the industrial areas something which is neither English law nor customary law: it is in fact no law, but merely a system based upon convenience, and we are asked to agree to three systems of law.'[19] It is clear that contemporary observers and subsequent commentators were able to see the changes and adaptations which Africans were making in their handling of 'legal' matters in the urban areas. What is not quite so clear is why there has been so much less sensitivity to the possibility that customary law in the 'rural tribal setting' was also a body of law 'created' and was also 'neither customary nor British', being evolved, like the new urban law, to meet new needs and to stake out positions. The perception is the opposite. The 'chiefly courts', Spalding

57

writes, 'whether recognised, or ignored, or suppressed by the colonial authorities ... followed patterns set long before the first white man laid claim to have discovered their existence'.[20]

As the colonial period drew to an end there was a focus on 'the future health of the customary law'. Suddenly, it seemed, it was being faced with a period of change with which it could not cope. Phillips doubted the capacity of the former guardians of the customary law, the Native Courts, to be 'capable of making a sufficiently dynamic contribution to the adaptation and development of the customary law'.[21] The care of its future health was to be put in the hands of its former adversaries, the lawyers, for whom it was now not a rival source of authority and a reactionary obfuscation, but the pennant of legal Africanity. This was the major obstacle in the way of the historical study of customary law because its *raison d'être* was now that it was a cultural survival. I have noted also that the common lawyers' notion of custom, which is essentially a-historical, impeded proper historical understanding. This is not to say that change in the customary law was never studied or noted, only that change was put into an evolutionary context – of a *development* of customary law towards something else, a development which was usually seen in relation to the influence of British law and procedures. While there was some recognition that the customary law might be changing, it was only seen as changing as part of a process of culture contact and legal acculturation. Elias noted that although in theory Native Courts were left uninhibited by technical rules, in practice they were all developing towards an approximation of English methods.[22] If one treats customary law as law, then the question here is, how far is the content of the customary rules influenced by the content of English rules? My problem is different: first, it is how far does the pull of English rule-form, exercised through dominant institutions, affect customary forms, and, secondly, how far is the content of claims new? Change through legal acculturation did take place but it also acted as a screen which obscured from view the changes which had always taken place, and which were still going on, as a result of group interaction, challenges and responses to power, struggles about statuses and resources, and responses to economic change. The problem lay basically with the view that the customary law had a substantive content of rules rather than understanding it as a strategy for legitimising control which assumed a 'legal' form when it was offered a 'legal' forum in which to operate. In this sense the customary law was never 'there'. When, however, it came to be an important part of cultural nationalism that legal integration would in some way provide for a strengthening of the African element in the new national law it was hardly likely that a perception of it would develop which 'relegated' it to a non-law position. Indeed the movement was in another direction entirely. If customary law was to be a viable part of a new integrated law, then the content of its rules had first to be ascertained. The problem of uncertainty came to the fore. The 1960 conference noted, 'One of the major problems in administering customary law today is in determining what is the appropriate customary law to be applied in any particular case.'[23]

Rubin and Cotran give a good indication of the approach of mainstream British legal scholarship. Their task was to provide 'a clear statement of the substantive rules of customary law'. Lawyers required the statement and exposition of rules and therefore 'the recasting and refashioning [of] the rules of customary law into a form which will enable them to be used in the context of modern Africa'.[24] This was comprehensible in terms of an English lawyer's understanding of law and its social tasks, but the emphasis on the ascertainment of rules which was apparent in the lawyers' writings in the 1950s and 1960s represents the ultimate failure to understand the customary law. It exemplifies the process which goes back over the whole colonial period: the British had looked for rules, and Africans, as this was realised, emphasised that the claims they were putting forward were in fact rules to be applied, not positions to be negotiated. Rules *became* the most useful strategy on the African side and thus both sides became rule-oriented.

It was the aim of the reformers that once the customary law had been ascertained and restated (it was to be hoped in a 'unified' form), it would be applied by local courts as part of a single legal system. The notion of application rested upon the idea that customary rules could be separated from customary processes as if they were not necessarily interconnected. Smith had pointed out that legal scholars have been obsessed with conflict-of-laws problems and indeed Allott has written that the complexities of choice-of-law problems 'may well be the strongest argument in favour of unification'. Yet conflicts problems seldom occurred in the urban customary courts, where English lawyers expected them to, because the courts did not separate rules from processes of settlement. Rules of law were not clearly articulated, Smith wrote of Northern Nigeria, and rule was not 'pitted against rule'. 'It was in the process of fact statement that the values and moral beacons which ultimately served as guide-posts of decision making emerged.' Similarly Epstein wrote of Zambia that the customary court 'deals with patterns of rightdoing and wrongdoing within the context of a given social relationship, rather than with the enforcement of specific legal rights and duties'.[25] Some lawyers also noted that African courts avoided conflicts problems easily but they did not draw the conclusion that this was because rules were not central to their activities. Instead they were led towards a new mystique – that behind the apparent surface differences there was an underlying unity in the rules of the customary law, which justified a unification and which spoke for the viability of a basic indigenous common law.[26]

REFASHIONED UNDERSTANDINGS: TOWARDS A LEGAL HISTORY

The revolution in African historical writing has not had much effect on the understanding of the African legal past. Legal history has not been written by general historians. While matters germane to it have been dealt with in the context of the political history of indirect rule it appears to have escaped the attention of those writers who have focused on African responses and initiatives under colonialism. We have therefore to turn first to the writing about the past by academic lawyers. Allott has written a general account of the development of East African legal systems during the colonial period in which he was concerned to emphasise that the 'key feature' of the systems was that they were 'dualistic', featuring on the one hand courts and law of western origin and on the other courts and law 'deriving from traditional institutions'. 'The laws of African origin', he wrote, 'comprised local customary laws varying more or less in detail from place to place.' Traditional law and courts were 'allowed to continue'. Central to his story is the struggle between the legal 'assimilationists' and the legal protectionists which I have outlined above. He discusses the development of Cameron's policy in Tanganyika which embodied the protective approach and the belief that the greatest danger to the 'unhealthy development of native law' was the tendency to 'mimic' the procedures of English courts. In the post-Cameron period the assimilationists gradually got the upper hand and, Allott writes, African populations came increasingly to do things the western way: 'the customary laws became progressively *emancipated* from their traditional form and background, and at the same time their rules . . . approached more closely those of the general English type law. In this way the *second* of the major features of the original colonial legal systems, that they *preserved the ancient African laws* for the African sections of the population, receded in importance.'

In his account, then, African law was just there to begin with, it was 'traditional'; and then it was 'continued' and 'preserved'. Where there was change it was first 'mimicry' and later real westernisation and emancipation. The development of the customary law was done 'to a very considerable extent' by the adoption of the 'advice and guidance' given by the district officers. Allott sees as one of the present tasks the 're-vindication of the African heritage of law'. But there is nothing in his account which tells us what this heritage might have been, or to suggest that it might have changed in the colonial period, not just through mimicry and westernisation but as a conscious expression of the ideological and social strategies of Africans.[27]

The most sensitive historical account of customary law in the colonial period is that by Read.[28] Read emphasises the political centrality of law in imperial ideology and he notes too the powerful mythology of success in this field which prevailed towards the end of the colonial period. The ideology of the lawgivers tended to mask the role of the courts in colonial Africa as part of administration. Read sees both the seizing of control over dispute-settlement procedures and the later resurrection of African fora as part of the establishing and consolidating of colonial political control. That the matter was administrative and political rather than professionally 'legal' is underscored by the wide divergences between colonial legal practices and the ideological model of British law, for example the absence of the separation of powers, trial by jury and the administrators' hostility to, and attempts to exclude, the legal profession. The need of the colonial state was for African institutions of authority, not for a known body of African law. By the end of the colonial period it had to be assumed that the rules that African-run courts were working with were African law. Customary law never had to be proved in the Native Courts as it was assumed that they knew what it was (which gave considerable leeway for invention). Judicial enquiry into it was piecemeal, occurring only in those random instances when a rule of customary law had to be proved before the High Court. The Colonial Office for most of the period under discussion did not encourage systematic investigation or written accounts for fear that the law would crystallise too early.[29]

Read's focus in his chapter on customary law under colonial rule is on those influences which formed the changing context of customary 'rules'. He points out that the 'fundamental axiom' of British rule overseas, that pre-existing systems of law continued in operation, raised a number of questions. If the law of the conquered was to become part of the law of the new state, how was it to be ascertained? Could it and should it be recorded? How far was it tradition? And how far should it be allowed to change? The word 'traditional', Read writes, when used in connection with indigenous systems, only has a 'limited, or hypothetical, connotation'. Intellectual reconstruction of pre-colonial systems was impossible as accounts, both European and African, were fragmentary and lack objectivity. Pre-colonial law was 'not articulated, defined or formalised' and was also the changing product of an eventful recent history: 'its mutations reflecting the often dramatic changes in the political or social life of the particular community: conquest and defeat, migration and absorption, famine and disease, triumph and disaster'.[30] In spite of all of this, Read shows in his summary of the colonial debate that pre-colonial law came to be conceptualised as an existing body of rules, a baseline, in contrast to the introduced law of the colonial government. Building on this misconception lawyers, administrators and anthropologists debated the difference between law and custom. Were all usages laws? Did tribal man distinguish law as a special category of rules? The very use of the phrase 'native law and custom' glossed over an unconcluded debate as to the nature of the rules designated. In any case the business of the administrators lay not in making academic distinctions but in governing. They enforced 'through new or altered institutions, customary law, which may not have previously distinguished law from custom, and in lending coercion of a new and powerful kind to the enforcement of principles of behaviour which had perhaps previously been unenforceable in any comparable way, they become potent instruments of change.'[31]

What is clear from Read's account is that customary law was neither 'there' nor traditional, and that in the colonial period it changed under the influence and through the institutions of the dominant legal system.

The inherent nature of colonial rule made it impossible to preserve traditional customary rules unchanged. With the introduction of a new source of ultimate authority, even for customary law ... came the appearance of new judicial institutions with new personnel. These included not merely judges and magistrates, administrative officers and police officers from Britain, but clerks, messengers and policemen who might be local people, 'native strangers' or Asians. The colonial regime provided new instruments of coercive authority mainly reflecting alien ideas. Even statutory 'native courts' of traditional pattern, were innovations: for, although in early days their membership and procedure might have had a traditional basis, the foundation of their authority lay elsewhere, and the means of enforcing it were new.[32]

It was not, in this view, changes in the contents of customary rules brought about by social and economic change, nor changes forcibly imposed through non-recognition by application of the repugnancy test that were vital, rather it was the fundamental change in the nature of the processes. The essence of the customary systems may be said to have lain in their processes, but these were displaced, and the flexible principles which had guided them were now fed into a rule-honing and -using machine operating in new political circumstances. Even the local clan and village tribunals which operated beyond and alongside the indirect-rule Native Courts began to take on the form of and to emulate the dominant system particularly because local litigants and judges knew that village fora were now a part of a broader hierarchy available for use in disputing strategies.

As Read points out, British administrators could not make up their minds as to how far customary law was supposed to be historic or traditional, and how far it could be legitimately innovative. In the towns there developed an 'urban customary law' out of the usages of town life which was, in terms of the 'historic' view of customary law, unenforceable by the courts because of the 'adherence officially to the notion of traditional, tribally based, customary law. [This was] particularly evident in the sphere of marriage and extra-marital relations.' The strength of Read's account is in his realisation of the transformation of custom through the changed processes and institutions which used it. The emphasis on rules isolated from structure, he writes, led to 'an undue emphasis on obligations of a merely social character'.[33] Some groups now had the ability to use the support of the colonial government to foist forms of behaviour onto others. Where ethnic groups were mixed this power, masquerading so effectively as legal rather than political (conflicts being conceptualised by lawyers as 'conflict of laws'), was a crucial instrument of political domination, the only legitimate weapon left with which to pursue ethnic rivalry in the colonial situation.[34]

This brings us to the questions which Read does not investigate and upon which I hope to throw some light. Why for example was customary law seen as legitimately innovative in the field of criminal law, yet legitimately 'historic' when related to marriage, land or succession? Given that customary law evolved under the general influence of the legalisation process, who benefited from and promoted rule-orientation, and who resisted it? What did the sections of African society which manipulated the new processes try to achieve with it? What did they try to establish as 'customary' and why?

It may be illustrative of some of the points raised by Read to look at Hooker's account of the Indonesian experience, which is written with an historical sense rare in the African studies.[35] In a parallel with the British experience, the early Dutch assumption that *adat* (customary law) would be superseded by a codified European law was replaced in the period after the first world war by an hostility towards codification and a philosophical and administrative fostering of *adat*. Van Vollenhoven, the leading Dutch authority on and protagonist of *adat*, objected to codification not only because he thought that it shifted the source of law away from the people to a book, but, significantly, because he thought that *adat* was essentially different from modern European law and could not simply be reduced to its forms. 'The law is nowhere individualistic like Roman law was', van Vollenhoven wrote in 1919; it was not about the exercise of rights regardless of community.[36] Societies were based on status, relationships were not determined by submission to 'predetermined rules of universal application within territorial limits'. *Adat* was not conceptualised separately, as western law was, its oral admonitions were 'vague and elusive', allowing a wide latitude of interpretation which permitted a variety of accommodations in dispute-settlement. Power, as Hooker writes, does not necessarily lead to sanction and the adjudication of conflict does not need the imposition of decision. *Adat* looked to a process of mediation: 'Rights and duties are not absolute as fixed principles but are relative according to the proper behaviour *adat* requires from specific individuals.' The individual was not a 'fixed point in a normative reference absolute and independent of circumstance'. Each judgement was regarded as 'unique rather than as an instance of a determinate general rule'.

These sorts of insights are of course a part of the British legal and anthropological writing even if the emphasis on essential difference faded under the lawyer's onslaught in the 1960s. But what is apparent from Hooker's treatment is how *adat*, even under a policy designed to foster its separate character, underwent a process of legalisation. *Adat*, he shows, was discussed by lawyers and administrators within a common set of European-inspired categories – marriage, inheritance, legal personality, delict – which imposed a new conceptualisation upon it. As it worked into the colonial legal mechanism some *adat* 'principles' turned into rules, the criteria for admissibility into this category being established by precedent, by already having been used by a judicial or quasi-judicial authority. A principle, if it could once be wielded persuasively in one forum, might come to be established as a rule if it was reinforced by use in others. The proponents and defenders of *adat*, like Ter Haar and van Vollenhoven, ironically contributed to its legalisation and the fading of its special character because they wanted to establish its use in legal administration. Van Vollenhoven's emphasis on its legal character was in a sense tactically necessitated if *adat* was to be firmly established as a positive law rather than be replaced by a Dutch-inspired code. Ter Haar appeared to see it as a sort of common law to be derived from decisions of courts at work, *adat* being embodied in decisions given by functionaries in an *adat* community acting in a judicial capacity. He emphasised the judicial function over mediation in pursuit of the aim of formulating principles on the basis of judicial decisions so that *adat* could be absorbed into the mainstream of state law. Hooker writes, in terms which are aptly illustrative of the African processes that I will be describing, 'There was a conscious policy and effort to preserve traditional institutions and to identify obligations in terms of indigenous systems. At the same time the organisation and administration of the state institutions could not treat *adat* institutions and obligation systems on their own terms.' European procedures and concepts of regulation 'formalised *adat* rules to an extent unknown in the traditional sphere'. 'Conflict of laws', which was not an issue in *adat*, became an issue with the creation of courts: 'it might be argued that the forum, because of its inability to follow indigenous principles of compromise made the conflicts question inevitable.' Furthermore, the situation in which low-level judicial processes were carried out in expectation of review contributed to legalisation. 'One of the results of this expectation will be the propounding of rules in full knowledge of later possible review and so there will arise a consciousness, if not of law making then of law declaration, the statement of which, whether accepted or not, is going to remain relatively permanent.'[37]

Instead, in Africa, the generally received historical picture has been one of the growth of legal dualism, with English and 'customary' sides. But even if one can make sense of this institutionally once colonial administration had created separate court systems, it does not adequately portray the content of the law, nor does it represent the legal world in which people lived. The concept of legal dualism, like that of the dual economy once favoured by colonial economists, may be conceptually neat, but people lived within one world in which all the parts were interrelated. People used and were subject to both sets of courts and courts operated with strong awareness of each other. Furthermore the law of the 'English' courts was not English at all. As Adewoye writes, it was one thing to introduce courts, 'quite another to maintain a standard of judicial administration compatible with the spirit behind these institutions in their homeland'.[38]

Adewoye, writing as an historian of West Africa in one of the rare works of African legal history, focuses on the operation of the courts rather than upon the substance of the law. He stresses that the role of colonial judicial system was essentially the stabilisation of colonial conquest. His picture is one of the interaction between 'imperfect' versions of English and African law, rather than one of part reception of English law and 'survival' of African law in a dual system, and is subtler than both the legal and the anthropological views of the past. Adewoye writes from the perspective of having lived with the colonial legal legacy, unlike many of the British administrators whose writing is imbued with the sense of that legacy being the summation of an achievement, which can be successfully built upon. Adewoye observes, in precise contradistinction to the oft-made British claim that the rule of law had been introduced into Africa, that it was not among the colonial bequests. 'The forces standing in the way of its operation are numerous,' he writes, 'a good proportion stemming from the absence of any strong tradition of legality . . . . the colonial regime did little consciously to entrench the rule of law. Traditionally, judicial administration was the preserve of the ruling elite, an adjunct of power . . . . people had recourse not to law as such but to the wisdom of their rulers and elders in the resolution of interpersonal conflicts.'[39] The connections between the absence of a strong tradition of legality in both customary and colonial law, and its absence in the post-colonial state, is of importance in regard to Central Africa. Much of Adewoye's book, like much of the writing on the British legal system in India, is concerned with the role of the Anglicised indigenous legal profession. The position of the local profession, vital in India and West Africa under colonial rule, is not part of the Central African story as the imposed legal system operated almost entirely without a legal profession. This drastic modification to the adversary process contributed to the absence in Central Africa of a 'strong tradition of legality'. Neither of the legal traditions in Central Africa, in parallel to Adewoye's comments on West Africa, had much to contribute to the idea of the rule of law, as neither English colonial law nor African law were concerned with the problem of limiting state power.

The perception of customary law as a continuing body of rules is, then, being replaced by an understanding of its formation in colonial processes. Other contemporary studies are also pointing in this direction. The observation that customary law is essentially a fiction even in the circumstances of the post-colonial state is beginning to take hold. Bohmer's study of the lower courts of Upper Volta, which was based on an acceptance of definitions of African law of Allott and Elias which stress that there was 'indeed law', separable and distinct in African societies, was unable to observe the use of it by the customary courts, which did not appear to apply it. Judges and assessors, she found, were ignorant of it and thought such knowledge to be irrelevant, disputes were solved by what 'seemed "fair" in the circumstances'.[40] This was not necessarily based on idyllic reconciliation: community values projected from the audience could be oppressive, so could judicial homilies, and scorned women litigants were led sobbing from the courtroom. Van Binsbergen, observing the post-colonial 'law' of the Nkoya in Zambia, concludes that courts and rules were peripheral to the judicial process and the settlement of conflict in those areas in which customary law is supposed by lawyers to apply.[41] Regarding inheritance, he wrote, there was not a set of rules but a set of expectations and no formal redressive action could be taken if they were not met.[42] 'The relatives are left with their resentment and are likely to turn to sorcery for revenge.' Action outside of a court arena might be taken by the headman to prevent this but he would be concerned not with rules and justice, or rights and obligations, but with the dulling of animosities. Conflict was regarded 'not as a matter of right or wrong against abstract, unalterable criteria of formulated rules of behaviour, but as a direct threat to group unity ... the awareness of continually being on the edge of disruption.'

Richard Abel's research also demonstrated that actual court cases were not concerned with the identity of rules and that courts did not develop a rule-orientation of their own initiative. He attacked both the older style of ethnography for producing disembodied rules which did not reflect actual practice, and the rule-directed interviews of the modern legal researchers. He urged instead the collection of contemporary court records because this case method would concentrate on the solution of actual controversies 'without being misled by perceptions of ideal morality'.[43] The ambition to get away from rule-orientation and to look at what litigants and courts really did in disputing was correct. Yet there was a weakness, which was that in the understandable effort to escape from the 'perceptions of ideal morality' and rule-orientation it did not ask about the uses of the ideational aspect of rules. If idealised rules, put forward by panels of experts, or by litigants, or by anthropologists' informants, are simply considered to be 'false' because they do not represent the 'law in action' then the content of the 'false' claims is not on the agenda for examination. Yet what is put forward in the 'false rules', in the stated customary law, although it may not be applied by the courts, represents important material and moral claims about a society in flux and it is in this sense that the rule statements must come back on the agenda for study. And it is through the study of the historical processes in which these statements were formed that we will understand both their form and their content. For this historical understanding of form and content we may turn to Snyder, who is able to liberate himself from the idea of customary law, a notion which, as he writes, 'implies historical continuity [whereas] its origins are actually comparatively recent'.[44] Snyder suggests that the customary law must be understood through the 'particular conjunction of class forces and ideologies mediated through the colonial state, and that this law simultaneously masked and contributed to a struggle over power and rural conditions of production.' He is able to show how the change in relations of production in the colonial period in Senegal is accompanied by, and necessitated, the transformation of local claims into legal forms acceptable to the French. 'Both the general conception of "customary law" and the specific legal forms it encompassed resulted from changing class relationships in the establishment of capitalist commodity production during the colonial period.' The departure from functionalism is complete and the focus is turned also from the individual in conflict and in dispute-settlement to the historical relationship of legal form with class and mode of production. My own historical analysis which follows seeks to add to this an emphasis on the peculiar institutional processes in which the emergence of the legal mode was shaped and to stress the active efforts made by Africans under colonial rule to use colonial state institutions. Because if one examines these efforts one is put on one's guard against a possible new evolutionism which might, in stressing the connection between market relations, new classes and the legal mode, overlook the ambivalent uses to which the legal mode could be put. Pre-capitalist forms were not simply dissolved by capitalism. Some fought for an accommodation which resisted dissolution. The legal mode was a weapon which could be used not only to define new relationships but to defend old ones, to fight a class rearguard action as well as to carve out new rights, and be used simultaneously to do both. Writing in a different context Washbrook has shown of British India how 'The conventions of the law . . . did not move very far or fast to accommodate the social imperatives of market capitalism. They served at least as much to shore up "antique" social institutions and rights as they did to pave the way towards a society based upon individualism and competition.'[45] New customary law in Africa could also serve both old ends and new ones.

Part II

Right and wrong

4

The lawgivers in Central Africa: social control

LEGAL THEATRE: THE WHITE MAN'S PART

The early years in both Zambia and Malawi were marked by a belligerent attitude to the administration of justice. The role envisaged for Africans in the trial of cases was a small one. The desire of the governments that their officers try all cases was an amalgam of an ambition to spread the British legal gospel as an integral part of the civilising mission and the need to have all the authority in the districts concentrated in the district officers' hands. The dismissive attitude which prevailed towards the pre-colonial situation is summed up in the words of the still extant official history of the judicial department in Malawi, 'Prior to the founding of the Protectorate, justice, such as it was, was administered by the native chiefs.'[1]

Lawyers worried about the basis upon which a dual system rested. For the first decade of administration the theory was that the law could not interfere with the indigenous administration of justice though officials were told to forbid the ordeal and 'inhumane and barbarous' methods of punishment. Death sentences were not to be carried out without the sanction of the deputy administrator and had to be done in the presence of a white official 'who will satisfy himself that the criminal is executed in a humane and decorous manner'.[2] Among the definitions of a protectorate was that it was a territory to which British rule had been extended in default of any regularly organised government, to supply the elementary needs of human society.[3] It was therefore the duty of the protecting government to define a system of law. In countries which were 'sufficiently advanced in civilisation' the protecting power could continue the existing system. But in Malawi the administration felt that 'there existed no legal system' applicable to 'members of civilised communities', though there was 'a definite though varying body of native law and custom which was known and understood by all and which had grown up in the course of an unknown period to regulate, more or less successfully, the conditions of native life'. The protectorate thus required two systems, first an African one, and secondly one both for the non-African population and to 'supplement the simple provisions of native

71

law and custom in cases where natives were concerned'. To this end the Order in Council of British Central Africa of 1902 applied to the protectorate the common law and statutes in force in England on 11 August 1902. Section 20 of the Order in Council contained the usual 'repugnancy clause' which provided that African law be applicable to cases between Africans where it was not 'repugnant to justice and morality' and it provided also that 'substantial justice without due regard to technicalities of procedure and without undue delay' should be done. Substantially similar provisions were made for Zambia. Though two legal systems were to be recognised, it was policy that judicial work should be largely in European hands.

The powers which the European magistrates could exercise were to all intents and purposes unlimited. Not only did the ordinances passed by the protectorate government create a wide range of offences but the criminal law, which regulated relationships between the state and Africans, and between Africans themselves, was not African law but the law in force in England in 1902. This included all of the wide-ranging and severe powers which the English common law gave to the state and the judicial authorities (for example over persons categorised as vagrant, idle, disorderly, etc.) without the safeguard of a jury system, or of the conventional restraints tempering use of these powers, and, because of the 'substantial justice' clause and the small numbers of administrators, all at best barely trained, without the protection of a highly technical court procedure.

The impressing of authority through the new courts was seen as an essential part of the establishment of the order part of law and order. The early district officers were few and isolated and in many cases, behind their overweening façade, were frightened and insecure. There was a slightly hysteric quality to much of early justice. A. J. Swann, for example, who was not an inexperienced young man nor particularly reactionary, described the rough and ready methods of early government, explaining that there had been no time for judicial niceties about things like murder. 'If life had been wilfully taken, the fact had to be recognised and punished at once, or a tribe might be annihilated. The slightest leak had to be *stopped*, not merely checked; pestilent weeds rooted up, not cut down.' If not the whole structure of European authority might have been broken.[4] Also a high premium was placed on the keeping of the peace between white and African. It was felt that swift action by the courts was necessary to prevent the white population taking the law into its own hands, for such action might provoke African revolt. In Zambia the secretary for native affairs noted that the first type of white men to enter a new country were 'as a rule the worst class ... derelict sub-contractors, unauthorised labour touts, migratory Boers, prospectors and mechanics' and he pointed to the danger of Africans taking the law into their own hands if they were not adequately protected.[5]

Following on the Orders in Council there were no African courts with legal powers recognised by the colonial state to enforce their judgements (the exception being the Lozi *Khotla*). Two systems of law were recognised but judicial administration was a theory unified in British hands. While it was recognised that village courts continued to function, their powers of coercion were not supported by the colonial state.

The basic commandment of the legal mission was the repugnancy test. Yet the way in which it was administered illustrates the tensions which were to develop between legal reformism and retreat. Some practices were ideal targets for the repugnancy test. A claim for damages, heard by E. S. B. Tagart at Mumbwe in 1916, was made by an older headman who had 'lent' a wife to a younger man for two years. In answer to Tagart's incredulous questioning the headman admitted that he had 'lent' his wife 'in accordance with Chila custom ... What I complain of is that he has taken the woman away with him altogether. She is still my wife.' Tagart pounced in defence of sexual exclusiveness. The headman had condoned and profited from his wife's immorality. The custom of lending wives was 'repugnant'.[6] The result must have been far from the expectations with which the claimant went to court.

In *R.* v. *Mendamenda* the High Court of Northern Rhodesia gave consideration to the question of repugnancy in connection with the age of consent. Customary law, it was said, would allow intercourse with a girl 'much below' the age fixed by the Criminal Law Amendment Act of 1885. But this should not be condoned by the Northern Rhodesia courts as it would encourage 'animal' habits. The aim ought to be to 'drag the native standard of morals up'. No reference was made to the relative novelty of the 1885 Act which was the touchstone of 'natural justice' or to the prior state of the English common law. Macdonnell J. rejected the idea that just because a custom was made by Africans for Africans it was natural. 'When the Order in Council bids us to submit customs to the test of "natural justice"', he wrote, 'it enjoins a more developed and therefore a more natural, standard than the native knows.' In spite of this tortuous thinking the experience of the High Court had not been, as Macdonnell admitted, that customs differing from English ideas had often to be struck down. The test was that they did not 'offend or scandalise' white morality. This offence was in the area of sexual behaviour and it is clear that the court saw the sexual disciplining of the population as a part of the white legal mission. Macdonnell concluded that not to raise the age of consent 'would be an encouragement to lack of self restraint in sexual matters among a race unrestrained enough in that direction already'.

Yet customs which upheld the kind of sexual morality and relationships of authority of which the white courts approved were not struck down. In one case the accused impregnated an unmarried girl, a headman's daughter, without his consent. Under customary law, Macdonnell wrote, this would have been 'punishable with the usual penalties of death, mutilation or enslavement'. Such offences in customary law would be treated by the white courts as crimes. The judge said, 'one can say at once that a custom which disapproves of the cohabitation with an unmarried girl *sans* her guardian's consent, amply conforms to the natural justice test.' Furthermore, though the new white courts would extend the protection of the law to all members of African society, they could continue the customary practice of imposing heavier penalties if the aggrieved was a chief, 'for native society is not egalitarian'.[7] Nor were the white courts going to make it so. Not only did the High Court continue to recognise customary status differences but the government, when indirect rule was established, did not interfere with the use by Africans of the Native Authority Courts to enforce these differences, which were not considered to be contrary to 'natural justice'. As soon as the Native Authority Courts got under way the district officer in Mumbwa reported that 'Natives are constantly being fined small amounts for cursing their father-in-law or other elders and betters.'[8] The working of the repugnancy test was not, therefore, basically in conflict with the essence of the direction which the system was to take, which was support for local hierarchies.

UNDERSTANDING PRIMITIVE LAW: THE ADMINISTRATORS

I shall now turn to the way in which the administrators viewed the indigenous customary systems. Though few had any legal training, many had in their minds a simple evolutionary scheme based on the contents of Maine's *Ancient Law* with its theme of the evolution 'from status to contract'. An additional assumption of many magistrates in the beginning was that 'primitive' law was simple, not technical and difficult like English law. At least one collector welcomed a proposal that a handbook be issued to guide magistrates for the white side of their judicial work because he felt out of his depth when judging cases between Europeans. As for Africans, he wrote, 'whose language, laws and customs are tolerably familiar to me, and whose affairs it is my principal business to administer, I feel on more or less certain ground.'[9] Early thinking on the desirability of a code often had as its premise the notion that an African law could be simple and free of the 'archaic niceties' and 'nebulous and heavy envelope' which surround English law.[10]

Some of the early district officers have recorded their reflections on early law and justice. Sir Hector Duff, for example, had read Darwin, on whom he based the view that Africans had had law but that it only applied within the tribe as a means of holding it together and that any act could be committed outside of the boundaries of tribal groups without exciting condemnation. However, while Africans did have this limited idea of law, almost all offences were punishable by death preceded by torture because 'savage governments can only be upheld by a policy of terror.' Since the establishment of British rule criminal law was no longer based upon terror but beyond that there had been little interference: 'justice is now meted out by Collectors of Districts after a decidedly patriarchal fashion, more in accordance with local custom and their own discretion than with any rigid judicial standard. Thus we have the remarkable spectacle of a score or so of

Englishmen who have received no special legal training at home, administering, in a most intimate and homely way, the affairs of nearly a million
human beings of a totally different race.' While, he thought, lawsuits
between Europeans called for trained lawyers, law for Africans could hardly
be too simple or direct. The absence of legal training was an advantage as
district officers were free from the bias of European precedent. This was
another way of saying that the minds of the district officers were full of legal
ideas which they imagined to be the basis of the law of their own culture and
which they thought of as universal. As Duff put it, 'The broad principles of
equity are the same the world over. It needs no special education to
distinguish *meum* from *tuum*, plain right from plain wrong.'[11]

In a law department circular issued in May 1909, for the benefit of district
officers, P. J. Macdonnell, then legal adviser to the N.E. Rhodesian administration, suggested that there were two maxims regarding African law to be
borne in mind. The first was that 'Primitive Man is muddle headed' and that
his 'legal notions are neither so simple, nor so clear nor so carefully reasoned
as our own.' Though customary law may make up an elaborate system there
would be within it 'illogicalities, and unnecessary and illogical distinctions
and deviations' and therefore 'to try to give to these conceptions a simplicity,
exactitude and reasonableness . . . is to substitute our own idea for those of
the native.'[12] The second maxim was that 'In Early Law all Crimes are
Torts,' which was representative of the thinking of virtually all English
jurists of the period and was, to them, as axiomatic as the progression from
'status to contract'. Its importance, Macdonnell felt, to the administration of
colonial justice was that it was one of the sources of African dissatisfaction
with the working of the system. Macdonnell remarked on the African failure
to grasp 'the (to us) clear distinction between the *civil* wrong which is
compensated by damages to the individual, and the *criminal* wrong which is
compensated by fine or forced labour exacted by the community'. Appreciation of this distinction may have been especially difficult for persons who
had suffered injury only to see the white man's court pocket the fine, and
though early on provision was made for fines to be used, at the court's
discretion, for the payment of compensation, this had no effect on cases
where the injury was a serious one and punishment was imprisonment or
death. In Zambia magistrates were advised by Beaufort J. to distinguish
between crime and tort by looking at the punishment which it had been the
custom to visit upon an act and where 'death, mutilations, beatings,
enslavement or exile' had been the penalty, 'then that act was clearly in
native eyes a crime.'[13]

Harrington, a district officer in the Luapula district, wrote in puzzled
fashion in 1910: 'they have no definite law as we understand it. Every
offence, even murder, is (or was) merely a civil action to recover compensation. Again custom was as often not followed as followed.' So their
customs could not be used to settle their cases. This gets at the heart of the
problem in the misconceptions and worryings which we shall see go right

through the administrators' attempts to understand 'customary law'. An injury gave rise to a claim in which 'custom' was one of the resources to be drawn on in the *milandu*, the public discussion, which followed. It was not a 'rule' which anyone could 'apply'. Yet white courts wanted to know customs because they wanted applicable 'rules'. And in this process rules were to be made.

The retreat in legal administration which resulted in indirect rule was to be parallel to a retreat on the substantive legal front. Administrators acknowledged the difficulties which they found in satisfying the local sense of justice, and found themselves supporting village decisions and the principles on which they were based. In November 1920 R. H. Murray reported a case where the defendant had refused to make a payment 'traditionally' due as the result of the death of his wife in childbirth, as it was contrary to his religious principles. The defendant, Murray reported, a 'mission native, claimed exemption from the payment demanded by native law on the ground that it was a heathen custom and so contrary to our ideas of morality'. But, Murray ruled, heathen customs were not *ipso facto* immoral, and the man's liability was not affected. All this was a far cry from the desire to free man from the thrall of savage superstitions by providing rational British justice in their place and it was the result of a combination of anti-*évolué* prejudice and administrative rationale. As the magistrate in the similar case of *Chitumbikwa* v. *Goodbye* remarked, the idea that African Christians could be exempt from legal obligations connected with superstition was, 'As practically all native customs and laws are in some ways connected with their superstitions . . . an extremely dangerous theory from an administrative point of view'.[14] Thus while government opinion was to move towards giving the headmen a greater role in the administration of justice, so it also moved towards a version of the customary law, aligning itself with the traditional leadership against the mission products. As the provincial commissioner explained to the Fort Manning District Council in 1930 'the old customs would be revived and made law provided that they were good, for instance he thought that Christian natives could be compelled to have their heads shaved on the death of a relation, and if they refused they would be liable to be put in prison.'[15]

In the prevailing conservative approach to law in the 1920s some thought was also given to the more general problem of what native law was. Murray, the provincial commissioner for the Malawi Central Province, pointed out that some people thought of native law as consisting of a series of laws adopted 'at some long distant but unspecified date' and thought 'the oldest inhabitant its best exponent'. This school would, for example, consider the payment of cattle as a necessary element in a Ngoni wedding now, as one hundred years ago. Instead, he argued, the true meaning of native law was not that it was a 'dead code' but that it was 'a living expression of native public opinion'. If this was the case of codification the law would soon become obsolete and would arrest development. Haythorne-Reed agreed with this flexible approach: a few people who kept the customs of their ancestors could not prevent another custom becoming recognised and codification would be a 'calamity, as it would tend to stereotype what would otherwise change for the better'.[16] Yet a rational flexibility with regard to customary law could not prevail. Traditionally minded district officers were in practice members of the 'oldest inhabitant' school as well as emotive supporters of it. In practice so too were the judges in the High Court who, faced with the problem of having to have 'native law' proved, resorted to old men as witnesses. But by the 1930s someone aged sixty would not have had first-hand adult knowledge of pre-colonial practices. And in any case, as A. T. Culwick wrote on the subject of people's views of the marriage law in his district of Tanganyika, 'the "past" they talk about is, say, 60, 70, 80 years ago. By that time it appears that the whole system had entered upon a period of confusion.'[17]

Nevertheless in spite of judicial validation of the 'oldest inhabitant' school, 'customary law' was changing. One government memorandum read: 'native custom is always in a fluid state as there is no fixed code of native law and . . . foreign culture is rapidly modifying the old indigenous ideas.' The present tendency was to imitate European procedure and with each generation there would be increasing dissatisfaction with the past and a 'growing tendency to imitate our principles'.[18] But modification of 'custom' was not only by acceptance of British ideas but also by rejection of them and by belligerent affirmation of an idealised past. This affirmation also tended to freeze further modification for it was a reaction not only against British legal ideas but one caused by competing African ones. Both, for example, challenged Ngoni and challenging Chewa took their stand on what they claimed had always been, and contending claims based on 'custom' led to rigidified interpretations of it. This process was furthered by the legitimation of indirect rule.[19]

The *nkhoswe*,[20] as Maliwa writes, had an importance beyond their role of guardians of a marriage; they were also the general guardians of the customary law. Their main concern was, she writes, to secure conformity with custom.[21] And as custom changed, so the ideas of its guardians of what it ought to be rigidified. Colson has written that the introduction of a European system of judicial administration could well have served to rigidify the customary law, as it was the European concept of customary law and its court system which slowed the rate of change in a changing system. But it was not so much that it slowed the rate of change as that it changed the nature of the norms. Giving to Native Courts the power to define obligations legally gave them the power to turn their conception of the ideal into something legally obligatory. There is much to suggest that it was the European rulers who wanted the customary law to be kept flexible and the African interpreters of it who wished to crystallise it.[22] Certainty in a customary system becomes more necessary if it is to form the basis of a defence against challenge from an alternative legality. Customary law, especially in a state of flux, could not afford to be flexible. It had to deal with changing circumstances, yet its claim to be law was that it was age-old custom. Thus newly made-up rules were quickly frozen. An illustration of this is a report by the district officer in Marimba in 1919.[23] Actions to recover debts were, it said, 'a source of considerable trouble as they are governed by a strange unwritten law known as the "custom of the Achewa." This must not be confounded with "native law and custom." It is an entirely modern doctrine based, apparently, on the idea that any change must be a change for the worse. It prescribes the payment of two bags of rice for tax and the curious sum of 27 shillings for adultery and renders any alterations of these amounts unthinkable.' As Fallers noted in Busoga in 1950, 'explicitness seems to increase as consensus about the law declines.'[24]

Melland, writing in 1923 after twenty-two years of service as a district officer in Northern Rhodesia, summed up the approach which was getting the upper hand in the 1920s. Of, for example, the payments which custom required on death he wrote, 'One needs to move warily before interfering with any part of religion. To do so carelessly is to invite chaos and to put the natives back in their evolution: nearer to the beasts of the fields.' The enlightened administrative approach was to see African life as a seamless organic web, slowly evolving. Native customs were sound, Melland wrote, 'but they have become or are becoming vicious partly because they are not written or codified, and also partly because our advent has hastened evolution unduly'.[25] Consequently he was concerned about an aggressively interfering approach to law. As he saw it, 'When religion, custom, morals and social fabric are all intertwined ... any new law or procedure has an uphill fight.' The British, he thought, were making a 'fetish of orderliness' and applying a policy of 'law, order and discipline', instead of one of moral and material evolution.[26]

Yet for all his dissatisfaction with his role as a keeper of law and order Melland's ultimate prescriptions for the legal front were in accord with the conservative direction in which British policy was moving. Detribalised Africans had to be encouraged 'to keep the fifth commandment, which is the first point in the native code which the educated native forgets'. The 'village aristocracy' should be strengthened against the 'element of *nouveaux riches*'. But, as Melland most acutely pointed out, so far the British administration had been dominated not by real law reform but by the creation of new order.

> In all the East and Central African Protectorates ... I do not know of any law promulgated by us *for the natives*. All our laws here, for example, are either for the whites, for the relations between black and white, or for the government and taxation of the black: not one for the blacks themselves. Whenever we had done anything direct we seem to have started on the wrong end: chiefly by trying to cure ideas and beliefs with a penal code.[27]

As if providing official confirmation of Melland's view, the secretary for native affairs wrote, describing the early colonial period, 'Chiefs were merely told that certain things were prohibited and few ... explanations were given for ... orders .... *Laws were simply things forbidden.*'[28]

SIN AND RULES: MISSIONARY JUSTICE

The formal structure for the administration of justice played only a part in the impact of white methods of justice. Before and after the administration came early settlers and, more importantly, the missions, and both played a role in the settlement of disputes either in order to impose their wishes or, when sought out by African litigants, to lend their prestige to an informal judicial settlement.[29] A good deal of the time of the early missionaries was spent in acting as judges. The first U.M.C.A. missionaries in the early 1860s were heavily involved in the settlement of disputes though they do not appear to have made a practice of imposing heavy punishments for breaches of a putative criminal code.[30] The judicial subsystem of the missions soon came up against difficulties. For one thing their desire to settle cases by the hearing of evidence and adjudication ran aground on the apparent determination of people to offer and demand ordeal trials. In November of 1861 Bishop Mackenzie, on the Shire Highlands, found that after he had listened to a case for a day and a half the defendant offered to submit himself to the test of a poison ordeal.[31]

Rowley's record of the early days abounds with accounts of missionary administration of a law made up from their notions of right and wrong according to a Victorian interpretation of the biblical law they had brought with them, and roughly adapted English procedures. Flogging was meted out for theft and the mission held what it claimed as the 'first trial by jury in Central Africa'. 'Before we left the country', he wrote, 'one or another of us had to sit in the administration of justice nearly every day.'[32] Chauncey Maples of the U.M.C.A.' held court at Masasi in the 1870s. Offenders, he wrote in 1878, sometimes 'have to be very severely beaten . . . I am not only priest or chaplain or missionary to these people but absolutely their ruler as well.'[33]

The foray of the Scottish mission in Blantyre into the field of secular jurisdiction is the most notorious. Before the establishment of the protectorate on the Shire Highlands the zeal of the mission's justice and the violence of their punishments led to a scandal in Scotland and a restructuring of the mission with specific instructions that it abandon secular jurisdiction. In 1879 they executed one man and flogged another to death in incidents which aroused horror in the mission world. Similarly in Tongaland lay members of the Scottish mission imposed a 'savage code of discipline' on station workers and ignored local African sovereignties. In October 1879 Douglas Laws noted with disapproval on his first inspection that 'there has been shown too markedly a tendency to decide native disputes' and that the problems of becoming a Christian colony were such that they detracted seriously from the essential work of evangelisation. 'The exercise of Magisterial functions by the head of the Mission', he wrote, 'hinders . . . his work as a Minister of the Gospel. In the eyes of the natives he is apt to be looked upon more in the character of a chief than as a teacher and friend.'[34] The mission was actively involved in secular judging, imposing widespread flogging and heavy fines in cases brought to them by headmen looking for a way to solve inter-village disputes. At Cape Maclear the mission built itself stocks in 1877 and a prison in 1878. One commentator wrote of judgements 'worthy of the traditions of an Eastern *kadi*. Theft . . . occurring on a public highway was punished by our sapient authorities by the wholesale destruction of the unfortunate villages in the vicinity . . . subjecting them to the loss of their all in the name of British law and dignity.'[35]

The exposure of the early excesses in the field of worldly lawgiving did lead to a change of policy. But the mission continued to be active as a conciliator in disputes. D. C. Scott, as head of the Blantyre mission, acted as a 'chief among chiefs', regularly attending *milandu* with his neighbouring rulers in Blantyre, Kapeni and Mpama. Scott had a far more sympathetic attitude towards local ways than did his predecessors and his experience led him to define *milandu* in his dictionary as 'a meeting for discussion of some claim or right . . . the most characteristic word of African politics, itself a charter of limited government and appeal to right and sufficient reason'.[36] In the North, while the mission was less active in the punishment of external 'crime' than in its first years, it retained its strictness in other areas of discipline. Its work discipline remained 'draconian', strict time and task control were enforced at the Overtoun institution, a rigid moral code was imposed and fines levied for infraction.[37] What is striking is the contrast between ideals in this early experience of clashing systems. On the one side the *milandu*, the discussion, on the other the resort to the enforcement of rules and punishment. Yet the assumption made by the missions both before and after the heyday of their active secular jurisdiction was that missionary justice would save Africans from a more severe retribution. In 1881 the Blantyre missionaries were instructed from Scotland that criminals, if caught, should be handed over to the local chiefs and that while missionaries might recommend that the punishments prescribed by native law should be less severe nothing should be done to undermine respect for the law and converts should be taught 'to obey and respect the laws of their country as far as Christians ought to do'.[38]

Yet rendering to Caesar was not so easy. For one thing many Christians came to feel that there were laws which they ought not to obey and respect and, as we shall see later, many were to come up against unsympathetic administrators with a developing zeal for the application of 'native law'. But this was not the only problem. For to many of the missionaries Caesar was not only a savage but a morally inadequate savage, and a wickedly superstitious one. Gradually all the missions withdrew from the field of strictly secular justice. Their ideas about crime and transgression were diverted from the sphere of peacekeeping to that of sin and punishment, and remained in this heightened form as an ingredient in the legal situation.

In 1913 Norman Maclean observed after visiting mission stations in Nyasaland that the missionaries, who were faced with the 'grim problems of heathen morality', were tempted as a result to exercise too stringent a discipline. He was startled to find in Central Africa 'the old stern discipline of the Scottish Kirk session' and warned: 'And with the exercise of strict discipline the desire grows for stricter and yet stricter discipline until at last the feeling is engendered that salvation is by discipline.' He had accurately captured the atmosphere of a part of the colonial mission. As Bishop Hine observed with satisfaction, 'We never watered down any of the strictness of Christian law and life; it is a hard law to obey, a hard life to live.'[39]

The separation of religion from law, which the western writers thought of as being so vital a part of their system, was not a part of the early colonial situation. In no sphere was this more important than the law of marriage and divorce, as the control of Christian marriage was an essential part of the missions' power. But the idea of transgression of the law being sin was also significant in the field of crime and punishment. Henry Rowley wrote in 1867 after his years with the first U.M.C.A. mission of the problems concerning Mang'anja ideas of right and wrong:

> Yet though they had this idea of a spiritual world, of the conditions of that world they knew nothing. They did not comprehend that this life was a life of probation, and they therefore had no belief in a future retribution. Though they did not think death annihilated they seemed to imagine that it reduced all to the same level; the murderer, and the thief, the adulterer and the liar, being no worse off than those unstained by such crimes . . . . whatever their idea of duty or law was, they did not believe in any future punishment for the violation of duty, or the . . . breaking of law, neither did they expect a reward for the faithful observance of both.'[40]

This is a revealing passage: it makes clear that to the mid-Victorian Christian law was closely bound up with a divinely ordained morality and that man's definition of right and wrong derived its overall legitimation from a judging god. To Rowley it was clear that the Mang'anja did not see wrongdoing in this way. He records a case in which Proctor successfully pleaded with people not to kill a slave wife and bury her with a deceased chief. Proctor asked the people if they knew what happened to them after they died.

> And when they heard that God was angry with those who killed their fellow creatures, as they were going to kill that poor woman, and that in a future state they would be judged for the deeds they had done here, and that they would then be punished, or rewarded according as they had obeyed or disobeyed God's will on earth, they were astounded and for a time they made no reply.

The genuine transplanting of British law thus seemed to depend on a successful transfusion of the notion of Christian guilt: to break the law was to sin; it was to offend not only against an earthly magistrate but against a divine judge. Arnot recorded in April 1883 how he had spoken to Lewanika of 'sin, death and judgement, and of God's love' and lamented of the Lozi that 'Goodness or badness, righteousness or sin, are not in their creeds.' He explained to Lewanika that in the next world the lowest slave might be seated in the palace of God and a king shut out, and was forbidden to say such a thing again. Nine months later he was explaining the same subject another way. God, Arnot said, would not accept the guilty after death, but would put them in a place of 'sorrow and burning'. When Lewanika asked why, Arnot referred by analogy to the king's judicial function and told him that when he was 'bad and wicked ... God judges you with the same judgement with which you judged your fellow creature yesterday.'[41] The local concept of sin was not congruent and both mission Christianity and British government failed to come to terms with it, setting it aside and confusing it with a package of apparent irrationalities labelled 'witchcraft'. Colonial law, for example, did not take cognisance of the efficacy of witchcraft and, much to the distress of the victims and complainants, did not treat purported killing by witchcraft as murder. To Chauncey Maples this apparently rational attitude was incorrect. One who purported to kill another by witchcraft, he wrote, was guilty of murder as a sin and had violated the letter of the commandment in the decalogue.[42] Of the people of Likhoma he wrote, they were 'people in whom the moral sense seemed almost non-existent, and whose lives seemed only a weary waste of evil and sin'.[43]

The promulgating of the decalogue as the new law was a not uncommon way of initiating missionary proceedings. In March 1886 Coillard held his first service at Lealui, employing the 'tactic of promulgating law, reading the Ten Commandments, the law of God.' The Bible appears as a book of law in the dramatic visit of Joseph Booth and John Chilembwe to Mbona's shrine in 1894. Booth preached a sermon. The people's response was that it was 'nonsense: they knew for certain that God had spoken to them through Mbona and they had no means of knowing whether God had spoken to Booth.' In reply to this Booth produced his Bible and read the Ten Commandments, which were carefully translated by Chilembwe. The discussion which followed focused on the issues of killing and stealing.[44] Douglas Laws, who dominated the Livingstonia mission, also emphasised the connection between law and biblical morality. 'I never found a tribe in Central Africa', he wrote, 'that did not know and recognise the second table of the Decalogue ... but the knowledge of and obedience to the first table of the Decalogue are fundamentally essential to the fulfilment of the second.' He emphasised the importance of frequent insistence on the Commandments, as did Maples, who advised stress on 'God's Holy Law' and the strictness of that law in sermons.[45]

Alexander Hetherwick of the Blantyre mission, who was rightly renowned for his liberal paternalism, returned to the same theme in giving his considered reflections on his time in Central Africa. Africans, he wrote, had no morality, by which he meant no guilt or consciousness of sin. They were restrained in their actions only by fear of consequences. This explained why, in African law, there was no crime, only tort. 'This lack of sense of crime and the punishment of it as an offence against society and the State, has rendered the institution of British law ... a matter of no small difficulty in the magisterial courts dealing with native cases.'[46] This analysis was by no means unique; what is of note is the connection made between crime and sin and the insistence on punishment for law-breaking in this light.

One case illustrates the way in which the informal and the formal mechanisms of white judicial administration could work together and how both could make use of existing ideas of equity in arriving at a settlement.[47] The confusions as to who had the power to judge, and what were the canons of judgement, were manifold, and well illustrate the complexities for all parties, as well as for the analysis of legal history. A man killed his half-brother by throwing a stone at him and fracturing his skull. Douglas, an Anglican who served at both Kota-Kota and Likhoma, sent the case to Swann, the district officer at Kota-Kota, who passed a sentence of two years for manslaughter. But, as Douglas wrote:

> 6 months of that time will be remitted on my informing Mr. Swann that the head of the family has made to the representatives of the dead man a *payment*, which is judged by me, acting in consultation with some native chiefs, to be sufficient to comfort them. That is how Mr. Swann combined the English and the native system of justice: the English say 'send to gaol', and a native says 'pay'. As a rule if a man is killed a payment goes to his mother's relations; but the difficulty in this case was that both parties had the same mother; so that according to native ideas, there could be no big payment.

Others, apart from the missionaries, found themselves in a position in which they pictured themselves as the unwilling dispensers of solomonic wisdom and necessary punishment. To the agents of the African Lakes Company after 1882 people brought 'all sorts of disputes for decisions'. 'Natives', wrote Moir,

> are inclined to be litigious, and *milandu* or palavers are very common. The commonest sources of trouble were runaway wives and decamping slaves. Even runaway wives generally accepted the decision to return to their husbands, usually with some provision that their treatment should be bettered. Many slaves were allowed to work for their freedom at an agreed price .... we sought ... to treat the cases brought before us on broad humanitarian grounds.[48]

If runaway slaves and wives took their cases to the missions and trading posts in the hope that these would be bent upon healing what Livingstone had called 'the open sore of the world' they might have found a careful circumspection about the new remedies. By the time of the Scottish mission unofficial agents of white justice were no longer the fervid liberationists who had got the Anglicans into so much trouble earlier. When runaway slaves presented themselves, masters were allowed 'to state their case. When it was made out to a reasonable extent, the slaves, if they wished to remain, were given work, with the proceeds of which they could buy their freedom, at an agreed rate.'[49] For the slaves, who found themselves working under new masters, and for the old masters, who lost their slaves, this was a little confusing and the missions were caught in a welter of accusations that they were acquiring the dependents of others. Once the administration began to establish itself the missions and traders were no longer the white courts of last resort but they were able to make use of the threat to invoke government power.[50]

Arthur Sim, who was the U.M.C.A. missionary at the former slave centre of Nkhota-Kota, recorded how the first district officer arrived in January 1895 and issued pronouncements prohibiting the capturing, buying or selling of slaves, and ordeal trials, and had then departed, leaving, Sim wrote, 'Matters more or less in my hands. I have had to administer martial authority.'[51] Sim became deeply involved in the administration of justice. Mutual incomprehension was a part of this new system. After the murder of a Makua soldier Sim recorded that not only the murderer but all the men in his part of town ran away, 'so little do they know of our idea of justice'. His first baptism was of a convicted murderer to whom he gave a course of instruction. Sim was not a man eager to rule in the secular world and lamented the position in which he found himself. Other missionaries, in particular when Christians were involved in family-law disputes, were more eager to intervene and continued to play a part even after the establishment of formal colonial administration. As one summed up after travelling in North Western Zambia in 1908, 'The position is not without an element of danger. The Magistrates are naturally jealous of their prerogatives, and the missionaries are glad to be peacemakers.'[52] Here was the germ of the later conflict between the missions, who handed down Christian judgement, and the colonial courts, which evolved their own mixture of wordly wisdom and customary law.

5

Witches and ordeals

Central to European accounts of the legal life of Central Africa is the ordeal trial. It is vital in several respects. One is that observation of the African world of witchcraft accusations and poison trials deeply affected the European view of the rationality of African justice. Another is that the colonial attempts to stamp out both accusations and trials left a hole in social defences against wrongdoing and deprived some in authority of a powerful weapon. No account of the interaction of legal cultures can be possible without an attempt to understand ordeal trial, in both its mythical and its real aspects.

This chapter describes the mutual incomprehension and the results of conflict between colonial government and governed over the ordeal. Recent writing has been characterised by defensiveness about the ordeal.[1] Epstein wrote in 1954 that there 'has been a tendency at times to see the judicial process as dominated by an appeal to the supernatural by means of oath and ordeal . . . . What does seem clear however is that these means were resorted to only in those cases where it was impossible to get evidence' and it was 'misleading . . . to conceive of the judicial process as dominated by mystical concepts'.[2] The basic assumption of this kind of writing is that the 'trial' was not only similarly conducted in both 'legal systems' but that trials concerned the same substantive issues.

In 1966 the International Seminar on African Law addressed itself specifically to the question of the places of reason and appeal to the occult in African law. They stressed that 'in the African view it is characteristic of men that they possess "reason," socially defined, [and] . . . that judges operate with reason in solving disputes.' They then suggested that there were special circumstances in which the occult was used: when executive power was weak; or as an evidentiary tool where evidence was poor; or when the offence complained of involved the occult. They argued that use of the occult was a shifting of responsibility away from the state's representative in some way comparable to resort to jury decision; or that it was used to deal

85

with problems which were not in any way soluble by judicial methods, problems for which judges were not used in Europe or America.[3] I cannot help being impressed by the general air of embarrassment; the desire to excuse by explanation. Lawyers, and legal anthropologists, do not believe in witchcraft. They clearly feel that to portray it as an important belief anywhere, rather than a fringe one, casts doubt upon the rationality of the people they are describing. The effect of this has been to make it harder to understand its workings and its possible perception by people as a central part of the process of controlling evil and handling conflicts, and clearly has diminished the appreciation of the importance of the effects of its outlawing.

In the late nineteenth century Central African societies, where many communities were struggling with the problems of slavery and assimilation in a conquest situation, structural conflicts and resultant hostilities meant that moral disturbances were built into basic relationships and structurally involved in a very wide range of important conflicts. It would seem also that the abolition of ordeal trial and the outlawing of accusations of witchcraft were to throw a far greater weight on the new notion that all conflicts be settled by a purely secular judicial mode than it could really bear. After British conquest, in the particularly difficult circumstances of foreign rule and increasing stratification, secular courts had to assume sole responsibility for the settlement of conflicts and the moral ordering of society. They were the only instrument approved by the colonial government, which frowned not only on ordealing but on other religious and ritual adaptations to its banning. This, apart from the often remarked effect of leaving people feeling that they had no protection from evil, had its effect on the emerging body of rules and notions and feelings which became the customary law and African legal culture. It combined with the effect of Christian morality in making the secular law into an all-embracing instrument with which to punish moral wrong, rather than limiting it to containment of social infractions. And it did not necessarily become any simpler to separate the supernatural from the secular in conflicts as the century progressed, nor were the moral disturbances eliminated from relationships. As we will see, disputes between kin concerning the separation of property, at first sight demonstrably secular, often had implications and overtones inseparable from accusations of supernatural manipulation. Other writers have depicted ordealing as a fact of life and considered its judicial functions without an attempt to shunt it into the sidelines.[4] Vansina stressed the judicial nature of the ordeal amongst the Bushong. But he underlines a crucial point obscured by those anxious about procedural rationality. More than a 'trial' is involved. The aim is not just to 'convict', with the ordeal as an evidentiary tool. It is to 'eliminate evil and death', i.e. to struggle against witchcraft itself, and the ordeal is in essence a ritual in this struggle between good and evil in the community, and not simply a sort of judicial procedure.

Considered historically, it seems clear that it had different uses in different circumstances, that it was not one institution but several, and that in one sense it was not an institution at all, being more of a random and erratic practice. And we must remember to distinguish the ideal version of what *mwavi* was supposed to be used for, from its actual use as a resource to be called upon in any escalating dispute. The European observations of the ordeal in action are many and important. At times the description is useful and illuminating and at others it is based on bare acquaintance and gross misunderstanding. But the most important thing is that the foreign observers' impressions of the African law influenced the way in which they judged and made legal institutions for African society, thereby creating the legal environment in which twentieth-century African law was shaped.

ORDEALING OBSERVED AND RECALLED

When Lacerda travelled to Kazembe's in 1798 he observed 'many human skulls and corpses cast out upon the road'; some of these had 'lost their lives for witchcraft, there being a belief in all of this part of Africa, even amongst many whites, (as I saw in Mozambique) that no man ever dies, except by sorcery. Whenever a Caffre accused of this crime denies his guilt – some coarsely confess their guilt – he undergoes the *Mave* ordeal. It consists in administering a tincture of some bark ... If the supposed wizard is lucky enough to vomit, his innocence is feted with great joy, and his accuser is fined,'[5] The tincture was an infusion made from the ground bark of the tree *Erythrophleum guineense* which was mixed by one skilled in its preparation, the *mapondera*, and administered under the eyes of a headman. Lacerda does not tell us that the mixture, if not vomited, poisoned the taker fatally: rather, he records, 'The Maraves burn their sorcerers,' that is those who did not vomit the *mwavi*.

There is a second account available for the Marave in the period before the conquests and upheavals of mid-century. Gammitto travelled through Marave country in the 1830s.[6] He at first records that, for suspected adultery and theft, ordeal was by boiling water or fire and that *mwavi* was used in cases of sorcery, but later he writes that *mwavi* was used in adultery cases where the offence was denied, and he gives a detailed description.

> *Mwave* is not only given to prove sorcery, but also in any case in which there is an accusation but insufficient proof, or even if this is present but is denied by the accused. In this case either the accused asks for it to justify himself, when the accuser does not have so much responsibility, or else it is proposed by the latter; but this happens only if there is complete certainty that the defendant is guilty.

Many other accounts exist which help us to build a picture of ordealing and of white understanding of it. There are no essential differences between the techniques they describe and the accounts given by missionaries, travellers and early administrators from the 1860s onwards. But from the later accounts we can build up a composite picture of the way in which white

87

observers understood the ordeal and we can see how its uses varied. Many stressed its ubiquity and the great faith which people appeared to have in it. It appeared to be demanded in the most trivial of disputes; to be connected with the detection of witchcraft; and, most spectacularly, to be a political tool of the new conquest states.[7]

Some observers specifically analysed a tripartite function of this kind, and the suggestion was also made that this represented an essentially temporal progression in which the ordeal had changed from a means of detecting witchcraft to an instrument of political control, to a routine judicial procedure.[8] It was also apparent that it was far from being an 'institution' in the sense of being part of a regular accepted system where all were agreed when and by whom it should be taken and what questions it settled.[9] African accounts appear to place less emphasis on procedure and more on what ordealing was meant to detect, and also do not make the separation between witchcraft and ordinary crime and between ordealing and ordinary trials which was implicit in the white approach. Daniel Malekebu, the first Malawian to be trained as a doctor in the United States, and who took over John Chilembwe's mission, wrote of the old law 'if you are accused of stealing you must prove that you are not a thief by drinking *muavi* poison .... if there are signs of intoxication, or even death you are guilty.' Malekebu made little distinction between secular and supernatural. 'Zinganga' (the doctor), he wrote, 'smells and points out all criminals, such as thieves and witches.'[10]

There are hints at the kinds of changes which affected ordealing in the recollections of men like Y.B. Abdullah and Saulos Nyirenda. Abdullah's account of the Yao, published in 1919, considers 'how we conducted cases at law ourselves and maintained law and order'. In the old days, he wrote, people had been 'sociable, generous, helpful and obliging' and 'in accord and united'. They had settled quarrels 'without rancour'. Minor matters within a village were settled by the chief by compensation of fowls, barkcloth or produce. If a fine ordered by the chief were not paid a man could be held until he was ransomed. In serious matters like attempting to steal another's wife, or incorrigible idleness, the punishment was banishment. On this level a system of discussion, judgement and compensation is perceived to have operated. On another level a different kind of wrongdoing is seen to be at work. After a death, in Abdullah's description, the 'lots' were cast to find the cause and 'afterwards they go to the chief to arrest the [suspected] persons and imprison them in the wizard's hut; to stamp out witchcraft, pay forfeit, or to burn the wizard to prevent him from killing others.' With the growth of the slave trade, of slave holding, and of the power of the slaving chiefs, the legal institutions of the Yao noticeably changed. Yao society became highly stratified with different ranks wearing different types of cloth. Those who Abdullah called the 'Wanyasa' were, in his eyes, enslaved: 'we consider them our property.' 'With them there was no political or social equality or intimacy.'[11] It is not surprising that in these circumstances the golden age of consensual judgement and compensatory settlement should give way to the suppressed expression of hostility between unequals and the consequent increase in ordealing to deal with what appeared to white observers to be mundane and trivial matters.

Large numbers of slaves and slave wives in owners' villages increased tensions, witchcraft and accusations. Vital social norms held only tenuously in the new and temporary slave societies: hostility, and challenge by use of the supernatural and by poisoning, were widespread. Responsibility for death and misfortune in this atmosphere of malevolence was detected by the ordeal. Finally slaves also came to be used as indicators in the same way as dogs or fowls were to be used in the colonial period. The truth of accusations and of evidence came to be routinely tested by the administration of *mwavi* to the accused's slave, a development which must have made appeal to the ritual and acceptance of it easier. The rulers of the conquest states lived with similar tensions and adapted the ritual to deal with them.

The vulnerability of slaves in communities like these is attested to by the recollections of a woman who had been a slave in Mkoma's country in the period before 1900.

> This poisoned drink is often given. I have twice taken it but the affairs for which I have had to drink it were not mine. The chief accused his brother. His brother denied it. So Mkoma gave me the poisoned drink; but I threw it up, so Mkoma said 'My brother is innocent; the poison denies his guilt.' The second time I drank poison was on account of one of the Chief's wives who was accused of unfaithfulness. She denied it, so the chief gave me the poison to drink. I threw it up, so the chief said, 'No, she did not sin.'[12]

Slavery and the ordeal, then, provided a combination of oppressions for some. Another former slave from Mkoma's country recalls how her son-in-law had forced the *mwavi* upon her daughter: 'he had made her drink the poisoned drink so that she had nearly died, for the villagers had called my daughter a witch. Nyondo [the son-in-law] would not allow this disgrace to rest upon himself and his family, so he said his wife should be judged by the gods by drinking the poisoned drink.'

To the increase in slavery can be added the coming of the conquest states. Nyirenda, the Tumbuka historian, who was hostile to the Ngoni and generally approved of the British for having conquered them and restored peace to Tumbuka country, saw the ordeal in a positive light, as did Abdullah, as a part of the old ways in a period of peace. Before the Ngoni came, he wrote, 'We do not hear that people fought together at random. There were poison ordeals and small village quarrels; in the morning they would be friendly in the place where they had wounded each other, there was no carrying the matter on.'[13] The conquest states, however, like the growth of slavery, magnified the potential of the ordeal as an oppressive instrument. There is a lengthy description of the use made of the ordeal in one pre-colonial Ngoni state, Chikusi's, which was witnessed by Moir of the African Lakes Company.[14] He first tells us that Chikusi accused two neighbouring sub-chiefs of attempting to bewitch him: one drank *mwavi* and survived, the other died. Chikusi then summoned the chiefs' wives from the villages to come and prove their innocence. A booth was erected for Chikusi and thousands gathered to witness the proceedings. Chikusi made a payment of cloth to the *maponderas* and 'several pieces of bark three or four inches square' were chosen from the medicine bags. Two old women and four young were accused of taking the chief's goods and of adultery. All the time, wrote Moir, Chikusi was 'laughing and joking with his men. Some of the women who had been fasting since the previous day were greatly agitated.' There followed a period of pounding, adding water, invocations, adjurations and dancing by the *maponderas*. After administration of the *mwavi*, apparently doled out impartially, two of the six died, and young men dashed off to kill their relatives and seize their property. Later the women, speaking to Moir, 'inveighed against the frequency of these orgies', which continued two days later with large numbers. Moir wrote that if a man accumulated goods or cattle those who feared or envied him (often the chief) would charge witchcraft. If an innocent man took *mwavi* and recovered, 'he believed in it all the more. If the innocent man died, all believed him guilty; and being dead, he could not contradict the allegation.' The tensions and conflicts of the Ngoni conquest states are evident here. The paranoid paramountcy; the fear of 'treason' by witchcraft; the oppression and disciplining of the Chewa women by witchcraft accusations; and the envy of rival power and property. The ordeal was a 'state occasion', a tool of the paramountcy.[15] It had been basic to the structure of the political power in the Chewa chieftaincies prior to conquest that the chiefs had had ultimate control over witchcraft through their monopoly of the right to use the ordeal. The supersession of this power and its jealous appropriation by the Ngoni was a crucial part of the establishment of the new states.

The observations of the White Fathers at Mponda's in 1890 give a picture of the use of *mwavi* at a time in which the polities were moving into a state of almost perpetual crisis.[16] The White Fathers observed *mwavi* as part of sorcery accusations, of crime and adultery, and high politics. In March 1890 a woman accused of stealing cloth herself asked to take *mwavi*. On other cases the diary reads:

> *Moave, moave!* That is how we were awakened by the town crier this morning. Some corpses had been disinterred and eaten. Two of the accused parties, a man and a woman named by the sorcerer, had to undergo the ordeal this morning. They drank the poison, failed to vomit and died, showing their guilt. 25 November 1890. Another case of cannibalism. Several people have taken the poison ordeal and it is said that one of them died from it. The taking of *mwabvi* is a very important ceremony held at the royal court. The elders and onlookers gather under the verandah while all the people involved in the case are lined up under the big trees, not only the accused but all their relatives . . . . Under one tree there are about thirty men. The women, more numerous, are under another, clapping their hands gently and singing lugubrious songs. Under a third tree is the sorcerer with the accused who are about to take the

90

ordeal to prove their innocence. On this occasion it is two old men, whose departure from this world will not be unduly hastened if the result is unfavourable .... He grinds up the bark of a tree like cinchona in a mortar. Finally everything is ready .... The women stop singing. He pours half the powder into a little calabash and fills it with a little water, stirs it with a straw .... The great master of ceremonies then enjoins those who have taken the *mwabvi* to leave the village until the poison has taken effect, and then declares the ceremony concluded. We learn in the evening that both the old men had the good fortune to vomit the poison.

In October Mponda himself was accused by his chief wife of killing the previous Mponda. Though he tried to avoid the ordeal he had no other way of proving his innocence, which, presumably, he judged vital to the continuation of acceptance of his legitimate authority. He took the poison and vomited it, proving his innocence. The Fathers were convinced that the dose was variable and that '*mwabvi* had precisely the effect desired by the sorcerer' (i.e. the witch-finder).

On one occasion four of Mponda's wives, accused of adultery, were submitted to the ordeal. One, who was heavily pregnant, died.

In another case observed, the slave who took the poison vomited it. The White Father's diary reads: 'Acclamations, singing from the women, and gunfire during the night .... We go to have a look in the morning. Several hundred women were dancing around the accused's hut, head, shoulders and breasts covered with ashes as a sign of repentance for having made a false accusation.'[17] In another case the man taking the poison as substitute died, rendering the original accused liable to pay a heavy fine.

New subjects and captive wives had not been easy to rule and did not easily accept their status. That they attempted by means of witchcraft to damage their masters seems very likely. Harm befalling the ruling members of the conquest states was therefore traceable to the machinations of their untamed subjects. Mass ordealing evolved to meet these circumstances. Likewise subjects would be anxious to take *mwavi* to clear themselves of possible complicity. This was not restricted to the Ngoni state systems. Smith and Dale observed of the Ila in Zambia that 'consciousness of innocence makes people bold enough to drink it willingly. If an important person dies very often all the people in the district wish to drink the poison to show that they had no hand in the death.'[18]

It may have been the case that towards the end of the century large-scale administration of *mwavi* in the conquest states was becoming more frequent, though it must be remembered that this is the first period for which many observations are available. Observation of the administration of *mwavi* as a conscious instrument of power raised for white observers the question of whether or not the dose was manipulated by the *mapondera* to make him both 'judge and executioner'.[19] We have no real evidence, however, about the death rate at mass administrations. But a variable dose does not explain the use of slaves to take *mwavi* for their masters, nor does it cover the other forms of ordeal in use, like fire and boiling water, in which a wicked witchdoctor could hardly change the temperature of the water. Arnot's and Coillard's accounts of the Lozi polity underline the theme of the rulers' fear of witchcraft and their defensive use of ordealing. Arnot's diary records a case in April 1884 when a woman accused of putting a crocodile tooth in the king's corn in order to bewitch him underwent the boiling-pot ordeal and was burnt as a witch. Coillard describes an incident in which the day after Lewanika's return from a hunting season, which had been a disastrous failure, he found the floor of his hut sprinkled with blood. 'Terror seized on everyone and spread everywhere like a tidal wave . . . . Everyone made a point of honour to wash his hands of it by submitting to the ordeal of boiling water.' As many pots as there were chiefs were set on fire 'and the slaves, always as proxies, plunged their hands into it by turns.' Coillard's witnessing was as troubled as Arnot's. Both were puzzled by the fact that on occasion none were scalded. Ordealing connected with the protection of rulers, and using slaves as proxies, had clearly been a part of the Lozi polity. Yet they were to have to make do without this protection. In 1890 Coillard reported that Lewanika had founded a sorcerer's village and that no one had been put to death for sorcery for three years.[20] The power of the Lozi ruling class would henceforth have to try to assert itself through the more bureaucratic forms which were acceptable to their foreign conquerers.

For all the varying adaptations of ordealing the basic evil of witchcraft remained to be combated. In the Reverend Ysaye Mwase's 'Notes on Native Law and Custom', only two fields were touched upon – family law, and the beliefs and practices relating to witchcraft. 'Witchcraft', wrote Mwase, 'means a great deal more than an ordinary man fancies to understand.' A *fwiti* (witch):

> is one who kills fellow men by look, wish or medicine . . . a *fwiti* is one who is believed to raise the dead before he eats them. *Fwiti* is the chief enemy of man . . . . Sometimes he dances at the doors of his fellow men believing that by that action the man or family within the doors are sure to die. However securely shut men's houses may be *fwiti* is able to creep in and do his dreadful business. No death in the world takes place by any disease but by *fwiti*.

The witch used a deadly medicine which could be turned into anything, 'fly, mouse, rat, snake, leopard, crocodile'. Witches were 'generally feared' by the Malawi community. 'The chief and highest crimes among the people are the habitual adulteries and *ufwiti*. No one would venture to redeem such sort of persons when convicted of the crimes . . . . To accuse a man of *ufwiti* is dreadful. The last possible degradation.'

Mwase then went on to give a full description of the various types of ordeal which had been used for the divination of witches. There was a procedure for piercing the ear; the water ordeal in which the accused plunged his forearm into boiling water and was acquitted if no harm followed; various forms of consulting lots; and the *mwavi* ordeal. ('Ceremonies of these ordeals are long and tiresome.') He also described a form of exorcism used to detect witches, continuing: 'Those who were detected by this method either they were caused to drink the *mwavi* ordeals, or burnt to death alive. Their surviving relatives were seized as slaves on the same charge to be sold or slaughtered at slight suspicion.' For a man who vomited the *mwavi* it was 'resurrection day.' And his accuser was liable to pay two or more slaves for the false accusation.[21]

If the ordeal had been an evidentiary tool in 'ordinary' criminal cases, or if it had simply reflected the weakness of an enforcing judicial authority, then it might easily have been replaced by the colonial court system, as the abolition of slavery and the end of the power of the conquest states did away with political ordealing. But the provision of courts with evidentiary procedures and powers to make effective judgements did not deal with the basic problem for which the ordeal existed. The problem was not in essence to decide who had committed an offence but to detect the presence of witchcraft and its use by the accused. (Similarly the medieval ordeal, which has often been seen as a means of extracting evidence or depicting its truth, was rather theoretically a way of revealing, through the intervention of divine power, the presence of sin in the accused.)[22] There was still a need to do this, increased perhaps by social mobility, the growth of new forms of wealth and new inequalities, increased inter-generational conflict and conflict between men and women. I deal at some length below with marriage and adultery and will just note in this context that this was a time of considerable marital instability and much of the continued use of *mwavi* was occasioned by accusations of adultery.[23] Not all adultery accusations involved a related charge of witchcraft and most were now settled through mundane procedures. But where an adultery could involve the blight of sexual or natal pollution, or where, more simply, social relations of power made it impossible for a woman to get her ordinary evidence heard or accepted, the only way she could clear herself was by taking *mwavi*. In a period of great tension, the British had outlawed individual ordealing, and there was no way of testing the veracity of an allegation involving witchcraft.

The European images of the 'legal system' derived from both the expansion of political ordealing and the spreading of witchcraft accusations consequent on the increase in slavery, the growth of mixed communities under conditions of political conquest and the abnormal conditions in crowded defensive communities. If we persist in looking at ordealing in the context of judicial procedure then liberal defensiveness about it is understandable, as it implies the absence of secular reasoning in African justice. But if we treat it in the context of control of the most serious wrongdoing – 'the chief enemy of man' as Y.S. Mwase tells us – then we can see that it was a central concern. The British legal offensive against the ordeal not only affected the British view of African justice, but it explains much about what Africans needed from the new colonial legal order, which was henceforth asked to provide what ordealing had provided in the past.

ORDEAL TRIAL AND THE COLONIAL COURTS

The Witchcraft Proclamations in Malawi and in Zambia were directed against the use of pretended powers of witchcraft for the purpose of defaming anyone, injuring person or property, or implicating anyone in the commission of a crime. Like the other witchcraft ordinances in British Africa, they were based upon the premise that there were no witches, that the evil to be eradicated was witchfinding, and that the villain was the 'witchdoctor', who held the villagers in thrall through the use of pretended magic powers. Witchfinding and consultation of a witchfinder to discover the perpetrator of a crime was made illegal, as was the ordeal trial and the receipt of remuneration for the pretended 'exercise of non-natural means'. The new law did not make punishable the use of non-natural means under the pretence of benefiting anyone, for example, by the provision of medicines. Nevertheless it became policy, where it was felt that a 'witchdoctor' was too powerful or rich, to use either the common law charge of obtaining money or goods under false pretences, or bring a charge of being a 'Rogue and a Vagabond' illegally claiming to be able to tell fortunes, under the Vagrancy Act.[24] The anti-witchcraft legislation reflected the development of the English law on witchcraft. Seventeenth-century legislation punished people for being witches – i.e. for possessing the powers of witchcraft. The 1736 Act and later the Vagrancy Act of 1824 abandoned this and henceforth punishment was to be for the *pretence* of possessing this power. The earlier law aimed at the practice of a real power, the later at the practice of a pretended one.

The administrative records cannot give us a full picture of the effects of the new legislation. In 1909 in Malawi it was reported that there appeared to be a decrease in the number of cases in which *mwavi* was used, though it was doubtful whether all were being brought to the Boma's attention. It appeared that in some cases *mwavi* was being used as a supplement to Boma justice and that an accused would drink *mwavi* after a Boma conviction, to prove his innocence.[25] The districts of Ncheu and Dedza, areas of high political tension where the Ngoni struggled to maintain their predominance, and where the mission presence was strong and aggressive, remained the only areas in which no decrease in the incidence of the use of *mwavi* was reported. Consistently, too, its increase was reported from the Mlanje district where the alienation of land for the tea estates and the influx of large numbers of Lomwe migrants posed problems for the Yao headmen, and increased social tensions. The 1919 report from Dedza district was to the effect that *mwavi* rituals were very common and that obtaining evidence to convict for holding them was next to impossible. 'Natives believe so firmly in the efficacy of the Ordeal,' the district commissioner wrote, 'in that if they do not take the *mwabvi* they are by their very refusal convicted of being *mfiti.*' There was apparently also an increase in accusations and ordealing in Northern Ngoniland after the end of the world war, perhaps caused by the influenza epidemic and the need to explain this disaster.[26] Similarly in the Mlanje area in 1924 and again in 1927 a large number of poisoning deaths occurred for which Boma courts failed to secure any convictions. People, it was felt, 'cannot fail to acquire the impression that they are not punishable and headmen have already protested that as *mwabvi* (trial by ordeal) is no longer allowed they have no means of discovering poisoners and have no protection from such criminals.' And it was not the pagans alone who clung to the old ways: 'even Mahomedan Yao headman have openly protested against the Government's prohibition of *Mwavi* as a means of discovering poisoners.' *Mwavi* drinking was still in use in rare cases by entire villages to detect those responsible for a series of unexplained deaths. In the Dedza district of Malawi, for example, an entire village under an Ngoni headman drank to discover who had been responsible for his death. Three died.[27]

The fact that the ordeal was not openly available does appear to have caused a significant amount of insecurity about the colonial ways of administering justice. And the fact that it was resorted to in certain cases affirmed administrators' ideas that indigenous trials had not proceeded by normal evidential procedure and so affirmed their views about the irrationality and cruelty of the indigenous legal order. The judicial department did have to make some adjustment to prevailing ideas. In 1909 it was decided that the courts should treat the administration of *mwavi*, followed by death, as manslaughter and not murder, because of the deep-rooted belief in it. In 1920 a judicial circular instructed courts to distinguish between a suspected person demanding an ordeal to prove his innocence, and the accusers requiring it to establish guilt. And even though the latter amounted to intention to kill in terms of the Witchcraft Ordinance of 1911, it was not to be treated as such. Ordeals, it was said, were 'so common' that to do so would be unduly harsh. As long as the ordeal was regarded by the population as a legitimate means of detecting and punishing those thought to be harmful, treating it as a capital offence would be neither understood nor just. Thus early reformist zeal, even in the prime field of witchcraft, was on the wane. It was all seen as part of the irrationality which pervaded the 'native mind'. As the district commissioner gloomily reported from the Lower Shire in 1932, the 'darkest superstition' was rife and years of effort would be required to stamp it out. 'The material and physical progress of the people we can judge with comparative ease. They are bound up with markets and trade . . . . But social progress is a different matter.'[28]

The North Eastern Zambia case-books show that the courts barely scratched at the surface of the problem. The pattern from the case-books seems to be that the person accused of wrongdoing requested the *mwavi* as the proof. But as the Boma treated administering the test more seriously than taking it, it was not likely that evidence would be given in court that the ritual had been forced upon unwilling participants. In any case Boma justice had not built up the reputation it wished for freeing people from the terror of the poison ritual. In one Fort Jameson case a man accused of arson preferred *mwavi* to the Boma: 'I shall take the *mwavi* and if I am guilty I shall die. Do not take me to the Boma,' he is reported as saying. In another, the threat 'If they do not take *mwavi* we will go to the Boma' underlines which may have been seen as the more frightening alternative.[29]

In ordinary legal administration the courts were not the arena for a spectacular clash between witchcraft and rationality. In a marked contrast to the cases involving slavery and divorce there is no evidence that people presented themselves in court or to the Boma to escape from a required ritual. The evidence points to the opposite: the desire to conceal the ritual from the Boma, and to continue to risk it in spite of illegality, even if the killing of those found to be witches was becoming less common. It was reported for North Eastern Zambia for 1910 that persons who had formally been killed after proof of guilt by *mwavi* were now being fined and driven from their villages.[30] But the anti-witchcraft laws did have an effect in that there was now an area of bitter disputes with which the legal system had no way of dealing and which could not often be satisfactorily solved clandestinely. The kind of case with which the new dispensation could not deal adequately is illustrated by one heard in Fort Jameson in 1904. Ndawambe, an Ngoni headman, was being plotted against by his Chewa wives, one of whom was a 'slave'. They called in a Chewa doctress to make a medicine to render him impotent. Here was a situation tailored for the administration of *mwavi* but this was now forbidden. Ndawambe wanted to take his complaint to the Boma but, as a witness told the court, he had advised Ndawambe 'that among the whitemen they would not believe in this medicine'. (Indeed, not only would they not have believed it, but his accusations against the women would probably have attracted a penalty.) So, turning his back on both *mwavi* and the Boma, Ndawambe had taken steps which led to his being tried with the unlawful detention and barbarous treatment of his wives. He was deported for two years. The Chewa wives (and witches) had won: the Ngoni husband was defeated.[31]

What could the new law, aimed as it was at witchfinders, do when people confessed to being practising witches? In 1931 at Kalomo a woman named Namangola was accused of causing a death by witchcraft. She confessed, and committed suicide. As the native affairs department pointed out to the attorney-general, a charge against the accusers would now seem absurd in local eyes. Indeed the dead person's family had recovered four head of cattle in compensation. But, although it was impossible to prosecute the accusers, it was ruled that at least they would have to return the cattle.[32] In 1933 in Kasempa six women confessed to being guilty of causing the death of others and of tampering with graves. The local administration took the case seriously. The graves were carefully examined in the presence of witnesses. Most were intact but one had only two bones remaining and one contained 'horns'. But what could the government prosecute for? One possibility was murder, but, as was pointed out, there was no evidence as to the cause of death. Nonetheless, in local eyes, six witches had been caught red-handed and had confessed, and interfering with graves was in 'customary law' punishable by death. Furthermore the women themselves wanted to be exorcised and cleansed. But if the government accused and convicted them it might be taken as a sign that it believed in their powers. They were suffering, the secretary for native affairs wrote, from 'hallucination and suggestion'. An uneasy compromise was reached: there would be no prosecution but the district commissioner would burn the 'medicines and adjuncts' of witchcraft.

In another case a man taken seriously ill accused another of 'stealing his spirit'. The person accused confessed and restored it and the sick man recovered. What could be done in the face of the confession? Who could be prosecuted? The Witchcraft Proclamation said the accuser, but in the light of the case history this would look ridiculous.

The Nyasaland administration reacted to similar cases with like incomprehension. In 1931 a police investigation into the disappearance of a woman from a village on the Upper Shire claimed to have uncovered a classic situation of midnight 'feasts' on the bodies of the dead 'attended by all *afiti* ... in a naked state'. To the investigator's embarrassment, 'An old woman who was one of the leading lights made a statement' but in the absence of corroboration the attorney-general was able to advise against prosecution. Four years later a Lomwe man and woman were accused of murdering a fourteen-year-old youth. 'When charged they both asserted that they were *Afiti* ... and that their desire for human flesh was so great that they decided to kill to satisfy this craving. They ... stated that they killed [him] by hitting his head against the centre pole of a hut and then twisting his neck. Medical evidence showed that death was due to injuries consistent with these statements.' The confession was corroborated by a woman who claimed to have witnessed the killing while the accused 'were in their supernatural bodies of *Afiti*'. But there were other witnesses who claimed that in spite of their confession the two accused were in another district at the time of the murder. Again the attorney-general would not prosecute. Conclusions were clearly drawn by the people from the attitudes of the legal authorities in both colonies. When a Mlanje man who had employed a witchfinder was taxed by the district officer as to whether he knew the Boma's law on witchcraft, he replied 'Yes, the Boma law is that the Boma must hear nothing about witchcraft.'[33]

Even more bitter were the escalated responses recorded by Marwick among the Chewa in Zambia. One informant told him that the road to the graveyard 'looks like a well-trodden road; and this is because of Europeans. If you catch a person killing his fellows with medicines, the Europeans ask "Did you see him killing?" and, if you lack words in reply, they set him free and arrest you ... and all they do is give the sorcerer a bag of salt with which to eat his relish.' There was also a popular myth, writes Marwick, concerning a man who reported a sorcerer to the district officer. The district officer imprisoned him and 'turning to the sorcerer, he discharged him and presented him with a bag of salt and a large knife, telling him to go back to the corpse he had been eating.' The whites had forbidden the ordeal, some said, because they were afraid of being detected themselves.[34] As a result cases involving witchcraft rarely appeared before any of the government's courts but they were still heard.[35]

There was a widespread feeling that witchcraft was on the increase and that government was doing nothing to combat it. Indeed all the government's measures seemed calculated to confirm this impression. While it continued to refuse to prosecute confessed witches, it added to its legislative prohibitions on witchfinding and allegations. In 1948 the Witchcraft Ordinance in Zambia was amended, making it an offence to assert 'that any person has by committing adultery caused in some non natural way death, injury, damage or calamity'. Prior to this amendment the Native Courts had made a practice of allowing people to sue successfully for breach of the taboos regarding adulterous intercourse. After its passing yet another defence had been outlawed. Yet, as Colson notes, the strains created by the fragmenting lineages and the shrinking of consumption and inheritance groups were increasing in severity. The confessions of guilt, as much as the accusations, were signs of severe social and moral disturbance, indications of conditions which made adherence to old norms impossible. As Turner wrote, the confessions of guilt were made 'by those who feel they have broken some crucial norm governing the intercourse of the living with the living or with the dead', though to officials they were simply confirmation of the irrationality with which they had to deal.[36] Native Authorities were firmly instructed that there was to be no 'active association' of members of the Native Courts or of court officers with the 'search for sorcerers'. The position of the local African authorities was a delicate one. If they were to retain a leading and convincing role in the combating of wrong, they put themselves at risk with the white administration. Of the two persons convicted under the Witchcraft Ordinance in the Southern Province in Malawi in 1935 one was a 'regular witchdoctor' while the other 'was a village headman who had assisted at the "smelling out" of witches'.[37] The early 1930s were a time when accusations and cleansing movements were becoming more prominent just when the Native Authority Courts were new and attempting to establish themselves. Yet they were entirely divorced from the processes of combating serious moral wrongdoing. They were thus left only with the area of sexual behaviour in which they could contribute to the affirmation of social morality.

The case of *R*. v. *Kasokera and others* which was heard in Ndola in 1922 illustrates well the inbuilt clash of logic involved in the law. After a man had died, Kasokera, the diviner, was called in to find out why. A witness described his style: he struck some horns in the ground, looked through an empty cartridge case and then announced that the deceased had been killed by the sting of a poisonous bee sent by someone whose wife he had enticed away. He concluded by sprinkling medicine on the bodies of the living relatives and was paid a gun and thirty-two shillings. In his evidence Kasokera stressed that he was a witchfinder, and no *mfiti*. He told the court that 'It is our belief that when a man dies the "thing" that caused his death still remains among his wives and property until the cause of death has been found out and the people properly cleaned by medicine.' If the successor touched them before this had been done they would die quickly. The headman's evidence affirmed that the cause of a death had to be established before a successor could inherit. It was, he said, still the custom when a person died to employ a diviner to find out the cause of death, though now people were 'afraid to have the person mentioned killed . . . or even to ask for compensation. The reason for still asking the cause of death is that the diviner can give medicine to drive away the misfortune, which killed the deceased, from his successor.' The court, in questioning, asked whether a man must be a 'wizard' before he could be a diviner, trying to establish a connection between the roles, but the headman remained firm that they were separate and opposite. Finally the Boma messenger explained that on the death of a spouse the surviving spouse had to have the cause of death established before the customary compensation would be accepted by the dead person's family. What sometimes appeared to the Boma to be disputes about the amount of compensation were, in reality, caused by dissatisfaction that the diviner had not yet been consulted. Finally 'the death cannot be taken off the body' without the diviner and 'until the death is taken off the surviving spouse is unclean and cannot re-marry or even co-habit with another wife if he has one.' Kasokera's explanation was taken as a plea of guilty and he was given a six-week sentence, a light one, influenced by the fact that the person he had named was already dead.[38]

Yet there was also an inkling of a better understanding. P.J. Hall wondered whether people took all of their 'superstitions' always very seriously: 'one finds superstitions, like customs, treated as life or death matters, or absolutely disregarded.' In anticipating Malinowski's publication of his 'discovery' that savages did not always obey their own customs, Hall cited the many existing marriages well within the prohibited degrees often proclaimed by customary law to be disastrous to breach. Claims about custom, then, clearly did not describe reality; the question was why, at particular times, they should be brought forth. Similarly with witchcraft beliefs, ordeals and divinations, the question was not one of an existing, indivisible package of superstitions, but why the charges surfaced when and where they did and what they were really about. But this sort of perception gained no ground. When the *Mchape*, a witchcraft-eradication movement, hit Zambia in the early 1930s the government's response was to see it simply as a continuing manifestation of the indivisible package of witch beliefs and divining. Though the government's files were full of descriptions of what the *Mchape* men were doing (that they dealt with whole communities rather than with individual accusations; that they promised to cleanse communities of adultery, jealousy and wrongdoing generally; that they destroyed all instruments of magic), the attitude of the Northern Rhodesian administration was simply that 'the whole trade savours of witchcraft and fraud' and was clearly a 'device of a non-natural kind to impose upon superstitious persons'.[39]

Administrators clamoured for prosecutions of the *Mchape* men under the Witchcraft Proclamation. The provincial commissioner at Fort Jameson thought that by allowing the proceedings the government was admitting that witchcraft existed. One Native Authority was punished by removal from office, and others warned, for allowing cleansing sessions at which calls for the production of 'medicines' and 'charms' were made. Across the border in Malawi, eighty-five convictions under the witchcraft legislation were recorded in 1931/2 arising out of the activities of the *Mchape* men. They put themselves unequivocally within the ambit of the law by denouncing as witches those who would not partake of the medicine. 'This is immediately taken up by the villages,' said a police report, 'and it is feared that trial by ordeal of the non-partakers may take place to disprove the accusations.'[40] The points about the failings of the Witchcraft Ordinance could in no circumstances be better made.

In the heyday of the indirect rulers there even appeared to be doubts on the subject of witchcraft and of the direction and efficacy of British efforts to eradicate it. Nothing is better illustrative of the retreat from the aggressive posture of the early colonial period and it was vocally led by commentators with Malawian and Zambian experiences. It was claimed that there was 'no other subject on which the races differ so widely' and that this was 'the most conspicuous instance of the superimposition of the white man's law and opinion'.[41] To the people at large, Melland wrote, 'we are on the side of the witches.'[42] But the new relativism did not reach the courts, which continued to sentence witchfinders but otherwise to ignore witchcraft. The section dealing with the law in Malawi in the memoirs of Sir Charles Ross, who served in the 1930s as senior Crown counsel, attorney-general and acting chief justice, is entitled 'Witchdoctors and Beerdrinks', which perfectly encapsulates what the criminal law looked like from the viewpoint of the High Court. The cases which it dealt with arose from what appeared to the judges as a tedious succession of assaults and killings which were the result of village drunkenness and of accusations of witchcraft. A general pattern which shows up clearly from the cases of murder which came before the Nyasaland High Court and on review to the governor is one in which the accused claims either to have been the victim of witchcraft which was responsible for his actions, or to have killed someone whom he knew was bewitching him.[43]

The problems associated with the banning of the ordeal as a means of witchfinding while the belief in and practice of witchcraft continued are well illustrated in the material gathered by Monica Wilson in Nyakusa country in Southern Tanganyika and Northern Malawi in the 1930s.[44] Witchcraft was seen as deliberate: 'witches act consciously', says one informant. Some of the visible signs mentioned are important indicators: 'What our parents used to say to us was "Pride". If a man is proud and is not sociable with his neighbours; if he boasts . . . he is a witch!' Also mentioned were 'hoeing a very large field'; or 'Being more wealthy'; or 'Eating fine food alone'. It is clear that these ideas were not left-overs from a traditional way of life but were related to increased social mobility and economic stratification. That they were not limited to those stuck in the old village ways is made clear by the account of the government clerk who was believed to be able to kill by witchcraft those surpassing him in seniority.[45] The insecurity of communities without defences against witches was being expressed in a greater movement between villages by people who believed themselves to be the victims of witches. The destructive use of medicines was also believed to have 'increased enormously'. The connection between witchcraft and the control of relations between the sexes seems clear. Three of the informants told her, 'Many wives were driven away for witchcraft,' that they were frequently accused and made to drink *mwavi*. One case concerns a woman who left her husband who then 'stirred "the horn" that all those concerned should die if they did not return his wife'. The offending man and his nephew promptly died and then the family 'drove away the woman in order to end the sickness among us'. It seems likely that increased female mobility, like increased stratification, would add to the number of accusations and cases. The cases still occurred. As one headman said, 'We judge them openly but we do not have them written in the courtbook.'

It has been suggested that the role of ordealing in the judicial process was to relieve weak authorities from the onus of decision-making and the giving of judgements which would alienate followers and which would probably not be enforceable.[46] But it may be more useful to think first about how disputes would normally have been settled where political power and formal institutions were weak. As I suggested in Chapter 1, we must depart from the implicit model in which a chief/headman administers a public decision for disputants, and think in terms of settlement within a local group or neighbourhood without such a public dimension. The chief/headman might be called in to administer the ordeal where an accusation of witchcraft had been made. In these circumstances they did not punish crime but administered *mwavi*, i.e. their power was not political or jural in the secular sense understood by British administrators, but ritual. Thus to an extent 'law' – in the sense of dispute adjudicated publicly beyond local groupings – was the administration of the ordeal in cases involving witchcraft accusations. It is not hard to see how, when describing these circumstances, both African and British evidence would overlap the ritual and judicial roles. The adaptation of these processes to the slave and conquest states has also been described. The oppression involved in mass ordealing and the consequent spread of the ordeal combined to present a picture of violence and irrationality to the incoming whites and to obscure the role of the ordeal in the struggle against evil. The need to engage in this struggle was not reduced by the white presence.

The passing of the conquest states, the establishment of the *pax Britannica* and the provision of stronger judicial machinery did not put an end to evil, jealousy and the desire to harm others. Indeed conflicts were sharpened by the pressures of colonial capitalism and the growth of the economic warfare of man against man. This was the greatest disturber of the villages' social peace. Young's Tumbuka informants put the ordeal in the context of the jealousy which arose as a result of economic inequalities. Significantly they presented it as something which occurred between clansmen (serfs were never accused of death-dealing intentions), an acute indication of the real problems for which the ordeal existed. Real conflicts would henceforth occur between people who owed it to each other to behave otherwise. In olden times they told him goods had been equally distributed but now persons ignored their poor relatives:

> mutual hatred began with stingy selfishness over goods .... they brought accusations of witchcraft against hoarders of wealth when one became niggardly with whom previously his group had shared things; now seeing how he was become in the matter of wealth they rose against him and accused the clansmen of evil intent. Now if he took the ordeal nothing remained but separation; they would never be together again.[47]

6

The courts and the people: law in action I

The early colonial period in both Zambia and Malawi was a time in which the administration of justice was chaotic and when the rhetorical ambitions of the lawgivers bore little relation to the reality. Harry Johnston, the Nyasaland protectorate's first commissioner, had early pressed the British government for a full-time judicial official, putting forward a 'dressing for dinner' argument that 'in the middle of all this barbarism I feel that we cannot be too fastidiously correct in our legal procedure.'[1] It was an inappropriate and unfulfillable aspiration. This point is emphasised in the first full report of the working of the judicial system in Malawi submitted by Judge Nunan to the governor in 1902. His approach to the problems faced was to be repeated across colonial Africa when the administrators' lawgiving came under the scrutiny of professional lawyers. Nunan demanded reform of the trial of African criminal cases, remarking on the admission of (and conviction on) 'flimsy evidence', on the 'possibility of innumerable irregularities' and on the 'summary disposal of cases of life and death'.[2] Across the border Judge Macdonnell composed a memorandum in 1910 the conclusions of which were similar to those which had been reached in Malawi. He wrote:

> Taken as a whole the standard of judicial work in the territory is a low one. The officials are without exception devoid of professional training, as is indeed the case with nine-tenths of the judicial work throughout the Empire. But here the inexperience goes further. Few of the men in the service seem to have read any law or to have thought about the problems of administering justice and nearly all of them give the impression of never having been in a law court in their lives ... the lack of knowledge does not so much matter; it is the lack of common sense and especially of consecutive thinking which is so depressing.[3]

It is important here to consider not simply the British failure to substantiate their own myths but the effect which the first twenty years of maladministration of justice had on the formation of attitudes toward the white men and their courts.

For this was not only the period in which the ambitions of the British were the most comprehensive, but the time at which the expectations of some of their new subjects might have been at their highest.[4] In the beginning, especially in areas which had been Ngoni-dominated, the collectors' courts were flooded with litigants trying out the new justice, and though district officers soon felt the load of judicial work to be too great, the administration in Malawi rejected the idea of devolving authority to the chiefs. Even where chiefs were allowed to hear matrimonial and succession disputes the feeling was that these should be heard at the Boma and not in the villages, and in these cases Africans were encouraged to apply to the white man for justice.[5] Experience in Zambia too was that 'enormous numbers' of cases were brought to the white courts[6] and the aim was that white justice should make its superior standards available to all. In the early years it was taken to be a sign of confidence in the government when large numbers of cases were brought to the Boma.[7] By 1910 in Malawi some of the early initial enthusiasm for judicial universality was beginning to wane and district officers had come round to the view that the large numbers of so-called petty cases which were habitually brought to the Boma could better be heard in the villages by the headmen. But even so the central government view was that on no account should a magistrate refuse to hear a case brought to him, however trivial, for it was by patient adjudication of small cases that the courts had won the confidence of the population.[8] This was very different from the attitude the government was to take later.

Thus in the early years white justice was held out as an ideal, and many flocked to take advantage of its offering. But its actual procedures were uncertain, unsympathetic and arbitrary, and soon there was a double withdrawal.[9] There was disillusionment on the part of the European magistrates, who realised the impossibility of the ideal role they had cast for themselves, and a realisation on the part of the Africans in the areas of the conquest states that if white justice was an alternative to that of alien chiefs it was not preferable to take advantage of the opportunity to resurrect old headmanships. People began to show increasing discrimination in their use of colonial courts. While women, especially in the mixed Chewa/Ngoni areas, and Lomwe migrants, who distrusted the Yao headmen under whom they had settled, used the courts out of choice, the Ngoni despised 'running to the Boma', and there was also deliberate abstinence where the Boma failed, for example in witchcraft cases. Yet the early years had seen legality of a sort established, though not the idealised version. The strict requirements of the law were sometimes seen as secondary to the use of the court to secure social discipline. As the acting commissioner for Malawi put it in 1905 when asked how a contract between an employer and employee could be enforced: 'It is perfectly true that there is no law existing which deals with this subject, but it is a recognised factor in the administration of this country that natives must be made to comply with the provisions of reasonable agreements . . . . [to do otherwise] would be to undermine the authority of the Government,' and he advised the use of the court to secure African obedience.[10]

It should also be realised that while the Native Commissioners' Courts thought they operated as courts of the first instance, they were often hearing appeals from the chiefs' courts.[11] When it had been decided in 1910 to revive the operation of the Native Courts and judiciary 'it came to light that they were already in being.'[12] But there was also another African judicial sub-system which was far less traditional. White administrative personnel were very few and relied upon African auxiliaries. Grouped around each Boma were a totally untrained police force, and a force of Boma messengers, who acted as 'eyes and ears' and who were responsible for collecting parties and witnesses in court cases, as well as the interpreters, upon whom the white magistrates relied. The powerful position of those who controlled this sifting process is illustrated by one Northern Rhodesian district officer's description of the scene on his arrival at his office in the years of the first world war: 'the litigants, accused and others with problems would have collected outside our offices and the messengers would have finished some sorting out of their own account to decide whether, and by whom, the individual should be seen.'[13]

Boma workers were often recruited from those hostile to their former overlords. The district officers' use of African auxiliaries caused suspicion and division among Africans, and complaints that the police and messengers turned away complainants to whom they were hostile, or that interpreters mistranslated or acted as attorneys for one of the parties in court, were common.[14] Indeed it was sometimes fear of the messengers and *askaris* that made people prefer to turn to the missions for judgement.[15] As one early district officer in Nyasaland wrote, because justice was administered 'by judges who could hardly understand a word of the evidence to parties who could hardly understand a word of English … [interpreters] really controlled the whole business of the district courts.'[16] Under these circumstances justice was maladministered well before those young magistrates who were keen to arbitrate judiciously, to settle wisely and to punish fairly even had a chance to render judgement.[17]

It is clear from the records that the employees of the Boma used their powers as intermediaries to block access to the courts or to grant it in return for fees. Witnesses feared the courts, fled when summoned and had to be captured, a process which could not have been conducive to building confidence in a new system of fair and orderly justice.[18] And once people were in court things were often not much better. The court records abound with references to accuseds, witnesses and parties to actions being nervous, incoherent and often uncomprehending in court. The practice of imposing fines on both parties when there was a clash of evidence, which seems to have been adopted in North Eastern Zambia, could not have set them at ease. The exposed position of those finding themselves in the Boma courts is captured in the outburst of an accused: 'What can a man say when he is alone, you Bwanas write down everything.' And the decorum of the new courts was not easily learned. One litigant, for example, is recorded as having received 'five lashes for repeated interruptions'.[19]

It is also worth stressing in this context, that 'tax collection was the *raison d'être* of the Provincial Administration: the organisation of touring and the work of junior officers centred on the twin duties of tax collecting and the upkeep of tax registers.'[20] This aspect of their work is not usually stressed by the district officers themselves. It is not as sympathetic as depicting oneself as an itinerant judge and solver of problems. Yet this major function of exacting tribute is likely to have affected perception of and receptivity towards the other incidental matters which a district officer handled on tour.

The Boma's judicial prestige rested therefore upon fragile foundations. The messengers were unpopular particularly because they were used as labour recruiters and frequent charges of extortion and violence were brought against them. Their period of service was noticeably short and the rate of dismissal for petty crimes, neglect of duty and abuse of position was high.[21] They did not have an easy job: as Croad, a district officer in Zambia, wrote, the messengers 'have often to travel unarmed by ones and twos into the villages to enforce orders with natives who often refuse them point blank'. The police in Malawi were no better. They were recruited locally by the district officer mainly from ex-soldiers. 'There was no system of training and each man became a policeman on being issued with a uniform and equipment.'[22]

Nevertheless from the kinds of cases which came before the courts it seems that the Boma's effective jurisdiction, particularly over village crime, was fairly far-reaching. Headmen were obliged to report crimes and arrest wrongdoers and court records show that time and again the headman appeared as the chief witness in criminal cases. But the Boma depended upon co-operation: as a law department circular put it in 1917, 'the delicate structure of the District Administration of the Territory ... depends very largely on goodwill.'[23] The headmen were law-and-order men themselves; they could also use the threat of reporting to the Boma with effect.[24] Thus the Boma court was an extra factor in local disputes: cases came before it not so much as a matter of course but where for legal or political reasons it was useful to add the Boma's weight to one's side.

There was in Central African societies an absence of judicial specialisation in the sense that other relationships between judges and judged, and knowledge and views external to those strictly relevant to a particular case in terms of the British notion of evidence, played a part in deciding cases. There is little doubt too that such social relationships and external knowledge entered, in a similar way, though to a different degree, into British legal processes as well. Yet when the British system was transplanted the instinct of its practitioners was often (rather as they dressed for dinner) to tend to fall back upon the extreme mythology of judicial detachment, a detachment which the British system did not and could not affect on its own ground. This stance, added to the huge social distance between the district officers and their subjects, and the incomprehensible and summary forms of procedure, appeared in practice both as harshness and lack of care. The generally adopted form of trial procedure was for the accused, or the parties, to make a statement, uninterrupted and unled, and then afterwards to be questioned on it by the judicial officer. The latter was told[25] that it was his duty in criminal cases 'to rebut the charge at the same time as he tries to establish it', and in general to defend the rights of the accused, a difficult task for an investigator, prosecutor and judge, especially one determined to uphold white authority and often possessed of a cruel sense of humour.[26] Proceedings tended to be summary and brisk. In 1913[27] the Northern Rhodesia law department reiterated the standard belief in the value of 'prompt and efficient justice [which] makes them respect and obey the Boma quicker and more thoroughly than anything else'. But, as Levi Mumba and others were later to show, summary despatch of cases was probably most unpopular.

The gap between the lawgiving ambitions of the early British administrators and the realities of life in the courts soon became clear. In the first year of its operation in 1897 the Native Court in Abercorn District[28] dealt primarily with serious crime like manslaughter, arson and slavery cases. After two years of operation it had settled down to convicting men for absconding from work and desertion from government service, and by 1900 'neglect of duty' cases were even more common as the court moved from 'pacification' cases to the process of backing up employers' authority. The court was run informally, charges were rarely recorded and punishments for lying and disobedience were freely handed out. In North Eastern Zambia other lower courts also appeared to settle down quickly to enforcing the social as well as the economic discipline of colonialism, especially in areas of white settlement where numbers of convictions for 'absence from duty', 'neglect of work', 'refusal to work' (sometimes 'with insolence') are recorded and magistrates appeared freely to use their judicial powers to punish their own servants.[29] Two administrators in Zambia at the time reported that Africans had an 'abnormally vivid' sense of injustice, which was, under the circumstances, not surprising.[30] A magistrate at Fort Johnston sentenced his own servant to ten lashes for stealing four lumps of sugar after an elaborate trial which well illustrated that the idea that justice was being administered according to a British model was a fantasy. When reprimanded by Judge Nunan, the magistrate wrote, 'I have often to be the Magistrate, Prosecutor, Defence and everything else, as you know, and I have, I think, exercised every function down to executions.'[31]

Of the early days in Zambia officials have recalled with nostalgia the lack of red tape, the 'amusement' and the 'freer hand' which they enjoyed when they were not expected to state the law under which an offender was charged and when there was no appeal.[32] A study of the records of the Fort Jameson district court shows clearly, for example, how the magistrates used the formal machinery of the law to discipline their domestic servants, and charges such as 'not being in the stable when required' were not unusual. The spirit in which justice was handed down is represented in Chomeley's memoir of the former administrator of N.E. Rhodesia, R. E. Codrington, of whom he wrote: 'The natives he regarded as children and he chose his officials from public school and university men who had entered the teaching profession. If, he argued, such men could produce a good testimonial as disciplinarians, over British boys, then these men were most likely to prove good and understanding native officials.'[33]

Court books sometimes read like a deliberate lampooning of colonial justice. Charges were not framed in terms of law; some taken from the Fort Jameson Court Book[34] were 'wasting time instead of buying food' – four lashes; 'sitting around fire instead of working' – five to ten lashes; one man was fined for absenting himself from the hospital while under treatment; another,[35] a Livingstonia man, for singing near the Native Church at 11.30 p.m.; some for being 'late for work'; some for 'gross disrespect' and two men five shillings each for 'constantly running away at the approach of the Boma official'. In general the central government and the judges were most anxious to curb the grosser absurdities of the district officers' courts but it had been an inauspicious beginning. As government became more routinised, charges were framed under the new battery of colonial ordinances or the huge reserve powers of the English Vagrancy Act of 1824, but the essential function of the lower courts remained that of discipline and punishment, especially in the field of taxation and employment. The Fort Jameson court, for example, dealt with 5,500 criminal cases between 1916 and 1918. About 5,200 were tax offences and approximately another 100 prosecutions, the next largest category, were for breach of employment contracts. It is not quite the picture of a court inaugurating a new era of justice. The grander visions had had soon to adjust to the realities of colonial life and crime, a process combining realistic disillusionment and unsympathetic misunderstanding which was encapsulated in Judge Beaufort's comments on Chiwali's case, 'Fight: no weapons no good reason: savages: no premeditation: ordinary daily life: 18 months.'[36]

A brief look at the Malawi criminal statistics gives an idea of what the pattern of constraint there was really about. Between 1906 and 1911 the number of convictions rose from 1,665 to 2,821, reflecting the larger number of statutory offences as administration became more systematised. By 1918, 3,511 were convicted, two-thirds for new statutory offences.[37] As the government got into its stride in the post-war years the nature and effect of the administration of law changed. In 1922 there were over 8,500 convictions of which 3,855 were for offences against the Native Hut and Poll Tax Ordinance of 1921, 1,609 leaving the protectorate without a pass and 705 for offences against the Employment of Natives Ordinance.[38]

In 1924 this total had fallen by two-thirds because of a new High Court ruling on the tax ordinance. The incidence of Boma justice must have seemed a little random. Otherwise in 1924 there were 35 convictions for unlawful killing; 441 other crimes of violence, mainly common assault; 794 crimes against property, largely simple larceny; 1,090 pass and employment offences; 882 against various colonial ordinances like the game laws, firearm laws, intoxicating liquor laws, township laws, district administration and cattle disease laws. There were 199 criminal convictions for adultery. A basically similar pattern is repeated in the years which follow. As Judge Haythorne Reed pointed out in 1928, about one conviction in five was for an offence everywhere considered as a crime. And he also noted that 'generally it may be said that the sentences inflicted in Nyasaland are much severer than those at home.'[39]

The legal framework governing the employment of labour in both territories was, throughout the period covered in this book, based on penal sanctions for the breach of labour contracts. This was considered to be a fundamental principle and when, during the period in office of the Labour government in Britain between 1929 and 1931, Lord Passfield (Sydney Webb) urged its abandonment, he met with firm opposition from the colonial governments of East and Central Africa, which all thought penal sanctions essential to the maintenance of the labour force.

In Malawi matters were governed by the Employment of Natives Ordinance of 1909 as later amended and the District Administration of Natives Ordinance of 1924. A contract had to be written if for longer than a month, wages had to be paid in cash, and any provision for housing or food had to be written into a contract. Penal sanctions were provided for both non-payment of wages and desertion or neglect of duties. Passes were necessary for people wishing to leave the territory and forced labour on public works could be required, at current rates of pay. In part to prevent the tying of employees through debt, credit extended to them was not legally recoverable. The position of those living on white estates was regulated by Ordinance 15 of 1928 which provided for the compulsory registration of tenancies and the payment of rent by labour services. In Zambia the legislation was in principle similar. The Employment of Natives Ordinance of 1929 adopted an East African distinction between major and minor offences by employees. Temporary desertion, drunkenness, neglect of duties, abusive language, refusing to work and giving a false name were minor offences, rendering a worker liable to a fine of half a month's pay, or a month's imprisonment. Major offences like causing damage to property, neglect of animals or permanent desertion attracted a fine of ten pounds or six months in prison. Ordinance 8 of 1929 provided for the arrest of deserters without warrant. For those living on white estates Ordinance 57 of 1919 was harsher than the Nyasaland ordinance as rent was payable only in labour services.[40]

The insistence on legal forms and the protection of written contracts must be seen in the light of the courts' practices. In 1909 the law department advised magistrates that the practice of giving employers a legal remedy in cases of desertion where there was only a verbal contract could not be pursued. Instead it suggested that an employee be asked to state in court what his terms of service had been and this could be put in writing and signed by him. With this written ratification of terms he might then be punished for desertion which had taken place before the written agreement had been executed.

Those who went to work on the Zambian Copperbelt found themselves subjected to yet another system of alien authority. Most of the workers were under the direct control of the mine managers who operated what was, in effect, a parallel system of legal authority. The compound managers were responsible for the housing and discipline of African workers, and managers and district officers accepted that 'no authority should be seen to challenge that of the compound manager.' The managers 'assumed some of the judicial functions given to district officers under the Employment of Natives Ordinance'. Breaches of discipline were dealt with inside the compounds and government officers saw only the most serious cases. As Berger points out, this further weakened the paternal role in which they ideally saw themselves. Charles Dundas, the chief secretary of the Northern Rhodesian government, said in 1935 that in industrial areas the district officers came into contact with the African population 'almost only in the guise of public authority and power – that is as the avenging magistrate and the Tax Collector'.[41] This parallel system of law and authority, which governed the lives of urban Africans in most important respects, may be compared to those systems of discipline on white estates and white missions. Any picture of the legal system in the colonial period must take into account these non-state systems of white discipline and white punishment, supported in the last resort by the state. Mine regulations, like religious law, imposed a legal dimension additional to customary law and statutory importations.

The temper of the district administration which was the broader context and example both for the white courts and later for the Native Authority Courts can be judged from some of the reports about the district officers' exercise of their powers under Proclamation 8 of 1916 in Zambia. Under this proclamation, which was the legal framework for the district administration until the introduction of indirect rule, native commissioners could punish as *criminal* disobedience to any 'reasonable order', which the law department defined as 'any order which circumstances may make necessary but which is not actually provided for in this or some other law'. But, as the law department had to point out, 'A Native Commissioner is not expected to use all the powers given by this Proclamation in season and out of season or to hunt and punish any minor infraction of its provisions . . . . It is discouraging to find . . . use [of] all the powers given by it and on all occasions trivial and great.' In reviewing the actions of commissioners under the proclamation, the department wrote that it 'has taken away from some men all sense of proportion'. That it was most often headmen who were being tried and punished for disobedience to orders must have given them a particular perception of how the new legal order, in which their part was soon to expand, did its work.[42]

By the 1920s the administration's legal retreat was evident. Partly it was a result of the tendency to move towards indirect rule and the recognition of the attractiveness of being able to use headmen as 'a strong buttress to the European Boma'. Partly it was based on a simple realisation that most civil cases and many criminal ones never reached the Boma.[43] This might have been the result of the changing balance of power in the countryside. It is not clear whether the falling off in the number of cases voluntarily brought into the white courts was primarily the result of dissatisfaction with the justice meted out there, or because of the ending of the nineteenth-century conquest situation and the greater 'indigenisation' of justice in the villages. The government's attitude was ambivalent: while it was uneasy about 'abstention from the Boma',[44] it did not want to interfere too much with the headmen.

The post-war period also saw changes in the administration of criminal law. There was a large increase in recorded crime, particularly larceny, due, some thought, to the 'demoralisation' of the people by the war or to the unprecedented prices charged for local requirements.[45] It seems to have been the case that the increasing mobility of people increased the rate of crime. Significant numbers of those accused were strangers to the district, removed from home restraints, in white employment, or porters. The district officers felt the strain of doing both police and trial work and heavier sentences and frequent corporal punishment were resorted to to defend the security of property. In addition an array of new colonial ordinances multiplied the number of statutory offences and offenders. Thus the load of criminal court work was increased, which provided district officers with an incentive to reduce their civil work. At the same time the heavier hand of colonial criminal justice might well have encouraged people to abstain from the Boma when they could. The consensus of opinion by the end of the 1920s was that although civil cases gave the officials 'a better acquaintance with native affairs and opinion than anything else',[46] the time had come to give formal recognition to African courts. The frustration of the district officers was increased by the fact that 'it not infrequently happens that Native cases already settled . . . are brought up after a lapse of some months or years.'[47]

THE 'NATIVE AUTHORITIES' AND THE ADMINISTRATION OF LAW

In 1928 Judge Haythorne Reed observed of Malawi that 'the fact that natives continue to bring disputes to their headmen in spite of the government having denied them the power to hear and decide cases points to the natives preferring their disputes being settled by their own people.'[48] Yet official African courts could not be created in isolation from African political power. As the Colonial Office told Governor Bowring in 1929, experience elsewhere had suggested that the native courts commanded far greater support where they could be associated with 'some revival of the traditional native organisation'.[49] There was some doubt as to whether the territory was 'ready' for such indirect rule on the ground that traditional authority had been much undermined. In 1930 the formal establishment of African courts

111

was postponed until an indirect-rule system had been created, because it was felt that non-recognised courts already functioned adequately.[50] As Bradley wrote of Zambia, indirect rule presented no problems as chiefs and elders were already settling cases and 'all that was needed was formally to give them criminal jurisdiction and equip them with clerks and simple records.'[51] But the formal renaissance of the African courts did also formalise the process of legal reaction for now the legitimate power to define the customary law had been given to those most likely to define it in an authoritarian manner and with emphasis on its punitive aspects. And their scope was wide, for the weight of British influence was no longer behind modernisation of the law or rendering it certain. In the words of Bradley's handbook on Native Courts in Northern Rhodesia, which was intended to explain the working of the Native Authority Courts to Africans: 'The Chief and Elders in the Court should hear cases in the same way as their fathers did. They should not copy the English way.' English law, he wrote, was 'all fixed'. African law was 'not fixed at all. This is better for Africans than the English way.'[52]

In order to create the new courts the territories were divided into a large number of petty monarchies. When the governor of Northern Rhodesia asked why the number of Native Authorities could not be reduced he was advised by Moffat Thompson, the secretary for native affairs, that this could not be done except by amalgamating the areas of chiefs who were of 'equal status' and 'entirely independent'. When the government had come to Northern Rhodesia, 'the tribes were in a very disorganised state', but since then a tribal organisation had been 'created'. An element of contradiction ran through the thinking about tribal authority. It was at the same time traditional and a fragile creation. When the courts were constituted it was emphasised that the chief should have sole jurisdiction. 'For some years past', one provincial commissioner wrote, 'care has been taken to foster the authority of each chief in his own Area, and it would be subversive of the tribal system and native traditions to give judicial power to anyone but a chief or a sub-chief.' And it seemed clear to white officials, in elaborating the constitutional theory of these neo-traditional monarchies, that while tribal elders 'sometimes take a most important part' in judicial life, 'in theory they are merely instruments of the chief.' A concomitant of this version of traditional government was an insistence on the primacy in African constitutional life of what was analagous to an hereditary aristocracy. The secretary for native affairs suggested that while it was advisable to have some 'educated and progressive' men on the Native Authorities care should be taken to see that they did not 'overwhelm the hereditary chiefs and elders'. A conference of Eastern Region officials agreed in 1929 that even the 'new men' on the Authorities should be 'of aristocratic birth'. They further emphasised that under no circumstances should headmen or elders be 'commoners' either. The problem of the intrusive, over-educated progressive 'commoners' could, it was suggested, be dealt with in the long run by educating the children of hereditary chiefs and headmen 'along the right lines' so that they could be the intellectual betters of their subjects.[53]

By taking as an example the Native Authorities of the East Luangwa district we can see the areas of activity over which the institutions of formal indirect rule were to exercise jurisdiction, and the range of the rules which were promulgated under the Native Courts Ordinance.[54] The Authorities had criminal jurisdiction over all offences against customary law which, though they remained undefined, were thereby made into crimes in the colonial legal system. In addition, they were to deal with the common law crimes of common assault, breach of the peace, affrays, petty larceny and public nuisance. The maximum powers of punishment were five pounds or three months for superior courts and two pounds or one month for subordinate ones. They also had jurisdiction over all civil matters excluding claims above ten pounds; disputes over title to land; and disputes where a Native Authority member was a party.[55]

Rules covered villages' cleanliness and sanitation, control of infectious diseases, control of fire, road-making, tree-felling limitations, tax registration, reporting of deaths, grass-burning, the killing of game and other administrative matters. But these rules were by no means simple in their form. The rule on tree-cutting for example encompassed and defined such matters as the width of trees which could be cut and permitted distances from roads and rivers. There were similar complexities in the rules on the use of streams and control of diseases. The rules, or similar ones, had been operative for some time under Proclamation 8 of 1916, but now control of the administration and judgement of breach of this technical set of rules, which did not easily lend themselves to negotiation and compromise, was being given to the customary legal authorities. The rules also controlled drinking and the carrying of weapons and freedom of movement. Proposals for East Luangwa included a general prohibition of permanent movement from area to area without a headman's consent and a specific prohibition of even the temporary movement of unmarried women.

District officers assiduously collected evidence from the chiefs and headmen, who were quick to assure them that customary law had, for example, given them total power of control over people's movement. 'The Mutatwa custom of old', officials were assured, 'as regard natives moving without the Chief's permission . . . was that . . . they were brought back and killed.' In Mpika Headman Chimbanga testified that 'the Chief, in the old times, if a man ran away without permission . . . would, if he said the man was troublesome, mutilate him: likewise anyone who did not give obedience.' These were claims of right, not tales of a renounced past, and they formed the basis of the 'customary law' through which the administration would support local authority.[56] Rules also required the cultivation of food, and they protected authority: 'Any person acting disrespectfully to his Chief or Headman shall be punished.' They also restated firmly many of the 'traditional' laws of marriage, for example: 'Any man marrying a woman

113

without first informing the woman's parent or guardian be punished.' The Watchtower movement was banned.

The banning of Watchtower in East Luangwa drew from the government the comment that while it might be difficult to uphold a conviction against the rule in any of the territory's courts, the Native Authorities could 'issue the order and the results can be awaited'. Similarly, the Native Authorities wanted a rule making it obligatory for villages to supply food to travellers at reasonable prices. Though the High Court had quashed a past conviction for refusal to supply food, the government's comment was that the rule could be given a trial, though there would be difficulties on appeal, if any. I stress this because the government was content (as in the case of female freedom of movement) to let the impression be given that something was illegal, even if it knew it was not. A careful concern for the civil rights of ordinary villagers was not on its legal agenda. The Native Authorities, it might be noted, were also given the power to arrest any person likely to commit an offence. As was noted in the secretariat, 'This power is very wide and goes much further than the power usually granted.'[57]

The experience which the Northern Rhodesia government had of the working of a recognised Native Court, the Lozi *Khotla*, was, from the point of view of the legal officials, far from encouraging. In terms of the initial agreements with the chartered company the *Khotla* had retained jurisdiction over everything but serious crime. By 1914 local officials had reported that 'Justice has never been dealt impartially by any *Khotla*.' The beer law, which forbad the brewing, selling, buying and drinking of beer, was not applied to the royal family; cattle were impounded at will; cases were not heard for long periods; and starving litigants and witnesses were detained at Lealui.[58] In 1929 the magistrates at Sesheke roundly condemned its laws and procedures. Laws were made 'without sufficient consideration'. Penalties, under laws like the beer law, were very severe and no attempt was made to make the punishment fit the crime. 'The evidence deemed necessary for a man to win his case', the magistrates reported, 'is often weak; particularly so perhaps in their matrimonial cases.' Cases 'often have to wait indefinitely' and the general behaviour of the court was extortionate because, since the abolition of slavery, tribute labour and tribute, 'the ruling caste must be feeling the pinch very considerably.' The magistrate made a number of recommendations: that all the laws in force should be reduced to writing; that the penalties should be clearly stated and be made widely known; and that the *Khotla* should be made to observe the rules of evidence. It is significant to note the kinds of things complained of and the kinds of remedies suggested. The magistrate was asking for the rule of law for Africans. But the government was moving away in the opposite direction. The policy of indirect rule was not concerned with the rule of law. It was as concerned with the maintenance, support and creation of relationships of authority, as the *Khotla* had been. The *Ngambela* wrote to the native commissioner in 1921 that former slaves 'were very insolent and contemptuous . . . . This according to our native law is a great offence and punishable by severe lashes and heavy fines.'[59]

That the interest of the new Native Authorities was in a similar direction, in authority rather than law, can be illustrated in the form of a vignette from the first meeting of the Namwala Native Authority in April 1930. The district commissioner addressed them on the subject of the law. He 'touched on the Statute Law . . . the "Law in the Book" and the other law resting on Custom [which was] changing as time goes on . . . . With the exception of old "sickening" customs which must never be heard of again, his Excellency wished them to uphold what was customary among them.' He concluded his talk with the advice that the Native Authorities now had new authority: that members should admit to meetings 'only those they desire to sit with them, and generally . . . show that a new state of affairs had now commenced'. The chiefs were quick to see that the main point lay in the latter and not in the first part of the address. After their meeting they came back with one main question: 'Whether the District Commissioner will reverse their decisions?'[60]

Once the Native Authority Court system was instituted all district officers were under specific instruction to temper their intervention and to support the authority of the new courts. The governor's advice was that 'No native has the formal right to appeal from a Native Court to a District Officer's Court.' He could petition for a retrial or review but district officers, while they should guard against 'extortion and oppression', should take care that the new courts were not 'degraded' in people's eyes by the perpetual interference of the Boma. Native Courts might well 'pass sentences lacking a sense of proportion and will fail to observe rules of procedure'. But it would be better when cases came up to 'advise' courts for their future guidance 'rather than to unsettle the minds of the natives and possibly undermine their confidence in the Court by reversing a decision'.[61]

Earlier ambitions to provide protection for one and all against indigenous abuse of power had been reversed. Concern was now for the authority of courts, not the victims of its misuse. The new courts seemed to realise this. In Mumbara in 1930 the Native Court fined a man for going to the Boma to appeal against a decision. The district officer could find nothing in the ordinance making this illegal. In another case a woman was fined, as the chief put it, for 'leaving me and going to the Boma'. The Boma took no action as the woman had not complained. District officers and chiefs had come together effectively to narrow women's range of appeal beyond the village. Female complainants who had earlier flocked to the new courts would now be circumscribed by the new rules and administrative arrangements.[62]

In the context of the tenderness towards the upholding of authority of virtually any kind one might note the comments occasioned by the case of *R. v. Shinga and Malia*. Proclamation 8 of 1916 imposed on headmen the duty to suppress 'matrimonial or sexual relationships contrary to the custom of the tribe'. A village court had dealt with an adultery case, ordering a woman to return to her husband. She remained with the other man. The Boma court gave her three months' imprisonment with hard labour for disobedience to a decree for restitution of conjugal rights. The legal adviser wrote, 'It is not thought proper in highly civilised communities to punish for this refusal. But it seems doubtful how far it is expedient to apply this in the case of natives where direct refusal to obey a decree of the court is clearly established ... in view of the necessity of upholding the authority of the court.'[63]

The problems of upholding the authority of a revived neo-traditional system and of using that authority as a routine instrument of administrative discipline can be illustrated too from the Malawi experience. In Malawi's Southern Province, Hailey wrote, a disintegration and intermingling of tribes had preceded European conquest, and when indirect rule had been introduced in 1933 some headmen had no traditional position at all.[64] He thought that it was a 'tribute to the essential strength of clan or tribal sentiment' that 'the traditional Native Authorities' had been able to regain so much influence, especially in an area of relatively high literacy and labour migration. Yet a closer acquaintance with the recorded workings of the indirect-rule courts show that their power was not as accepted as might have been hoped, and that when it was it owed much to the backing it was given by the district officers. The administrators appeared to feel that the new courts were successful because, before their introduction, there had been large numbers of appeals from the informal courts of the village to the white court at the Boma, while since, to give A. G. Hodgson's example of the Northern Province of Malawi in 1935, 9,665 cases were heard, 11 were revised by the district officers and 67 went on appeal.[65] The public had been quick to apprehend that the new courts, unlike the old informal African courts, had official status and support, and that appeals rarely succeeded.

One can detect behind the general satisfaction with the workings of the new courts an emerging disquiet about their effectiveness. The basic question raised in my context is how far the judicial activities of the new court system were 'real' and how far 'fictional'. In 1933 the Nyasaland Native Affairs Commission reported of the new courts that 'All experienced a little difficulty in enforcing their judgements, particularly in the matter of payment of compensation in civil cases and consequently often required active support from the District Commissioner.'[66] In 1936 it was remarked again that the most difficult problem was the non-payment of compensation in civil cases. 'Modern life in a native community is a vast honeycomb of debts .... Non payment of compensation in response to a court order must tend to lower a court's prestige and the list of outstanding debts of this nature grows longer every year.'[67] Yet another report refers to the 'main problem' of the new courts as being the difficulty in enforcing judgement debts. Courts did not order imprisonment in default, nor did they exert themselves to see that damages were paid. With the exception of the cattle-owning people of Northern Malawi, judgement debts remained unsatisfied for months, even years.[68] A year later it was suggested that the greatest menace to the success of the Native Courts was non-compliance with judgement.[69] When the Native Authority Courts handed down a judgement in a civil matter they were couching their decisions in a new legal form, one which was not dependent on a negotiated settlement. That the new form was slow to find acceptance is suggested by the observation made of the North of Malawi in 1936 that there were 'unrecognised courts of headmen functioning collaterally with the recognised courts of the Native Authorities'.[70]

Yet again, in 1946, when the courts were no longer new, a district report remarked upon 'the difficulty, perhaps the diffidence, of the Chiefs to enforce their own judgements'. They had all been advised that after time limits had expired action should be taken, and, if necessary, instalment payments should be ordered, but still many cases of failure to obey court orders were brought to light. And the explanation given in 1948 was that the courts lost interest in matters once judgement had been given and judgement debts were not collected because they saw this 'as a personal matter between the parties rather than a function of the courts'.[71]

In any case, as Colson observed, people simply took their cases from court to court.[72] On this level it seems that the new courts and legal forms did not 'work', that there was an element of charade in legalistic adjudication according to, and the application of, 'native law and custom'. It also appears that it was not just a matter of unacceptability of judgement rather than mediation which was the problem. For the new courts were struggling as well to establish their authority. It seems clear that other 'courts' were functioning, just as they had done before the creation of the Native Authority Courts, and that the latter aimed at monopolising judicial business. One Nyasaland official recommended the recognition of the headmen's courts as 'courts of arbitration' and advised that they should 'still function as a recognised part of the judicial system. Any attempt by the Native Authority to force all petty cases into his court for the sake of the revenue should be discouraged.' It should, he thought, be made known that the setting up of a Native Authority with a court book did not do away with the traditional courts of the lesser headmen.[73] But this was not official policy.

There was also a tendency for some chiefs designated as Native Authorities to limit and narrow the composition of courts (which was not prescribed in the ordinances) and exclude traditional councillors. Lord Hailey warned that the drive to monopolise judicial power in this way could affect acceptability. 'It would be dangerous to allow any departure from the traditional character of the courts,' he wrote, 'as representing an assembly of elders or other persons whose judgement commands acquiescence and respect.'[74] The problem of the struggle for power emerges also from the apparent commonness of contempt charges. As one report put it, 'Evidence is not lacking that the courts do not invariably receive the respect to which they should be entitled. Convictions for contempt are not uncommon and two members of a certain court recently applied for uniforms for the stated reason that they would thereby achieve added dignity, and would not be so liable to be laughed at by members of the public.'[75] It seems likely that the Native Authority Courts were identified increasingly as political rather than legal instruments. In 1945 it was reported that 'complaints have been heard from Chiefs that there is a growing disrespect for the traditional solemnity and dignity of the courts. This attitude is reflected in quite a large number of convictions for contempt.'[76] This was taking place in the context of the creation of local councils, much resented by the chiefs, and the beginnings of active agitation by nationalists against the authority of the chiefs. Thus part of the problem of legal effectiveness was that of the lack of acceptability of the legalisation of judgements, but the context of the problem was also the competition for prestige and authority generally, and the rejection of a neo-traditional chieftaincy. On the one hand we can see that the legalised style of the courts did not 'work', on the other that the political context was forcing them to choose between accepting a certain ineffectiveness or becoming stricter and more formal in an effort to impose and defend their status.

And at the same time the official courts had to defend themselves against village settlement agencies. These two themes seem evident in the remarks of a Tonga councillor remonstrating with headmen in 1947. 'Here at the Court we do the work of the Government. We get the law of the Government .... If you fight with us, you don't fight only with us. You are fighting the Government.' In spite of the reluctance of district officers to hear appeals, their political interference was invoked by both sides in cases. As Colson put it, 'In a sense the district officer sits in every court, influencing its judgement.'[77]

The reluctance of the new courts to use imprisonment as a sanction was also remarked upon. In 1934 the Lilongwe district commissioner pointed to the 'serious error' prevailing of punishing thieves only by compensation awards against them. 'A Chief's main object in all cases is to satisfy the complainant,' he wrote, 'but clearly the thief is not punished as he should be, and in many cases it is the thief's relations who pay the compensation with the result that the wrongdoer continues to commit crimes. I have frequently emphasised the evils of the system but Native Courts do not seem to be convinced.'[78] This picture of customary practices battling for survival with the new legal machinery is, as we shall see, very different from the retributive idealised version of the customary law being contemporaneously put forward. In 1935 it was reported that in spite of the rapid increase in criminal cases, with which the courts were willingly dealing as their authority became established, there were in a full year in Malawi's populous Southern Province, 'only' ninety-six imprisonments and two whippings. It was a 'notable fact' that the Native Authorities were 'most reluctant' to whip.[79] Imprisonment, it was said, was still rare though 'the advantages of this form of punishment as a deterrent have been pointed out in several cases.' To an extent what we are seeing is a nervousness about authority on the part of the middlemen in the colonial government's enforcement of order, but there seems still to be the element of a different practice surviving, for even many of the new statutory rules, breach of which entailed criminal punishment in terms of the government's law, were enforced by the Native Authorities in a way which 'invariably involved restitution in a practical form for the actual damage done. Thus, damage to reserved timber was punished by the offender having to plant and maintain seedlings in replacement.'[80] All of the nearly sixty rules and orders passed by the Fort Jameson Ngoni Native Authority were model rules drawn up by the colonial government. The courts, wrote Barnes, 'do not always see the reason for the introduction of new laws, they may forget about them.' In any case they were poorly equipped to deal with them, as they 'think of themselves as an arbitrating, rather than as a law enforcing body'.[81] Lord Hailey observed of the new courts that much of their structure and procedures 'still follows the forms dictated by tradition', with changes more apparent on the criminal side 'since we are endeavouring to introduce to the African the conception of the public offence . . . and . . . punishment . . . instead of . . . compensation and other forms of arbitral adjustment'.[82]

It should also be stressed that the kind of record-keeping required of the new courts itself contributed to the development of a rule/judgement system. Early on the complaint was registered of the Nyasaland courts that their major defect was not so much evident in the judgements given as in their methods of recording their decisions. There was complaint by administrators of the incompetence of the court clerks, who were not sufficiently literate and were often relatives of the chiefs. Clerks, it was said, often arrogated the powers of the courts to themselves, yet also struggled to master the new forms required of them. One district officer wrote that the recording of cases in writing seriously impeded the capacity of the courts to work through their case load. 'The amount of time spent in recording a few lines', he observed, 'has to be seen to be believed.' It seems likely that only the barest bones were conceptualised for the written records. (Investigation of the few records of these courts extant bear this out.) Court clerks were told over and over again that their methods of keeping the court books with facts and judgement alone were defective and they must write down the facts of each case *plus the rule of customary law relied upon* plus the decision of the court. Thus rules had to be made explicit, simplified, and made *applicable*.[83]

But what rules were they to be? So far as the actual civil rules of customary law went the broadest imperial perspective was in favour of promoting evolution towards uniformity. 'Our only interest', wrote Hailey, 'is to see that an unduly conservative composition of the courts, or the establishment of case law by administrative officers . . . in the exercise of appellate and advisory powers does not place an artificial check on this process.'[84] Like many imperial effusions, this had little relevance to the native courts struggling with the imposition of a rule/judgement format and responsibility for statutory rules. The same men, in the same courts, in the same circumstances and atmosphere, administered both colonial rules and customary law. And we cannot understand how they went about these tasks if we consider them separately. Nonetheless the attitude at the top did have an important effect in that it discouraged colonial governments and district officers in this period from building a systematised body of law and precedent. There were good reasons for so refraining but it did mean recognising, *de facto* and *de jure*, a plastic law and very wide powers of chiefs to create it. The Nyasaland administration recognised the chiefs had powers, which were 'inherent in native law', both to give orders to particular persons and to make rules of general application.[85] A district report recorded in 1935 that offences against native law and customs 'varied in the extreme' and included preaching without the Native Authority's permission, knocking down an old woman with a bicycle, and shaking hands in public with another man's wife.[86] This looks far closer to a mundane and random exercise of authority than the official theory described by J. E. Ellis in 1936 that 'Native Law and Custom is of necessity in a state of flux, and this power to make rules enables tribes to crystallise their customs into substantive law and evolve for themselves in time a common law of the people.'[87] It was precisely this legal creativity which was to provoke the African representation for the customary law to be written down, which I discuss below. In Hailey's terms, the process of 'vitality and evolution' provoked uncertainty and led to attempts to make a written record to 'crystallise' the laws.[88] Thus even a policy designed to prevent a rapid legalising and freezing of custom by the new courts had the effect of promoting it.

Yet in spite of hesitancy about the extent of their authority, occasional lack of sympathy with the rules they were required to enforce, and a tendency to arbitrate rather than to judge and punish, the new Native Authorities were swept along towards a growing legalism on the tide of statutory offences which flowed into their courts. The overwhelming preponderance of offences against statutory rules specifically related to the colonial order as against 'ordinary crimes' is the pattern throughout the 1930s, and the reproduction of this pattern henceforth became the primary responsibility of the Native Authority Courts.[89] In 1932 there were, overall in Malawi, 1,912 people imprisoned without the option of a fine, and 1,023 of these were for tax evasion. There was also a considerable increase in convictions under the Forestry Ordinance (no. 12 of 1926) which aimed at restricting tree-cutting on mountain slopes, river beds, etc. Eight hundred people were convicted for cutting trees in forest reserves, cutting protected trees and cutting and cultivating on river banks. In 1933 there were 1,516 convictions for offences against the Penal Code and 4,700 for breaches of local legislation, including 2,197 tax offences, 776 against the Forest Laws, 387 against the Township Regulations and 227 for breaches of the tobacco and cotton uprooting rules.

With this preponderance in mind we can look at the picture another way,

120

from the aspect of the work actually done in the new courts. In 1935 the Northern Province Native Courts in Malawi dealt with 6,092 civil and 3,573 criminal cases. Only 4 people out of 4,581 came before them in criminal matters and were acquitted. Offences against the person numbered 756 and against property 347, making little over a thousand for the main 'petty' crimes of assault and larceny. Offences against local ordinances number 1,214, against Native Authority Rules 504, against native law and custom 280, and marital 'offences' 1,456. If (and it is a highly qualifiable if), we count the latter two categories as falling within the ambit of 'custom', then the profile of the courts' activity is:

Crime	1,103
Offences against ordinances and rules	1,718
'Custom' (largely marriage)	1,736

The major offences under the Native Authority Rules were for breaches of the sanitation rules, 99; the rules regarding general village cleanliness, 62; the liquor rules, 33; and migrating without permission, 21. The preponderance of cases therefore were either marriage cases (in dealing with which, as I will show in the next section, there was a tendency towards increasing strictness) or offences against the colonial government's rules. Offences of this nature, and also petty crime, were not easily manageable except by punishment. The Northern Province court imposed fines on 3,085 people, sent 41 to prison, and in 279 cases imposed both a fine and a compensatory payment. A tendency towards a routinisation of petty legalism – rule, offence and punishment – presents itself. And the weight with which it was felt depended on variations in administrative enthusiasms. Two years later a big increase in the proportion of criminal cases was noted, due to a largely inflated number of convictions for offences against village sanitation rules. There were 1,556 cases involving assault or larceny under the Penal Code (i.e. ordinary crimes): 1,424 marriage cases and 9,275 offences against colonial ordinances and rules. The profile of offences and the way they were dealt with is similar for the Southern Province courts. The 1937 reports contain self-congratulation for the success of the administration's 'ceaseless propaganda' on forestry and conservation and for the 'numerous cases' heard in the Native Courts for breaches of the sanitation orders. It was noted that the big increase in the number and proportion of criminal cases was 'at variance with the well known native preference for treating all cases civilly if possible' but that it was due to an 'awakened interest in forestry matters' and a larger number of prosecutions on the Lower Shire for failure to uproot cotton. Thus modes of judicial preference aside, the kinds of task the new courts had to do compelled them towards dealing with cases 'criminally' rather than 'civilly'. Of the 6,724 convictions recorded, nearly 4,000 were for offences against statutory rules, and another 500 odd were for marital offences. Imprisonment was imposed in 94 cases, a fine in 5,829, and compensation as well as a fine in 609.[90]

By way of comparison convictions for offences against the Native Employment Laws (for breach of contract) matched the figure for major crimes, as did those for Liquor Law offences, all in the range of 100–200 per year. The only important Penal Code crime to be above this figure was larceny with approximately 450 convictions which put it in the same league as Forestry Law convictions and Township Law convictions. Then there was a huge leap to 1,500 for tax offenders.

One Northern Rhodesian district officer described well the process on the district level in the post-war period. Native Courts were having busy times because of more frequent touring by district officers who exerted pressure upon the Native Authorities to enforce their rules. In 1948 in the Chinsali district there were 99 civil and 390 criminal cases. In 1951 there were 135 civil cases (of which 119 concerned marriage) and 1,760 criminal cases, nearly a five-fold increase, and resulting almost entirely from health and conservation prosecutions. He wrote: 'From the foregoing figures it is apparent that in the recorded cases of the Native Courts there is little of what could be described as "native law and custom".' He thought that this could be because customary law continued to be administered by unrecognised headmen and family heads or because 'the conception of native law is changing to such an extent that statutory law is replacing traditional tribal law as the means of controlling society.' Africans, he observed a year later, 'claim that their law had always been in existence' but in modern society new sources of law were springing up alongside the old: legislation, Native Authority Court rules and orders and precedents, and case law, affected by the growth of literacy. The anxieties which people felt about the processes of legalisation in the Native Authority Courts was evidenced by a reluctance of people to bring to Native Authority Courts cases connected with inheritance and personal property, preferring to have them settled through other agencies of society which avoided 'judgement by decree which has become a feature of the Native Courts'.[91]

Through the implementation of policies and rules about taxation, sanitation, forestry and conservation, employment and labour, plant disease and agricultural practices, Lord Hailey's goal of the inculcation of the idea of the public offence proceeded apace. Administrators soon began to remark that the Native Authority Courts were adapting to their role as administrators of a 'criminal law' in a peculiar and inflexible way. The courts were, it was said, more at home in civil than criminal matters, as was evidenced by the 'singular lack of elasticity in the sentences imposed'; little allowance being made for circumstances and a 'tendency to impose a flat rate fine for specific offences', for example three shillings for a stream-bank cultivation, five shillings for liquor offences.[92] Seven years later it was remarked upon that 'in the exercise of criminal jurisdiction sentences imposed tend to conform less with the requirement and circumstance of the individual case than with a rigid formula.'[93] The following year the district officer at Karonga wrote of the failings of the courts:

122

The first is the fixed scale of punishment . . . . the father of a daughter who has been seduced knows that, if he can prove his case, the offender will pay him one cow or two cows depending on whether or not a pregnancy ensues. The Court likewise has a standard fine for such cases, itself an interesting fact as it automatically tends to invest what is by English law a purely civil case with a criminal aspect. There does not ever seem to be an enquiry by the court . . . whether a first offence has been committed . . . . It has been represented to the chiefs that each case should be judged on its merits, but it will be some time.[94]

In large part we can see that the courts created for the policy of indirect rule functioned as an increasingly resented administrative agency of colonialism. The picture that emerges is one of maladjustment and inflexibility with regard to 'crime' and statutory infractions, a lack of ability to enforce judgement of civil compensation, and the co-existence of unofficial courts both in the village and in the towns to which many people clearly turned. Epstein has described how the mine compound elders, whose 'courts', though supported by management, were not recognised by the government, distinguished themselves from the official Urban Courts. The elders saw their task as the restoration of relationships and the giving of 'moral instruction'. Elders worked for nothing, they said, while court members worked 'for the salary they get every month', and gave no instruction but only fined and imprisoned people. 'At the Boma', as an elder put it, 'there is no charity.' If the elders found that a man had wronged another, they told Epstein, they might tell him to pay over five shillings compensation 'so that they may be eating together, and that there may be understanding between them'. But if he would not pay, the elders would threaten to send him to the Urban Court 'where they will make him pay much money'. But while the first generation of migrants may have preferred such arbitral and reconciliatory proceedings, both the unofficial elders and the tribal elders who were appointed to the official urban courts were under attack from a younger generation who were not satisfied with reconciliation based on the enforcement of a customary rural morality. Urban representations were made in favour of rules and against the cumbersome proceedings and irrelevancies of both the elders' courts and the Urban Courts.[95]

In one sense it seems that the courts did not develop as they were supposed to, as institutions which would evolve what would eventually be an African common law. On the other hand it is clear that while many civil cases were resolved at an unofficial level, large numbers did use the Native Authority Courts in spite of the relatively high fee – in Malawi in the 1930s it cost one shilling to bring a case to court, at a time when the annual tax payment was six shillings. Thus the important question becomes in what circumstances and why did people want to use the courts in spite of their increasing aura of punitiveness and formalism? The answer is plainly that many matrimonial cases were brought to the Native Authority Courts, where a foreign legalised form of defining and enforcing rights was becoming dominant, because people wanted these kinds of rights enforced in this way. The 1930s and 1940s are towards the end of the period in which property interests were necessarily defined and enforced through 'marriage' laws and these laws carried a particularly heavy strain with the rapidly increasing commercialisation of agriculture. A legalising court system was therefore particularly appropriate to those enforcing these rights.

7

Africans and the law

The white courts had brought a routine oppression rather than a liberating justice. Yet what was explicit about many of the African responses to the new legal dispensation was not that it bore too heavily upon transgressors but that it was too lenient. Like accounts of witchcraft and slavery, tales of pre-colonial terror were most popular during the imperial period and they are crucial to an understanding of legal history because they played so large a part in the conceptions held in the early colonial period of what life had been like before the white conquest, and, therefore, of how the purposes and results of the new law were measured and judged. The thinking of both whites and Africans about the pre-conquest past contributed, as did the experience of the first decades of British rule, to the fashioning of African responses.

Lacerda's account of the journey to Kazembe's that he made in 1798, translated with gusto by Richard Burton, provides something of a model for views of pre-colonial African kingdoms that we can combine with those of the witch-ridden peoples discussed earlier. Lacerda recounted that offenders suffered amputations and other physical mutilations.[1] Similar accounts exist of the Bemba and the Ngoni. Their accumulation over the nineteenth century was behind the views of the early administrators, like Duff, that 'among primitive people where the moral sense is exceptionally feeble, legislative retribution is of necessity exceptionally severe.'[2]

Many of the early British accounts stressed the absence of a moral sense in the African population and depicted a society in which the entire social fabric had been held together only by the severest of deterrent punishment for infraction. (From this it followed of course that British justice if it was to be understood and effective had to be severe.) The harshness of the criminal law in England, which until 1837 had exacted death for so wide a range of offences, and which still rested firmly on deterrence, might explain why so many of the English commentators were ready to believe in the ferocity of the African criminal law and in the ubiquity of death as a sanction. There

125

often seems to be a dissonance in the accounts of morality and punishment, combining as they did the notions of a general absence of morality and the fierceness of sanction to impose morals. The British observers were largely from a ruling class and drew, perhaps, analogies from the current opinion at home on these matters which by and large thought of the sexual appetites of women and the criminal propensities of the lower orders as being kept in check only by stern control from above. At the root of the problem was considered to be the lack of discipline in the upbringing of African children. Smith and Dale and Macdonald all complained of the leniency with which children were treated, and Hetherwick too regretted the absence of corporal punishment of children. Missions regretted that their schools could not use it as parents objected. Administrators also noticed that life was gentler for the young than it was in England. Hodgson, for example, wrote: 'the castigation and discipline of the Chewa boy ... is so small in comparison with that considered a necessary part of the education of his English brother.' And J.P. Murray, who believed that in customary law a father had the right to inflict reasonable correction, thought it 'a lamentable fact that native fathers do not: it would be better for the race if they took Solomon's dictums anent the rod more to heart.'[3] It is not easy to reconcile this absence of punishment for the young with the brutal restraints that these same children were supposed to have undergone when adult. Rowley, who spent three years among the Mang'anja twenty years before the start of the colonial period, found them to be of 'gentle disposition ... averse to deeds of violence, and by no means given to bloodshed'.[4]

Nonetheless the official white view of pre-colonial times remained that of rapine countered by terror.[5] The Nyasaland government, in 1912, saw African morality as having been entirely imposed by savage punishments, and suggested that the European dilemma was how to moderate this without causing social breakdown. When London directed the government's attention to the fact that floggings imposed by the Nyasaland courts far exceeded the norm in the rest of Africa, officials took refuge behind the argument that Africans were used to the severest punishments and the relaxation would mean the breakdown of law and order.[6] Indeed Duff specifically diagnosed the cause for what he believed to be an increase in thefts and adultery as the abandonment of the supposedly traditional death penalty.[7]

This view of the colonial past was also held by many Malawians during the colonial period and is an important part of current thinking about law. The past, of course, was not simple and uniform. It contained oppressive states and slavery as well as village-level reconciliation. Representing the past involved choices. White administrators' accounts generally looked back to the oppressions. In the minds of Africans the two are sometimes run together.

Abdullah's account, for example, combines and confuses an idyllic timeless Yao past with the violence which accompanies the development of the

126

slaving chieftaincies. His account of the state of the law under Mataka is in the Darkest Africa tradition.

> In the law court a man who had violated the harem of a common man was fined 30 yards of calico; of an elder five slaves; in the case of a chief's wife, the whole village was enslaved and the guilty parties, both men and women, were executed by having their throats cut. A Wizard was either burned or drowned. That was when it became the custom to cut off people's arms, legs or ears, to castrate them, inflict wounds on head or body with knives; cutting a man's throat was merely play . . . . All this was done to instil fear into people so that they should tremble at the very name of Mataka.

Abdullah was a U.M.C.A. convert and member, part of the new Christian elite, and allowance must be made for the tendency of the new Christians to dwell in hyperbolic delight upon the savagery from which they had been delivered. But there was a multi-tier past to look back to and the violence of the immdiate pre-colonial period could be put together with a 'golden age', and in an ironing out of the rough spots, a composite memory of both peaceful compromise and firm authority emerged. Yet the real immediate pre-colonial past of Yao 'law' is encapsulated in Abdullah's description of Mataka on the march, slaves in sticks accompanying him: 'the bound slaves were for settling law suits and for buying food on the way.'[8] Slavery, violence, retribution and reciprocity were interdependent, rather than contradictory. A Tumbuka informant reports that after fighting, wounding or killing: 'On the following day they would pay damages for whoever had died; they used to exchange men or women in compensation, or perhaps goats, or hoes, or bundles of cotton, or baskets of salt.' The image is one of calm compensation rather than savage revenge but it depended on the power to 'exchange' men and women. And it depended on having the status and wealth necessary to mobilise support, for, as the account continues (describing compensatory payments for adultery), 'an unbefriended person they used to kill or burn simply.'[9] The spirit informing much of the feeling about the law which prevailed in the early colonial period was one which looked back to an era of retribution not with horror or regret but with approval. Donald Fraser recounts an interview with an Ngoni chief: 'gradually he got excited, and after referring to the lack of ready obedience, he cried "In the old days if a slave would not obey his chief he would be killed."'[10]

Gluckman wrote of the Lozi during the colonial period that 'the greatest change in Barotse law was the passing of most criminal offences under the control of British officers.'[11] For the rulers and elders of African society this was a profound change and an erosion of their authority at a time when they had reason to feel that it was most needed.[12] One of the results of taking criminal jurisdiction out of African hands, of reducing their control of malfeasance, was to produce a demand for others to act. In calling for the recognition of the seriousness of wrongdoing from rulers who seemed not to recognise it the stress was necessarily on strictness – 'this is how we would have acted' – in the past. By the early 1920s this was widespread. Mackenzie noted in the far North of Malawi that people were complaining of British 'softness' towards evil-doers. In 1919 from Lilongwe the resident reported that people were telling him that customary law allowed a man to kill when his food was stolen and in 1923 the Central Province provincial commissioner wrote that larceny of crops was punishable by the loss of right hand or death.[13]

Confirming that the officials had gathered their 'custom' correctly the West Nyassa Native Association told the government that for larceny of crops 'frequently slavery and death were the result thereof' and that the 'case' was sometimes 'shared' by relatives of the thief 'who had to forfeit sisters and brothers and became slaves for a small stolen thing whatsoever it was'. In 1928 village headmen in the Dedza district were complaining that persons sentenced for two to three months for larceny returned to the villages and continued to steal, and they pressed the government to inflict more serious punishment.[14]

The mission churches and the Bible appear to have been major ideological influences in the escalation of notions about punishment. A close identification was not uncommonly made between African society and the conditions of life described in the Old Testament, the 'native laws and customs as contained in the first five books of the Christian Bible' as the African National Church put it.[15] The first five books of the Bible are full of savage and retributive punishments for wrongs and as the Bible became the major influence on the early literate witnesses to the pre-colonial legal system, and as they believed it to describe a state of things not only applicable to Africa but also divinely ordained as correct, so the retributive side of customary law came to be emphasised.[16]

Donald Fraser emphasised that a Christian consciousness of sin was the more necessary as a buttress of moral behaviour as 'Magic penalties which were supposed to follow certain sins against society no longer terrify.' The 'removal of old magical and communistic restraints' needed to be 'accompanied by the creation of a Christian law and conscience'.[17] The missions approached this task with an absolute self-confidence. Rowley recalls Bishop Mackenzie's initial announcement that all who lived on the mission could only have one wife 'because we had God's word; that our custom was more in accordance with God's word than theirs.'[18] Morrison's description of the 1914 meeting of the Livingstonia presbytery bears upon this point. The presbytery was discussing marriage and divorce when 'A more highly instructed member rose to a point of order. The Presbytery, he said, had already settled the law of marriage. Upon this Dr. Elmslie started to his feet. "It is the law of Christ! ... he repeated [it] in the native speech, with a passionate vehemence.'[19] The law was no longer man's but God's. Its transgression was no longer to be considered simply as a social wrong, but as sin. There is much that is suggestive in Rothman's discussion of crime in colonial New England to help us to understand what was happening in

Central Africa. He writes regarding the definition of deviant behaviour that there was an:

> equating [of] sin with crime. The criminal codes punished religious offences such as idolatry, blasphemy, and witchcraft, and clergymen declared infractions against person or property to be offences against God . . . . The identification of disorder with sin made it difficult for legislators and ministers to distinguish carefully between major and minor infractions. Both were testimony to the natural depravity of man and the power of the devil. By linking murder with sin and sin with every transgression against man and God, clergymen taught the colonists to find terrifying significance in even casual offences.[20]

The inheritance of 'customary law' was mixed and what it had meant in action depended upon circumstances. Compensation was a possibility, so was retribution, particularly in the conquest societies of the immediate pre-colonial period. That this latter aspect also came to be idealised seems to be a process resulting from a combination of African loss of control over wrongdoing in a situation of rapid change and, for some (consequently), chosen features of the missions' message. It is hard to escape the conclusion that the emphasis on punishment in Central African law was escalated by the coming of Christianity. In the nineteenth century people paid compensation, or were killed as sorcerers, or were mutilated to deter or intimidate, or were acted upon in revenge. That a basic feature of the law was the payment of compensation by the wrongdoer by handing over other people would seem to argue that the focus was not on exacting a toll on the conscience of the offender. It was the neo-traditionalists, animated by a very fiery version of the Christian conscience and under the pervasive influence of the Old Testament, who turned deterrent mutilation or the penalty for sorcery into punishment for sins.

One might note in this context Iliffe's point about Christianisation in Tanganyika: 'A powerful strand in the converts' thinking was a Manichean view of the world as a struggle between light and darkness.' He recalls Monica Wilson's remarking that Nyakusa preachers were constantly harping on the contrast between heaven and hell and 'the rewards and punishments of the future life'.[21]

This escalation of the consequences of crime and the tendency to equate it with sin and to demand appropriate apocalyptic punishment can be illustrated from G.S. Mwase's account of conditions in prison, where he concludes his comments on the kindness of the treatment in prison with the following remarks:

> I wonder if divine treatment towards sinners is like this one which our local government is doing to its sinners. I think the divine punishment to sinners is more better than the Government man do. Picking out from what I am taught, the divine punishment is very cruel. There is no mercy or grace towards a convict, who is to be convicted by the divine court . . . . Out of what I am taught is clearly that once you are convicted by the divine court and sentenced to

129

everlasting punishment [you have] no food, cloth, water, or physician to see you or attend to you.

In Mwase's view the missionaries' hell was more justly the sinning criminal's deserts than the Zomba prison.[22]

AFRICANS AND THE COLONIAL LEGAL SYSTEM

One experienced white observer wrote of Malawi that 'Every part of native life hinges on meetings in the court, and everywhere people seem always to have taken a special interest in their lawsuits.'[23] The lives of ordinary people were, therefore, widely affected when things began to go wrong in the area of law and justice. As local African associations became vocal they protested pointedly on these subjects and while some of the protests have an *évolué* ring about them, in that they focus on discriminatory practices, many reflect widespread feelings, as people at large demonstrated by their 'abstention from the Boma'. Fear of the new force of colonial police was widespread. Among John Chilembwe's reasons for rebellion in 1914, according to Mwase, was the complaint that 'The Boma knew that the *Askari* were pure barbarians, and would do brutality on the villagers, yet allowed them to trouble the villagers as much as they could.' Eliot Kamwana's evidence on grievances to the commission of inquiry into the rising asked that 'Native tax collectors and policemen should stop to extort and ravish in the Districts.' In the context of a discussion of the injustices done to Christians who took seriously the commandant that they should not work on the Sabbath, Charles Domingo gives us the flavour of the police operations; 'The native police will come and arrest them; they will be severely punished for their *disobedience* and Christianity will not sweeten them. If they are arrested they will be thrashed with *chikoti*.'[24] Police 'government' was experienced in the towns as well as in the villages. From Blantyre as early as 1923 local African civil servants petitioned about 'the very awkward method the policeman takes' who enters 'every neighbouring house and puts everything in disorder'. In Livingstone in 1932 an African public meeting complained of the African police 'They are always ill-treating the people .... When a person is handcuffed they beat him badly.'[25] Barbarian, extorter, the strong arm of white employers' discipline, the terror of the urban elite, as Morrison observed, 'The native policeman is now a power in the land.' The police thought so too. Mission teachers, themselves white auxiliaries and claimants to new status, complained that the police told them, 'You are nothing. Your work is nothing. We are the government.'[26]

The African 'new men' also complained bitterly of the racial discrimination in the new legal system. Mwase attributes to Chilembwe anger about the practice of whites sending Africans to the Boma 'with letters for punishment'. The letters were treated by the magistrates as evidence, and sentences and punishment inflicted on their bearers. If, complained Chilembwe, an African disputed the white man's version, the magistrates would be 'angry' and would say 'the white man does not lie . . . . There the natives wondered why a white man should not lie, is he not a descendant of Adam and Eve from when, every kind of evil has started from, including lying and other sins thereto why a whiteman should not . . .'[27] The complaint referred to common circumstances. As Mwase wrote, in the early days of the colonial regime, the white planters created the law on their estates, and the Bomas punished whoever was disobedient: 'The whiteman was not to appear in court at all but only by his letter. A native could be punished by the letter's evidence, which evidence, he could not cross examine it . . . . [this] clearly showed that the whiteman had to buy the law with respect of his colour.' And, with a keen appreciation of British susceptibilities, he summed up the system with the words, 'This was Law Market, as that slave market.' In 1923 the Petition of Native Civil Servants of Blantyre complained that

> various cases in this country are judged by favour and not in accordance with the law. For instance if a European assaults a native a case is brought before the Court, generally the case is in favour of the European. Likewise when a European has any reason against any of his servants, he only writes a note which he sends his servant to the Boma, where without the European complaint appearing in person the boy is convicted but only receiving the false statement.[28]

In January 1928 the Central Province (Universal) Native Association, in which Mwase was a dominant figure, at a meeting of sixty-five persons, resolved;

> 1. That the giving of chairs to European offenders in Courts of Justice, while the Native (blackman) is standing induces the native to feel slavishly at his side and freedom to the part of his European offender.
> 2. That the following evidence by a letter from Europeans against Natives in court of justice should be considered to be unjust.[29]

The Lilongwe resident countered these last complaints with an explanation that 'Europeans as a rule are busy men' and that letters from Europeans were not used as evidence but as a basis for cross-examination, which was a distinction which might not have appeared obvious to the complainants. In March the association warned that 'the effect of inability through any cause to make the law good is to loosen all authority.' They rejected the explanation that seating arrangements in court were a matter for the magistrates' discretion and that letters were not accepted as evidence. It was the word 'discretion' which aroused their suspicion. 'Because of wonder and knowing', the association wrote, 'that justice has no respection of race, colour and language, we appeal that the Magistrates in Court of Justice should work at laws of the Court and not only at their discretion which in many cases led to the governed to blame the Government.' 'Laws', they said, 'are made to be observed by both lawyers and others.' They objected to the bureaucratic brush-off which they had received from the resident, saying 'no man requires rethatching of his house while no rickages [sic] are going

131

on. We have been rained on therefore require remedy. So please you should act thoughtfully that we should be quenched by your explanations and not with a running pen, which seeks for no cause of subject.'

Africans did not expect to be treated in the same way as others by the courts and discriminatory practices aroused not only pique but anxiety. In 1928 the Southern Association expressed 'deep regret with all alarm' at the light sentences imposed on an Indian and a European for manslaughter of Africans. Europeans and Indians, they said, would 'find the way open to them for killing the natives, with straightward belief that nothing serious will happen to them.'[30]

Anger about discriminatory treatment also features in Levi Mumba's thoughtful memorandum on administration of justice in Nyasaland:

> Let us see how the natives fare in cases between themselves and Europeans. The optimism and credulity of the native led him to accept assurances of British justice on their face value .... he looked to the Government through the magistrates for the so called protection in cases between himself and the whiteman .... It is no exaggeration to say colour is the deciding factor – Being confident that his brother at court would not go against him, the European usually takes the law into his own hands when dealing with a native, deliberately commits a crime, and even tells the native after he has soundly mistreated him to go and report to the Boma where to his disgust the native finds that the door is banged against him, or that the Boma supports the European. The educated native who has been taught that everybody is equal before the law, that justice is blind to anybody and everything, now knows that in this country at any rate it is not blind but has got eyes to see and therefore it has ceased to be 'justice blindfolded' and has instead assumed viciousness.[31]

Many of the complaints made about the administration of law were occasioned by the new courts' attitudes towards evidence. Reflected are the groping misapprehension with which the colonial administrators investigated cases and their consequent impatience with 'petty native matters', and African dismay at the rules of evidence of the white courts which, when they operated, seemed to be designed to limit artificially the search for truth. Morrison wrote that 'the natives contrast the procedure of the Church courts, where a man has the freedom to speak all of his mind, with the civil courts where the witness is abruptly cut short, and his meaning often distorted by the native interpreter'.[32] Levi Mumba made a more potent contrast between the way in which cases had been heard by Africans in the past and the apparently callous and summary procedures of the new era.

> There once had been ample time for the circulation and discussion of a case before it actually came to the headman or chief's court. This gave the public a chance to weigh the evidence with tribal law and custom and for the exchange of views on which the judges set their verdict .... In court all were given the privilege to speak and very little interruption to the speaker was allowed .... The following may be taken as typical of native court procedure:-
> A, has killed Z, the relatives of Z take something to the chief with which to report the case and give an account of the circumstances leading to the death.

Acceptance of this thing is taken that the hearing of the case will take place – a day is fixed. It is inadvisable that the committer of the act should be present. When all are assembled A's and Z's parties as well as those of the chief's court, a capable person of the chief's opens the case at the same time warning all to give full chance to each speaker. When this man sits down one of the plaintiffs (Z's relatives) gets up and comes forward to sit or stand at the same spot as the previous speaker, narrates the case with approval here and there from his party. When he is finished one of the chief's men asks the defendants (A's relatives) to put their defence; when they are finished the court then asks for witnesses from both sides. After this to make the facts more clear another of the courtmen will get up, repeat the statements made by the plaintiffs and defendants without adding to, or lessening them. He then refers the case to the audience, sits down or is asked by the court to go on and thrash the case out with assent where approved until the guilty side is clearly shown when the case is handed over to the chief or his deputy for judgement. In the judgement though heavy compensation may be awarded reconciliation plays an important part, the parties being made to drink from one cup when the compensation and fine had been paid in full.

Things were very different in the Boma's courts. Cases were isolated from social context and quickly despatched.

If a case of stealing comes forward now it is only necessary to substantiate the charge by a witness without 'bothering' about the relatives of the offenders. I use 'bothering' advisedly, since some magistrates are fond of interrupting a speaker by the retort of 'I don't want to be bothered with his yarns' as if they were not appointed for this sort of work .... Another point is that the magistrate is self satisfied with his view of the case irrespective of the applicant's tribal law and custom. He likes very much to hear cases unassisted by any native assessors. All the instinctive points which has [*sic*] for years guided the native in his mode of living which may eventually lead to crime are ignored on the assumption that he looks on the case from an enlightened view. Generally in the European courts freedom of speech during the hearing of native cases is at a minimum. Often one witnesses cases of appeal 'judged' in 5 to 10 minutes, sometimes before the parties have finished speaking. Some vigorously protest against this on the spot, refuse to leave the court until they are heard and have to be dragged out by court messengers. The reason given for this action is that enough information has been received on which to form a judgment, or that the parties give facts which are irrelevant to the case. The truth, however, is that there is altogether too much superciliousness on the part of magistrates who think it is a waste of their time to take much pain in investigating all native cases and the result is that there is general dissatisfaction all over the country with the way cases are heard. The respect which a native chief had for his councillor or village headman does not exist in the relations of the magistrates and their native chief subordinates in the practice of justice.

Mumba had captured well the essence of the British colonial courts. They were oppressive in a distinctively legalistic way, not simply randomly unjust. That the differences between colonial judicial systems were appreciated can be seen from Mwase's descriptions of the workings of the criminal law in the territories around Malawi.

The Germans, he wrote,

are very cruel, for a very small matter they flog, not less than twenty-five. They do not like to take evidence in court carefully, word by word, as the English men usually do. Perhaps they do so only between white to white only . . . . What I am commenting, are the native cases. Any word a chief has said, or told to do, to his men, or women, does not matter how bad it stands, that must be observed. If one will put an argument, that person will be flogged twenty-five.

Yet he also claimed, and endorsed, a preference among the people for the way in which the Germans treated homicide cases. The Germans 'were not imprisoning the life of a person, as the English men often do'. People told him that the Germans themselves frequently warned them to beware the English because of this. But, wrote Mwase, 'The Germans were not putting a person in prison more than five years for a big case.' (Though for a 'very bad case' they exacted the death penalty.)

It appeared, on the other hand, that there was nothing to say in favour of the Portuguese:

> The Portuguese are the people who can put a person on remand in prison without hearing the case, sometimes four or five years, and afterwards when hearing the case, found him or her not guilty or found him guilty and sentence him to two months or so. They often take evidence from the first person, does not matter what kind of lies the first person has spoken.[33]

The Germans were systematically cruel; the Portuguese oppression was randomly a-legal. British oppression was contained partly within the legalism of its legal system, and also partly in the failure of this system to live up to its promises.

Yet even with a satisfactory police force, more careful procedures and equality before the law, the real heart of the anger and disarray might not have been touched. Mumba's memorandum provides our best guide. He introduced his essay on the administration of justice in Nyasland as follows:

> In dealing with this subject it is better to understand first the growth of a social native community before the Europeans came. Differing from the European a native East African is not an individual. He is a member of a body which may vary from one to a thousand and which must be dealt with together as a unit. That is to say, if you start a quarrel with a member of the clan, unless such quarrel is a local one – You can take it for granted as certain that the whole clan will be at arms; if one is marrying, the others must assist in dowry, and where this is not the custom they must stand as 'sponsors' for the marriage; or if one is fined by a court, the payment must be demanded from the clan as a whole; damages and compensation paid in shares by all.

Mumba's version of the African past was not one of pre-colonial violence and disorder but a vision of communal solidarity and moral community.

> The ties binding a native to his relatives were born with him and though he was capable of standing trouble which was caused by his own indiscretion he was always careful not to do anything which would unnecessarily involve others as custom would inevitably demand their inclusion. Therefore before one did anything the others were consulted for their information, opinion and ruling.

According to our methods no matter what the case may be every native is a minor at law, he cannot prosecute, nor be prosecuted by any one, except through his clan head, village headman, councillor or chief. In this way a check was kept on the action of individuals prompted by selfish motives and so the peace of all the members of a clan or tribe was preserved.

This was 'excellent way of the old times', which, Mumba recognised sadly, 'cannot now be redeemed'. A fundamental change had come. He continued:

Early in the nineties European methods of administration of justice were introduced. From that time, unwittingly perhaps, but all the same effectively the communal structure of the native was destroyed. No more could a clan be considered as a body. No more could a father speak for his son or vice versa; the offender must come forward in person. In this the European came with his individualism and thrust it on the native. If there is any one thing more than all others which has changed and spoiled a primitive people with no education for guidance, it is this individualism. I hate individualism because it has suddenly torn the son from the father, or one man from another. I hate it because it gives a false air that a person should not consider the feelings of others in his action. I hate it for its selfishness and because it has propagated crime. But individualism has come to stay and has to be faced. The native shook itself and found that after all his relatives have not adhered to him .... So the vices of the native have been let loose and off he goes for crime. Where a mere twig served to keep watch on a garden or over anything thorns and guards cannot keep away thieves now: where a grass door with a piece of wood across kept burglars away, 'alonda' and doors with locks and safes inside are insufficient now: where compensation paid by many lessened murders, hanging of the criminal has increased it: where a mere word sufficed of old, 25 lashes fail now – All this is the result of individualism, and it proves that the punishment by individual imprisonment and flogging where applied to people who live according to a collective system is a failure and other means should be sought to check the growing crime.[34]

Mumba was by no means alone among African opinion in his expression of feelings of anxiety at the apparent social breakdown. To him increasing punishment was not the answer and he looked for 'other means', but this was unusual. More generally African opinion, basing itself on a view of the past kept in order less by moral community than by authoritarian firmness, favoured an increasingly punitive legal order. Mumba was rare, too, in his perception that the golden age could not be restored. But how was a moral community to be rebuilt? People were seeking to create from the disarray a new order of authority and solidarity. Morrison describes the young as being in danger of throwing off all restraints, and the elders as 'bewildered' and having 'lost hold'. He describes a Kirk session where African elders discussed the new Christian morality. 'Every case was a test case to be settled on first principle; every subject was touched at its roots. Here were men laying the foundations of the Christian home and Church and social order of the future.' As the missions saw it, out of the anxiety and disarray, on the basis of a new moral and religious education, would be born a 'Christian law and conscience'. I would suggest that there is a hint of the processes at work

135

to be gleaned from Morrison's picture even if it did not turn out the way he desired. I have said already that the morality of mission Christianity was an ingredient of the moral and legal order which was being created, as new 'oughts' were being born and a new ideology of social control formulated. The style of white administrative *fiat* was another. But the main ingredient was to be the developing of neo-traditional ideology and its application as the new 'customary law'. Mumba blamed the British for giving the Africans 'too much latitude in hearing cases himself in a foreign way which even he himself did not fully understand'. But the adaption to the 'foreign way' was being made. It was not an adaptation from a communal justice to an idealised British model or one from a past of rapine and murder to one of order and freedom. It was made by men both anxious and authoritarian, determined to rebuild. Their materials were the summary and technical legalism of British forms of justice, a remote and despotic legal style, a fiery view of sin and, above all, the vision of a strict and moral golden age. From this amalgam the customary law was made.

TOWARDS A CUSTOMARY LAW

The experience of and response to the coming of colonial courts and legal forms was by no means uniform. Variations in the average length of a district officer's stay in a particular district and, more importantly, the relative wealth of the community; the strength of its indigenous organisation; and its degree of tribal homogeneity, appeared to have influenced local response to the new courts.[35] Nonetheless certain themes emerge as common to the responses described in the previous chapter, and in combination they contributed to and developed towards a process of an increasing legalism in African life. Once African courts were officially recognised, in the 1930s, administrative worrying about the kind of law that was being used increased. The consensus at the end of the 1920s and during the 1930s was that codification of the 'customary law', though desirable from a legal point of view, ought to be postponed. A premature codification would, it was thought, rigidify the law and halt its forward movement. But in the absence of a codification white disquiet grew. Lord Hailey's report on the workings of the Native Courts in Malawi endorsed the view that '"native custom" administered in the courts has ceased to be a matter of precedent and has become just common sense.'[36] The implication was that the Native Courts were cutting loose from an accustomed rigid adherence to an outmoded law and reacting pragmatically to the circumstance. But this was a misunderstanding. For the settlements of the indigenous courts had rarely been based simply on precedent. Only the white courts, when they used the 'customary law', had worked in this way. A memorandum on customary law produced in the Northern Rhodesian administration after the second world war takes up the same problem.[37] It ponders on the nature of the answers given to someone enquiring about customary law:

After long and patient investigation he has ascertained . . . that some wrong or injury to a chief by a commoner would be sufficiently compensated by payment of a beast or a few goats when the witness will confound him at the end of his statement by the saving clause 'but if he were a strong chief he might take all the offender's property and have him killed in the bargain.' The power of a chief was always a factor to be considered in estimating native rights and liabilities, and in such a case, as in others, it introduced uncertainty. Was a particular rule, however arbitrary and tyrannical, a part of the law or was it the chief's power overriding the law?

This was a part diagnosis of the crucial failure in understanding. This lay in the belief that if the search was careful enough there must be rules to be found. In observing other people's systems the administrators and the lawyers revealed how peculiar was their understanding of their own. Law to them was about the certain application of rules without the intrusion of the element of arbitrary power. That it was thus neither in Britain nor in Africa did not occur to them. The memorandum observed that experienced Africa hands were against codification. But does that mean, it asked, that the government was to be content with uncertainty in spite of the maxim that where there is no certainty there is no justice? The facts of uncertainty and power in African 'customary' settlements could not, in this view, be a part of the 'law'. As the memorandum observed, Africans said that the penalty for adultery was death. They were referring to the right of private vengeance. Europeans translated this into the notion of a chief's court imposing the penalty.

To make 'customary law', a jump had to be made from the facts of private vengeance and chiefly power to an ideal world of regular rules, fines, courts and penalties. White administrators made this jump hardly noticing that they had done so. They needed to do so in order to create customary law for the courts to use. And if Africans were going to use the new fora and forms properly, they too had to make this jump. Legalisms had to be fashioned out of the raw material of 'customary' life. The memorandum complained that Africans did not seem , 'even when they have copious law, to have thought out the topic to its final conclusion'. Even when they had law, that is, they did not know what it really was. But it was now in the process of being 'discovered'.

Disaffection with the workings of the white courts led to an assertion of an African right to control the hearing of civil disputes, but this soon developed complications as to which Africans should control the courts and what 'law' they should be using. In 1929 the West Nyasa Association drew up a memorandum entitled 'Who is able to decide cases between natives?' The newly elected president of the association, Chief Marenga, claimed in the association's name that 'It goes without saying that it is one who is acquainted and understands the history, customs, manners, habits and language of the people. In short it is the native himself.' European incomprehension, the memorandum went on, meant that lawsuits 'very often are

137

summarily dismissed as useless, to the disappointment of the natives concerned'. The association resolved that 'all cases, civil and criminal, with the exception of murder, should be settled by the chiefs.'[38] There were many other indications of the desire to take back control of the judicial process. In 1929, Chikulamayembe, advised by Edward Manda, proposed that the government should codify the customary law for each part of the North, partly in pursuit of the goal of delineating Tumbuka from Ngoni. Chikulamayembe wanted to limit the right of appeal from his court to the Boma and he felt that decisions were less likely to be overturned at the Boma if both were based upon the same law book.[39] It was not easy for interested Africans to know what the protectorate's laws really were. They were not easily available. In 1920 the Momberas Association pressed unsuccessfully for copies. In the case of another association the fact that they had succeeded in collecting government gazettes with ordinances in them was cited as evidence of their general attitude of disaffection. It is also important to stress that the laws were only available in English, except for the District Administration (Native) Ordinance, which was printed in Chinyanja as well. Legal understanding therefore had to take place in a foreign language at its most opaque, and African legal concepts and representations had likewise to be pressed into foreign forms.

Alongside of the conflict between chiefs and government there was also developing a germ of the conflict between old rulers and new men about control of the law which was to be so much more acute where and when a class of professional lawyers became more numerous. As early as 1923 there were signs of a rift between the chiefs and the mission graduates in the Momberas Association. Some who took cases to the Native Courts, the new men said, were not helped as 'some of those who settle cases are very shallow and ignorant of this important work.' Consequently, it was suggested, chiefs and councillors should select to help them men with 'wider views of points'. Many cases, the complaint continued, needed appealing to the Boma and even this was not satisfactory as the district officers often used as an assessor the chief being appealed against, or the chief insisted on attending the court and intimidated appellants.[40] In 1927 the Central Province Association, as part of a general attack on abuse of powers by the headmen, complained of the corruption of their courts. The headmen, they said, concealed ninety-eight per cent of crimes in return for payments and they were responsible for holding the *mwavi* ordeal.[41]

Government policy as we have seen aligned itself firmly with the traditional rulers. Over forty years the early British impulse to westernise and improve had evaporated. The new orthodoxy, retreating in its expectations and hostile to the 'new men', aimed at leaving village justice in village hands. In 1932 the then Governor of Zambia, Maxwell, wrote that, although the African courts were not likely to reach the high standards which the British had been accustomed to impose, they must not be interfered with: 'while endeavouring to maintain our high standard we must learn to make allowances for others who not only live on what we would call a lower plane but who are content to live on that plane.'[42]

Yet it was clear that all the people were not so content. The official indigenisation of the law by placing its interpretation and administration into the hands of resurrected chiefs' and headmen's courts did not satisfy the 'new men'. In 1936 the journal *Zoona*, in Malawi, registered a complaint not uncommon among the 'new men'. 'There are many today who favour Government by Europeans because they know that if they take their case to the Chiefs' Village Courts the Chiefs will not give just decisions. Many of the Chiefs cannot be trusted with anything, many others are grasping, others quarrelsome.' In local disputes, the magazine continued, 'Chiefs seized the opportunity for private gain and favoured relatives over strangers.'[43]

Elite African opinion was allied with a part of 'liberal' British opinion in wanting a more technical and legalised system of justice. Levi Mumba called for a classic separation of the powers – a division of the magistracy and district administration. Norman Leys attacked the administrators' wisdom, claiming that Africans wanted, indeed had had before, a technical law: 'It is a complete mistake,' he claimed, 'to imagine that natives prefer the personal prerogative of a benevolent local despot to the law.' Leys was writing in 1918 and for most of the next two decades this was far from orthodoxy. Most pro-African opinion was bound up with the policy of indirect rule, of encouraging the building of an African element in government and courts, and allied to anthropological and administrative opinion that this was not to be done through the pursuit of legalism. But the experiences of indirect rule and the emergence of an African elite cut off from its processes began to make clear that favouring indirect rule was not the only way of being pro-African.[44]

By the 1930s the new African elite was beginning to move from simple disaffection, to line itself up on the side of the lawyers and liberal opinion. All wanted more legalism, and to African new men this was a more important priority than Africanisation. The administrators, and conservative opinion which had now come around to appreciating the value to the empire of indirect rule, continued to want the law to be less 'legal' and 'technical'. This not only suited the needs of administration, but also, in their view, made the law more 'African' and therefore closer to what people needed and wanted. Yet the chiefs, though they continued to want to retain the courts in their own hands, also took part in the demand for legalism. While the administrators continued to duck away from codification on the grounds that it was too early, the chiefs began to lend their voices to a demand for more law. In the Northern Rhodesian African Representatives Council in 1947 new men and chiefs joined in support of a motion that the Native Courts should have 'code of law in their Courts in order to help Chiefs in deciding cases'. Chief Kopa, in support, recounted that two years previously he had asked the district commissioner to give him some law books but that the request had been refused. The (white) council president then intervened to enquire whether Kopa wanted the 'law books of the Territory which they have in the Bomas or do you mean that your own laws should be written down in books?' There were, he told the council, two types of law, 'English law which is written down in books' and 'your own laws and customs', which were not. Kopa replied, 'I was under the impression that our Native Customary Laws have been codified but if that is not so then how do the District Commissioners come to the conclusion that cases have not been decided in accordance with Native Customary Law? I must say I am confused.' He had a right to be. If the customary law was not written down, who should know it better than the chiefs? They were, however, Kopa complained, frequently being reversed by the Boma courts, which used law books. Law in books was, therefore, the key to control of the process: written law took precedence over unwritten, and so, as another chief said, 'we want law books for our customary laws.'

Edward Sampa, one of the prominent 'new men', spoke for those in the urban areas of the Copperbelt. What the chiefs had been asking for, he said, they had been urging in the Copperbelt, without knowing that the chiefs too wanted the customary law put into writing. People whose cases had been decided in the Native Urban Courts constantly felt aggrieved that the 'case has not been properly decided on account of there being no written law. If there had been a written law the complainant even if the case had gone against him might have been satisfied.'[45]

This was not an isolated expression of opinion. A year later the African Welfare Association Abercorn discussed the Native Courts and the numerous appeals which were made from them to the Boma. They asked that 'Native Courts be supplied with code books, containing penalties for each offence. An African has begun to despise the workings of the Native Courts ... [because] he sees his case judged without reference to a book, and when he appeals to the Boma his case is taken in a different and satisfactory way and the sentence either reduced or increased or sometimes the case dismissed'.[46]

Control over the development of an unwritten 'customary law' was no longer sufficient if Africans, both elite and traditional, were to use the law to re-create a lost coherence, authority and stability in African social life. The institutional structures, which had been supposed to separate the English 'law in the books' and the fluidly developing unwritten customary law, were themselves producing the demand that this gap be closed. Where there had been no need previously to 'think things through' even where there was 'copious law', demands were now being made for written precision. Legalism was wanted, and seen as necessary, to establish in the only way now possible the legitimacy of the normative claims being made. To be the controlling norms they had to emerge as laws in the book.

Thus African opinion, both traditional and new, joined lawyers and liberals in the push for legalisation. To the latter white groups the aim was to make the legal system more like that of an idealised English 'rule of law'. To the traditionalists it was to ensure the primacy of their definitions of right and wrong. At the end of the colonial period, the African elite and African lawyers took over control. They wanted to make the law both more legalistic and more African. Yet the African element that they were to emphasise had been bequeathed to them by those they had vanquished, having been formed by the neo-traditionalists as their weapon, in and through the structures of the white administrators.

Part III

Men and women

8

The lawgivers in Central Africa: marriage and morality

I have shown in Part II the general way in which the customary law, far from being rules handed down from the pre-colonial period, must be understood as an historical product created in colonial institutions. I will now pursue this theme focusing upon the 'law' of marriage and family. It was through marriage that people gained access to land and, in most societies, men lost the use of land through divorce. It is an area crucial to the understanding of social history in that it is basic to an understanding of the ways in which Africans thought their societies in this period should be ordered. And it is also crucial to legal history because the law related to the family is often regarded as being quintessentially an area in which the African customary law 'survived'. Yet what I will be describing will be less a survival and more a development of new tools of control to meet the needs of a new situation. The context in which the 'customary law' of the family developed out of the shifting structures of kinship of pre-colonial societies under stress was, first, that of the intensification and then abolition of the slave trade and slavery; secondly the conquest of matrilineal peoples by patrilineal and their subsequent liberation by the British; thirdly the early intervention of British courts into African family disputes; and fourthly the impact of the colonial economic system with cash cropping, labour migrancy and the formation of urban communities.

COLONIAL ADMINISTRATION AND MORAL REFORM

Over the whole of the colonial period cases concerning conflict between men and women took up most of the time of the colonial courts. Indeed in terms of the time which officials claim to have spent on it this was one of the colonial government's most important interventions into African life. Duff noted that in Zomba 'Much more numerous than all other judicial cases put together are those which have to do with women.' Far away from Zomba on the Zambian plateau and in quite a different local political situation Gouldsbury and Sheane recorded that 'Dissensions regarding marriage, divorce, abduction and the like constitute nine-tenths of the daily

145

work of a Native Commissioner.'[1] All the evidence suggests that a major disturbance in relationships between sexes was taking place. In this situation African claims and attempts to formulate new rules for the new situation were adjudicated by white courts with their own peculiarly dissonant prejudices about female status and male authority. We must therefore look first at what white views of African marriage and the position of African women were, as they were to be an ingredient in the blending of the new law. In this process we can also note the intrusion of legality into the sphere of kinship and family and the way in which it came to dominate it. For we are looking at a process in which the 'family law' is moving from the private to the public sphere. The British officials undoubtedly underestimated the role of dispute-settling within and between families. They were unable to consider the role of chief or headman without official judicial capacities, and 'private' justice, internal to families, seemed to them to be no justice at all. So family 'quarrels', which had previously been settled within a lineage, became public 'cases' to be settled outside. And 'cases' implied 'courts', and 'courts' implied 'laws'.[2]

Initial white judgements of African morality, because they led to a willingness to intervene in African marriage, had an important effect in Central Africa. African sexual morality and the position of African women were severely condemned. The white man's mission thus appeared to be both the liberation of women and the improvement of morals. These were not necessarily compatible. Some African peoples appeared to the new administrators to have no sexual morals at all. Lomwe morality was said to be of 'so low a standard that adultery is not considered as an offence . . . . they often have their women in common.' Of the Mang'anja it was reported that 'the chastity of women, or their feelings on the subject (if they have any), is not considered; it is their custom to occasionally change wives with each other and also to loan their wives to a friend or for money value to a stranger.' From Fort Johnston it was reported that the Yaos were 'generally and distinctly immoral. No man between Mvera and Monkey Bay dare trust his wife out of sight for any length of time.'[3] Smith and Dale (a linguist and a missionary) wrote of the Ila: 'how fragile the marriage bond is . . . . women are bandied about from man to man; and of their own accord leave one husband for another. It is no unusual thing for a woman scarcely out of her teens to have had four or five husbands still living.' Sexual amorality was seen as combined with the fragility of the marriage bond. Reverend Guillaime observed of the Bemba, 'For the smallest reason the woman quitted her husband's house.'[4]

The observations of marital anarchy among some people were put alongside an admiration of the sexual discipline believed to be maintained by others. François Coillard contrasted the 'marriage by cattle', which he had known in South Africa as a 'blessing . . . a barrier against corruption and a civil contract', with the Lozi situation as he found it where marriage was a 'union of nothing but caprice, which ill temper may break tomorrow'.[5]

Firmness in the protection of marriage was admired. There was an element of ambivalence and suppressed approval in E. D. Young's account of the Makololo practice of cutting off hands, or exacting the death penalty, for adultery. Young reminded his readers that: 'It would be impossible to take one of these men whom we were about to employ through many of the parts of London after dark without a feeling of shame and humiliation which the native need never feel when the stranger . . . comes to his village or his hut.' Twenty years before the first white magistrates were working, the admiration which white men felt for the results, though not the methods, which some African men appeared to have achieved in imposing a morality on women was already evident.[6]

The sexual morals of conquerors, like the Makololo and the Ngoni, were given most approbation while those of the indigenous peoples were disapproved. Donald Fraser wrote of the Northern Ngoni and their Tumbuka subjects:

> I do not for a moment profess that the Ngoni were a moral people. Murdering and plundering were the trade of their tribe, but breaches of the 7th and 8th commandments within their own villages were punished with the utmost severity, death and frequently death by hideous torture being the common penalty. Parents also maintained a strict control over their children. On the other hand the social morality of the Tumbuka was very low, and the marriage tie easily broken.[7]

The results of the mingling of Ngoni and Tumbuka had been that:

> The two tribes have reacted on one another in this moral sphere [and] while the composite people may exhibit a distinctly higher type than that found among most Central African tribes, and than that which obtained among the old Tumbuka, they do not nearly approach the strictness of the old Ngoni.

Fraser clearly sympathised with 'the old men' who told him that 'the ancient domestic purity, honesty and obedience, had disappeared before the insidious effects of Tumbuka influence.'

The combination of rampant immorality and morals imposed by firm punishment and the subjection of women made the African woman's 'position in life, from her childhood to her grave, one of gloom, discouragement and disgrace' as one missionary wrote. Duff wrote that native law gave a man the same rights over a woman as 'over sheep and cattle'.[8] Typically objected to were the great disparity in ages between husbands and wives and the 'manifestly unjust' practice of 'inheritance' of women.[9] Officials therefore saw their dilemma as being how to moderate the savagery of the punishments and improve the position of women without causing social and moral breakdown. One of the judges in the Nyasaland government wrote:

> In the olden days, before the advent of European government, the heaviest of punishments, mutilation even death, were meted out in certain cases of adultery. The result was that in some tribes adultery was almost unknown. Such penalties could not, of course, be tolerated by a civilised Government,

but the result has been that the pendulum has swung from one extreme to another . . . . As a consequence the marriage tie has been weakened . . . . This result is not peculiar to Nyasaland: it is universal when European civilisation has affected native life. When a stop is put to the cruelties by which the marriage bond was safeguarded we have only done half our work.[10]

'No-one is quicker than a native to note the slackening of old bonds,' wrote Gouldsbury and Sheane, aptly reflecting the concern of those in authority.[11] A substitute had to be found, then, administrators thought, for the 'cruelties by which the marriage bond was safeguarded', which would still safeguard that bond. This was to be the 'customary law'.

Between 1907 and 1910 the Northern Rhodesian government collected the views of district officials on various aspects of African law. There was much concern with the apparent dissolution of African marriage. One officer was of the opinion that this was the result of a breakdown in authority in general, which was 'indirectly the result of the white man's government' and was 'partly [due] to the quite unnecessary diffidence on the part of the officials in assuming along with the other powers that have been taken from the chiefs, headmen and elders, the regulation of the native's social life'.[12] Parents, he wrote, allowed their daughters far greater freedom because a misconception existed that officials would not listen to the views of parents and elders if they clashed with those of the girl. Coxhead, who was a district officer at Fort Jameson in the early years, wrote similarly in 1914 in an account of the 'Native Tribes'. The dominant Ngoni system, he said, had allowed polygamy, had had no need of female consent, allowed inheritance of wives, pre-puberty transfer of women, and their corporal punishment. Nowadays, 'excessive' punishment was forbidden, female consent to marriage 'to some extent' required, and child marriage 'generally discouraged'.[13] This seems limited, but he was regretfully sure that 'our recognition of and insistence upon the rights of women have much to do with the increase in divorce'. The decisions of the chiefs were usually in favour of the man in a marital dispute, while the British efforts to improve the African law 'by the introduction of more humane rules have so far been productive of an increase in immorality, a weakening of the marriage tie, and a considerable amount of discontent among men, especially the elders'.

One remedy which both officials suggested for this state of affairs was a closer observance by white courts of supposed African legal formalities. The first memorandum concludes that the government would have to take a more aggressive role in cementing the old social order: 'Unless we are satisfied that one result of our Administration be the rapid and universal dissolution of a certain class of moral ties, it cannot be too strongly urged upon us to do all we can to encourage and insist upon the due performance of the old obligations.' One way this could be achieved was to 'refuse absolutely to recognise any claims whatever of a "Husband" who has not properly married his consort'. Coxhead noted what he thought of as a decline in the observance of marital formalities (which appears really to have been a switch from Ngoni to Chewa forms). The government should itself force compliance with the African laws of marriage.[14]

This swing from liberating African women from the tyranny of fearful punishment to controlling morality by an insistence on legal formalities was endorsed by the law departments of both countries. By 1907 Judge Griffin in Malawi had come to the view that 'A native looks upon all infractions of his marriage contract . . . as a serious wrong which he is quick to resent and punish, and I am strongly of the opinion that every assistance should be given him for the maintenance of the security of his domestic rights.'[15] In 1914 the Northern Rhodesian government advised that before parties could have a case concerning marriage heard in a Boma court they must produce proper evidence of the marriage in accordance with 'native custom'. Courts could not deal with temporary unions even if these were condoned by parents, and had to enquire into the ceremony by which the marriage had taken place and whether it was recognised in 'customary law'. The circular detailed the types of requirements like the consent of relatives, the necessary payments, and so on. While all these were apparently being widely and willingly ignored by those whose 'customary law' they were supposed to be, the white courts were detailing them as necessary to a legal marriage. Those unions which did not amount to marriage were 'immoral connection(s)', and any redress granted by the courts 'is to uphold immorality'.[16]

Charles Dundas, who was one of the more reliable of the administrative observers and who published the most thoughtful of the early accounts of the East African law in English, wrote in 1915 that the marriage law had been the first to fall into disuse as a result of the European impact. European law, Dundas wrote, by giving rights to sons and to women, 'falls like a thunderbolt into the midst of native society. All precedent and custom are cast aside, and the controllers of society are disabled.'[17] African marriage in his eyes had degenerated and the morals of women had declined. The British had 'loosened the ties of matrimony . . . . We have freely granted divorces in favour of frivolous girls, and permitted them to run from one man to another, heedless of the bad example thereby set.'[18]

The Northern Rhodesian courts, in mobilising the law against 'frivolous girls' also grasped the connection between the control of sexual behaviour and the authority of the 'controllers of society'. In a circular on judicial policy regarding African divorce Macdonnell advised that 'divorce is a matter of grace rather than of right . . . . normally a marriage is not dissolved and is not meant to be.' All marriages, he wrote, involved a proprietary interest and proprietary rights should not be disturbed without good cause. He continued: 'Indiscriminate divorce would break up tribal relations. At present marriage is an integral part of tribal organisation. If divorce were made too easy tribal rule would break up and disappear. Already complaints are heard from headmen that the young men . . . take women without regard to tribal authority and recognised custom.'[19] The white courts' policy of establishing a 'customary law' of the family became part of the fight to

149

resurrect the defeated African authorities and to defend them against change. Both British and Africans were to see the field of marriage, adultery and divorce as crucial in this struggle.

The retreat from a protective attitude towards women's rights is nowhere better exemplifed than by a case from Namwala, in the Kafue district of Zambia, heard by J. Gibson Hall in 1916. A woman, beaten by her husband, found her father willing to take her back, which was rare enough. But the father was belaboured by the court, for the evidence had been that she had been beaten for committing adultery. 'Do you really mean', the court asked the father 'that because [the husband] wishes his wife to be a pure woman and because she wishes to be immoral, you say you don't want her to live with him? . . . Morality, as regarded by the majority of human beings', Hall concluded, 'is unknown to the Baila. Here is a case where a father denies his daughter to her husband, because that husband wishes her to be pure'.[20] African women would have to look elsewhere for sympathy in their efforts to loosen male control.

SIN AND RULES: MISSIONARY MORALS

The Christian missions in Central Africa saw themselves as fighting a dramatic and intensely important battle on the marriage front and the atmosphere of conflict and dogmatism, of moral approbation and condemnation, which this battle engendered, was another ingredient in the formation of the new customary law of marriage. It became a part of the context in which both Boma and village courts operated and in which the *nkhoswe* handled family disputes. The battle for Christian marriage, monogamous and indissoluble, was fought all over Africa. Hastings points out that at the World Mission Conference of 1910 some tolerance was expressed for polygamy in Indian and China, but none for Africa, and he quotes from *The Church in the Mission Field*: 'Our correspondents in Africa view with unanimous intolerance conditions of life which are not only un-Christian, but are at variance with the instinctive feelings of natural morality. With them there can be no question of polygamy. It is simply one of the gross evils of heathen society which, like habitual murder or slavery, must at all costs be ended.'[21] In Malawi Arthur Glossop, on Likhoma island, which was in many ways an Anglican mission colony, wrote in 1898: 'What is the one supreme difficulty? The marriage question: that is the rock.' It was not an issue on which missionaries could see a way to compromise between Church principles and local practices and in consequence they fell back upon a defensive rigidity. As Glossop wrote, 'The pressure is great to allow exception . . . . Yet one also sees that exceptions are impossible. The least sign of explaining away this or that brings up a crop of more applicants for dispensation.'

In similar vein Bishop Weston wrote from Karogwe in 1910 that 'the most pressing problem . . . is that of the women and girls. An ideal of Christian womanhood is the overwhelming need of our young Church at present, and we must win it in the face of tribal customs, unholy rites, semi-Muhammaden influence and natural apathy.' The difficulties seemed enormous but there could be no weakening. Weston wrote, 'The Western law of marriage is indeed a very hard teaching for one whose fathers and brothers are polygamists, and whose wives have themselves no desire for lifelong union. Yet we have to keep up our standard.'[22] Hine, who was Bishop at Likhoma, and later in Northern Rhodesia, wrote: 'The Christian law of marriage is a hard law for primitive man in Africa to obey; but from the first we raised that standard of life and purity, and required Christians to conform to it.'[23]

At first the missions, like the Boma officials, had been protective towards women. The first mission on the Shire Highlands was continuously involved in the protection of female fugitives. Proctor's diary entry in July 1862 sums things up: 'Mobita came to us to complain that one of his women had left him and come to live with ours. He said that all their women were leaving them and coming to us.'[24] As the mission presence became more obstructive, so conflict with African men over control of women became more acute. The missions based their position on the idea of Christian marriage based upon formal consent. W. P. Johnson recalls a case on Likhoma island, in 1886, of a girl in a mission school claimed by a suitor who had redeemed a debt for her father and had thereby become her 'owner'. The mission appealed to the chief. 'One of our leading Christians pleaded on our side before Chiteji, and, alas! it seemed that he had been more impressed with the way our wishes often traversed their customs than with the fundamental principles of the Christian marriage law.'[25] But Chiteji had perceived correctly that the heart of the matter was a dispute over who should dispose of the destinies of women rather than the principles according to which it was done.

However, as the missions began to build up a community of converts and catechumens the emphasis changed. It was no longer on the freeing of women from enforced unions but rather on the building up of unbreakable monogamous marriage. This contrasted obviously with the Boma's approach which, while it too swung from protectiveness to stability, made no issue of principle out of polygamy or divorce. (The Boma also remained slightly more concerned with the issue of female consent.) There were now two broadly differing white approaches to the matters of right and wrong in marriage and there was also being created an African Christian elite in the villages with a new conscience on these matters. In some areas Boma and mission attitudes were congruent. Both thought African marriage a less noble conception than Christian, as African unions involved no true companionship or real affection and both thought that through the reform of African marriage the status of African women would be improved. Donald Fraser, of the Livingstonia mission, in his account of the life of an early convert, Daniel Mfusu, in the 1890s tells a dramatic story of village resentment of Mfusu's monogamy and how he had to resist the 'Determined efforts . . . made to drag him into polygamy'. Fraser's view of African family life is shown in his explanation of village pressures. 'For every daughter born there had been a special welcome because she would increase the possessions of her parents by her marriage .... Now the girls were to be on their hands, consuming food and bringing in nothing.'[26] Neither patrilineal nor matrilineal marriage appeared to be consistent with the missions' desire for monogamy and indissolubility. While the perceived desire to get rid of daughters in patrilineal bridewealth marriages brought pressures for polygamy, the apparent desire to retain control of them among matrilineal people seemed subversive of marital stability. Arthur Glossop analysed the problem among the latter as follows:

> The difficulty from their point of view is this: they marry very young and their parents arrange their marriages for them, perhaps before they are Christians; each marriage is contracted only on the understanding that it can be dissolved at any time by the return of presents. Then the relatives have such power over the wife they can always be recalling her .... You can say of an English mother-in-law that it is no business of hers but you cannot here; by native law they all have the power over the wife, much more than the husband. This is directly subversive of Christian marriage and is the great difficulty.[27]

The Churches, in their efforts to impose indissoluble marriage, would be opposed to the power of maternal relatives in matrilineal marriages, and this would be an influence limiting of female freedom and increasing of male authority.

The Boma, with its administrative priorities and its lack of Christian fervour, was an unreliable ally for the missions in the battle over marriage. Often the administration found itself closer to African practice than to church prescription. Bradley recalls travelling in the 1920s through North Eastern Zambian villages 'filled with pathetic women left without money or help or a man', as most adult males were labour migrants. The circumstances in which these women found themselves angered Undi, the Chewa paramount, who while touring a Catholic area with Bradley spent hours every day granting divorces to them. A few weeks afterwards Undi complained to the administration that Catholic priests had been following him through the area telling Christians that there was no such thing as divorce and that the decrees were null. Bradley immediately sent for the bishop who agreed that priests should not interfere with 'customary law' that had received the approval of the government, and who disowned the religous fervour of his missionaries with a worldly 'What can I do when these priests of mine are mostly ill-educated Polish peasants?'[28] But not all clerical opinion was so accommodating. On the Malawi side of the border central region headmen decided in response to pressure from women for divorce that a two-year period of absence would suffice if no money had been sent. The Catholic missions resolutely refused to recognise this, resulting 'in intolerable hardships for deserted families'.[29]

The Nyasaland Missionary Conference complained in 1910, in a confused precognition of the novelty of customary law, that 'The general principle that native questions should be dealt with according to native law or custom came to be a serious matter when "native law" or "native custom" came to be interpreted as "Heathen native law" or "Heathen native custom" ignoring the rights of a Christian native to have a Christian native law or Christian native custom.'[30] Alexander Hetherwick, of the Scottish mission in Blantyre, like the other missionaries thought that the new conception of Christian marriage raised questions which were 'the most difficult' to deal with. Among the difficulties Hetherwick pinpointed the unreliability of the Boma courts and the unsympathetic policy of the Colonial Office. The legal problem, as he saw it, was whether polygamy was 'contrary to morality and justice' and therefore fell into the category of 'native laws and customs' which were, in terms of the repugnancy clause of the Order in Council, not to be applied. How would a magistrate look upon a Christian's claim to this effect? 'Would he view it from the Christian or the heathen point of view ...?'[31] The magistrates did not, on the whole, think much of 'native Christianity' or claims thereto, particularly as they moved towards support for 'customary law'.

The missions fought a prolonged battle with the colonial administrations everywhere on the subject of marriage laws. I do not wish to deal at length with the various conflict-of-laws problems which arose out of the coexistence of different types of legal marriage, as these were lawyers' questions which affected only a small minority and were not vital to the development of the customary law. The legal position after the establishment of British rule was that African marriage was to remain the basic 'law' of marriage while the new statute law of Malawi and Zambia provided in addition for marriage for the 'civilised' communities. This statute marriage did not simply involve monogamy but also had implications for the marital property regime and for inheritance which, if such a marriage were entered into, would be ruled by English law. The missions, which fervently wanted monogamous Christian marriage, pressed in Malawi for the recognition of a third type of marriage, which could be performed by a Christian minister, would be legally monogamous, yet for property, inheritance and other purposes, would be marriage according to African law. While the Nyasaland administration was prepared to grant this request, the Colonial Office was not, and it insisted that it was desirable 'where natives are married with civilised ceremonies, whether religious or purely civil, any property to which the parties to marriage may be legally entitled should devolve after death according to English law.'[32] The missions, because they were of the view that a transition was needed between full Christian marriage and African marriage, and also because many refused to marry couples under the ordinance which provided for western marriage so long as it recognised the possibility of divorce, confined themselves to blessing 'customary' marriages.

The consequence was that virtually all African marriages were marriages according to African law. This position was regularised in Malawi in 1924 by the Registration of Marriage Ordinance, which recognised a Christian marriage without effects in civil law. The Boma courts continued to treat marriage as marriage according to 'customary law' and were reluctant to treat Christian marriage as if it had any legal consequences. The result, Hetherwick claimed, was that the law 'fell into disrepute among the natives themselves .... this one Ordinance [affected] the respect of the native for the whole legal system of the country.'[33] Only a few would have noticed but it seems a possible area of confusion and resentment for some of the Christian elite so affected.[34] In Zambia, where there was no legal provision made to allow for the conducting of marriage ceremonies by missionaries, the hostility between Boma and Church could be such that in 1916 in Fort Jameson the Rev. M. D. Groenewald was convicted and sentenced to six months in prison or a fine of ten pounds for having conducted a marriage service which, according to the court, gave the impression that it was a legal marriage. In North-Eastern Zambia the legal position was that marriages 'according to native law and custom' or civil marriages, conducted by a registrar (i.e. 'English' marriage), were the only possible forms. The general missionary practice was to insist on a Christian ceremony once the village marriage contracts were completed. But the danger from the Church's point of view of village marriages being the prior and preferred form was, as the Dutch Reformed Church petition following Groenewald's conviction said, that many 'lapsed into heathenism'. The weapon of monogamous marriage was much blunted by this priority. While the government claimed that Africans could not understand the consequences which followed upon monogamous marriage, the Churches viewed 'with alarm the destruction of their efforts to plant some sense of the sanctity of Christian marriage in the minds of their adherents'.[35] The flavour of the conflict between government and mission on the question, and of the courts' assumption of the role of protectors of African women, can be no better illustrated than by quotation from the judgement of Mr Justice Beaufort in *In re Paulos*, a dispute regarding the custody of a child which came before the court in November 1909.[36]

Paulos was a migrant worker from Malawi who came to Zambia leaving his first wife behind him, as was usual. In Zambia he married again and had a child. He then became a Christian and, as the mission required, renounced all wives but his first. His second wife then went to live with another man, taking her child with her. Paulos, with missionary support, claimed the child. The mission's argument was that Paulos had acted entirely correctly, indeed morally, and that the woman he had set aside was in moral turpitude.

Beaufort J., in a judgement from which I quote at length because it is redolent of the prejudices and attitudes of the judicial officers was scornful of both local custom and mission morality, which were, he perceived correctly, lined up together in this case against women's claims:

> Now I am advised that by Native Law the children generally belong to the father, and the real result of which is, that the father annexes any increment

arising from them. This is natural. It follows from his views of the status of a wife – a cook, gardener, drudge, slave and concubine in one.

Here is an Atonga, from Nyasaland, with an Atonga woman in Nyasaland as his senior wife, who comes to work here, and while here provides himself at some small expenditure with a native woman of this country as drudge, cook and concubine. She bears the child as a result of such intercourse. He tires of her and – regardless of his obligations to support her – adopts such a course of conduct that she thinks she is free to ally herself with another protector, and then he claims the offspring. He abandons the women in the name of religion and actually finds white men of undoubtedly high religious and moral standard, to support his claim and to ask the approval of the court to conduct, at once heartless, sensual and selfish on the grounds that it was done with a good motive, as a necessary preliminary to becoming a Christian. He is an industrious respectable native: he is still sufficiently pagan to be allowed much latitude, he is not sufficiently Christianized to be too rigidly judged. He must become a Christian at any cost – though a grave wrong is done to one or more unoffending women .... I know I am at issue here with not only the Dutch Reformed Church, but with the Universities Mission of the Church of England and very likely with other missionaries from David Livingstone downwards. The status of the woman, her rights and claims, are already sufficiently lightly esteemed among natives without invoking Christianity to give it the further blow of holding that the salvation of one man is to be procured at the price of cruelty to several women.

We should not be surprised then that the missions found the Boma courts to be unsupportive. But the Boma courts were not all that missions had to fall back on. They had their own court system which could judge the convert community and apply to them fully the strictness of the missionary position. The Christian concept of marriage and its regulation by these mission courts was a relevant part of the context in which the customary law of marriage developed. A few hard-core church members attempted to abide by the very strict application of marriage law and doctrine which the missions demanded and they were often people who, usually through slavery, had become cut off from their original localities and families. But the majority of mission adherents were trying to maintain a footing in both Christian and village communities, which meant a village marriage but one which would be recognised and accepted by the Church. Richards wrote in 1940 that the 'Christian sex ethic' was to many Africans 'the chief content of Christian teaching, since it is largely by keeping or failing to keep the Christian sex codes that a convert wins or loses membership of his church'.[37] Furthermore the denominations differed in their attitude towards customary marriage and divorce. The Catholics and the U.M.C.A. did not allow divorce, and while the Catholics just disregarded customary marriage, the U.M.C.A. insisted on the observance of customary marriage requirements. The Dutch Reformed Church, on the other hand, was positively against customary observances, but allowed divorce.

Yet village family life and obligations and the causes of the Church did not necessarily mesh easily together. And in their regulation of the conflicts which arose in this field the missions' courts introduced another set of marriage 'laws' into an already crowded field.[38] I shall look at one such court, the matrimonial court of the Universities' Mission, primarily because it has left a printed record, and the only one of a Central African court in action on the level at which ordinary disputes were dealt with. This record gives us an opportunity to look at both the marital histories of the applicants to the court and the legal culture which they met there.

The basic legal principles which the court applied were not only monogamy but indissolubility, the latter being probably the more revolutionary and the less applicable under local conditions. Applications which came before the court, therefore, were treated not as applications for divorce but for nullity or for Pauline licence.[39] The style in which the judgements were reasoned, and the results at which they arrived, were almost a caricature of amateur legalism, a strict adherence to principle even exceeding that of the early district officers' courts. Hine recalled that 'Bishop Smythies laid down for us that we have always to think first of the purity of the Christian Church, and not to be biased by sentiments of pity for individuals.'[40]

We might look, for example, at the case of K.O. and S.J. K.O. was a 'heathen' with a 'heathen' wife, who left him. A few years later, after his baptism, he married a 'slave woman' (S.J.) and had two children by her. Then her relatives came and claimed her, redeeming her for fifteen shillings. The assumption seems to have been that if K.O. had wanted his marriage to continue, he would have gone along to live with his maternal kin. But he did not. His application was for Pauline licence in the first case, and nullity in the second, on the grounds that the woman's consent was not properly given. But the court would not take the easy way out in the second case. K.O. was now a Christian. His marriage must be preserved, taking precedence, it must be noted, over the redemption of a woman from slavery. The court did not think 'there is anything inherent in the conditions of slavery out here to constitute an *impedimentum dirimens*. I should say that a slave out here is as capable of giving consent as any woman.' It ignored the realities of the claims of the female's kin, saying, 'it is open to the wife to "leave father and mother and cleave to her husband."' Watkins' *Holy Matrimony* was consulted and it did not say that slavery was an impediment to marriage. 'The fact that S.J. has now been persuaded by her relatives to desert her husband does not affect the case. K.O. must therefore be regarded as the husband of S.J. and unable to marry anyone else during her lifetime.'[41] Both the Boma and village courts would have ended the marriage, but if K.O., and others similarly pronounced upon, wanted to remain under the mission's patronage, they had to regulate their marital affairs accordingly.

The case book presents a source of descriptions of the marital patterns of the mission's adherents and also one of the workings of the village courts in judging marital matters for many of the cases had already been the subject of adjudication in the villages. We can see that there was a hazy area between slave status and marriage which was not easily dealt with by western legalism

156

and which the Church's emphasis on marriage overrode and obscured. This can be illustrated again by the case of a woman who was given by her clan when a small girl as a slave in order to redeem a male clan member who had been captured for committing an offence. When she grew up she had been given away in marriage, and baptised. Then her relatives exerted their right to buy her back. 'In order to remove all taint of her period of slavery her people have absolutely refused to allow her husband to follow her, and in order to clinch the matter immediately married her off.' Once again the marriage was more important to the Church than the redemption from slavery. There was surprise at the inability of the woman and her family to see that what had been done was wrong, and at the impossibility of arbitration because of 'horror of anything suggestive of slavery'.[42]

The kind of circumstances involving the survival of the status of slavery and of 'inheritance' of wives with which the missions had to deal can be illustrated from further cases. They show how the initial condemnation of these local institutions was replaced by the aim of preserving marriages so that the mission's interest came around to be centred on the observance of the technicalities of local practices. In case no. 50, B.O.'s 'real wife' was a slave woman who was taken away by her owner in 1915 and 'reported to have been either killed or sold to the coast'. B.O. then took another wife F., but the Church refused to let them take communion because his slave wife (note that this marriage was treated as valid) might not be dead. B.O. later inherited another wife and abandoned F. His marriage by inheritance, as it was legitimate in village eyes, was that which the mission endorsed, ruling that his marriage with F. was null. In case no. 14 in October 1918, T.W., a Christian, inherited a Christian woman, K., from his uncle, and entered into a 'village marriage' with her with a goat sent in witness of the agreement to the 'continuation' of the affiliation of the woman to the family she had married into. The woman was very much older than her inheritor and there was no cohabitation. After six months K. decided to return to her own family, who returned the goat as was customary when inheritance was refused. In 'customary law' and in real life the marriage was over and one might have expected a mission, which had earlier inveighed against the low status of women and the 'inheritance' of wives, to regard it as over also. But they would not. The marriage

> was made publicly, in accordance with the ordinary native customs; and a public contract of marriage between two Christians is, according to Mission custom, binding. The Christianity of the two parties is taken to imply that the contract they make is a monogamous, indissoluble union.
>
> According to Watkins' *Holy Matrimony* the fact that the marriage was not consummated is not relevant; the essence is the public contract.

The 'only ground' the court could see for nullity 'is that there is no explicit consent to a monogamous indissoluble union . . . but this conclusion would have very far-reaching effects . . . . Normally Christians who marry must be presumed to have a Christian intention.' This absurd presumption was not

157

treated as reality by the law of England, but to many of the missionaries Africa was a kind of *tabula rasa*, upon which the first principles of religion, morality and law could be written.

What I suggest we can see happening here is a parallel to the course taken by the Boma courts. The mission court used the observances of a proper village marriage as evidence of an intention to form a life-long union. It therefore became important for village priests, as they were unable to conduct marriages themselves, to insist upon the observance of formalities. Here their pressure combined with that of the Boma for a rigidity and technicality which had to be imposed over an apparent reluctance to observe custom properly. As the U.M.C.A. court remarked in case no. 3, there was 'great laxity and confusion of ideas' on marriage questions. A customary order would have to be imposed to form a base for the superimposition of Christian marriage.[43]

It is clear from the cases that those on the fringes of the Church were not prepared for the pitfalls which accompanied their pattern of sexual unions. It could not have been obvious what kind of association the Church would not turn into an indissoluble union, making future changes of partner and continuing Church membership incompatible. In case no. 8 a man and woman lived together and had a child. The man went away for two years, and on his return they had another child and lived together. In 1920, six years after the union was formed, the man left. Here was an obviously real marriage but the Church court treated it as void. No formal permission had been given by the *nkhoswe*; only one goat had been paid. It could not be 'presumed' that the man had intended a Christian marriage as he was only a catechumen. 'The evidence', the court said, 'seems to show that he hardly meant as much as an ordinary native marriage but merely a union a little better than open sin'.

The cases also illustrate much about the lives of the parties. Long periods of male absence are common in the case histories. In no. 4 the petitioning husband was away from 1910 to 1915 during which time his wife went to live with another man. In no. 7 the parties were separated by the war from 1917 to 1919. The woman married again with the consent of her relatives. The case was dealt with in the village court which ordered the second husband to pay compensation of three pounds, ten shillings to the first. (The Church court ruled that the first marriage was indissoluble and continuing.) In another the husband was away from 1920 to 1922. In his absence his wife fell ill, was reclaimed by her relatives, was remarried and refused to return. In another the wife returned home to her mother's village when her husband left for work and petitioned for nullity. In another the husband left for South Africa and 'In the village this was held to annul the union,' and the wife soon remarried. In another the husband was away for six months during which his wife, with the concurrence of her relatives, went to live with the mission storeman. (That this was seen as a conclusive remarriage was evidenced by the fact that the storeman had her entered on his tax paper.) The first husband brought suit in the village recovering two pounds but not the woman.[44] In another the husband had been absent two years, his whereabouts unknown. He was not a Christian, and his wife, who was, made an application for dissolution under Pauline licence, in which she succeeded. But one of the assessors commented, 'Husbands stay six, or even seven years away often. They ought to support their wives when away, but do not. Sometimes the Boma gives a divorce. If this was allowed by us a hundred wives at Likoma could apply tomorrow for nullity, a Divorce, or Pauline licence.' The Church was preserving the bonds of dead marriages which was the price women had to pay for membership.

Indeed it seems that it was women who eventually paid a price for the Church's principles, which had offered them so much at first. The Church's principles, just as they did not fit at all into the kind of life-patterns described above, did not fit with the real position of women. In Masasi in 1893 Bishop Hornby advised the wives of polygamous marriages when he was baptising them that they had to tell their husbands that cohabitation must cease with them if their husbands went off with others. 'I knew it was quite against the custom of the country for a woman to take any action, but it is for the church to establish new customs . . . . I hope some of the women will take the highest line.'[45] The pious hopes of improving the lot of women and the condemnation of local marriage were not for long the ruling notes. Accounts like Johnson's and Proctor's from the early period,[46] from which it appeared that much of the missions' time was occupied with the protection of women, soon became less frequent.[47] Missionaries, like government officials, became disturbed and irritated by the apparent lack of discipline among black women that the white presence was causing. The attitude of G. E. Butt, who travelled in North Western Rhodesia in 1908, became representative. Young women, he wrote, neglected their homes and defied their husbands; 'some even thrash their husbands . . . . the women need the Gospel here, not so much to save them from the tyranny of men, as from their own degradation.'[48] Though the missions remained a liberating influence on the lives of a few women, mainly full-time adherents,[49] they aligned themselves, as far as village women were concerned, with the forces of a male-ordered stability. The hostility of the mission churches and their courts and synods towards divorce; the atmosphere of holding the line against a flood of breaking marriages; the practice of explaining and discussing decisions in order to impress Church law on communicants and church elders, all these created a climate of enforced marital discipline. After the initial attack on pagan marriage the Church was inflexible about those it had blessed and its policies contributed to the growth of legalism out of local arrangments. Many of the early leaders of African colonial society were converts. They shared with the older leaders a common interest in marital stability, whether Christian or pagan, and they grasped as a new weapon the rule-ordered discipline of their new rulers, both sacred and secular.

9

Slaves and masters

For the first decades of the rewriting of African history, slavery in African societies was not a fashionable subject of study. The particular sensitivities of African studies were such that slavery as a term was reserved for something done by whites to Africans and the anger and outrage aroused by this part of the African historical experience obscured the existence of slavery in pre-colonial African societies. Miers and Kopytoff have noted the hesitation of western scholars 'to dwell upon institutions such as slavery or human sacrifice for fear of contributing to the unfavourable stereotypes held by the wider public' and the tendency in discussing African slavery to 'present it as almost entirely benign'.[1] African scholars were early on the defensive. As Sarbah wrote in 1904 of West Africa, 'On proper analysis of the incidents of this condition, one is quite reluctant to give the name "slave" to persons in bondage.' Proper analysis generally pointed to the slave as 'part of the family', living happily and in terms of virtual equality with the rest of society.[2] This approach has been common in recent writings. Munro, for example, wrote; 'Kamba slavery was of a mild form: women captured on raids became the wives of Kamba men, although they had a lower status than Kamba wives, and the children were brought up as members of a family.'[3] Slaves, wrote Turner, were not 'markedly exploited' though 'female slaves were often taken as concubines' and 'slaves had to work in the gardens of their owners.'[4] This looks like the fullest sexual and economic exploitation the organisation of the society offered. Slave status was fiercely resented and 'slave wives', that happy mixture of sexual and economic exploitation achieved only by the most daring of planters, left their 'husbands' in large numbers as soon as opportunity offered. That there was a connection between slavery and the other institutions of kinship is correct, but this had little to do with the benignness or otherwise of slavery. This has been nowhere better expressed than by Henry Maine:

> What then is meant by saying that the slave was included in the family? Not that his situation may not have been the fruit of the coarsest motives which

160

activate man. The simple wish to use the bodily powers of another person as a means of ministering to one's own ease or pleasure is doubtless the foundation of slavery, and as old as human nature. When we speak of the slave as included in the family, we intend to assert nothing as to the motives of those who brought him into it or kept him there . . . [only that the] ideas of mankind were unequal to comprehending any basis of the connection *inter se* of individuals, apart from the relations of family.[5]

In their illuminating introduction to *African Slavery* Miers and Kopytoff underline the connection between slavery and kinship institutions generally. The realm of kinship and marriage in Africa, they write:

> is characterised by the acquisitions of various rights-in-persons, including rights to the whole person, in exchange for wealth . . . . What gives African 'slavery' its particular stamp, in contrast to many other slave systems, is the existence of this 'slavery'-to-kinship continuum . . . . 'Slavery' in Africa is simply one part of a continuum of relations which at one end are part of the realm of kinship and at the other involve using persons as chattels. 'Slavery' is a combination of elements, which if differently combined – an ingredient added here or subtracted there – might become adoption, marriage, parentage, obligations to kinsmen, clientship and so forth.[6]

More recently, approaches to African slavery have become considerably less restrained.[7] There is a new emphasis on the inequalities in pre-colonial African society, and in the elements of force and power necessarily involved in the master/slave relationship. Analysis of slavery in terms of its essential feature – as a labour system – has contributed to these shifts in perception. In contrast to Munro and Turner a recent account of Lozi slavery emphasises the 'terrible hardships of the slave condition', the 'complete contempt' for slaves, and the cruelty and exploitation.[8] Miers and Kopytoff have been attacked for a relatively euphemistic approach.[9] Yet while I think that the newer efforts to break with the absurd image of a benign slavery can only increase understanding both of pre-colonial societies and of the effects of abolition, it may be that a concentration on the unpleasantness of the position of slaves might, by default, be overemphasising the difference between 'slavery' and 'freedom'. Lovejoy's lower-key realism expresses the narrowness of the difference well: 'Slaves and peasants were similar,' he writes, 'but slaves worked more and harder.'[10] And Balandier reminds us, in the context of relations between generations, that 'Inequality was . . . rooted in the very heart of the relationships governed by kinship.'[11]

Thus while recognising power and exploitation we must, I think, retain the emphasis on slavery as part of a continuum of relationships involving differential status, control and constraint. This emphasis is vital for the point which I want to make, which is that we cannot understand the effects of the 'abolition' (or preferably 'non-recognition') of slavery by the legal system of the colonial power in isolation from kinship institutions like marriage, parentage and so on.

If one wanted to express it in conventional lawyers' terms one could say that slavery was an important institution of the family law. When it was no longer available as a recognised justification for control the other institutions of the 'family law' would be affected and would respond. Miers and Kopytoff write, in the context of the emergence of slavery, that there was a 'strikingly high demand for people, expressed in a general high circulation of people among social groups, – a circulation not simply of acquired persons but of women, adoptees, clients, relatives. The high demand is related to a view of people as a resource.' The development of a customary law cannot, therefore, be understood outside of the general context of the struggle for control of persons. It seems clear that, as the economic changes which accompanied colonialism began to alter the material basis of Central African society, the demand for control of persons would alter also, but in the period with which I am dealing, the early colonial period, this was not yet apparent to anyone. Ways of acquiring control over persons were still seen as crucial following the abolition of slavery and they were made the more so by the early perception that white courts were assaulting marriage laws in general. The abolition of slavery, combined with the turmoil in the area of male control over women generally, were responded to together by the development of the customary law. 'Africans continued to seek to enlarge their households and kin groups, to increase the circle of relatives, to acquire more wives and children, more clients and dependents,' write Miers and Kopytoff, commenting on the 'relatively undramatic' consequences of the abolition of slavery. But in doing this they had now to make use of a set of rules about the control of others which would be legitimate in the eyes of white courts.[12]

While the analysis in *African Slavery* points us in the right direction regarding the necessity of seeing slavery in the context of rights in persons generally, it hugely overemphasises the precision with which these rights were defined. Rights were, they write, 'precisely defined in law' and 'while all social systems in the world can be analysed in terms of such rights Africa stands out *par excellence* in the legal precision, the multiplicity of detail and variation, and the degree of cultural explicitness in the handling of such rights.' But 'legal precision' and multiplicity, complexity and cultural explicitness are not the same and treating them as if they are obscures the process by which 'legal precision' emerges.[13] All the rights in persons in the slavery to kinship continuum, while analytically describable as rights, represented enforced or negotiated relations of power. Legal precision, in the sense of rules invented prior to and outside of actual relationships, was demanded only by one group, the white magistrates and judges. Their demand for the pre-definition of rights was contemporaneous with their assault upon one area of legitimate power over persons. As 'legal precision' gradually came to be given to 'rights in persons', therefore, they embodied the attempt to make good the loss of a legitimate claim to control of slaves.

162

SLAVERY OBSERVED AND RECALLED

During the nineteenth century in Central Africa the demand for, and trade in, slaves, both for internal use and external sale, mounted.[14] I am concentrating on the second half of the century. With the rise of the Ngoni and Yao and Bemba states, and the growth of Swahili trading enterprise from the East coast, the numbers of conquered, captive and unfree in Central African society, and the risk of losing one's freedom, increased. Slavery thus became a growing social institution: first in the sense that the pool of powerless who could be traded became larger (and, as the opportunities to trade increased, so more people were at risk), and secondly because of the large numbers of women captured by the newly dominant states and forced into 'slave-marriages' in which their kin were powerless to protect their interests and their children became slaves of the captor lineages. As one Chewa author recalls, as the trade grew 'Certain of the villages called up serfs they had and sold them to the traders .... Everyone was obedient to the chief or headman. One reason for this was that when the Arabs came seeking slaves any person who was unruly or troublesome would be sold in exchange for a gun, or for cloth, salt or beads.' The trade was not only connected with the maintenance of authority: after the Ngoni wars, Ntara writes, 'It was a pleasure and prestige to own slaves. It was a source of wealth,' and people traded them for guns and cloth. 'This was not all. Usually slaves were used to pay for damages or fines just as it is with people who have cattle.'[15]

This is a crucial point, with implications throughout the 'legal system'. For a system based upon reciprocity and compensation for loss caused can only exist where adequate compensation can be given, and as people became a viable currency, so their exchange in the settling of disputes increased. One Portuguese account of a Yao slave caravan from as early as around 1820 describes not prisoners of war: 'but all are the victims of some crime, either real or supposed; and among them there are crimes which, though committed by only one individual the onus falls on his entire family, and most remote relatives; thus it is not rare to see father, mother, sons, daughters, nephews etc. being sold in the same fair'.[16] It is probable, as Alpers says, that the increased demand for slaves caused criminal liability to be more widely defined and also caused compensation in the form of slaves to increase. As Phiri tells us, powerful lineages took advantage of weaker ones to acquire dependents. In the event of a legal dispute the weaker side would be forced to surrender a child in addition to the normal compensation in goats or hoes.[17] As Mwashitete recalled of life at Mkoma's:

> Girls are sometimes given in payment for quite small offences. For example if the chief calls his people to work in the fields, and one of them does not come, he may have to pay for his absence with his daughter. If a man is forbidden by Mkoma to set the grass of the pastures on fire and does it, perhaps by accident, he may have to give his daughter.

163

Power was obviously a crucial factor in what was 'customary' compensation and it could be randomly exercised, as is clear from the recollections of a woman from Karonga: 'People do that in our land. If a man has a claim on another and it is not settled, he seizes goods or children, and he who has been made to suffer innocently must go and beg the accused until he gives satisfaction.'[18] Early white observers were puzzled by the apparent flexibility surrounding the statuses of slave and 'free', which to them were of such paramount importance and so widely different. Proctor found most confusing 'the condition of slavery which prevails here, permitting those who have owners, but are not wives or workers (the latter being chiefly children) to live in the village like free inhabitants'. Rowley, writing of the same period and area, thought that people could be enslaved for debt or for breach of custom and that 'The Mang'anja were most ingenious in devising means for the forfeiture of their own freedom.'[19] Johnson remarked on the ease with which status could be altered: 'a free man whose position had been acknowledged on all hands, would submit to become a slave, perhaps after the decision of a law suit.' His status could be restored if his kindred redeemed him.[20] The combination of the growing slave trade and the centralised power of the conquest states building upon societies with status differences had implications for dispute and compensation as a whole, and abolition likewise would have far-reaching effects on such a system. Melland remarked acutely, 'since we have de-monetised the high currency of the country – slaves – it is very hard indeed to pay the high fees exacted in smaller currencies – goods.'[21] Powerful persons who had come to rely upon the exaction of slaves in the settlement of claims, and whose power had been buttressed by the ability to sell dependents to traders, had now to seek new means of control.

ABOLITION AND THE COLONIAL COURTS

Slavery in Central Africa in the second half of the nineteenth century had become important in a basic way to economies, polities and lineages. As McCracken remarks, 'The central reason why slaves continued to be sold in Central Africa was that slave labour was a fundamental feature of most Central African societies.' Land was plentiful, labour was scarce, and early white observers noted slaves put to use in agriculture, building, and rural crafts.[22] MacDonald's observations on the Malawi highlands were typical, that female slaves, more valued than men, became a man's 'junior wives and he keeps them busy in hoeing the farm, and all such female duties.'[23] The conquest states incorporated large numbers of slaves, and social systems like that of the Ngoni were built upon and ideally adapted to the acquisition of slave wives both for the building up of numbers within the patrilineage (which was far harder if substantial dowries had to be paid for wives) and for use by the chiefs to distribute among followers as part of the essential cement of political leadership.[24] And once the pool of unfree became larger and more negotiable so slavery became an important part of political power and lineage growth among 'matrilineal' peoples as well. For the chiefs in a matrilineal polity the accumulation of slave wives was the only way of building their own lineage because the children of their 'free' wives were subject to their maternal uncles.[25] For matrilineages cannot normally grow in the same way as patrilineages by the accumulation of 'free' women; their numbers of women are finite. The only way a matrilineage can rapidly expand in numbers, as Miers and Kopytoff pointed out, is by acquiring 'slave' women. Thus, if slave women were available, they were a vital acquisition for 'matrilineal' as well as 'patrilineal' men, and slave wives were widespread in Central African society. In nineteenth-century Chewa societies women were 'a special target of the slave hunters', the most highly valued being females of child-bearing age. Slave marriage was widespread and early in the twentieth century, 'Chewa elders still spoke nostalgically about it. They maintained that women who had been captured in war, or purchased in slave caravans made better wives than those married under regular matrilineal custom. They were the property of the husband.'[26]

The greatest impact of abolition, therefore, was upon marriage, coming as it did in combination with early administrative and missionary aims towards improving the position of women, and with the breaking of the power of the 'patrilineal' conquest states over 'matrilineal' subjects. One of the most important bonds attaching women to men was under attack. Slave marriage was a distinctive form of power over women in that it gave to men not only command of the labour of women but also control over the fruits of their reproductive capacity without any of the payments or reciprocal duties involved in ordinary marriage. A slave wife, having no kin, could not divorce her husband and, obviously, no question of uxorilocality was involved. Clearly then lineages which had lost control of their women in this way had suffered an important loss and would be eager to redress it when opportunity offered.[27] I should stress, however, that marriages cannot simply and clearly be divided into 'slave' and 'free', that the boundaries of slave status were not easily fixable and that 'regular' marriages were commonly in a state of incompletion, confusion and dispute as to the rights and powers of the lineages making the exchanges. Also, of course, slavery did not only affect women, and slaves were not necessarily always acquired for a predetermined purpose, and their function and position would change in the course of their lives. Peter Kilekwa's autobiography is illustrative. He was captured as a child near Lake Bangweolo and sold to a 'man from the coast' who took his purchase back home only to find that the boy's mother could not afford the eight yards of calico ransom which was asked. Only then was he put into a slave caravan which was unsuccessfully attacked by the Ngoni, and which took him to Lake Malawi, north of Mponda's, where his owner died of smallpox, bequeathing Kilekwa to a friend. A year later he was bought by a Yao and, after a period of work as a house servant, was taken to trade at the coast. Once there he was sold to an Arab and put on a

165

dhow for Muscat, being rescued in sight of land by the British and taken to a mission school.[28] He might, of course, never have reached the coast, being redeemed as a child or remaining, and living and marrying, as a man of slave status in the Yao community, which he might have sought to leave once the British had come.

Thus all kinds of rights in property, of male/female relationships, and ideas about status were thrown into confusion by the establishment of a superior authority which did not recognise the legality of servile relationships. As Swann experienced it, 'Thousands who had been carried away as slaves in their youth, found old relatives still alive, and a general migration ensued from one district to another, bringing all kinds of intricate relationships and claims to be adjudicated in our law courts.' Only by bearing this in mind can one hope to understand fully the type of cases which were brought to the white courts for judgement and the uses which people sought to make of the courts. One of the early missionaries, still holding court at Likhoma in 1900, found that he was 'constantly having to hear and decide cases – lawsuits – which at the root involve their notion of property in persons . . . . I don't know what the marriage customs and laws would be without it.'[29] 'Freedom in thousands of cases set whole families at variance,' Swann wrote, 'their claims being so well balanced as to make it no easy task to decide in a British court.'[30]

In the face of a flood of complex litigation Livingstone's heirs gradually retreated from moral fervour and abolitionist sentiment. Some 'slavery' cases were reasonably simple, for example those involving a political readjustment between Ngoni and their former subjects. The Boma found that it had to intervene more than once in cases where slaves had fled and were later reclaimed. In 1908, for example, a group of Tumbuka moved from the Mzimba district in Malawi. Chimtunga raided their village. The complainants told the court that they had been 'Chimtunga's slaves' but now wanted to be independent once more. Similarly Kamzoole's, a Chewa village, raised a complaint that they had been 'Mwase's people and taken in war by the Angoni', and asked to be freed. In the case of *R.* v. *Munanka*, heard in Kafue, the accused was tried criminally for seizing children in compensation for an unpaid debt. A man had died and the chief, having killed a cow for his funeral, laid claim to a beast in return from the dead man's relatives, taking the children when it was not paid. Evidence was given that, failing the payment, 'they would remain with him and become his slaves,' i.e. they would work for him and he would control their marriages. It is notable how long it took before the Boma court was approached. The incident took place two years after the establishment of white rule in the area, and it was not until 1915 that a claim for the return of the children was made. The case was heard by E.S.B. Tagart, who took a moralistic line. The chief, he said, 'speaks clearly of the Chila custom . . . if nothing were given him they would remain with him and become his slaves.' A three-year sentence with hard labour followed.[31]

166

Declaring serf villages 'free', punishing fresh seizures and taking no notice of slave status in criminal proceedings involved few problems. (The plea that the complainant was a slave, raised as a defence to a charge of assault, appears several times in the court books.) But there were more complex issues. In North Eastern Zambia in 1907 a case came before the court in which a man claimed the freedom of a female kinswoman who had been captured by the Ngoni. P.E. Hall, the magistrate, ruled that the claimant 'must offer a reasonable sum for the redemption of a slave of long standing'.[32] This, rather than a wholesale liberation which ignored former claims, became policy generally. As one of the native commissioners, Coxhead, wrote of the Ngoni and Chewa areas of Zambia, it was difficult to tell whether someone was a slave or 'pure-born', and that while slavery was not recognised by the government 'in the native court civil actions still occur connected with property or marriage arising out of complications, the result of some of the parties having been slaves, or children of slaves, before the British occupation. The native courts, therefore, have to recognise slavery as having been "legal" until the year 1898.'[33] In most of North Western Zambia:

> the principle adopted seems to have been to take no notice of the existence of slavery until a concrete instance presented itself in the shape of a slave asking the Native Commissioner's Court for his or her freedom. The Native Commissioner would then ask what redemption price the slave or relations were willing to give and whether the owner was willing to accept the price offered. Agreement being arrived at and the price paid or promised, the slave was declared free.[34]

A similar attitude appears to have prevailed in Malawi. Though from the records it seems that few cases came before the courts, slavery did not die a sudden death. In 1917, for example, a case was reported from Nkhota-Kota concerning a headman who had died, leaving 'several slave wives'. These had all been inherited by his heirs, though one, who was a Christian convert, had refused marriage by inheritance to a Muslim and her refusal had been endorsed by the Boma court. This refusal did not change her status in the eyes of her inheritor. In 1917, when she was about to contract a Christian marriage, the brother of her former husband appeared and took her away as his property.[35] Yet on the whole there was not much which troubled the administration. In 1923 when two children were apparently offered for sale in the Chiradzulu district the magistrate reported that 'a mild form of slavery' continued to exist. The secretariat minutes commented imperturbably, 'there is not much that is objectionable from a native point of view.' Normally the district officer did not interfere beyond 'refusing to uphold any claims to control the movements of a slave, and announcing when occasion arises that there is no slavery in British territory and everyone is free'.[36]

Yet this missed part of the point. For some of the disputes, and interest, arising out of the status of slavery concerned not the freedom of movement of persons but claims arising out of the incidences of slave status. The

167

difference between slave and free in the community did not concern western notions of personal autonomy but were about whose lineage children belonged to, who controlled their labour, who had the right to bridewealth and other incidentals like the passing of property or compensation for death or injury. A neat illustration of this comes out in the evidence of a Chewa headman on marriage law, given in 1915, where the difference between slave and free is seen simply as being a matter of which lineage children were to belong to:

> 'Years ago, if a man met a woman lost in the bush she was called his slave wife,' he said tactfully. 'If after having borne children the mother died, the children would go to the father or his relations. If anyone wished to marry that child they would ask the father's family. For a free wife on her death the children would go to the wife's relations with a present of cloth. A suitor would approach the wife's relatives.'[37]

The continued recognition or non-interference with slave status meant that the marriage and kinship consequences of slave marriages might still be regarded as legal in the Boma courts, even though the political power which held these marriages together was broken and the slaves themselves were seeking 'divorces' in large numbers. Even where women were 'freed', they could not necessarily claim their children. Furthermore, 'freed' slaves were not always able to move elsewhere. As I have shown above chiefs claimed a control over the right of movement and settlement of persons, and this piece of customary law was eagerly seized upon by the new district administration, itself anxious to control movements and prevent the splitting of villages. Though the Lozi case is a special case in the story of abolition I will describe it briefly because it differs mainly in that the administrative arrangements institutionalised what was happening elsewhere. The Lozi country was not subject to the repugnancy clause but in 1906 the North Western Rhodesian administration prevailed upon Lewanika to issue an abolition proclamation. Yet none were to be free except on the payment of a two-pounds ransom, a rule which was strictly enforced. The proclamation recognised the right of chiefs to demand unpaid labour; and it also provided that 'No man or woman set free . . . may leave the kraal of his or her late master to reside elsewhere without the permission of the head of the kraal.'[38] It was not until 1916 that the administration decided for Zambia as a whole that no claim founded upon slavery would henceforth be recognised, that the two-pounds ransom was abolished, and that dowry and compensation claims arising out of slave status would be dismissed. In Ila country in 1917 the administration made an effort to explain its refusal to recognise slavery, and as a result 'scores claimed their freedom.' Among the Lozi, the administration believed, slave-owners were 'accommodating themselves to the new state of things.'[39]

The government's optimism about the Lozi was misplaced. In response to the abolition of the two-pounds ransom the Lozi *Khotla* tightened the law on chiefs' control over movements, requiring persons to make an application through their headman to the *Khotla*, and it proposed a law punishing people 'who shall by reason of being free be insolent or contemptuous towards his chief, *induna* or headman'. Former slaves, the Ngambela explained, 'disregard the authority of the *Khotla* . . . they . . . behaved very rudely.'

Lozi slave-owners were far from reconciled to the freeing of slaves and were determined to use their customary legal institutions to maintain the relations of subservience between slaves and their former masters. Those who would not accept the continuation of servile relationships the *Khotla* sought to expel from their country with their families, and without their property, to their 'homelands'. In 1921 one former slave attempted to claim the freedom of his son and daughter – 'freeing persons and taking slaves from their owners', as the *Khotla* put it; 'who gave you the right to free people here in this country . . . . you have no right to free anyone here because you are a person carried off as a slave.' In the Lozi master's view the slaves had to stay and 'obey the laws of the *Khotla*', or leave. But this was a harsh alternative. As the 'slave' in this case replied, formerly the Lozi had refused to let them go, while now they were trying to drive them off to places from which they had been carried off as children, and where they were now strangers.[40]

We must feel the temper of the Lozi response to the attack on the relationships of authority and subservience, for it was not an easy adjustment anywhere and the resentments aroused are an integral part of the context of dispute and disruption in marriage and kinship with which it is contemporaneous. The way in which marriage, inheritance and slavery continued to be interlocked in disputes can be illustrated by the case of Chimfia heard in Ndola in 1915. Chimfia had been married, and then, of her own accord, divorced, refusing to live with her first husband, who wanted also to marry her niece. But her family were not able to pay to redeem her from her first husband, so Sukama married her, paying in strings of beads, hoes and cloth. But Chimfia fled to her home, and Sukama, following her, was killed by a lion. Sukama's brother Shapera demanded compensation, and the family, unable to pay, handed Chimfia over as a slave. Shapera's wife, Changa, described as a 'Mlamba headwoman' then became ill. Her illness was blamed upon the widow, Chimfia. As she related in court, 'Changa said her husband . . . must pay her something. He paid Changa with my daughter, Mubolwa, and said that if Changa got well it would prove the reason of the sickness and he would pay her more'. Changa recovered and Chimfia was handed over to her. This last transaction took place after the establishing of the Boma at Ndola, but Chimfia 'had no thought of complaining there'. 'Chimfia has never been redeemed,' Changa told the court, 'and is still my slave.' In evidence of customary law, the headman and others assured the court that Shapera had a right to pay Chimfia to Changa because she was the widow of his brother and had not been redeemed, and that Changa had a right to compensation as Chimfia was 'recognised as her slave'.[41]

Forms of servitude and consciousness of servile status continued to exist even if last-resort legal power to enforce them had been taken away. Turner found that slavery had been clung to tenaciously long after its abolition; that in the late 1920s cases in which people were trying to repurchase relatives were still continuing which were kept from the Boma, that feelings against recalcitrant slaves ran high in the 1920s and 1930s, and that slaves were being compelled to remain in their owners' villages. The difference was that while in the past all free Ndembu had hunted runaway slaves, after abolition by the Boma no one dared take action against slaves who emancipated themselves by flight.[42] Resentments continued on both sides. As Arthur Douglas discovered, in what he supposed to be a trivial case, a reference to the former slave status of a mission teacher erupted into a most serious matter and a 'howling and infuriated and bludgeon-armed mob' invaded the mission.[43] Mitchell observed in 1949 that 'though the institution of domestic slavery ceased to exist, the system of values upon which it was built still survives and still affects the social structure of the modern Yao.' 'Slave descent', he wrote, 'still markedly affects social relationships in modern Nyasaland.'[44] Van Velsen reported in the early 1950s that one of the villagers had told him in confidence that he was 'only a slave. The secrecy shows the humiliation inherent in the position of a slave.' Even in the late colonial period the question of slave status was 'a very live issue among the Tonga'.[45] There was acute awareness of the issue of slavery. Slaves still found it necessary to claim that it had been abolished by the Europeans and that therefore owners had no rights to their labour. On the owners' side 'blame is attributed to the Europeans who caused slavery to be abolished, thus allowing upstarts . . . to break away from their rightful owners.' While the slaves resented reference to the former status they were not in a position to do much about it.[46]

For, as Kandawire writes, while abolition had resulted in 'a large measure of free movement by ex-slaves . . . it did not necessarily restore their traditional claim to the new land to which they went to settle.'[47] Van Velsen wrote that while British law had abolished the slave trade 'it could not by itself abolish the status of slaves. The status of slaves has never been so much the result of law, theory or decree, but rather a consequence of people being cut off in space and time . . . from their kith and kin, and therefore at the mercy of the strangers among whom they lived.' This situation was not simply remedied by a change in the law if there was nowhere else for the slaves to go.[48]

Claims to land could only be made effective if the former slaves returned to settle amongst clansmen. But many were separated from their former homes by long distances, or were not first-generation slaves and had no claims in former 'homes' which they had never known, and therefore, like the former Lozi slaves, did not see return as a real alternative. As Miers and Kopytoff remark, the majority of slaves remained where they were after abolition; 'the paucity of new economic riches into which they could move *was matched by the paucity of new social riches available to them. The major change would lie in the redefinition of relationships* either into a form of clientship or in the more desirable direction of moving further into the kingroups and becoming more like kinsmen.'[49] The former masters were then given a steadily increasing role in defining the laws governing these relationships, and in administering it in the villages, and the spirit in which it was done was not one of egalitarian reconciliation.[50]

171

10

The courts and the people: law in action II

As we have seen, the European Bomas were flooded from the beginning
with marriage cases. This is explicable early on as slaves and conquered
peoples sought release, but the long-term interaction between the courts of
the colonial regime and disputes about African marriage, previously a
matter for family heads, needs some accounting for. What was African
marriage to the administrators, or the view of the administrators on marriage, to Africans? One basic context was the system of taxation: for in both
Malawi and Zambia men were responsible for paying, as well as the poll tax
on males, the taxes of their wives living in their hut or huts, with a 'plural tax'
on every wife after the first. Under district regulations all marriages had to
be registered with the Boma for tax purposes within six months of their
taking place, and failure to register was a punishable offence. While the
governments insisted that such registration was not a valid test of marriage
and that valid marriage required compliance with customary law, nonetheless registration and the receipt for tax paid came to be looked upon as
evidence of marriage. It also made crucial a definition of divorce, for only a
proper and complete break, legally acceptable, could free the husband from
responsibility for tax transferring it back to the men of the woman's family.
Chitosi, a chief in Northern Rhodesia, was described as saying in 1910,
'Divorce questions are not brought to him to settle nowadays . . . . there is
the hut tax paper to be altered which only the Boma can do.' The connections between marriage and the tax register involved the district officers in
constant enquiry into people's lives. One Zambian report is of a 'sense of
outrage caused by the personal and domestic inquisitions, such as the
examination of women's huts for signs of a male occupant.'[1]

Besides tax administration, there was a more fundamental reason why the
colonial administration interested itself so much in the preservation of
African customary marriage. For it was consciously perceived that there was
a connection between traditional social organisation and authority and the

172

stability of the colonial regime. As one of the Nyasaland judges commented (in the context of his support for the rights of *Nkhoswe*):

> It must be realised that the mingling of tribes, the slackening of discipline, the introduction of Christian rites and kindred results of European occupation have had a weakening effect on all native customs and on marriage especially .... We can either strengthen the old organisation ... or we can aim at an 'educated' community of the Americo-Gold Coast type. It is a question for Government, but facets of it appear whenever a case involving native custom is heard.[2]

Yet not only were there competing systems of marriage but people were taking advantage of the British conquest to free themselves of undesired bonds. What kind of 'customary law' would the Boma, in this fluid situation, support? Officials were conscientious in their support of 'custom' (especially against the missions) but their own views of marriage, the relative positions of men and women, and sexual morality, inclined them towards a particular definition of the customary law. Furthermore, in most cases, as Dundas was later to put it, they were not exactly experts in this field: 'we were wholly ignorant about connubial life among Africans (for that matter any connubial life, being bachelors).'[3]

In the mixed Chewa/Ngoni areas of North Eastern Zambia it was as early as 1904 that the administration expressed its embarrassment at the flood of matrimonial litigation. In the Fort Jameson district the marriage question was discussed at an *Indaba* where the administration urged elders to insist on the maintenance of custom 'to stop women causing trouble'. In 1906 the administrator complained that adultery cases were far too common and, clutching at the most commonly exchanged piece of Southern African ethnographical currency, advised that 'Chiefs and old people must insist on the payments of *lobola*.' The complaints were repeated in 1915. In Malawi also it appears that in the areas of mixed Chewa/Ngoni population more marriage cases were brought to court than in predominantly Chewa areas.[4] The evidence suggests that from the outset the former subjects of the Ngoni found it advantageous to use the new Boma courts to free themselves from marriages imposed under Ngoni rule. The simple adjurations of the administrators that this should stop were ineffective because the Boma courts, by recognising the jural identity of women, had effected an alteration in the customary system which no repetition of old rules could withstand.[5] It seems to have been women who sought divorces. Barnes wrote of Ngoni marriage that 'A woman could not on any ground secure a divorce. All my informants agreed on this point.'[6] Escape could only be procured from the Boma. The Boma, however, once adjustments had been made for repugnant usages and allowance given for female consent, was concerned that it should be applying the customary law. In theory this was simple, the logic of 'patrilineal' and 'matrilineal' systems could be discovered, and their rules applied to the appropriate peoples. But where 'patrilineal' conquerors had seized and incorporated the women of 'matrilineal' peoples, whose law applied to contested marriages? In any case, the logic of a system of personal laws broke down as it was not clear who was, for example, Ngoni and who was Chewa. As the prestige of the Ngoni declined in the Central region of Nyasaland after the British conquest, so the numbers of persons claiming to be Ngoni declined also. In the North of Nyasaland, where the Ngoni chieftaincies were not conquered, their prestige remained high with their Tumbuka subjects, and, as Cullen Young records, Ngoni marriage was adopted by young people as they 'set up a fashion of "being Ngoni"'.[7]

Thus it must be borne in mind that not only were the 'laws' in flux once the conqueror's authority had been overthrown, but the boundaries of ethnicity were themselves vague and fluctuating. Finding and applying the customary law in these circumstances was difficult. It does seem to have been the case that Ngoni-type marriage was ceasing to be the norm in the years following British conquest in Malawi as well as in Zambia. Even in the Mzimba district, where the Ngoni chieftaincy remained strong, it was noted in 1919 that the custom of completing payment of bride price before marriage was 'largely disregarded' and that this was 'deplored by all Ngoni elders'. From the Central Province the district officer at Nkhota-Kota reported in 1919 a 'break-down of the dowry system', while five years later the provincial commissioner wrote that bridewealth had fallen to an insignificant token rather than a substantial transfer of 'slaves or cattle' and that marriages were being arranged through the *nkhoswe*[8] in the Chewa manner, tendencies which he perceived as a 'decline'. In spite of these developments he insisted that marriages were invalid unless the old forms were carefully followed. Chewa women, he later wrote, had 'many more rights than those of other tribes' and he recommended that in cases where bridewealth had not been substantial (which the Bomas accepted as evidence of a Chewa, or other 'matrilineal', marriage) courts should rule that 'the woman has the right to custody of her children.' In 1917 Hodgson, the district officer in Dowa, another mixed Chewa/Ngoni area, reported that the marriage age of girls was dropping and marriage was beginning 'to follow the custom of the Achewa'.[9]

Yet there was confusion as the directions of change were neither uniform nor uni-directional. In 1926, Foulger, a district officer with the Tonga in Malawi, wrote that their marriage was 'practically a matter of purchase', that the *nkhoswe* were unimportant, and that the father had the right to the children after divorce. He tempered this picture of a uniformly Ngoni-type marriage with a warning that the courts should not enforce it to the letter 'particularly with regard to Ngoni claims from Momberas' (the Ngoni who had been overlords of the area prior to British conquest), an indication of the prevailing conflict over marriage systems and control of women and children between Ngoni and Tonga men. Only three years later another white observer, W.M.G. Turner, wrote that Tonga marriage was arranged by the *nkhoswe* and that after divorce 'all authority over the children rested in the woman's clan.' In the space of three years, two white 'experts', giving considered advice to government, had described two opposing systems of marriage among the Tonga. Both gave indications that they understood the pitfalls of trying to pin down the customary law of a defined tribal group. Turner warned against the term '"native law" for the latter expression connotes to our minds an idea of fixity which does not apply to native thought . . . . native ideas are fluid.' He had caught on to the processes of change but Foulger with his recognition of 'Ngoni claims from Momberas' was equally to the point. It was not only that ideas were changing, it was also that there were sets of ideas in conflict[10] and neither formed a regular system of 'customary law'. As Foulger complained, 'The irregular habit of paying *chimaro* after marriage is to be deprecated; it is increasingly common and leads to much litigation.' Once Foulger had identified this as a marriage payment a legal logic required that it be paid first: actual practice was 'irregular'.

Yet while there was a reluctant recognition by some district officers that there was a valid kind of marriage in which a large bridewealth was not paid, and in which the husband's control over the woman and children was not so great, on the whole the Boma tended to regard 'matrilineal' non-bridewealth marriage as a lower and irregular form and looked upon its re-emergence as a step back in legal evolution. There were many areas in which it was actively discouraged. In the North of Malawi in M'Mbelwa's area, Ngoni rule had long been established but Ngoni law had not penetrated down so far as to affect marriages among the subject Tumbuka and Chewa, which continued according to 'matrilineal' patterns. But in 1904 the first British magistrate, a man with experience of the Zulu 'patrilineal' and bridewealth system, arrived and, after four years of apparent perplexity, ruled in 1908 that only Ngoni bridewealth marriage would be recognised in future by the Boma.[11] A similar pressure was exercised by H. Harrington in the Luapula district of North Eastern Rhodesia. He reported on marriage in 1910:

> This is very definite. The only valid marriage is by dowry. There was at one time a great deal of trouble over improper marriages. The woman would leave the man and take her children with her. The man would bring an action to recover the children. It was after much of this that I got together some of the Chiefs and others and they demonstrated to me that among the general public . . . marriage by dowry was the only valid marriage. Any man who takes a woman without marriage by dowry (even if the woman and her guardian agree which they often do for reasons I will show) the woman can go off at any time and take the children and the man cannot recover them. This is the law on the subject of course it is not always followed now though it was when the natives were living in their more natural state . . . . The women are the worst offenders in this, they will not properly marry if they can help it, they want children in their own right . . . . If she marries the father of the children disposes of them.[12]

A number of points are apparent from this: that non-bridewealth marriage was alleged to be the 'norm', though even the consequences of this were not regular or automatic ('This is the law on the subject of course it is

175

not always followed'); that non-bridewealth marriage was far more to the advantage of women and their lineages; that bridewealth marriages increased male claims; and that the administation supported that part of the population which was asserting that bridewealth marriage was the norm. It is also clear that there is a puzzled conflict in Harrington's mind (as in the minds of others) as to the effects on women. On the one hand the advantages to them of the non-bridewealth system are clearly appreciated, but precisely because of this are deprecated. Giving too much freedom or legal advantage to women is seen as reducing their status. 'Still women are very plentiful and cheap and easy to procure,' Harrington wrote, 'hence the men have little respect or value for them. Anyhow the time will come when the status of women will be raised and the marriage dowry raised and a proper marriage insisted on. Then the social life of the people will be raised.' The model in his mind was bourgeois and patriarchal; the man in control, the woman bought, tied and valued – an unbought 'free' woman being accorded neither value nor status.[13] Yet he was also aware of the dangers involved. Women, he wrote, needed to be protected by a limitation on bridewealth in case the amounts paid by wealthy aliens became so large as to be unrepayable by her family if she sought divorce.

This was not a new problem. The payment of bridewealth tied women into marriages. Elizabeth Colson reports the recollections of a woman conversing about divorce: 'When we were young there was no argument. If a woman told her parents that her husband beat her, her mother would say, "you stay or we will beat you: we have already . . . accepted bridewealth for him. It is for you to return to him." '[14] Or, as Monica Wilson writes, 'A girl sent to her husband or a widow inherited by his heir, often found little sympathy if she ran home to her father.' As one of her informants said, 'I, the father, would help my son-in-law; I would beat my daughter. If I could not make her go back to him I would return all the cows and then insist on her marrying again to get all the cows from her new husband.' A chief's senior wife among the Nyakyusa told her, 'Some wives run away when their husband beat them but then they may be married to another who also beats them . . . . It is because of the cattle . . . . it is that which binds us.'[15] The impact of wage-earning and cash-cropping compounded this problem. It was now possible for individuals not belonging to chiefly lineages to accumulate marriage wealth beyond that of the marriage cattle circulating amongst their kinsmen, and it was possible for agriculturalists who had previously had no way of accumulating marriage wealth at all, now to be in a position to marry by payment of bridewealth. Harrington picked out the problem of wealthy aliens; another district officer on the line of rail in Northern Rhodesia, where the cattle market had made older cattle-owners rich, encountered another. 'When I was at Mazabuka some years ago', he recalled in 1927, 'a large crowd of women came to the Native Commissioner and complained that they were being forced into marriage with old men who had already one or more wives as the old men were the cattle owners and could afford to pay big prices.'[16] The same memorandum also observed the beginnings of this process among the 'matrilineal' peoples of the area. Under the *pax Britannica*, it claimed, parents were no longer afraid that women leaving home would be treated as slaves. 'Matrilineal' people were therefore willing to accept large sums in bridewealth and give up girls and their children.

Another district officer's report of the confused state of affairs on the Luapula gives an insight into the way the Boma intervened in the developing conflict between what was actually being practised and what was claimed as 'custom'. Chapman wrote that 'although immorality is very noticeable, the essential marriage customs necessary to make the union valid are religiously carried out in detail.' This might suggest that there was a clearly delineated working 'system' but, as he continued, 'Many of the unions of today are not marriages by native custom, but amount to the immoral union of the two contracting parties; the correct people with whom rests authority to consent to the union are totally ignored . . . . sooner or later the woman realising the fact that she is not married . . . by native custom deserts.' This done, there was no legal redress. The picture which emerges is by now familiar, a rigid and definite 'law' is being insisted upon by some in the face of it being widely ignored by others. This was not a customary legal 'system' but a situation of conflict into which Chapman wanted the administration to step by insisting on one set of claims (the ignoring of which was 'rapidly increasing') and thus making marriage prerequisites strictly observed and divorce difficult. Yet it is noteworthy that he saw fit to warn against the natural tendency of Boma officials to insist on bridewealth payments before a 'proper' marriage, in pursuit of enforcing the customary law of marriage. Bridewealth, he wrote, has 'in such cases . . . been known to have been returned by the girl's people who regard it as a purchase price'.[17]

It is now apparent that an understanding of the developments and conflicts in marriage in this period must go beyond the picture of 'matrilineal' and 'patrilineal' and systems adhered to by particular ethnic groupings, for not only were the boundaries of ethnicity blurred by conquest, intermarriage and reconquest,[18] but the boundaries of 'system' are blurred also. It appears more accurate to say that in our period no people were either 'matrilineal' or 'patrilineal', and that the kinds of marriages entered into reflected relationships of power and, above all, of wealth. It is generally the case outside of Africa as well as in it that there was a difference between the marriages of rich and poor. The former are far more likely to have been 'legitimate', with ceremony, property transfer and stability, the latter less formal, less stable, and with less in the way of specific property arrangements. The influence of the women's family of origin and their connection with children remained larger among the poor than among the rich, where the husband controlled property, wife and issue. As Monica Wilson discovered among the Nyakyusa in 1934, marriage was supposed to be patrilineal, virilocal and validated by cattle bridewealth. Yet there was a 'lively tradition' of non-bridewealth 'matrilineal' marriage, which was 'regarded as a poor man's expedient which condemned him to an inferior status'. The marriage of poor men left the control of children with the woman's lineage, and the man had far less authority over his wife. A poor man, said one of the informants, 'cannot beat his wife much. He will wrong his father-in-law who gave him the girl. She will run to her father and her father will say "Why do you beat my child? Did you give marriage cattle?" Then he takes his daughter away.' As Gouldsbury and Sheane reported of the Bemba, where the majority pattern was 'matrilineal' but where the bridewealth alternative existed: 'Parents . . . who accept a large dowry are considered to have sold their daughters and to have reduced them almost to the status of slave. Hence we frequently find fathers refusing a substantial *mpango* and surrendering their daughters to poorer, but more complaisant suitors, as against whom they reserve the right of recalling their daughters and revoking the contract.'

'Relationships between generations and between men and women', Wilson writes, 'are bound up with the control of wealth,' and wage-earning and expanding markets for produce increased wealth and altered the balance between men and women. As, 'marriage with cattle spread among the Nyakyusa the freedom of women diminished,' and 'the form of marriage was harsher in 1935 than in 1875.'[19]

As Richards noted, a Bemba woman when married did not pass completely into her husband's control and when he was absent as a labour migrant she still lived among her own people. On the other hand, when large payments had been made and marriage was virilocal and 'patrilineal' she was left living with her husband's kin and 'the heavy marriage payments made the husband and his relatives . . . anxious to maintain their control over her.' Bemba women told her, 'Ngoni women are afraid of their husbands.' Yet it appeared to her that even the relatively freer position of Bemba women was changing. She found that 'cases of wife beating are quite a common occurrence in Bemba villages and an examination of court records show that husbands claim to be able to divorce their wives for disobedience.' She attributed this to the contracting period of matrilocal residence, increased marriage payments and the consequently stronger position of husbands who were able to remove wives from their families earlier. The picture she presents is, like that of Monica Wilson, one of a decline in the position of women as marriage payments grew in value.[20] A similar picture emerges from Barnes' account of Ngoni marriage. It is clear that specific systematic rules were absent, that there was a great variation in the types of behaviour which were accepted as legitimate and a very wide gap between the behaviour and the most firmly stated norms. Contrary to the norms which the Ngoni stated, there was a low incidence of bridewealth payments and great uncertainty as to where the children 'belonged'. Even where bridewealth was paid there was no hard and fast rule on the affiliation of children among the supposedly 'patrilineal' Ngoni, whereas, among the supposedly 'matrilineal' Chewa, wealthy men, who hoped to leave an inheritance to their sons, were paying bridewealth to secure 'patrilineal' rights and prevent their sisters' sons from disputing the inheritance. By the 1940s, Barnes found that there was in operation 'no overriding principle, such as agnatic descent or a state enforced code of law, to which all decisions can be referred'. On the subject of residence, while 'in describing where a couple ought to live, Ngoni always speak in virilocal terms,' some spend their married life virilocally, some uxorilocally, with slightly fewer than half of the extant marriages in Barnes' sample being virilocal. Generally there was 'a wide variation in the norms held or . . . expressed . . . and an equally wide variation of actual behaviour. Men select their own course of action by reference to the total situation in which they find themselves when they marry. A man may try to enforce one rule on one son-in-law and another rule on another.' And in spite of their 'patrilineal' norms, the Ngoni, when faced with the increasingly common problem of the stranger man marrying a local girl while working in her area, and wanting to take her and her children back home when his job ended, reacted just as 'matrilineal' people did. Ngoni courts denied the father's right, supporting claims by the wife's kin to keep the children.

It is apparent from Barnes' account that while patrilineal norms continued to be expressed by the Ngoni of the colonial period in North Eastern Zambia, a system in which bridewealth secured rights over children was a figment of an idealised past. The position of Ngoni women was therefore not much different from that of 'matrilineal' women, though normative pressures favoured the husbands' kin. In these circumstances Ngoni women were also vulnerable in the face of increasing marriage payments. In the atmosphere of rising concern about female indiscipline a new, non-traditional 'legalisation' payment came to be accepted, and was formally legislated by the Ngoni Native Authority in 1944. The most important right established by the payment was a right to damages in the event of adultery. While the rights associated with 'traditional' bridewealth had declined in importance, the new payment grew in both value and significance, and was seen as giving to marriages the 'mark of stability'.[21]

While it is evident that in areas where the power of 'patrilineal' conquerors had been broken by the British, 'matrilineal' patterns began to re-emerge, and while this re-emergence was assisted at first by the abolition of slavery, the British insistence on 'consent' to marriage, and the early willingness of Boma courts to grant divorces, the general trend for the rest of our period appears to be that noted by Wilson. The increase in negotiable wealth, the growing sympathy of the Boma courts towards marital stability and male claims; their increasing impatience with women; the tendency towards formalisation of marriage; and the assertion of African men; all contributed to the growing control of husbands over wives and children. It is evident that there was not one regular 'legal' form of 'matrilineal' marriage and that practice varied according to the payments made. A Chewa headman, Nyongo, told the Fort Jameson court in 1915, 'Sometimes they married without a present passing; then, there would be no damages if a women left her husband. Sometimes the father received a present, but refused a consideration for agreeing to his child going to her husband's village . . . . Then the wife could return at will to her parents' village.' But finally, 'The girl's parents would pay full damages if after receiving *Chimalo* and removal consideration the girl refused to live with her husband later on.'[22] There was a drift towards the third pattern, and beyond it. Foulger noted of the Lakeside Tonga (with a high percentage of migrant workers among whom more cash was available than was the case in neighbouring areas) that there was a tendency to increase the cost of bridewealth to 'an unreasonable extent'. Turner, writing in 1919, found that 'The tendency is for greater and greater sums to be demanded' and while previously the man used to build in the wife's village, now, with the increase of bridewealth, he sought to build at his own. But marriages and children were still under the guardianship of the woman's uncles or brothers and after divorce 'all authority over the children rested in the woman's clan.'[23]

The conditions of urban life also favoured a drift towards increase of bridewealth. It was no longer possible for a man with a job in town to obtain the consent of a woman's family by a prolonged period of residence and service in her village. This was replaced by payments of cash and cloth made at the beginning of the relationship. Consequently, Godfrey Wilson observed, the payments 'are swelled out of all recognition and have a new legal significance'. And, as Richards noted, the increase in the money payment would 'greatly strengthen' the father's right over children. On divorce, repayment 'has become a matter of great importance in native eyes, owing to its increased size'.[24]

In the later 1920s, the Nsenga in the East Luangwa district of Zambia took matters yet further, demanding to be allowed to change their 'system' of customary law. The provincial commissioner reported: 'The Nsenga wish to relinquish their ancient law and custom of matrilineal descent for patrilineal descent and primogeniture. Exchange their custom of Matrilocal for Patrilocal residence and award the custody of children after divorce to father.'

Whether the Nsenga practice was as old or as tightly knit as the Boma's idea of customary law and the commissioner's perception required, it was clear why a change was wanted and why the commissioner approved. 'I do not think we should stand in the way of an alteration of the law of inheritance,' he wrote. 'The attitude the women have taken and the lack of discipline amongst the younger generation have I think led the elder men to consider this solution to retain the custody of their children and curb the immorality of their women.' The alternative, he advised, was to enforce the 'old native law' of restricting the free movement of women and tightening the law of divorce. But changing from matrilineal to patrilineal would have the desired effect 'and would not be contrary to our ideas of equity'.[25]

The desire to increase the husband's control was by no means isolated.

180

Colson noted later among the Tonga on the Northern Rhodesian plateau that 'the increase in the value of bridewealth has been seized upon as a justification for increasing the father's (i.e. the husband's) power.' She also noted the alliance of district officials and African husbands in the pressure for patriarchy: 'one or two of the farmers said that the Tonga had begun to think in these terms under the influence of District Officers. "They told us we were foolish to pay large bridewealth when we had no power to keep our children. They suggested that we should change the law." '[26]

Yet this was not a uniform tendency and there were influences, both white and African, in the other direction. Not all officials were out of sympathy with matriliny. As Moffat-Thompson, the secretary for native affairs, noted on the Nsenga proposal, 'The suggestion has no doubt come from the males.' When the urban courts in Zambia had to face the difficult problem of creating a customary marriage law the Eastern Province provincial commissioner advised that as matriliny was the normal institution throughout the territory 'urban courts should lean towards matrilineal marriages.'[27] While vocal male opinion demanded paternal custody for children after divorce, the High Court of Northern Rhodesia resisted.[28] Peter Simfukwe, from the 'patrilineal' Mumbwe, and Miriam Mufula, of the 'matrilineal' Bemba, were both pupils at the Church of Scotland school in Livingstonia, in Malawi. Mufula became pregnant and both were dismissed from the school. Simfukwe paid a large sum in damages and the pair were married in the church. Having had four children they separated. The Urban Court which first heard the dispute over custody acted in classic compromising fashion, giving each parent custody of two children. Simfukwe appealed to the Boma where a more legalistic approach was taken. Ruling on the basis of 'native law and custom' that Simfukwe's payment had been bridewealth, which gave him the right to control of the children, both the district officer's court and the provincial commissioner's court gave all four children to the father. (Patrilineal pressures were favoured in the District Courts and appeals would be rare.) But the mother succeeded in appealing to the High Court, where Robinson J. gave custody to her. His ruling was actually based on the finding that there had been no marriage in customary law; that the payment was damages for seduction and not bridewealth and that therefore the children were the mother's. But the judge also took the opportunity to travel to Bemba country to hear evidence on Bemba 'law and custom'. Simfukwe claimed that he had paid a large sum in bridewealth which was customary where a 'patrilineal' man married a 'matrilineal' woman, to get control of the children. But the Bemba insisted to the judge that foreigners had always to conform to Bemba custom and that no custom existed of paying bridewealth and taking the children as a consequence. Robinson believed them. The customary law, he wrote, was not immutable, but changes in the area of family law 'would be very slow indeed'.

I retail this at length because what was at issue here was the whole theory on which the legal administration rested, which was that each tribe had its own separate and complete body of law and custom, which altered slowly enough to be always recognisable and in force, and which could be discovered by enquiry from those who knew it. It was this emphasis on the existence of a customary law and on the recognition and preservation of ethnic identity and separateness which took precedence over the generalised approval of the drift towards male authority. The government's emphasis on the preservation and separateness of the customary law of each 'tribe' found a warm echo in the Native Authority Courts. For it was vital to the power of each Native Authority that it was the body which knew and applied to all in its area a particular body of 'customary law'. The assertion of identity and the assertion of law were connected, indeed the first in a sense took precedence over and 'created' the latter. Barnes observed that 'Ngoni say that children ought to live in their father's village, but this is a statement of the same order as the oft re-iterated remark that the Ngoni pay bridewealth. Ngoni make these statements because they are part of the index of their tribal identity, not because they have observed them to be true.'[29]

The administration lent its support to the Native Authorities, especially where a breakdown in observance of the supposed system was occurring. In reaction to the erosion of Ngoni marriage in Northern Nyasaland M'Mbelwa's council issued an order in 1933, supported by the authority of the district officer, which claimed that 'As every tribe in M'Mbelwa's district is incorporated with the Ngoni', only Ngoni and Christian marriages were henceforth to be performed and anyone 'going beyond this is a lawbreaker'.[30] Colson noted in the late 1940s that when foreigners settling among the Tonga wanted to follow their own law the Tonga courts would not let them; that the 'sense of tribal unity was increasing' and that tribal lines were 'beginning to be more strictly drawn'.[31] But these developments were taking place precisely because the claims being made were new. In a situation of economic change, British intervention and inter-ethnic contact there were no almost impermeable, slowly changing bodies of tribal law, if there ever had been. The 'law' was not there as a system of discoverable rules, in the way in which Robinson J. found it; it was made up of conflicting claims, and it is therefore crucial to understand the process by which, and the context within which, these claims were made.

MAKING CUSTOMARY LAW

The problems caused by the ambiguous and ambivalent intervention by British administrators into marriage and inheritance, the conflicting claims and the temper in which they were made, and most importantly, the processes by which custom was turned into law can be illustrated by cases revolving around inheritance of women. Here, one might think at first, was *par excellence* a custom repugnant to the proclaimed aims of the colonisers' law as it apparently treated women as chattels and ignored their right of choice of spouse. But repugnance was not quite so simple. As Tagart pointed out, the Boma courts had not found polygamous marriage to be repugnant, nor bridewealth payment, nor the necessity of guardians' consent' but had held repugnant the lending of wives, and the forced cohabitation of widows with heirs. In any case, the criteria were not fixed: 'What may not have been repugnant to good government ten or fifteen years ago may quite well be so today,' he wrote. But there was much hesitation in the approach to inheritance for fear of the effects that this would have on the discipline of women. 'It must be kept in mind,' as one magistrate, L.C. Heath, wrote, 'that by giving women . . . freedom hitherto denied them, we are doing something very contrary to long established native views, and such freedom is liable to misuse.'[32]

In November 1920 two cases involving inheritance of widows came before the Namwala Boma court. Heath pointed out that before the courts had made plain that a woman could not be forced into a marriage there had been no problem. Where marriage by bridewealth payment existed, once bridewealth had been paid a man was entitled to a replacement if his wife died, and if he died, his heir would inherit an estate with a wife. But as it was becoming more and more common for a woman to refuse to stay with the heir, difficulties arose. If she married someone else, her father would receive a second bridewealth payment while the heir's estate would be 'empty'. So it seemed that the original payment should be returned to the heir. But the payment had normally been passed on, to acquire wives for other men in the family, and would not be there for returning. So far as the British courts were concerned the answer could only be found through an enquiry into 'native law and custom'. Judge Macdonnell, careless of the effects upon the reality of female choice, instructed the Namwala court that no 'natural justice' was involved. 'If it is the custom that the claim for return of bridewealth lies against the widow's father, then that is the custom and our courts should uphold it . . . . I would make the party state his custom very exactly and prove it properly.'

So, 'custom' regarding a basic institution, already irrevocably altered in its working, was to be 'established' by a series of hypothetical enquiries from those who had been adversely affected by the change. The careful process of 'proving' the custom was embarked upon by the Boma court. 'Objects are taken to represent men and women and the matter slowly and repeatedly explained' to the witnesses, the local chiefs, and hypothetical questions posed to them. What would have happened if a woman had refused to be inherited? Would the bridewealth have been returnable? 'Yes', said one witness, but 'others might not demand back the dowry,' if the widow's relatives were 'still friendly towards him he would wait and see.' It is vital to note that in answers like this which are descriptive of real life, there are two parts, one a categorical statement, and the other a set of qualifications. The first part was useful to the court because it could be hardened into a rule, the second was not, and was forgotten. As this witness continued, 'It was much more common to persist in claiming the woman, than in demanding back the

183

dowry.' A man would only demand dowry back if he wished to sever relations entirely with the woman's family. Could a customary right to return of bridewealth be constructed from such answers if it was something that was not demanded in practice? The witness continued to stress the unlikely nature of such a demand, linking his answers to a disquisition on sexual morality: adultery used to bring mutilation, a man never divorced his wife; reclaiming bridewealth could only mean, now, that he had an eye on his neighbour's wife. A woman's relatives would never have taken her back as this would be an admission that they wanted to marry her to someone else. 'The woman would never be able to leave the husband's family; she would remain theirs until she died.' And, warming to his theme of sexual possession, he concluded, 'The matter of return of dowry has come in with the white man; this is not our custom. A woman married then, really was married for life.' This was in contradiction to his initial 'Yes' but though it was probably closer to reality, it was not the sort of answer that was of any use to the court's 'proof' of custom. What the court wanted was to work out the logic of the Ila marriage and inheritance system so as to be able to give effect to a rule which would be consistent with that logic, even though a part of the system was no longer operative. But, as the answers indicate, this type of rule and logic were not a part of 'customary' life, in which rules and rights were less prominent than the continuing flow of inter-lineage relationships. Even on the death of the woman, as the witness continued, bridewealth would never be taken back. A successor would be claimed, and if not provided 'the matter is left as the matter does not end it will be hoped that a successor will be provided to the family one day.'

This was all a long way from settling a case according to rules, which is what the Boma court wanted to do. As the magistrate burst out at another witness, 'if you leave the matter for years and years it is impossible to do anything at all.' While the Boma saw itself as finding out the customary rule with which to decide a case, the local perception of what was happening was different. Chief Mukobela was asked whether a son could sue for his mother's bridewealth if she refused marriage by inheritance. The exchange is recorded as follows:

> *Mukobela*: Today he will – because of the Europeans – but long ago he could not.
> *Court*: That is not so because we have made no such law. We have made no such laws about your manners we have followed your own customs.
> *Mukobela*: Some you follow – some you don't.
> *Court*: Explain.
> *Mukobela*: Long ago if your son married and you paid his dowry for him – and after a time [the son and his wife] parted – You the father would take back the dowry. But today if you so claim the official says – Not at all.

It is important to see what was at issue here. The court's perception is that it is administering the customary law, while Mukobela's is that it is standing in the way of parents' power. The magistrate put it to Mukobela that once a man had paid bridewealth for his son it was surely appropriate to allow him to marry again with the bridewealth he had been given. No, it was not, Mukobela replied 'because you paid dowry for your son and he, if his own heart desires to part from her – why should he? If he does so you say – I will take my cattle back – pay for yourself if you want to marry. And if they are returned you hand them back to those who helped you to pay them for your son.'[33] The customary practice (i.e. the 'customary law') of pre-colonial times was elders' authority and control over marriages. Bridewealth cattle were a lineage asset, provided by the lineage for its members, but they were more than simply a negotiable material asset, they were also a means through which authority was exercised, as Mukobela's answers show. It was this kind of practice that he wanted the Court to continue to enforce as 'native law and custom'. But the court laboriously sought to 'discover' rational rules – in this case treating bridewealth cattle as if they were money which, once given to the son, could be freely used by him – the result of which would be to replace elders' discretion and control. Once hypothetical cases and logical deductions were teased out of the witnesses the conclusions were not always in accordance with 'custom'.

Customary practice, however, as it was not rule-bound, was not necessarily regular. So we must go back again to our original question and ask why a particular version of custom should be vocalised at the time the courts were making their enquiries. It is clear that what was bothering the customary authorities in Namwala in the early 1920s, when they were asked about how to adjust the bridewealth claims arising out of widows' refusal of inheritance, was the context of marital breakdown and sexual indiscipline. As Mukobela told the court: 'We are grieved when the women leave us as we want to be married for always – And a man is angry when his son leaves his wife . . . . If a woman comes and says she wants to leave her husband and he says he wants her tell her to go back to them . . . . If you would imprison them others would fear.' Imprisoning of difficult women was not something that the new legal order would do but nonetheless a version of custom could be 'found' which would in effect make it difficult for women to leave bridewealth marriages and then enter into less restrictive arrangements of their own volition if their male relatives disapproved. As Macdonnell J. put it, 'we do not compel the widow to marry or cohabit with the Inheritor; we give her her choice.' She could remain unmarried, which he admitted was an unreal choice, or she could remarry properly. But, he asked, 'Must we . . . allow her to abuse the freedom so given her?' If she did, 'we are justified in enforcing as much as we can of the inheritance customs against her.' Under the new dispensation too, then, bridewealth had its uses as a form of control. For if the Boma was to enforce claims for its return, families would be most unwelcoming to returning women.

The Boma courts also accepted the (somewhat less onerous) redemption payments to free widows of non-bridewealth marriages among 'matrilineal' people. Before the white man came, the Ndola court was told in 1915, 'she was redeemed by a gift of clothing, or perhaps a slave.' Nowadays money, clothes or a gun were required, 'to set her free. Until this is done she is under certain obligations to her deceased husband's relatives, such as providing them with food and working for them.' No man who was not a relative of the dead husband could have sexual relations with or marry her; if they did, 'the relations of the husband may seize the man's sisters and make them slaves.' It is noteworthy that as soon as the Native Authorities were given a chance to propose rules, the East Luangwa Authority put forward a legislative proposal that 'Any man marrying a widow, the parent or guardian of whom has not returned *Chimalo* to the deceased husband's relatives, shall be punished.'[34] The 'customary law', it is clear, had been about the practices followed by men in their disputes about their rights over women. But once in the colonial period women became *sui juris*, the nature of the rules had to change. For they were now rules which defined not merely men's claims to women but women's claims about themselves. The aim was to ensure that these were defined in a way satisfactory to men. This was to be the role of the Native Authority Courts.

THE COURTS AND WOMEN

The Marriage and Divorce Ordinances of 1902 and 1905 in Malawi made female consent (which could be given by the father, who would not normally have been the guardian) necessary for a valid marriage and lack of consent grounds for annulment. These gave legal backing to the early ambition to establish the free status of women. In the mind of early administrators the status of a 'free woman' was something to be defended against the institutions of African marriage, with its apparent ignoring of female consent, and with the 'inheriting' of widows by the husband's heirs. There are however relatively few cases reported in which women specifically complained about the kind of restraints which the administration would interpret as absence of consent. As women, usually through their matrikin, appeared to have brought all other kinds of matrimonial cases to the courts, the few consent cases that did come to court must have been those which involved the special perception of status of the newly converted Christian women who were complainants or reflected the spread of bridewealth marriage. The mission churches, and the early administrators, did put an emphasis on the autonomy of female consent to marriage and regarded many of the rights and duties existing in all forms of African marriage as conflicting with this. Emily Maliwa has written that the deepest conflict between Malawian and British ideas about law was over marriage and she emphasises a total conflict between the missions' idea of marriage and the 'traditional' one. Women, she writes, looked to the missionaries as protectors and to the missions as a ladder to greater equality of status. Chiefs and male adults generally much resented, she says, the erosion of their authority inherent in the way the missions treated women.[35] But Christian marriage and mission influence affected only a small minority, as Maliwa herself notes. While the Churches may have improved the marital position of a small number of women, this was not the main thrust of 'western' influence.

In February 1931, as a consequence of the interest being taken in Britain and at the League of Nations in the position of women in tropical Africa, district officers were circulated with a questionnaire on the rights of women.[36] It seemed clear to them that women were free. In the eyes of the chief secretary it was precisely the establishment of the jural status of women at the Boma which had given them this freedom. 'One of the strongest arguments in support of the claim that native women have much independence', he wrote, 'is the way in which they bring cases, and often win them, before administrative officers or in the Courts.' There was general satisfaction that there were no forced marriages or inheritance of widows; that women could own property; and that 'where complaint is made of slavery it is usually the insult that is objected to and not the fact of slavery.' Some of the answers commented on the advantages women enjoyed in predominantly 'matrilineal' areas. The Blantyre district officer reported that the lot of Yao women, who lived with their *nkhoswe* in their own villages, was far happier than that of Ngoni women, and others emphasised that Ngoni women, unlike others in the protectorate, could not hold property independently, could not inherit, and were normally inherited. In 'matrilineal' areas, the Mlanje report said, the mother took the children after divorce even where she had been 'entirely to blame . . . exceptions to this are very rare: and almost always due to European influence.' This gives the essential clue to British attitudes. While they saw themselves as having established the free status of women, they were not at all enamoured by what they appeared to do with it. From Cholo the district officer wrote:

> In my opinion Native women in Nyasaland have much, in fact too much, independence. Husbands find it increasingly difficult to maintain order and good behaviour in their households. Women often attend beer drinks, dances, and similar functions against their husbands' wishes and neglect their wifely duties. At the slightest remonstrance or correction they are apt to fly into a rage, become abusive, cause a breach of the peace, and then fly to the Headman or the Boma and complain of cruelty.

In the face of such an attitude jural status was not going to be particularly useful. This is a lurid example but the current was running in this direction. The governor of Malawi, Kittermaster, assured the secretary of state that 'the native girl of Nyasaland is as independent and as little subject to discipline as the young Englishwoman of today', and Dundas, deputy-governor of Zambia, advised London that far from there being reason for concern about women's rights in Africa, 'anxiety is felt because girls are becoming too independent.'[37] This anxiety was felt, as the Blantyre district officer reported, by 'native male opinion', which was hostile to the female custody of children after divorce, indeed to divorce at all, and this opinion, as it became increasingly vocal, caught the ear of the government. By the end of the 1930s both the Nyasaland and the Northern Rhodesian governments shared the view that women's rights had gone too far, that marriages were becoming 'increasingly temporary' and that it was of 'the utmost importance that such a tendency should be checked'.[38]

The liberation of African women was no longer on the colonial agenda. The exposed position of the 'patrilineal' male aristocracies which had seized local wives had been well appreciated by the Ngoni Chief Chibisa's reportedly hostile reaction to a suggestion that a school be started in this area. If we agree, said Chibisa, 'we shall have no power over our women . . . . Those who are our slaves shall take over our women.' The coming of the Boma courts had helped to re-establish the patterns which had existed before 'patrilineal' dominance. But, as Hodgson, the Dowa district officer, remarked, 'The Mchewa, although matri-potestal, is not an ardent feminist.'[39] The Boma did not popularise new ideas about female rights and status but it recognised the rights of men in women's lineages. Thus the European conquest had created the conditions under which 'matrilineal' men re-established control over their women. It gave scope for the assertion of a new group of male claims, themselves as I have shown expanding in ambition, which joined those of the challenged 'patrilineal' men in asserting what the 'real' traditional law had been. These were the claims which became the customary law in the 1930s when the Native Authority Courts gained a greater degree of autonomy.

Richards wrote, in her study of Bemba marriage, 'In the old days divorce was a matter of family arrangement, more often than not.'[40] Cases were handled by family councils, or heads of families, not referred to chiefs' courts. Cases might have been referred to a chief by the inhabitants of his village or by members of his family, and if so, he acted 'in his capacity as head of the family or local group . . . rather than as head of the legal court'. Godfrey Wilson noted that the Ngonde paramount 'played little or no direct part in the maintenance of common law', and local chiefs little more: 'even they usually left whole areas of the law untouched to be enforced by the common people among themselves: the laws of marriage, for example, seem to have been normally enforced by the two families of each married couple concerned, with the advice and assistance of their neighbours.' Leaving aside the obvious conceptual problems with law and enforcement, this is an understanding like that of Richards', of marriage matters handled in a private, rather than in public, judicial realm. And Barnes too wrote that marriages were established without reference to the Ngoni state and 'in the past, before the growth of the Native Authority bureaucracy had begun, many people were divorced in the village. Kinsfolk of the two parties meet together in the village of one or the other party, discuss the marriage, and agree among themselves that the couple are to be divorced.'[41] Yet, as they all noted, the colonial administration of law now insisted on the all-embracing judicial functions of the chiefs. Also an increase in marriages over greater distances and an increase in people's mobility meant that often they could no longer rely on near neighbours and kin to, in Godfrey Wilson's words, 'give legal validity to, or place legal restraint upon, marriages'. Where men took wives whose homes were many miles from theirs, and once they could escape family discipline simply by moving, control of marriages would have to be maintained by a hierarchy of authorities stretching beyond home and neighbourhood.[42] Richards also observed the transformation in the handling of marriage disputes, which were increasingly referred to chiefs and headmen. The colonial government would no longer tolerate what appeared to them to be the summary punishment of people by members of their families.

These pressures for institutional juridification were helped along, as I have shown, by the legalising influences of the white courts. Richards shows how in 1914 Gouldsbury attempted a codification of Bemba law which gave the impression that in pre-colonial Bemba custom 'certain definite guiding principles governed the settlement reached at divorce,' and he applied these in his court. Grounds for divorce and grounds for the award of custody of children were prominent in Gouldsbury's codification and in his court there was, for example, an established tendency to award custody to the father in cases involving a woman's adultery. But Richards found 'it highly doubtful from the statements of elderly informants that a definite ruling, viz, that the guilty party lost the children on divorce, ever existed, or that it took as precise a form as he indicated.' And the manufactured custom came into being, she thought, not only because white officials favoured patriliny, but also because the Boma court was a venue well suited to the interests and aspirations of relatively well-off men in government employment whose cases predominated before it.

Barnes wrote of the Ngoni Native Authority Courts that while they, like village meetings, thought of themselves as being primarily concerned with 'teaching people to live well together' they were also:

> unlike the village, concerned with reinforcing the power of the Native Authority bureaucracy and upholding the authority of the chiefs. Hence the court gives greater weight to the formalities of marriage and the theoretical rights inhering in the different payments. The chiefs, councillors, assessors, clerks and police who make up the court are all men, whereas in the village meeting old and important women give their views and they are listened to with attention. My impression is that women are less favoured in the courts than they are in the village.

Both institutionalisation and legalisation occurred at the expense of women's interests.

These developments in addition took place in conjunction with circumstances which made it more likely that women's interests would be treated unsympathetically by the Native Courts. We have seen that considerable strains were put on marriages by the high rate of labour migration, and it is not surprising that Native Authority Courts were protective about the rights of absent husbands. Among the Ngoni, Barnes found, the adultery of a woman whose husband was absent was not condoned, wives were watched closely by their husband's kin, and courts would not entertain divorce proceedings without long delays for attempts to contact absent men. Native Court members were 'anxious to show that they do not divorce women too easily'. District officers, Barnes writes, were far more sympathetic to the pleas of deserted women than the Native Courts, and when on tour the district officers divorced 'batches of women' whom the Native Courts had turned down. Richards found the same reluctance in the Bemba courts and an atmosphere in which Bemba women who had been left behind in the villages refused to accept parcels of clothing from absent migrant husbands, 'knowing that the gift would be considered to bind them before a Native Court'.[43]

Two other developments were contributing to the tightening of Native Court attitudes. One was the gradual movement of women into towns away from the disciplinary control of families. The other was the not unconnected increase in the importance of property transactions in marriage. Richards thought that the rise in marriage payments continued because 'Bemba husbands feel it gives them some control over their wives in these uncertain days,' and property disputes figured even more largely in divorce cases. So did actions for damages for adultery. Richards questioned whether damages had been awarded 'customarily', and related them to the new circumstances. One can feel, she wrote, 'from conversations with Nyasaland clerks . . . how much they cling to the idea of damages to protect their interests under urban conditions and with wives who claimed a matrilineal kind of freedom'. Furthermore, she found, the chiefs were shocked by what they saw as the increase in sexual irregularity and tried to stop it by exacting high damages, the norm being between five and seven pounds, when the pay of an unskilled labourer was ten shillings monthly. Damages awards were rising, adulterous women were being beaten, regulations were being passed purporting to control the movement of women, and divorces were being refused. Richards concludes, 'both the native courts and the district commissioners are giving decisions in marriage disputes under the influence of a strong desire for social reform, in a situation that both authorities consider alarming.'[44]

It is important to note also that men's ambitions were not simply a form of sexist atavism. This is a period which sees the beginnings of profound economic changes and increasing amounts of property becoming involved in the cases concerning marriage, divorce, custody, dowry and inheritance. When the law of property and the law of contract in these regions come to be written about, as they must be when the period in which the appropriate economic transformations occur is dealt with, they will have to be placed in the context of their development within and emergence from the 'law' of kin relationships. Property was stabilising marriage, as Wilson shows, not only by bridewealth tying women, but by the increasing value of land reducing available rights to cultivate, and thus making it harder for people to divorce and still keep, or reacquire, cultivable land. Also changing was the nature of lineage property. The notion of lineage assets fraternally circulated and inherited was changing to one of separate property.[45] As an informant told Monica Wilson, 'even the sons of one mother quarrel now. Each one consumes his own property; he milks the cows which come from his daughters alone and his brother keeps his property separate.' The economic underpinning of the world of kinship was collapsing. In these circumstances, the law emerged.

11

Africans, law and marriage

LAW, CUSTOM AND ADULTERY

By the middle of the colonial period, many of the men of Central Africa perceived relations between the sexes to be in a state of crisis. It was in this context that the institutions of the new state pulled marriage from the 'private' to the 'public' sphere and local men struggled to assert their control over women in the new institutional processes. I will examine in this chapter two aspects of this struggle, the making of a 'customary' criminal law of adultery and the drive to fix 'customary' prerequisites for marriage, through a system of registration. Yet the male ambitions could not be directly transformed into new customary law because they did not control the colonial state and had to interact with an ambivalent British officialdom. And neither African men nor British officials could control the pace of economic transformation. The lack of power may have made the reaction more strident.

Both British administrators and African leadership were apprehensive about the social effects of economic change. This was illustrated by the policies with regard to the development of urban legal institutions which aimed at retarding the growth of an urban population and trying to ensure that urban workers were kept 'in touch with their tribal life as long as possible'. Under the Native Registration Ordinance of 1929 in Zambia, which went into effect in 1931, every man was registered in a rural area, in which he was liable for tax and in which, in theory, he was permanently resident. In terms of the Vagrancy Ordinance of 1929 men out of work in the towns were supposed to return home. After the 1935 riots a system of compulsory deportation and repatriation to 'home' rural areas was considered and an ordinance was drafted but deferred pending an enquiry into labour conditions. Repatriation and deportation were not supported by the 1938 report on labour conditions in Zambia, but in 1945 the government adopted a policy of administrative deportation without passing an ordinance. District officers were to use 'discretionary pressure rather than legal authority'. An even more severely extra-legal approach was taken towards

192

the deportation of unattached women from urban areas. The government decided in 1938 to support the native authority's practice of rounding up women and forcing them to go home, though this was not legalised until 1952.[1]

There was bound to be a difference in relations between sexes under the transient conditions of the new urban life as compared to village marriage. As these differences developed so the conflict grew between the customary controllers of village mores, marriages and alliances, and the inhabitants of the mining towns. The customary authorities drew upon an idealised version of traditional marriage, honed down into 'rules', with which they sought both to preserve their position and to provide the necessary moral stabilisation for urban dwellers. The urban dwelling men themselves, though their objective conditions were different, also relied heavily upon a newly developing customary legitimation for their strategy of establishing control over women and the stability of marriage in the towns. The battle was fought under the banners of custom but it was not to be settled until the new weapons of imported legality were brought into play.

The prolonged and angry controversy in Malawi and Zambia over how the law should respond to adultery gives us an excellent opportunity to study the way in which outraged attitudes were transmuted into the process by which the customary law was claimed and made. Both African and white authorities viewed the rate of adultery as a sort of index of moral decline and they were concerned to use the law and courts as weapons to punish and control it. Many of the district officials appeared to see the law as a leash restraining outbursts of black fornication, while African authorities consistently blamed the whites for not tying the leash sufficiently tightly. For these purposes claims about custom were particularly well suited as they provided necessary legitimation for the control of sexual behaviour. The claims were fed into the court system where they were given in evidence and 'proved' and whence they emerged as customary law. The groundswell of African male complaint about white leniency towards misbehaving women translated itself into the presentation of a 'traditional' severity to adulterers and into a pressure that the colonial legal system abandon its initial practice of treating it as a civil offence, compensatable by a cash payment, and punish adulterers as criminal instead.

The treatment of adultery was prominent among the issues that the Malawi Native Associations raised for the consideration of the administration. 'In the olden days before Europeans came in this country – adultery cases were of serious nature,' the Southern Province Native Association said in 1923. Formerly 'they used to throw the adulterer or both (man and woman) in the deep waters' and cases were therefore rare. But nowadays, they said, magistrates treated adultery matters as 'small cases', little compensation was given, and the women were given a choice between the husband and the adulterer. They warned that 'This should be realised that murder cases originate from this side.' After a 'heated discussion' (compare the Momberas Association's 'very hot discussion' of marriage law) the Association called on the courts to punish both men and women with imprisonment and heavy liability for compensation.[2]

The West Nyasa Association in 1923 put 'Divorce, Adultery or Fornication' at the top of its list of legal matters on which it addressed the government. African law, it claimed, made no distinction between adultery and fornication, which, before the white man came, had been extremely rare offences, owing to the 'strict and terrible' punishments which had been inflicted. An offence resulted in 'nothing more or less than war or death of the criminal', fighting could take place between relatives, and slaves exchanged as compensation. In the case of a repeated offence a man, although a 'free man, yet his uncles and relatives would be disposed to give him over to be burnt up alive in an open field, without mercy in the presence of a great crowd of people.'[3] In the same vein, G.S. Mwase wrote of adultery that it was the major instance in which there were:

> a lot of doubts in the way the whites decide it. [By] the country's law, this is one of the capital charge or the capital crime which [was] followed with death sentence by consuming the both culprits with fire . . . even a spear would play his flesh or her flesh until they were both perished . . . . And sometimes both culprits were to be given away by cutting parts of their bodies such as ears, arms, nose or something else in the way of emasculation . . . . But the whiteman's law is very much relaxed in dealing with this case.[4]

The scenario by now is familiar to us.

The witnesses who gave evidence about customary traditional law in the colonial courts were similarly emotionally moved and expressed themselves with the same strength. But as we come to look closely at the statements about the treatment of adulterers which were collected from witnesses in the colonial courts we will notice again the division between the extreme statement of the desired norm and the qualifications, when a note of reality creeps in as both memory and sense intrude upon indignation. Chief Mwanamkupa told a court in 1913 that:

> According to old Awemba custom adultery was criminal, the offenders being punished by mutilation, confiscation of their goods and enslaving of their relations. This applied to both Chief and common people, but the more severe punishments were generally inflicted for adultery with the wives of chiefs. In the majority of offences committed among the common people compensation was paid to settle the matter.

Similarly Mpeseni, the Ngoni paramount, told a court:

> Suppose adultery was proved, both guilty parties, man and woman, were put to death at the order of a chief. There was no question of redress by damages being paid to the injured husband . . . .
> Adultery cases could be settled, as it were, out of court, by payment to the injured party . . . if it was agreed that the case should not be brought before the chief.[5]

194

As I have shown before the chiefs and headmen presented to the courts at times a form of retroactive fantasy in which they acted in the normal course of events as judges in all cases. From the British point of view that was how a legal system worked: what the customary law was would have been what the chiefs did in their courts, while what happened outside the courts was 'extra-legal'. But in real village life there was no such clear-cut distinction between the realms of public and private. In the evidence of both chiefs we can see that the picture of the chief hearing cases and sentencing to death was qualified by a creeping admission of reality, that cases could be and were settled out of court for compensation. But it was the first picture which gradually established itself as an account of what had been the 'law'.

Some witnesses made a clear distinction between what happened in cases involving a chief, and cases involving commoners: others have a more complex picture of an interplay between private settlement and chief's power. Among the Chisenga, a court was told, death was the penalty for adultery with a chief's wife, though among commoners an offender might be 'compelled to pay heavily in slaves and goods'. In Ndola in 1915 Chief Chimwala gave his version. Before the white man came the case would be taken to a chief and 'the accused would be made to pay heavy damages and flogged and perhaps even hung. If he was a slave and had no one to pay for him he would be sold . . . . If he was friendless and unable to pay, he would probably be made a slave.' Chewa evidence gave the chieftaincy a lower profile. Chinunda told the Fort Jameson court that the Chewa had settled adultery cases by compensation which would be considerable, perhaps a slave:

> but if no compensation was forthcoming the injured party might . . . kill the adulterer. The injured man might or might not bring the case before the chief. It is quite likely he would kill his enemy first and then report it. Such a course would not involve him in much trouble. The chief would question him and he would be told to bring a present after which the matter would be closed.

Another Chewa headman said that the adulterer might run to the chief for protection and he would be ordered to pay compensation. If he could not do so he would be sold into slavery. Another said that a man would kill another who had slept with his wife but that if he did so without reference to the chief, he would have to compensate him. Another was explicit that a private demand for compensation would be made first, and that only if private negotiation failed would a 'case' be taken to a chief, who could order the offender's kin to pay compensation, or order death. For vengeance against an adulterer offending a second time, 'It was not a heavy penalty if the husband killed the adulterer.'[6]

Thus the raw material out of which the customary law of adultery was to be built by the courts was varied both as to whether it was normally compensatable or punishable by death and as to how far it was in the

195

'public' and how far in the 'private' realm. Some of the differences regarding the latter might be attributable to differences in pre-colonial political structure but they may be better understood in the light of the interest which chiefs and headmen had in the colonial period of exaggerating their 'traditional' powers. While Chief Chaolikila of the Lungu claimed that before the whites came an adulterer was brought to the chief, 'who could order his death or mutilation ... [or] also very heavy damages', the 'old men' of Walungu gave evidence that the punishment for adultery was beating and compensation, regulated by the 'old men', and that a chief would not attend.[7] Yet to the administrators and later, as we have seen, to many anthropologists, only a model of public power which included a 'judicial' and an 'executive' function was comprehensible. If there were chiefs they *must* have had judicial powers; if there were laws, they must have had government to carry them out. Yet an understanding of the chief's role is more clearly expressed by the witness who said, 'If the husband has no relations he reports the matter to his chief.'[8]

The administration strove to pluck law out of the confusion and the anger. They accepted from the witnesses that adultery had been treated as criminal in pre-colonial times and that only since British administration had been established had it been treated as a civil matter with the possible consequences of divorce or damages or both. As early as 1910 the North Eastern Rhodesian administration reported that adultery had increased and that damages for adultery were 'received with unfeigned satisfaction' by husbands who connived with their wives for self-enrichment. Other factors cited were the long absence of men from home and substitution of civil penalties for penal ones like flogging. Regulations were proposed providing for imprisonment for up to two years, and whipping.[9]

In 1916 the public prosecutor of Northern Rhodesia revived this proposal. To make adultery criminal, he advised, 'is not to introduce any new principles. Among the customs of most native tribes it was always seriously regarded and visited with severe penalties; it was a crime punishable with death, mutilation or enslavement.' He warned that there had been a 'distinct weakening of the marriage tie among natives' and he was supported by the legal adviser, P. J. Macdonnell, who advised that the criminalisation of adultery was needed for 'maintaining the structure of native society'.[10]

The legal administrators in fashioning a traditional crime out of the distemper of the chiefs and husbands were assisted by the courts. In the case of *R*. v. *Uliakawa* in August 1916 it was 'proven' by evidence from witnesses in customary law that the Basala custom was to put a man to death for adultery with a chief's wife, while among the Ila that offence was punished by cutting off the offender's hands. That this would have been better described as the chief's revenge – as an incidence of power rather than a rule of 'law' – did not occur to the court. Adultery with a chief's wife was a crime, Beaufort reasoned, and should therefore be treated as a crime for all men's wives. Authority now existed, without extra legislation, for treating adultery as criminal. But what were to be the consequences? Who would be punished? Would compensation cease? British administrators were at heart unhappy about compensated adultery, especially where no divorce followed. They saw adultery as a moral wrong, particularly in women, which it was correct to punish, and, this being the case, the women must be punished too. It was a little hard, though, to make a customary law to fit this. The 'proofs' of customary law, as collected in court, were confused about the punishment of women, for women were not seen as offender or offended. Mpeseni's version had the women put to death but most accounts ignored the woman entirely, concentrating on whether the husband would avenge himself by killing the man who offended with his wife, or by claiming compensation from him. It is clear that adultery was not a reproved act simply because it was sexually illicit. Sexually illicit acts committed against women were not thought to be too serious. The same Chewa chief who gave evidence concerning death for adultery told the court that 'For the rape of an unmarried woman the offender was not heavily punished – he paid a fowl.' Another said that for such an act a man was warned, never killed. And yet another recounted: 'If a man had an unmarried daughter and some man lay with her the father might insist on the two marrying. If the man refused he would beat his daughter but leave the man alone.'[11]

But the new law was founded on the male alliance against female indiscipline. Both African and British men were now emphasising not the offence against the husband but the need to punish the women. As one chief complained at an *Indaba* in 1916, 'The women should be punished [but] when we punish them they run to the Magistrate and complain.' In 1917 the Lozi put forward legislation in a situation in which it was reported that owing to an increase in labour migration and an influx of money the marriage tie was being increasingly lightly regarded. The Lozi, it was said, 'all agree that the woman should suffer as well as the man.'[12] Uliakawa's case made the proclamation unnecessary, but the Lozi persisted and the *Khotla* eventually passed a law fining all women adulterers one head of cattle or, failing payment, requiring them to hoe for the local chiefs. Only a civil claim would be available against the man. British officials objected, both on the ground of inequitable treatment of the sexes, and because women had no cattle to pay, and the result of the law would be the spread of the enforcement of compulsory labour at chief's headquarters about which there was much sensitivity following on the recent strains accompanying the abolition of slavery in Barotseland. But the Lozi presented their effort in the context of a general tightening of the marriage law to deal with the migrant situation. Marriage was only to be recognised by the payment of bridewealth; on separation bridewealth must be returned; in case of adultery the offending man must pay two pound or two head to the husband, or three pound or three head if he took the woman. The woman, who suffered nothing from these payments, was to be fined. While there was objection by the officials to the last suggestion, on the whole they received the Lozi proposals sympathetically. Officials usually favoured, as I have shown above, the spread of bridewealth marriage and were willing to help the Lealui *Khotla* in attempting to enforce a bridewealth.[13] The new Lozi law was very protective of the absent migrant interests, and reflects, perhaps, the reaction to pressure for easier divorce from wives of migrants which appeared in other high-migrancy areas. Bridewealth established their rights in women and their rights to damages, and the development of the penal adultery law might well be understood in the light of the defence of the migrants' interests by the local Native Authorities, against invasion of their paid-for rights by the local population of women and unmarried men. One might also expect that the anxiety of men to have their rights defined and vigorously protected in their absence fuelled the growth of rule-making and punishing.

Yet for the British officials the problem was not solved by the imposition of new punitive rules. They continued to worry about the morality of compensation. Over and over they insisted that there must be something immoral about compensating a man for the injury of his wife's adultery if he continued to live with her. To them the offence was not one committed by one man against the rights of another, but an offence committed by a woman against her marriage and they were not able to accept that the husbands were acting honestly, if they wanted monetary damages but were willing to go on living with a sexually impure and unfaithful woman. As Tagart put it, men must not be allowed to gain from their wives' adultery or 'the inevitable result will be the disappearance of the last vestiges of respect for marital obligations.'[14]

Yet this was again very far from an understanding of male opinion. The Reverend Ysaye Mwase wrote for the Nyasaland authorities an account of African marriage, strongly coloured by golden age-ism, which was also a plaint against the monetisation of marital affairs. 'With our fathers', he wrote, 'marriage was not a question of valuation, nor money. Where marriage becomes a question of money value the community degerates [i.e. degenerates].' Turning the tables on the British, who so often regarded African marriage as a question of purchase, Mwase implied that only in colonial times had a monetary value been put upon women. In the past if a wife proved herself unfaithful, the husband could demand her back, and 'cause the usurper to pay double, otherwise he must revenge the purity of his bed by serious troubles. However much goods the seducter [*sic*] paid – he was never permitted to keep the woman on condition that he paid so much to her former husband.' Thus while adultery was a most serious transgression, it did not break the marriage. The colonial courts, as we have seen, treated the matter differently – as if adultery was an offence easily commuted by monetary damages, while at the same time it could be irrefutable grounds for the breaking of the marriage tie. Mwase wrote:

> In nowadays a native does not understand when he fails in the circumstances in question to find that the seducter of his wife takes advantage over him. According to native law the seducter is punished for his crime – not that the pay

is the value of his wife, as if it was the wish of her husband to expose her for public sale. This encourages the commission of the sin instead of diminishing it.[15]

Gratefully the district officers in Northern Rhodesia seized on the excuse offered by *R. v. Uliakawa* to treat adultery as criminal, which they coupled on the civil side by giving divorces to husbands to rid them of adulterous wives. While African men were in support of an administration of law which would punish women, they were appalled by the way in which divorce became a consequence of bringing an action for damages for adultery. Witnesses on customary law were at pains to insist that divorce was not a consequence of adultery.[16] So far as the white magistrates were concerned they thought they were adopting, in response to African demands, a more punitive attitude towards adultery by divorcing adulterous women and allowing 'criminal' punishment under 'customary law'. But in the minds of African men they were achieving the opposite, in allowing adulterous women the liberty of leaving their husbands. Complaints were also vocalised in the towns, where adultery cases most commonly ended in divorce. 'A man may live with his wife for ten years an award of 15/- shillings damages is made,' said Thomas Mukamba, of the Nkana advisory committee, 'This is no use.' Other members criticised the courts which allowed adulterers to keep the women with whom they had committed adultery. There was general agreement that adulterous couples should be sent home to their families and not be divorced in town. 'It is not good,' said Edward Sampa, Chitimikulu's grandson, 'that wives should change hands ... just for payment.'[17]

In the midst of this turmoil Hall J. issued a judicial circular in 1933 withdrawing the authority given by *Uliakawa*'s case to treat adultery as criminal.[18] Unlike Beaufort J., Hall did not seize upon the alleged punishment of adultery with a chief's wife by death or mutilation in the past as an excuse to bring penal sanctions to both men and women. There was, he wrote, no reason to treat it as a criminal offence now under entirely different conditions and against the 'modern trend'. Three years later the central government again issued explicit instructions that adultery be treated as a civil matter only. Yet this apparently had little impact in the districts. The majority of secretariat and district officials remained firmly in favour of a criminal treatment of adultery under the 'customary law' (as one put it, treating adultery as criminal was 'clearly' not repugnant) and most chief's courts, including the Lozi courts, continued so to treat it. Officials advised that to change the law would result in an increase in immorality and would cause 'serious antagonism' between African authorities and the central government. There were African complaints that the urban courts were not punishing as strictly as the rural ones.[19] Ten years after the judicial circular of 1933 the effective law of Zambia was still that the Native Courts could and did treat adultery as criminal, claiming customary law as their authority. In Malawi too throughout our period there grew the desire to use the new

199

courts as punitive instruments against both male and female offenders. One of the first complaints of the Momberas Association was that 'only the man is condemned and heavily punished' and thus the women were encouraged to continue. They agreed that men and women should suffer the same penalty and that both should pay compensation to the injured husband. When not at first successful the Association took up the matter again, claiming that 'In olden days, especially in Zwangendaba's time, if man and woman were found guilty of adultery they were both punished by death.' By now they were demanding not only that both should be liable to pay compensation but that there should also be equal imprisonment for men and women. The other Associations also wanted the courts to punish female as well as male adulterers. The Southern Province Association had a 'heated discussion' on the subject; the West Nyasa Association a 'prolonged discussion'; both ended in similar demands to this effect. Feeling ran high outside of the Associations as well, and traditional leadership supported the treating of adultery as a criminal offence by both parties. In 1929 in the Fort Manning district, the Ngoni headman, Mlongeni, complained that before the Europeans had come 'adultery was looked upon as the most serious offence after murder and both parties were killed if found guilty.' Mere compensation was not a sufficient punishment. It was agreed with the district officer that a new 'native law' treating adultery as criminal would be enforced.[20]

In Malawi in the 1930s it was noted that in the Native Courts there was 'a growing tendency to treat adultery as a criminal offence' and a 'definite increase' in the number of cases in which fines and compensation were ordered. In the rural districts of Dowa and Kasungu, for example, courts were 'very lenient except in adultery cases, in which the maximum fine is nearly always ordered . . . with scant regard to mitigating circumstances such as the neglect or absence of husbands'. Both the increase in the number of cases, which came to dominate the Native Courts, and the increasingly punitive response were attributed by officials to the high rate of migration and a tendency towards adultery by the plural wives of absentees. During this period the treatment of adultery as criminal had been formally authorised by a judicial circular but in 1940 and again in 1946 the High Court ruled that it could only be a civil matter. Musgrove Thomas J. in *R. v. Roberts and Aluwani* based his ruling on the view, time-honoured in legal thinking on 'primitive law', of the inability of the 'native mind to conceive that the state is angered by the breach of its Laws . . . . Native law knows nothing of what we call criminal law . . . it knows of wrongs to the individual for which he can in the appropriate court receive compensation.' In *Joseph Lumbandi* v. *R.* in 1940 the court voiced another concern. While on the civil side of customary law policy amounted to allowing a relatively uncontrolled and flexible development, the court objected to 'a haphazard development of native criminal law by primitive courts operating separately'.[21]

In neither Malawi nor Zambia were the rulings of the High Court of real effect in the world of the Native Courts. And likewise in both there was an increasing tendency towards making women pay. One district report from Malawi after the High Court judgements records that group and village councils had been debating whether women ought to be called on to make a contribution, 'and in some courts this practice has begun.'[22]

In Zambia, too, after *Uliakawa* the trend in the Native Courts continued towards increased criminalisation, and towards fining in place of ordering compensation. Not only was it the feeling that women should be punished along with men, but demands were made that female adulterers should be fined more heavily than male because 'a man pays dowry and that means that the women had no right to go with another man.'[23] Officials who knew this was strictly speaking illegal, and who appreciated the problems involved in basing contemporary law on alleged custom, were in a difficult position. As the chief secretary wrote of one area, in former times the penalty was said to be a slave, 'Now that slavery has been abolished . . . apparently no punishment is legally possible.' What was to be done when those fined by the Native Courts for adultery appealed? Adultery had been effectively criminalised through the transmutation of male outrage into law via the process of 'proving' opinion in the courts and then allowing its adoption as 'law'. I would stress the effects of the process of 'proving customary law' in the white courts. The lengthy process of taking evidence and cross-examining chiefs and elders (even Boma messengers) led to a stating, defining, clarifying, a *regularising* of customary practices (both real and manufactured) in a way which was designed to turn fluid accounts of relationships into rules. It must be seen, in other words, not as part of the process of discovering the rules of customary law but as a vital part of the rule-making process. What kinds of rules would be made out of this process, and how and whether they would be applied, depended on a combination of circumstances: the rules would reflect the current anxieties and aims of the witnesses, and if these coincided with the moral predilections and administrative purposes of the officials, a 'customary law' might become established. When the Western Province regional council in Zambia met to discuss how adultery should be handled in the multi-ethnic urban communities the chairman told the meeting that: 'The law relating to adultery and its punishment was an African customary law and in urban areas it was for the Urban African Courts to decide these matters following the principles of the established customary law on the subject.'[24] The 'established customary law' had by then, as we have seen, been born from a particular set of angers and anxieties.

TOWARDS A CUSTOMARY FAMILY LAW

The opinion of African men about the state of law on family related matters was voiced through the Native Associations and other representative bodies, as they developed, and through the courts. The anxieties which they expressed were by no means a matter of simple conservatism. I have shown above how there was willingness to change the 'law' to respond to the strains imposed by migrancy. Even the Momberas Association representing the self-consciously 'patrilineal' Ngoni district of Northern Malawi agreed in 1920 that although it was Ngoni law that once bridewealth had been paid children belonged to the father, if he had been absent for more than three years his wife could keep the children. (The Association still thought that she should surrender them to the father's family if she remarried.) This sort of flexibility on the subject of patrilineality and matrilineality was distrusted by the officials as it went contrary to their views about stable traditional systems on which customary law was based. Added to a pragmatic flexibility was the strong Christian element in the new African leadership. This could express itself in various ways, sometimes as a literal condemnation of polygamy, more often as a general increased sensitivity towards female 'immorality'. In the context of the contest for validity between 'patrilineal' and 'matrilineal' systems this led to various problems. The Ngoni leadership, for example, supported both polygamy and a restrictive 'Christian' approach to the chastity of women. The Chewa were more likely to be monogamous, but in the view of missions, and Ngoni, immoral in their sexual habits. As Barnes wrote, 'In chastity the missionaries were allied with the Ngoni against the Chewa; in monogamy the missionaries fought against the Ngoni allied to the Chewa.' Customary law, when it was defended by the Association, was an idealised morality, and often more than that, a morality idealized in a way which made it compatible with the new mission morality. The 'glorified past', as Barnes observed of the Fort Jameson Ngoni in the 1940s, in terms which have a wider application, 'is reinterpreted in terms of new values which have been acquired in the interim'.[25]

It was the observance of idealised modes of behaviour rather than the administration of specific laws that was really wanted. Marriage should be serious, the elders respected and women dutiful, and as African authority was now powerless to secure this, it was the responsibility of the Boma to use its authority in the administration of law to see that morality prevailed. Thus each demand for moral observance was made in the form of an assertion that it was a demand for the law to be followed.

In May of 1926 the Momberas Association was in despair: 'the marriage law among the Ngoni is now relaxed, so many people marry early and die soon.' This general feeling of declining standards of behaviour and a loosening of the moral bonds is apparent in the picture drawn by the Reverend Ysaye Mwase in 1927. In some ways, he wrote, however rude and superstitious people had been in the past, people in the present were 'below' them. Men had once to be worthy of the name of husband before taking a wife. 'Women based themselves by domestic works – such as cooking and pounding: fetching firewood and water . . . helping their husbands or fathers to sow or plant in the cultivated gardens – and bearing or bringing up children . . . [and] were loving and amiable in their homes.' The marriage price was very low because people were unwilling to sell their daughters as slaves; polygamists were few. Marriage took place only after maturity disciplined by service. 'Their marriage did not hang on goods . . . but on mutual love and service . . . . Divorce was very rare.' A man hesitated to dismiss his wife and found it difficult to remarry if he did so. Also 'Where the authority of parents or chiefs is obeyed implicitly, who count it disgrace to tolerate such a state there could be no common divorces. Where women became aggressors in the case in question they were prevailed upon to be reconciled to their husbands.'[26] A loving, working, domestic compliance, under the authority of parents and chiefs, characterised the life of women, their aggressions controlled and 'reconciled'. The contrast with the new world in which chiefs and parents were ignored, women were frivolous and adulterous, and indulged in their behaviour by the white courts, could not have been greater.

It is not surprising that the white man's law and courts should bear the brunt of the blame for the new behaviour which it appeared to license, rather than underlying changes in social and economic circumstances which were not so easily identifiable. But there was acuteness, nonetheless, in the diagnosis that it was the change in nature of authority, and what authority would allow, that was of considerable importance. The substitution of white courts, which entertained (or so it seemed) women's whims, for the *Nkhoswe*, who controlled them, appears at the heart of complaints. The Southern Province Native Association in Malawi, in complaning about the decisions of magistrates in marriage cases which 'although according to the law' were not 'to the satisfaction of the natives', objected particularly to the failure of the magistrates to call the *Nkhoswe*.[27] Levi Mumba complained bitterly about the lack of care in the courts' handling of divorce cases, objecting particularly to the lack of consultation of *Nkhoswe* and the willingness to entertain the wishes of women.

> One is also surprised to see that in some marriage cases the men who stood surety at marriage time are ignored. Lack of sense of gravity on the part of the magistrates is also revealed by asking questions which on the face of them are very silly, e.g. cases of adultery the woman is often asked which husband she prefers!!! This is a funny experience for any Bantu husband and creates a desire in him to do what he hesitated before, i.e. kill the adulterer if he can by any means possible. This encouragement of dissolution of marriages by magistrates has given the native woman a liking for this course when she wants to leave her husband . . . .
>
> The truth . . . is that there is altogether too much superciliousness on the part of the magistrates who think it a waste of their time to take much pain in investigation [*sic*] all native cases and the result is that there is general dissatisfaction all over the country with the way cases are heard.

He concluded his complaints with a description of an entry in the case book of a first-grade magistrate for a divorce case:

> there were no *ankhoswe* present, the evidence of both parties including his judgement, were summed up and recorded in 4 lines only !!! This shows how much care is given to the most important case in native life.[28]

The judicial styles of the British courts and those of face-to-face community justice were far enough apart to cause major mutual incomprehension. Yet added point is given to Mumba's complaint by the district officers' accounts of their doings. Duff wrote with some pride of his work in Malawi and of the great changes that had come to the people in the matter of adultery cases. Seducers used to be killed, he said, and women tortured in order to name the man. 'What a contrast to the procedure now adopted. A short discussion at the Magistrate's office, a note entered in the judicial minute book, a little paternal admonition, – perhaps a small fine to be paid as compensation to the injured husband . . . the incident is closed.' Bradley gives a picture of his first happy-go-lucky tour of duty as a new district officer. After stressing his ignorance of everything African he writes, 'I enjoyed myself hugely . . . . Among other enormities I granted divorces to about 50 ill-treated or deserted wives, although I had as yet no jurisdiction as a Magistrate.'[29] There was also, as time progressed, the growing fashion for the 'liberal' view of African marriage which insisted on the ease with which people accepted divorce. By the 1930s the up-to-date district officer no longer thought of African marriage as a field of anarchic sexuality restrained by terror but as a matter-of-fact economic relationship. A. T. Culwick, for example, who had taken thousands of matrimonial cases and claimed a 'very clear insight' into African marriage, wrote that Africans did not expect 'the mutual affection, sympathy and comradeship' which was the English ideal and that there was a striking absence of emotion even in contested divorces.[30]

Though G. S. Mwase was at pains to emphasise at the time he wrote (the early 1930s) that the 'whiteman's law is very popular', and though he acclaimed the abolition of trial by ordeal, he attacked the treatment of adultery and the law relating to women generally. He was unhappy about the way in which the new law not only proclaimed female consent to marriage in a negative sense, but also treated women as if they could arrange their own marriages. While the parents of a young woman were looking for someone proper for her to marry, wrote Mwase, 'Another whimsical fool wheedles her and falls into adultery with her without the permission of her parents. This is . . . a case which the whiteman's law say absolutely nothing against it. It is said that both are free agents.' Mwase felt that the man, in such cases, should be treated as an adulterer.[31]

A similar feeling is evident in the reaction to the attempt by the missions to persuade the Nyasaland administration to recognise that marriages performed in church were indissoluble. In a letter to the government in 1936, the Blantyre Native Association affirmed that two kinds of customary marriage, *lobola* and *Nkhoswe* marriage, existed in Malawi, and that 'These customs have been practised from time immemorial' and had been recognised by the Churches when they first entered the country.[32] Where *lobola* marriage prevailed, the Association wrote, representing the ideal rather than current reality, no marriage was recognised unless bridewealth was paid, which was 'not buying, but giving an assurance that the man takes responsibility'. In the rest of the country, while it was the case that 'According to English Law a girl of twenty one years of age or over do[es] not require to obtain the consent of the father or guardian to marriage, amongst the African no girl, woman nor widow can admit any marriage unless the *ankhoswe* agreed.' Not only was their consent necessary and not only did they act to 'safeguard' the marriage, but 'They have got absolute power to dissolve the marriage when sufficient cause is given.' The control of the *Nkhoswe* over marriage, existing from 'time immemorial', was being asserted against the individual woman's right to consent and the state's right to divorce, as well as against the Church's hope of substituting Christian for customary marriage. The Association pointed out that the Churches had previously not accepted marriages 'of which *unkhoswe* has not been established', and objected to the practice of church marriage which, it claimed, people did not understand but accepted only in fear of being otherwise 'erased off from the Church membership'. And Christians, they pointed out, married not only among themselves, but married non-Christians: 'both the man and the woman are not educated, especially the latter does not understand the meaning of the whole institution of church marriage.' They rejected the idea of a Christian native marriage according to English legal principles, urging instead that church marriages must be performed in accordance with the 'people's customs'. The government, on these matters quite willing to support custom against Christianity, agreed. But it is clear that the 'customs' were not compatible with the jural categories of English law where the primary will to make and unmake a marriage was that of the parties to it, not that of their elderly relatives.

The Zambian elite added a different kind of complaint when they focused not on casualness and lack of care in legal administration but on inter-racial marriage and racial discrimination. There were calls either to stop inter-racial marriage or to compel white husbands to respect the authority of their wife's matrikin. Following the acquittal of a European who successfully pleaded impotence to a charge of raping a black woman, the Livingstone Association complained of lack of a careful investigation.[33] Complaints of this sort were hard to make and ineffective. When the Association called for a law compelling whites who had children by local women and then abandoned them to be made liable for their support, the government told them that such a law already existed, as part of English law which applied to the territory. But, as the Association pointed out, such a law had 'never been interpreted to our native women and to the Native Community as a whole'. The chief secretary replied, 'It is impossible to supply the native community with copies of the whole body of English and Statute law.' The community were deemed to know the law, yet they were ignorant of the whole body of English common law which automatically applied to the territory and they had no influence on that area of 'legal culture'. But the attitudes expressed could make themselves felt in the area of customary law.

205

Expressions of the anxiety of the African urban elite about marriage can be found in the early 1930s. The 'question of native marriages was one of the most important functions of this organisation', said the Livingstone Native Welfare Association, in giving vent to its unease about the way in which the new town marriages were being arranged. Formerly men had found husbands for their daughters, looking for the 'best and respectful character', and daughters had been compelled to take the choice. Now they were not able to do this, 'but one thing we must realise is that the evil which we see resulting from leaving the choice of a husband to the girl is that they are soon divorced.'[34]

The resolution passed in 1933 by the Lusaka Association reflected the same dissatisfaction with the conditions of urban marriage. The instability of marriages between persons with conflicting customs required special care from the courts. But, the Ndola district officer reported, the prevalence of 'mine marriage', which couples exploited to gain adultery damages, and the tactics of women who married a different 'victim' for his cash every two months, were entirely undermining the law. The 'more thoughtful natives', including those actually married according to customary law, were disadvantaged, because ' "mine marriage" cases appear so frequently before the District Commissioner that he tends to consider all matrimonial disputes with suspicion.'[35] The Association was more to the point as to remedy. They 'unanimously' resolved that 'a man wishing to marry a woman in the industry centres should first seek the consent of the woman; having got it, he should pay whatever dowry is asked for in accordance with the African custom, after this the marriage should be registered at the Boma.' If it were later to be the case that the marriage broke down, the husband should only be able to reclaim his bridewealth if the wife were at fault. The Association thought that the adoption of their suggestion 'might materially help to tighten up marriages between Africans in the industry centres'.[36]

The demand for registration was favourably received by white officials and it was one which was being raised not only in urban but also in rural areas, where some of the Native Authorities were already doing it. As I have shown above, in the period when plural wives were taxed, the necessity of registering every married woman on the tax register had drawn the whole question of customary marriage partly out of the 'private' and into the 'public' domain. While the law had been passed for revenue purposes, people had regarded registration as evidence of a valid marriage and a divorce had to be proved before the tax register was changed. All this, as one official wrote, served the useful purpose of bolstering up customary marriage, while the later abolition of the registration of women's names for tax purposes had weakened marriage in that separations could now take place without reference to the chief, or to the Boma.[37] But the crucial question raised by the new request for registration was, how would the registering authority establish, before issuing a certificate, whether the marriage was valid according to customary law? An increase in the formalities like registration, would inevitably mean the need for the establishment of more formal rules of marriage, and if registration was to come, the customary law would have to be spelled out.

In 1934 it was reported that the necessity of a system of registration was being felt in townships along the line of rail where inter-ethnic marriages were 'so often dissolved with impunity' and resulting unfairness. In 1936 the registration proposal was raised by district officers at *Indabas* around the country where the chiefs were reported to have received it with enthusiasm, as they viewed 'the gradual loosening of the marriage tie with grave concern'. But while ready consent would be given to something presented as a scheme to stabilise marriage and to prevent the movement of unmarried women to the line-of-rail and urban areas, there were serious misgivings. Matrilineal authorities clearly saw the proposal as one which would increase the power of husbands over wives. As the Mpika district officer reported, the wife's family retained considerable power over a marriage, reserving the right to take back the woman if the husband proved unsatisfactory. 'A certain amount of fear is felt lest this right should be lost to a husband who holds a certificate of marriage.' And while women's families might fear loss of influence over a man bearing the authority of a state-certified marriage, so also, as the project unfolded, did many women. Not only would a registered marriage be more difficult to leave but the suggestion that the registration be done in the woman's home area would revive the authority of her family which emigrant women had often sought to escape.

While during the 1930s some of the newly institutionalised Native Authorities, which were so far only operative in rural areas, were allowed to adopt registration procedures, the issue of compulsory registration was postponed. But by the end of the decade the urban elite revived their demands. When the native advisory committee met at Nkana in September 1939 the 'chief topic of discussion' was native marriages. There were complaints that town dwellers had 'lost respect for their tribal customs'. One member urged that women in the towns who left their husbands and looked for other men should be sent home, and this was generally approved. Thomas Mukanta of the African Methodist Episcopal Church 'agreed that the chief problem on the mines is the loosening of the marriage tie. All the government's schemes have had no effect – The women become proud and leave their husbands. *They do this because there is no Government law binding them to their husbands.*'[38] The drive for the criminalisation of adultery, the demands to control the movement of women, and the concern to preserve and protect 'customary' marriage, all were really subsumed under the wish for a 'government law binding [women] to their husbands'.

During the 1930s some Native Authorities had begun to operate non-compulsory marriage registration. The general practice was for the Native Authority in the woman's home area to certify that her parents as guardians had consented to the proposed marriage and that arrangements had been made for the payment of whatever bridewealth was traditionally required.

The general aim was to ensure that women would not enter into marriages, or float around from liaison to liaison, without parental consent, and to establish a measure of control by giving the receivers of bridewealth an interest in the preservation of marriages, even those in urban areas. Native Authority rules put into rule form in each area what the requirements of a valid marriage to which the guardians could consent were, and these were then promulgated by the Native Authority. The question of requiring express female consent before a marriage could be registered was raised in the secretariat, and then allowed to lapse. It was not anywhere to be stipulated. The consent which all interested parties – an alliance of white and African Christian bodies, rural Native Authorities and urban elders – were pressing to have as a legal requirement was the consent of parents or guardians.[39] On the whole it appears that voluntary registration was not a great success. The Ndola district commissioner diagnosed a rural/urban split. Marriage registration, he thought, appealed to 'the less sophisticated' as a 'settling effect' but was 'unpopular with the bulk of natives living near the centres of employment'. Another reported that men considered it shameful to count out the amount of bridewealth in front of the chief. From the Central Province the official view came that women disliked the marriage certificates 'as they would impose greater disabilities' upon them than on men. The provincial commissioner for the Western Province advised that 'Responsible Africans ... continually ... urge Government to compel the general compliance .... the main objection to registration comes from the least responsible elements and ... is based on the fear that once a marriage certificate is taken out the marriage will be more binding than they wish. The women are particularly inclined to hold this view.'[40] Others were said to have objected to the certificate for fear that it connoted an indissoluble marriage, like a mission marriage. Thus while the Native Authorities and the advisory councils continued to press for a compulsory registration system, response at large appeared apathetic. From the point of view of Government there appeared to be divided aims. On the one hand the stemming of the perceived disintegration of customary marriage was seen as a priority by those who viewed the bolstering of the 'customary' social system as vital to the overall political order of the territory. On the other hand there was the apparently more limited objective of the urban authorities described by the Kitwe district commissioner as simply that of 'eliminating the unattached women from the urban areas'.[41] As another official wrote: 'Registration of marriages should be introduced as early as possible after which no woman should be allowed to come to the copperbelt even at her parent's request unless she can prove possession of a certificate.' Certificates should only be able to be cancelled in the girl's home district because only there could responsibilities be properly assessed. His diagnosis of the reasons for his recommendation go to the heart of the matter and remind us of the pride in women complained of in the African councils: 'So long as women are in a minority on the copperbelt, they will wield a power they have not got at home and will want to shed their husbands for trivial reasons . . . for reasons she would never dream of advancing at her home village.'

Godfrey Wilson's analysis also reflected this view. The disproportion of sexes in the towns meant that women had 'alternative mates readily available'; trivial disputes led, therefore, to women leaving their husbands, and this 'helps to keep the relative economic status of wives high'. The idea that women in urban areas wielded extra power is singular in revealing the depth of the insecurity and resentment involved. For women in towns were potentially in many ways in a more vulnerable position than in the villages as they were cut off from their matrikin, unable to support themselves by growing food, and virtually entirely dependent on a share of the husband's wage. As Wilson observed in another context 'it is on getting a job, not on getting married, that a young man's living now depends,' and this was a crucial factor in upsetting the balance of power between men and women. A man in town did not depend on the land and support granted by a woman's kin and was free of labour obligations. Instead his wife needed his money.

Though urban administrators and the African elite saw the remedy in an officially backed process which would ensure that women would find it much harder to assert themselves, registration and marriage certificates seemed to be irrelevant to village tribunals. For the formalisation and the nature of legality that it implied had little to do with customary marriage. The provincial commissioner reporting from Kasama wrote that the people's reaction had been that the issuing of a certificate could not 'confirm a person's heart'. He wrote: 'The African has not the same sense of the importance of the letter of the law . . . . Marriage certificates are useful to produce to Compound Managers and Town Police but are of no proof in a Native Court.' He recounted a case in which parental consent to a marriage had been given and a certificate issued. Yet the chief's court, in the face of parental insistence that a proper marriage had not taken place was unable to settle the case. 'To a legalist the case was perfectly simple, but . . . all the parties argued around the point and continually used the word *chifupo* indifferently for marriage, engagement, concubinage and cohabitation, in a way which to an English lawyer would have been begging the question.'

We can cull from this a sense of the difference in procedures and in attitudes towards legalism between the village process of creating a marriage and the newly formalised 'customary' law. In a sense what we can see is a resistance to legalisation. As he continued, the problem was with the meaning of marriage. 'To us marriage is a fact provable by a ceremony before witnesses. To a native marriage is an indefinable state reached gradually over a period of time.' Certificates were not seen or accepted as crystallising processes or confirming a person's heart. Their purpose was more mundane. Those who wanted them wanted to be able to establish rights over women; rights to damages; rights to have a marriage recognised by the colonial courts, primarily in the urban areas; rights to accommodation in compounds and locations. But this desire and need to prove and hold

209

demonstrable rights by a piece of legal paper, rather than to establish them by a course of behaviour, was bound to spill from the arena of urban courts and compounds into life at large. For many people, it was acutely pointed out, the validity of a marriage was dependent on the 'performance of some obligation over an indefinite period'. It was not clear at what point, if any, a marriage could be registered as complete. It should be possible, officials thought, to fix a common point, like the consent of the parents and the passing of bridewealth or a token. One summed up the process which the demand for registration was hurrying along: 'The natural tendency will be for the continuing indefinite obligation to pass away. It is not workable in the new conditions which are arising and there will inevitably be a growing demand by the men to know the definite minimum required of them to safeguard their homes.'[42]

There was a basic ambiguity in the demands being made by the African elite, and the aims of officials. They were trying to establish a mode of control of women and marriage suited to new conditions but they sought to do this by an apparent strengthening of rural 'customs' and authority. Some officials were aware of this and doubted whether 'tradition' was a suitable weapon with which to stablise urban marriage. This view supported a formalisation and legalisation of African marriage but considered that this should be achieved by means of legislated reform which would provide a framework for freeing the marriages of urban dwellers from impossible customary constraints, observances and procedures, and in particular make 'inter-ethnic' marriages easier by legalising a sort of common denominator form for urban marriage. The object of a marriage law reform, as the secretary for native affairs saw it, would be to 'tighten up marriage contracts in the interests of African society' and to enable Africans to marry 'without having to observe all the old native customary laws'.[43] Another pointed out that if the Native Authorities were failing to prevent people from entering into unions which they considered irregular 'then it would suggest that the native customary law has lost its force in this respect, and some other system of legalising their marriages must be sought.' Ndola's district officer thought that the crux of the matter was a conflict between tradition and modernity and that the conservative Native Authorities and the urban population were unconsciously opposed. The way of reform seemed to him to follow the path of modernity. He wrote: 'The introduction of registration of marriages by repute and cohabitation would be a blow at the African idea of marriage as a social factor in a communal society and a step towards the African acceptance of marriage as a contract between two persons.' Yet another official also saw things in this light. The tendency in Europe, he wrote, had been to eliminate the Church's power and to reduce marriage to a simple contract. The same should be done in Africa and the 'sanction' of customary law should be eliminated.[44]

But modernisation was not to come to the law of marriage in this way. Even among officials a more traditionalist conception prevailed. In relation to the majority of the population which was 'matrilineal', the chief secretary urged officials that: 'Sight must not be lost of the fact that a native marriage is a contract between three parties, and that the woman's guardians form a very important party. It is clear that the contracting of marriages without the consent of the guardians is not desired by the majority of thinking natives.' Hastings Banda summed up: 'with the Chewa people a woman marries the family, not the man.'[45]

The strains created by the conflicts between 'matrilineality' and 'patrilineality'; the tearing of the webbing of customary marriage arrangements by migrancy; the development of an urban society with a transient, multi-ethnic 'stranger' population – these were not identified by African men as being the nature of the problem they had to deal with. The essence of the problem seemed closer and more obvious – it was women: the 'new independence and self-assertiveness of the young women' which manifested itself in women defying village restrictions and moving to the urban areas, and their greater readiness to leave unsatisfactory marriages.[46] Men's reactions to the practicalities of the marriage problem were shot through with this perception of its nature. Voluntary registration of marriages was not working well among those who did not need the certificates, but even though the government remained dubious about compulsion a new pressure appeared which made it advantageous, if not necessary, for those intending to work in the mines to have registered marriages. The desire on the part of mine-compound managers to control the number and sort of women allowed onto the compounds and the advantage, under the controlled system, to men in being able to claim married quarters and live, licensed, with a woman, combined to give the certificate a new value. It was as an essential piece of paper evidence for compound managers, rather than for courts, that certificated marriages caught on. Pressure of this kind was operative wherever there was much labour migration. In 1935 it was reported from the Ncheu district in Malawi that marriages were being voluntarily registered by men going south with their wives because 'it is desirable that an authentic document should be obtainable for display to the authorities [where] native marital relations are liable to be subject to scrutiny by officials.' In 1938 uniform rules regarding voluntary registration were approved by the Nyasaland administration for the whole of the Northern Province. In 1945 rules were promulgated for compulsory registration with a certificate to be issued detailing the name of the parties, the parents and *Nkhoswe*, and the amount of bridewealth if any. Though it was recognised that local courts might continue to settle disputes without the certificate, it was felt that it would be of the greatest use for courts and compound managers in Southern Rhodesia and South Africa where, it was claimed, it was common for parties to marriage cases to deny that any marriage existed and where women were left destitute because they were unable to prove their relationship. But there was to be a clear spill-over from this evidential requirement for officials. As early as 1939 a Nyasaland district

211

officer observed that a marriage without registration as evidence that customary formalities had been observed was 'no marriage under customary law and merely an irregular union'. This, he wrote, 'was an important point when dealing with the allocation of married quarters and payment of such things as marriage allowances and gratuities on death'.[47] It was to become an important point with regard to the incidences of marriage as a whole.

Yet once there was a real advantage in registering a marriage (more real than evidence of the right to claim adultery damages which court personnel emphasised) the cumbersome procedure which had evolved out of the agitation by the Native Authorities for control no longer appeared viable. If a man married before leaving his rural area it was simple, relatively. He had, in order to obtain a certificate, to get the consent of the woman's parents before the Native Authority, and register with that Authority the amount of bridewealth and any other arrangements required by 'custom'. The woman could then follow or accompany him to town, bearing her certificate. If he was in town, and wanted to marry someone 'back home', the necessary arrangements had to be made in the woman's area. But the real problem concerned those migrant men who in town met the women who rode the lorries from the country in defiance of their Native Authorities and who, instead of entering into an informal liaison, now wanted the increasingly valuable certificate. For the system required that both should return to the area of the woman's Native Authority, where the consent and bridewealth formalities would be gone through. Then there was the question as to what court would have authority if anything went wrong. It was the practice of the new Urban Courts to hear adultery cases (for which they began to demand the certificate as evidence of the right to claim) but there was strong resistance from the rural Authorities, and, indeed, from many in the towns, to the idea that the Urban Courts should grant divorces. The Urban Court members themselves were not, it was reported, anxious to extend their jurisdiction over divorce: 'they considered that they could not take the case in the absence of the in-laws who had agreed to the marriage contract.'[48] Divorce, it was agreed, would be much less likely if the couple had to return to the rural Authority which had overseen the marriage. Yet men and women in the towns wanted certificates issued and divorces granted by the Urban Courts.

African rural leadership made its views plain. Young girls, it was said, should not be married by the Urban Courts; 'they are wanted at the villages to be trained as they do not work properly if they marry too young.' If Urban Courts married and divorced, girls 'can go from one man to another without the parents knowing – this is a very bad thing.' The Central Province African provincial council in Zambia passed by fifteen votes to three a motion that 'marriages through urban courts are not legal in accordance with Native Customary law and all marriages should be conducted direct by the Native Authorities, whatever hardship this may impose on individuals.'[49] At the next meeting of this council, however, disagreement emerged. The Broken

Hill urban member asked that there should be a European marriage officer on the line of rail who would marry women there in accordance with a 'proper Marriage Ordinance'. When the chairman pointed out that this would be ignoring customary law and that when these people went home they would not be considered married the Broken Hill spokesman answered acutely that 'the chiefs had no written law regarding marriages.' Customs, he urged, should be changed to meet the line of rail circumstances. Chief Mailo from Serenje disagreed. No one, he said, should be married on the line of rail, all should be forced to return home, and women should be handed over to the custody of their parents who would be instructed to look after them. All the rural members, said Chief Mailo, 'emphasised that there is no short cut to marriages at home. Even if the man is at work he must go home and get married properly. They have no time for the Urban Court marriages on the railway line.'[50] Feelings about the marriage situation continued to run high, and it was discussed with much animation at the first session of the African representative council in November 1946. Two Western members put forward a motion calling for compulsory registration with one law for the whole country. Alton Sitambuli said:

> In the past if an individual wanted to spoil another person's marriage he was restricted from doing so because he was afraid of the Chief. In our Councils we find that the marriages of today are useless .... We would like to have a law which would provide for marriages to be tied in the same way as they used to be tied in the past ... [when] people were afraid of doing something bad with another man's wife.

He was supported by the next speaker, Chief Musokotwana of the Tonga, who claimed that formerly when a marriage was 'spoiled' the 'spoiler' was punished. He dragged in the complaint that these cases, which had been treated as criminal in the past, were now being treated civilly. 'There is no proper law,' he complained, 'laying down that after marriage there should be no separation.' One Bemba member wanted 'the Government to pass an act providing for a heavy penalty to be imposed on an individual who deliberately spoils a marriage'. Another urged that a magistrate should tell people getting married 'that if something should occur to separate them, they will be severely punished'.

There was a certain lack of congruence in what was fuelling these demands, a desire to keep women married, and the law being campaigned for. For strictly speaking neither registration, nor a Southern Rhodesian-type marriage ordinance, which the council eventually asked for, said anything about the dissolution of marriage. But the general feeling was clearly that any extra input of officialness would intimidate people from both adultery and divorce.

There was a connection between the processes of legalisation, increased payments and the control of adultery. Barnes noted of the Ngoni introduction in 1944 of the thirty-shilling legalisation payments to be made before issuing the registration certificate:

Informants said that the law was introduced so that women as well as men could be punished for their adultery. It was argued that in a marriage in which no bridewealth had been paid, and only a few shillings as the legalisation payment, the women's kin could not in equity be called upon to pay damages on her behalf to her husband when she committed adultery . . . . By making the legalisation payment a considerable amount, equal at the time to two months' wages, it became possible to punish the woman in the same way as her lover.[51]

As Barnes observes, the attempt to check adultery by increasing payments was in general agreement with the wishes of both administration and missions. But disagreement remained as to who should exercise this official power. Some wanted the Boma to take over control of marriage altogether; others suggested that the Boma handle the registration but that Native Authorities control divorce; and others wanted the Authorities to handle all of marriage. Chief Ikelenge said, 'Before the Europeans came to this country people were getting married and their marriages had to be solemnised before Chiefs and Councillors.' This was a prime example of the invention of a bureaucratised past in its loss of capacity to imagine social life uncontrolled by an official administrative act, and its presentation of the powers of pre-colonial chiefs as if they were magistrates at the Boma. Hastings Banda was to observe explicitly in 1946: 'It is only since the Indirect Rule was introduced that Nyasaland chiefs have been performing marriage ceremonies of non-Christian Africans.'[52] But the import was clear. The powers of the chiefs over marriage were to be extended in an untraditional way. The government, said speakers, had first taken marriage from the chiefs, and then later handed it back. It should not take it from them again. The council accepted the principle of registration, yet a motion that the Boma and not the chiefs should control it was defeated by sixteen votes to ten. The implications were clear – that the procedures of bureaucracy would now invade and finally dominate the world of customary processes. The Draft Marriage Ordinance of 1947, though it contained provisions which had not exactly been campaigned for, such as the need for female consent, the banning of intimidation of women and the prohibition of the pledging of minors, made registration in the woman's area compulsory and required the woman's guardians to witness and register the marriage consideration. It was by these last provisions that the open webbing of custom would be tightened into a rule system as it became tied to the formal requirements of a registration system.[53]

The demand to control women and to reconfirm male authority had further weapons still beyond the criminalisation of adultery and the legalisation of customary marriage, and both had implications for the making of the customary law of marriage. One was the expressed demand by the male elite for the raising of bridewealth. I have already shown, in the context of the abolition of slavery, how bridewealth was perceived as a means of tying women into marriages and inhibiting divorce, and indeed the formalisation of payments under the registration system was anticipated by some as having

214

this effect. But in addition to simple formalisation there was a demand for a legislated increase. The matter was debated by the Zambian Northern Province provincial council in 1946. Joseph Pardon of the Fort Roseberry African Welfare Association said that it was cheap marriages which led to easy divorce. Four pounds should be the minimum bridewealth. And he harked back to the system in which kin would be involved in the circulation and accumulation of payments and would thereby retain their authority. 'A man would have to work hard to earn enough money to obtain a wife,' said Pardon, 'and would probably need help from his relatives and would therefore respect them more.' And he went on, 'Men were willing to pay seven pounds, ten shillings or eight pounds for a bicycle and four pounds can be found by a man honestly determined to marry.' Joseph Chipepa, a senior tribal councillor, emphasised that councillors considered that there should be a minimum bride price of four pounds, though he conceded, 'the mass of the people did not agree . . . in this matter as they liked cheap marriages.'[54]

These demands for a legalised increase in bridewealth payments in order to discourage divorce were also made in the other provincial councils[55] and they were encouraged by the judges of the Urban Courts, which gave preference to the payment of a substantial bridewealth as proper evidence that a marriage had taken place, over 'matrilineal' practices, such as cohabitation in the woman's village. Men on the Copperbelt were sometimes eager to pay higher prices, explicitly so that women would not be 'proud and cheeky'.[56]

The second weapon was the demand which began to surface for a change in the practice of observing 'matrilineal' patterns and giving the custody of children to women following divorce. Much has been made of pressure for changes in the law related to inheritance and the demands made for the right to make a will,[57] and the pressure for male custody can be seen in the context of the emergence of individualism, of limitations and changes in ideas of kinship obligations, of a new concept of private property and of family. But it can also be understood in the context of the Sena 'decision', which I describe above, to 'change' their pattern of descent from 'matrilineal' to 'patrilineal'. It is clear that an obvious way to control wayward women was to prevent them from taking their children with them. It was perhaps the most effective way of establishing male control over females under conditions of industrialisation. In the village the 'custody' went to the males in the woman's family, i.e. authority in the last resort was theirs, not hers. But in nucleated family circumstances, a 'matrilineal' woman retained her children, and her male kin were absent. Authority effectively was hers. Thus the demand, which surfaced in the provincial councils, that the government should make the rule for all of Zambia that the man retained the custody of children on divorce, was a potent call to restore control of the family to male hands. Men who married on the line of rail were finding that they had no way to compel their wives and children to return home with them when their labour period was over. As early as 1931, reflecting urban opinion on this matter, the Livingstone Native Welfare Association complained that the Boma's interpretation of the law meant that men who came to town to work and who acquired families either had to stay in town permanently or leave their families. The Boma, they said, should not side with the families of women who prevented them from leaving: 'it is a good native custom [that] children are the man's property, and it is against the custom of many tribes ... to give children to women.' The Association resolved unanimously (ninety-one members being reported present) 'that the Government be approached to confer with the chiefs that a proper decision of granting custody of children, no matter be he a foreigner or not', be 'granted to the father' and that, when the time came to leave for 'the home of the husband, no objection be accepted from the parents, the woman and the children be allowed to accompany the man wherever he wants to go'.[58] Twenty years later the African representative council was to debate a motion calling for the abolition of the matrilineal system entirely.[59] Though it was defeated in a split council, we must keep in mind that this assertion of the father's right is a continuing pressure in addition to those already operating – the criminalisation of adultery; the registration of marriage; the increase of bridewealth. This is the context in which the juridification of customary marriage takes place.

Part IV

Discussion

12

Writing African legal history

ANTHROPOLOGY OF LAW REVISITED

As I point out in an earlier chapter western writing about African legal institutions stems first from a dismissive, and later from a still dismissive but progressively evolutionist, viewpoint. Savage societies were thought at first to be without government and anarchic. Later experience demonstrated that this was not so, and that a meritoriously unanarchic and regulated social life prevailed. The question which then arose was, how was this order kept? The British model of civilised government was one in which the state secured obedience and order by command: not a command which enforced itself by capricious terror, but a rule-bound command. Nineteenth-century British jurisprudence emphasised that law came from the state but that it restrained power; that it was the main means of control in the social order; and that the alternative was anarchy, which was not a good thing. Law was seen to be essentially about order and obedience, rather than about the expression of social solidarity, the facilitation of market relations, the legitimation of power, the manipulation of symbols, the definition of inalienable rights, or the expression of class interests, all of which have been the foci of other traditions of explanation. The importance of this is that it is from British jurisprudence that the anthropological writing about African law with which I have been concerned derived its ideas about what law was and what it did.

When Malinowski published *Crime and Custom in Savage Society* in 1926 he aimed at establishing that savages were rational men who lived in a rational social order, not one dominated by fear, superstition or blindly followed habits. To do so it appeared necessary to him to show that they were obedient to a rational law, though, unlike the law of western states, it was obviously not a law of 'codes, courts and constables'. 'Law', therefore, Malinowski enjoined, 'ought to be defined by function and not by form.'[1] Whatever was found, in other words, doing the work in a society that law was thought to do in western societies, was law. But what did law do? To answer this Malinowski and many after him turned to the British jurisprudential tradition, which conflated the questions of law and order. Most of

219

the anthropologists went to jurisprudence in the first place to find out what law was. They then did a functional study in the field assuming that the jurisprudentially defined function was the right one. They used the results of their study to refute a culture-bound, western, state-oriented positivism, to show that all sorts of mechanisms did what jurisprudence said that law did, and that law was not always present to do these things. The question that was far less fully worked at was whether law did what jurisprudence said it did in western systems.

This means that in place of an evolutionary history, which saw primitive societies as either lawless or containing embryonic law, and advanced societies as having developed 'real' law, there was a functionalism which ironed out both historical change and the appreciation of significant differences between societies, by defining law as having a universal function – social control – and therefore as necessarily being a part of all social orders. Evolutionary history was replaced not by real history but by no history at all. The presence of law universally was established by functionalism's dialogue with British jurisprudence. This ruled out an historical approach which would have been able to treat law, like other social institutions, as a specific historical product and link its emergence to the economic changes undergone by the colonised world, and the imposition of new state forms.

The next step in the movement away from an historical approach came with the development of case and dispute studies. Clearly if law was a universal way of resolving conflicts and if it was not conveniently written down, then the way to find out what it was, was by studying what people did to resolve their disputes. The logic of fieldwork, combined with the dictates of a fashionable American realist jurisprudence, that law was what courts did in practice, led to concentration on the observation of cases in courts, and later to the extended study of disputes from pre-court genesis to post-court resolution. This yielded, of course, much rich material about conflict resolution but far less about the long-term changes in legal forms and categories such as property, right, duty, legal personality, contract. But more important was the general failure of disputing studies to address themselves to relationships of power so that the settlement of disputes and the invocation, use and manipulation of norms were not analysed with emphasis on the interests served by the processes. Gluckman's cases have already been reworked to demonstrate that a study of results, rather than a stress on the reconciliatory ideology which apparently rules the process, shows a clear pattern of winners and losers – that is, a pattern of social power.[2]

Tribally bounded ethnographies of 'law' went out of fashion as the 'tribes' were incorporated into new nation states. The lawyers who now were studying the new states were practical men with a mission, which was that of using 'law' to aid 'development'.[3] Most did not doubt that both the means and the goal existed. One of the ways of proceeding was to identify the way in which customary legal systems (which earlier anthropological study had assured them were 'there') impeded the economic changes which were perceived as necessary to development, and adapt them accordingly (for example, customary land law). Another was to assist in the integration and modernisation of the legal systems of the new states in the belief that this was a necessary step towards nation-building, itself a necessary step towards economic development.

The onslaught of development law, modernisation and unification which was promoted by the new states led some of legal anthropology into a sort of 'opposition'. What the developers and lawyers had identified as a messy situation of legal pluralism calling for rationalisation, or as 'traditional' impediments to modernisation, could also be regarded as necessary defences of local autonomy. In this way the former world of the student of the anthropology of law, the 'customary' systems of 'tribes' and 'regions', appeared as the embattled legal world of the peasant struggling with the twin oppressions of capitalist change and the new state. In the colonial period folk and customary systems had been seen in an idealised light because they were co-opted as part of the proof of the rationality of the supposed savage; now they were once again seen in an idealised light when contrasted with the new legal oppressions from above. The glare of the oppressions of the imposed systems made both people and researchers look for relief in the shade of the folk systems. The unpleasantnesses that might lurk within this shade were again not the object of study. Once more an opportunity to study the legal form in its process of change in folk systems was not taken and once more their role in the legitimising of power on the local level was not the focus of study, at least until the recent development of a feminist-oriented anthropology.

It was from the development of sociological studies of law in western societies, rather than from the unifiers and developers of non-western ones, that the next major advances in understanding of non-western legal systems were to come. The jurisprudential notion that law flowed outward and downward from the state as an all-embracing system which was western industrial society's major institutionalised form of social control came under close examination in the growing corpus of law and society studies. The 'discovery' was soon made that things 'really worked' differently: that difficulties of access, expense, formalism, and the coexistence of a thicket of different parallel systems and sub-systems for dispute-managing cast increasing doubt on the notion that law was, or was even meant to be, society's main system of conflict-resolution. Suddenly it seemed that people in the neo-colonial states and those in industrial societies were in a comparable position, facing plural systems of 'rules' and 'agencies' for settling their conflicts, among which they chose in the process of maximising their individual interests. Law just jostled along in a crowded universe of tactical resources for disputing and modes of social control.

For both western and non-western societies this has had the beneficial effect of pushing the study of law off its pedestal at the centre of western conflict-resolution and making it clear that in both types of social system legal things cast their shadow over only part of the area they were once assumed to cover. In its contribution to this realisation the anthropology of law has perhaps been at its strongest but the realisation leads to another question. This directs our attention to that shadowed area of which we need to ask, why is the legal form in use here? For what is it specifically appropriate? In terms of the new states this raised the obvious question as to why they should be pursuing centralisation and ironing out local-level 'legal' systems when the model of the western state which they were trying to emulate was so badly misconceived. The answer has been thoroughly pursued by neither anthropologists nor neo-colonial politicians. It is that legal forms enable particular people to gain particular types of power over others, and particular sorts of economic advantage.

As disputing studies developed subsequent to this they focused on the choices made by the 'actors', or litigants, regarding their disputing strategies and tactics. While this had the advantage of correcting the former over-emphasis on harmony within small groups, the disadvantage was in playing down the power of class, and of cultural, symbolic and institutional structures. In addition the real content of substantive rules remained much less important to this type of anthropology of law than the process of disputing.[4] Earlier writers had done the valuable service of pointing out that the formal content of rules, written or oral, often had little to do with the ways in which disputes are resolved and that even where 'rules' are 'applied' their content-in-action is often negotiable. Nonetheless the rules in action tell us not only what people want but how definitions of partial advantage are defined in terms which are both morally and politically legitimate. They are a clue to both interest and ideology in the study of conflict, not simply to be 'listed' in the definitional way to which many anthropologists rightly objected. Sally Falk Moore has reminded us of the 'partial' nature of law. To put it simply, the societal model of law *or* anarchy is false: even with law the social order is full of anarchy. Law is not, as Weber would have it, a 'gapless' system which even potentially regulates the whole of social life. This approach seems to me to raise the questions of the use or non-use of law, of its absence or presence, in a context quite different from that of the old value-laden debate about the cultural worth of law.

In this context we can consider the imposition of the law of the state onto the law of local communities as a meeting of distinctive modes of social ordering. Considered historically it is a struggle between modes formed by and made distinctive by differing historical experiences. Whether or not, in some pure definitional form, law must be connected with the state or the domination of society by a particular form of commodity relations (and clearly as a matter of definition there is no reason why it should be) the real historical process through which many of the 'subjects' of the anthropology of law have lived and are living is that of the domination of a state/ commodity law, a peculiar *combination* in time of forms of definition of

222

rights and a state apparatus. This dominant form, spread by capitalism and imperialism, has reshaped and re-formed modes of social control at all levels. This is not to say that the local levels eventually simply reflect the dominant mode, for there are resistances and adaptations, but all have changed by its power. It is from this perspective that there is an advantage in identifying the differences between the newly dominant form and those of the societies which are now its subject. (And it is clear too why, if the historical perspective is ignored, it seems less important to stress the differences.) To say that there is value in preserving the concept of law as one specifically distinct from other forms of social control is not, therefore, to make claims about its superiority, or say that it is *the* way in which western disputes are settled, or to accept the lawyers' definition or self-image. One does not have to buy any or all of the pervasive western illusions in order to preserve the idea of law as a distinctive cultural and historical category.

An analogy might be sought in the development of the anthropology of medicine. Western medicine, like western law, has been celebrated by those convinced of western superiority as a distinctive feature of western civilisation. As law was seen as a delineator of western political and ethical culture, setting it above non-law cultures, medicine, based on the germ theory of disease, has been a flag of the scientific culture of the west, embodying its superiority to those modes of thought labelled non-scientific. From this point of view western medical practice was understood to be concerned with the scientific diagnosis of disease, and with scientific chemo-therapeutic treatment, based, so far as was possible, on exact knowledge of the body and its process, and of the responses of particular organisms to particular drugs. And, just as the non-literate societies of Africa and elsewhere did not have shelves of law books, so they did not practise this kind of medical science. The original perception was that they had, as well as no law, no medicine. But they clearly had healing responses to disease and affliction. At first these were dismissed as witchcraft, mumbo jumbo, folk remedies, often dangerous and certainly not understood in the sense that anyone really knew why 'traditional' remedies acted in the way that they did.

But with the waning of imperialist ethnocentricism closer attention began to be paid to the practice and processes of non-western medicine in its societal setting. (This attention began far later than the development of legal anthropology because medicine in the form of establishing public health programmes and health services in new nations became a governmental problem later than law.) In place of dwelling on the lack of scientific understanding of disease and drugs, attention was paid to the many thera-peutic processes and rituals which, it became apparent, were both subtly understood and highly effective in the relief of a wide range of affliction and suffering. The practice of healing in society, the 'disease-relieving process', became the focus of this interest. This study of medical activity as a social process not only changed understanding of the response to affliction and disease in non-western societies, but was hugely rich in insights about western medical practices. No longer could medical practice be exclusively understood in terms of its scientific self-image. The rituals of interaction between patients and their healers are now understood as an important ingredient of the medical process. The roles of various forms of non-drug therapy and of placebos came to be better understood. In short, when analysed as a social process of 'disease resolution', many western medical practices were seen to have features in common with the social practices of non-western medicine. There are other striking similarities in the literature on law and medicine. The shift in medical anthropology to studying the patients' perspective of illness parallels the move towards 'litigants' perspective' in the legal writing; the shift towards placing disease in its context as experience lived in and by communities, rather than individual cases of pathology, parallels the development of the extended case method. These are valuable insights. They have rescued the western understanding of non-western healing from its opaque dismissal of it as hopeless mumbo jumbo. They have produced a better understanding of western medical practice than its scientific self-image alone could possibly do. Seen as a social process of healing the shared features become obvious. But even with this understanding it would be foolish to forget the essential differences. While its function might be the same, there remains an essential difference between the 'form' of western medicine, i.e. its self-consciously scientific basis, and its partners in the field of healing. A fascination with things in common should not obscure the essential differences in defining problems and solutions.[5]

An historical approach leads us to a clearer appreciation of how the now dominant legal level forms the other levels in its image and how disputants are not simply strategists with interests but people struggling with ideas about human relationships which are often incompatible with the dominant social and legal forms of the societies in which they now find themselves living. The processes at which we have been looking are those between 'status' and 'contract', where obligations towards persons were turning into rights in things. And it took place under alien rule and the spur of an intense pace of economic dislocation. This meant that the forms, institutions and processes of a 'contractual' legal system were imposed upon local societies rather than 'evolved' by them. The new concepts and procedures were therefore available not only to meet the needs of the new relationships of 'contract', but also to defend and reformulate the existing relationships of 'status'.

IDEOLOGY AND LAW IN COLONIAL CENTRAL AFRICA

In the heyday of nationalist historiography the developing political ideologies of colonial Africa were perceived as being essentially radical. In part this was because virtually all manifestations of anti-colonialism were assumed in some way to share a common radical ground and in part it reflected the use of history to provide roots for nation states which used a rhetoric which appealed to the sympathies of radical pro-African and anti-colonial historians. African nationalism clothed itself in a radical garb, tailored and admired by those who were writing African history. A suspicion existed, perhaps, that only an unsympathetic conservative would write about conservatism and authoritarianism in African societies.[6] After all, why draw attention to it except to weaken the nationalist thrust towards a future unembarrassed by outdated traditions, tribes, customs and attitudes? A progressive African future, moreover, could not be grafted onto such a stock.

The development of Marxist historiography, which had suspicions about the class nature of the new African leadership and the class nature of African colonial society, made writing about non-radical Africans more possible. It became possible to write about the conflicts among Africans about the nature of the social order which were produced by twentieth-century changes. To this we can add a sensitivity to the effects of the African engagement with the new economy, the disturbances caused by migrancy, the uncertainties of collapsing markets and fluctuating prices, and confusion in the face of the decline in the value of money.[7] Recent experience in the industrial world has underlined the connection, in certain circumstances, between depression, inflation and the strength of conservative ideologies. A profound sense of disorder in the economic world can be linked to attempts to strengthen social order. African colonial societies were in many ways divided, distrusting and defensive, and the illumination of these facets is something to which this socio-legal history may be able to contribute. Africans under colonial rule wanted both change and the creation of social order. The same people often pursued both goals and emphasised different political and social values when they spoke of change and when they spoke of order. Historians have concentrated so far more on what was said about change than what was said about order.

In the understanding of the development of social and political ideologies in any society, the ideas about control of wrongdoing, about punishment, and the ideas about the position of women and the regulation of sexual activities, seem to me to be of fundamental importance. They are also prime indicators of attitudes towards and responses to change. In our period the pace and direction of changes appeared to be beyond the control of local communities. Attitudes towards fundamental changes are complicated. People can welcome new developments which promise material rewards and greater freedoms, while at the same time deeply regretting the effects on basic personal relationships, and will rarely appreciate the connection between the two phenomena or the contradictory nature of their responses. Political opposition to alien rule can also unite different classes and generations with widely differing interests and ideologies, which are not at the time self-consciously realised or manifested. What appears to emerge from socio-legal history, with its study of local-level conflicts and its access to basic

225

ideas about social behaviour and social order, is the high level of anxiety about change in Central African colonial society. Anxiety and disquiet, as much as hope and vigour, must be read as a part of the African response to the unfolding future under colonial rule. It was not simply British officials, but many Africans too, who perceived and feared social disintegration.[8]

The anxiety regarding marriage and the family was expressed in a struggle to maintain aspects of systems of kinship with their accompanying values and obligations. But if kinship is the medium through which the working economic relationships of a society are expressed, and without which relationships of exchange of labour, goods and resources in people have no rationale, then we can see the struggle as being one to maintain not simply customs or sets of values, but the very form of the material organisation of the society. The penetration of colonial capitalism disturbed the economic relationships between generations, increased the prominence of money in place of service, and made disputes about money in marriage more frequent. It was an invasion of capitalist modes of relationship into the most intimate sphere of life, an area perceived in terms of moral values and judged in terms of the total state of rightness and wrongness of the society. So the anxiety was particularly marked, and the misconception of the causes peculiarly strong. And, as the old basis of relationships was dissolving, so the need and the effort to re-create them was at its strongest, and it could only express itself in a neo-traditional idiom.

These fears are less obvious if one's studies of the history of the colonial period focus around political activity and organisation, or economic change, though they may be suggested indirectly by some religious history. But they appear far more strongly when one looks at the responses to challenges to what was felt to be the existing order of things in areas like 'crime' and 'family' where one is given an indication, through the fashioning of the customary law, of both anxieties and proposed remedies, of the attempts to knit together the tearing social fabric. I have emphasised the strong element of gender conflict in the creation and enforcement of the customary law and generational conflict too must not be underestimated. Mary Douglas' observations of the Lele of Kasai in the late colonial period serve as a reminder. There was, she wrote, 'a barely veiled hostility which marked the relations between generations of men' as there were 'massive but precarious privileges which the older men had an interest in protecting'. While this hostility had existed, she thought, in earlier times also, 'in those days the old held the system more tightly in their grasp, and so hostility was more controlled.'[9]

In spite of the conflict which produced the customary law it has also at times appeared to represent a unified response to externally imposed changes. In this aspect it has appeared as something embodying an essential Africanness, representing a core of African values and institutions which survives throughout the colonial interlude. But one conclusion which can be drawn from this history is that the customary law is not a part of such a core.

226

It is more a part of events than of structures. This is not to say that the customary law of the family as it developed in the twentieth century was totally different from the custom which preceded it. Indeed a comparison of the recent Re-Statements of African Law with that of the earliest statements would show that this is not so. But this form of similarity is misleading for it is the spirit which informs laws, which directs the ways in which they are used, which gives them content in action. The law in England, for example, relating to the consequences for marriage of adultery, while outwardly similar in 1900 and 1950, had quite different meanings in practice. The fundamental tendency of the classical works of African anthropology was to describe working 'systems', and customs, or laws, in this scheme of things were the expression of social structures. If we add to this the sensitivity which has developed about the differences between 'structural time' and 'events' in historical change, i.e. an awareness that basic structures may change but slowly during times of fast-moving events, we compound the difficulty in accounting for changes in customary law. It has been located as part of a structure whose change is not simply to be accounted for in a stream of surface actions, but, if and when it happens, has to be conceived of as part of a basic structural shift. Yet if we develop doubts about the coherence of systems and, consequently, an awareness that customary law is not only to be understood as a manifestation of structures, then we must also to an extent change our view as to where it is located in historical time-scales. If we locate customary law within the competitive world of action, conflict and events, we have the potential to develop a better picture of its plastic and political nature.

The themes of gender conflict, anguish and disquiet which we have traced throughout our period were markedly present at its close. Epstein's study of the 'domestic domain' on the Zambian Copperbelt in the years 1950–6 emphasises the 'sexual canker' at the heart of relationships between men and women, and the 'anxiety' and 'insecurity' present in relationships between husband and wife.[10] He found a 'deep sense of moral concern even outrage' about developing urban mores. For many people it appeared 'as though the entire field of relations between men and women had been transformed into a sexual morass'. And it was not simply relations between men and women, but between old and young, among kin generally, and even between neighbours, that were becoming problematical and uneasy. Around the towns roamed the swaggering gangs of male youths with their emphasis on physical toughness; 'To the parental generation ... this was sheer anathema: here were their own children, insolent, violent and without any sense of *mucunshi*' (respect).

These disturbances in basic relationships were, as I have stressed, experienced as a crumbling of the social order as a whole. Epstein writes:

> Over the entire field of personal interaction, there was probably no indigenous concept of more fundamental importance than that conveyed by the Bemba term *mucunshi*. *Mucunshi* is commonly glossed as respect, politeness, good

227

Discussion

> manners and the like, *mucunshi* ... marks off what is distinctive in human behaviour postulating a standard of propriety that should govern all of one's conduct toward one's fellows ... but what also needs to be stressed is the way *mucunshi* is tied to a distinctly hierarchical view of social relationships.

The breakdown in human manners was connected to the subverting of the hierarchies which were perceived to be basic to social life, hierarchies which were, in Epstein's words, 'deemed to permeate almost every social relationship'.

And not only was there a collapse of respect but new circumstances placed great strains on those who still valued and tried to carry out correct behaviour. Epstein writes of relationships between husbands and wives in the towns that 'when people move into a strange environment, they will try to structure it along lines already familiar to them,' but that new circumstances are 'likely to generate pressures and demands so that the role expectations of the past no longer provide a basis for mutual understanding and adjustment but become rather a source of conflict'. This was also true of a broader spectrum of relationships. He notes the 'complaint' and 'resentment' with which people, who still acknowledged and shouldered the burdens of kinship, fulfilled their duties. Reciprocity was still an active mechanism but 'one of its major by-products was to introduce a watchfulness into relations of kin, a feature marked by a general readiness to perceive slight or take umbrage that often brought a high level of tension to the every-day conduct of these relationships.'[11] Thus not only was abandoning the good old ways productive of conflict, but so were the very efforts made to keep to them in a changing social environment. For that new environment contained at its heart the tendency towards isolation, and the watchfulness and tension with which kin relations were conducted, also typifies relationships with non-kin neighbours. 'In a word', writes Epstein, 'men tended to be guarded in their relations with neighbours' and trivial incidents often led to violent responses.[12]

Epstein is here writing about urbanisation on the Copperbelt but it seems that these are themes present in relationships in the rural areas as well over a considerable period and that they represent the development of new economic rather than simply urban relationships. And it might well be that the earlier signs of transformations in basic relationships caused more apprehension than they did once they had become a ubiquitous part of life, as on the Copperbelt. Epstein stresses, as I have done, that it is only in this context that one can approach an understanding of 'norms'.[13] 'At so many points', he writes, 'one was confronted with such uncertainty, ambiguity and conflict so far as norms were concerned' that the question was not what were the norms but 'how in such a seemingly inchoate situation rules were formulated and came to be acknowledged'.[14] It was the inchoateness of the situation which made people uneasy. They were both anxious about social breakdown and guardedly watchful in their relationships in a way which made them more exacting in their definition of what they perceived to be their due. These forces pushed in the direction of a formulation of rules.

CRIME AND COURTS IN COLONIAL CENTRAL AFRICA

The colonial nature of the system of criminal justice, in its authoritarian approach to administrative problems as well as to crime, and in the nature of the offences it penalised, stands out clearly. It cannot at the end of the colonial period have been possible for people to regard the state's courts as agents of justice or opponents of evil when they had devoted themselves assiduously for so long to punishing offenders against the range of ordinances regulating daily life. While the district officers saw themselves as bringers of justice, this image was not clearly reflected in the minds of others. 'The Boma', as one Malawian wrote, 'was a terror to all the people.'[15] It was not simply that life became highly regulated but that run-of-the-mill regulatory activities were carried out in a disciplinary fashion. The governor of Nyasaland, for example, in 1930, wrote to the secretary of state for the colonies urging that more punitive measures for breaches of tobacco-growing regulations (the purpose of which was to help the production of a better crop) be introduced. His argument was that 'obedience' needed to be enforced to ensure the 'moral development' of the growers. This curious cast of mind, which affected even those regulatory activities which were primarily conceived of as helpful, was fundamental to the administration of criminal justice at all levels. The early reforming spring of the lawgivers was to peter out in a dry scrubland of punitive ordinances.[16]

The Native Courts, developing under the aegis of the Boma, developed also in its image, aiming at securing obedience rather than arbitrating disputes. A look at the profile of activities of one court over a period of a few years shows how much the Native Courts depended on administrative direction. In 1948 the Native Courts in Chinsali district in Zambia heard only 390 criminal cases. Of these, 143 were convictions for infringements against health orders and 70 for breaches of forestry and agricultural orders. In 1949, 'with more frequent touring by District Officers and more pressures being brought to bear on Native Authorities to enforce their own laws the numbers of cases brought before the courts ... increased considerably.' That year 768 cases were heard and by 1951, 1,760, 'due mainly to pressure exerted'.[17] Of these 1,608 were for failures to obey Native Authority rules and orders, 684 were for 'health' cases and 244 for forestry. 'From the foregoing figures,' wrote the district officer, 'it is apparent that in the recorded cases of the Native Courts there is little of what could be described as "native law and custom".' It might be, he went on, that 'true' African law was being administered outside of the official courts, or it might be a 'combination of both processes by which traditional law and its administration is becoming divorced in the Africans' mind from statutory law and its administration'. Indeed many Africans avoided taking sensitive family and property cases to the Native Authority Courts to avoid the 'judgement by decree which has become a feature of Native Courts'.

As the Urban Native Courts developed they occupied themselves similarly. A study of the Northern Rhodesian courts[18] showed that, of the nearly 25,000 cases dealt with by them in a year, only about 10 per cent concerned anything like crime in the normal sense. The largest category, one-third, consisted of charges of unlawful residence in the urban areas, as the courts became the agency of colonial controls on urbanisation. In Malawi in the 1950s a similar profile is evident. Some 15 per cent of cases concerned ordinary crime, while 40 per cent of offences were against the taxation laws and another 25 per cent against other 'colonial' disciplinary ordinances.[19] As a pointer to the dependence of the courts on administrative direction it may be noted that taxation convictions disappeared altogether in the first year of independence.

The Native Authority Courts, therefore, dealt with the bulk of the criminal (and civil) work in the territories, which meant punishing, under administrative pressures, a vast number of minor offences against colonial discipline. And they punished harshly. African courts, wrote Clifford, 'dealt with such offences very firmly and these "technical offenders" were often very heavily punished.' It appeared to him that the Native Courts 'lean heavily towards punitive measures not only to discourage offenders but also it seems to maintain the prestige of the court'. Indeed maintaining respect for the courts was something of a problem and convictions for contempt were frequent.[20] Quite apart from using the power to punish to maintain a generalised respect, there were great advantages in controlling a court. Beidelman has described a local situation in Tanganyika, concluding that 'The courts were the major political institution ... whereby those in authority maintained their power: courts provided the only means whereby local leaders could coerce strongly dissident elements without risking the disapproval of the colonial administration.'[21] The chiefs and elders wished to keep this control over the Native Court system in the teeth of developments in colonial policy designed to professionalise and bureaucratise the local administration of justice. In Malawi, for example, they strongly opposed the appointment of the Native Courts adviser, an official foisted on rather reluctant colonial governments by the Colonial Office in London to work on the integration of customary and official legal systems.[22]

PROPERTY, POLITICS AND THE DISINTEGRATION OF COMMUNITY

I have traced above the emergence of a customary 'law of persons' through a process of the interaction of British institutions and legal ideas with African social and economic needs, and through the use Africans made of the new institutional forms. The economic revolution which made these needs take the form that they did also in time produced new pressures on the use of land. As land came to be seen as a scarce economic resource the control of which could be turned to monetary advantage, competition to use and control it grew. And, in a process which I suggest was to replicate that of the development of the customary law of persons, the customary law of land tenure began to develop.

In pre-colonial society, as Colson has written, people were linked to land through their membership of groups. It was their group standing which gave them access to land and consequently their concern was with maintaining their position linked to other persons rather than with rights in land. There were obvious limitations on the extent of land that a household head could cultivate. Large acreages were manageable 'only if [he] had control over the labour of a numerous following who looked to [him] for other reasons than their land-holding'.[23] Links to and rights in persons through whom land was acquired and by whom it could be used were crucial, not rights to land as such. But through the period I have been considering, rights in people as a resource were becoming less enforceable and negotiable, which meant that rights in property had gradually to be differentiated from rights in persons.

As control of land, particularly once it could be worked by contract labour, became an important source of wealth, it became the subject of specific rights. People began to resort to courts over control, sale, lease and boundary disputes. As Hailey noticed when he was compiling his memoranda on native administration there were emerging by the 1940s in Central Africa 'new practices with regard to the holding of property', characterised by an increase in 'individualistic tendencies'.[24] Overcrowding in Malawi, for example, was leading to 'a tendency for natives to assert, and for Native Authorities to admit, individual ownership in land'.[25] The Native Courts were making new customary law: 'The process frequently involves entry into a field where the customary law itself affords no precedents.'[26] Historians of East Africa have commented on the same process. Iliffe observed of developments in the coffee-growing areas of North Tanganyika that Chagga customary law on the subject of land was 'vague, contentious and mutable'. But as the land hunger of the commercial farmers grew, so land disputes multiplied in local courts, as did claims that freehold tenure was 'traditional'.[27] People in Kenya, Kitching writes, had by the early 1930s come to conceptualise past and current use of land in terms of ownership, purchase, sale and tenancy.[28] Mayer shows how conflicts arose among the Gusii when individualisation led to the seizure of clan bush lands. At the start of the process, he stresses, there was no law. Elders tried to settle disputes without the guidance of rules, or by adapting rules relating to bridewealth. He emphasises that the law suits came first and the substantive law afterwards. Law suits without law were 'open trials of strength with no possible decision by precise legal rules'. As with 'family' and 'marriage' cases prior to the establishment of British courts, so with land disputes 'a seal of law was sought for an arrangement which grew out of a trial of strength between families.'[29]

Yet this process did not take place in an institutional vacuum. Hailey, for one, was most anxious that it should not. A generation ago, he wrote in 1940, native tribunals had no custom on sale, hire or interest. Now they were dealing with these matters, ostensibly by custom, but really by 'a somewhat crude law of equity'. He envisaged a conscious use of the Native Courts to bring about the change, but they could not simply be left alone to do it. 'We cannot leave the African to devise,' he wrote, 'without any guidance from us, the means by which custom can, through the operation of the native courts, accommodate itself to conditions which are making something like a revolutionary change in the habits and ideas of society.'[30] But while there was an occasional element of conscious guidance it was by no means the dominant way by which institutional factors made themselves felt. It was, as in the case of family law, the feeding of claims into a court system dominated by British ideas which produced the customary law relating to land. When conflicts about limited land resources began to be taken to court, 'adjudication encouraged the rapid development of fairly comprehensive bodies of customary, though untraditional, law.' The courts could not simply settle trials of strength without rules, nor apply a crude law of equity, for they were 'under the ultimate jurisdiction of colonial officials who expected the courts to enforce long-established custom rather than current opinion. Common official stereotypes about African customary land law thus came to be used by colonial officials in assessing the legality of current decisions and so came to be incorporated in "customary" systems of tenure.'[31] Like the customary law relating to marriage, the customary law relating to land cannot therefore be understood without the officials' contribution. People with desires to acquire new rights in land were quick to turn the ideas of British officials to their own use. As Kitching writes, changes in African conceptions about rights in land resulted in part from 'Africans drawing lessons and parallels from the material consequences of settler land "ownership"'. By confirming white ideas about African land 'tenure' they hoped both to get back land lost and protect land held.[32] Sometimes, as Colson points out, it was officials seeking to protect African land usage who were 'tempted to give a precise legal definition to the vaguest claim'. In response to the onslaught of settler interests (and in the light of the Southern Rhodesia precedent where African concepts had been ruled to have no legal effect because they were insufficiently law-like) some officials approached the question of African land tenure with European concepts of tenure in mind 'which they were prone to interpret as universal legal principles applicable everywhere .... In particular they assumed that the full range of land rights, covered by the concept of proprietary ownership, must exist in Africa as in Europe.' Again the analogy with marriage can be drawn: once a marriage-like institution was identified it was assumed to have, and gradually made in law to have, the range of rights and duties of a European marriage. As Colson points out there was an analogy also with political authority in that, as it was assumed that people must have chiefs even where they had none, so it was assumed that land must have an owner, even where rights had never been defined.

The search for owners created systems of communal tenure 'with precisely defined rules'. 'The newly created system was described as resting on tradition and presumably derived its legitimacy from immemorial custom. The degree to which it was a reflection of the contemporary situation and the joint creation of colonial officials and African leaders . . . was unlikely to be recognised.'[33]

Thus one could say that law came to persons first, and then to property. As courts and rules replaced arbitration for certain parts of the law of persons, particularly the formation and dissolution of marriages, so, by the end of the colonial period, courts rather than arbitrators were beginning to be used for property disputes. Colson observed in the 1940s that while many cases were still being settled out of court, occasionally with the Native Court officers themselves acting as arbitrators, the new class of wealthier farmers were inclined to take their cases to the Boma courts, and the Native Courts themselves 'urge their people to come to court on any matter where the transfer of property is involved so that a proper record can be made'.[34] The problems involved in this process of legalisation and the effect on concepts of property and rights were serious and confused in the area of family property and inheritance which fall, as it were, in between the law of property and the law of persons. Western legal systems have struggled, and still struggle, with the problem of division of family and marital property, and African courts and families, under the pressure of new economic forces and legal institutions, found these problems no easier to solve. We have already seen how the earning and accumulating powers of individuals created conflict over who owned the money and goods acquired, and how tensions increased with the nucleation of families. These conflicts tended to come to a head at death, where relatives of dead men descended upon their widows, commonly seizing goods and dismantling houses, and, in more esoteric cases, demanding gratuities and workman's compensation payments. Neither the Boma courts nor the Native Courts were capable of settling these conflicts, for which no customary law existed, and in both countries legislation was eventually to be passed legalising African wills, and protecting the inheritance rights of widows and children.[35] This was an area, then in which no customary law had emerged in our period, there being no group or interest sufficiently powerful to create one (as in the case of marriage and land), and, unlike land and marriage, no correspondence between those interests which were being expressed, and a suitable image of a customary law of inheritance in the minds of British officials. Indeed the Native Courts, which the Boma required to state rules when deciding cases, specifically, it seems, steered clear of settling cases connected with inheritance, personal property and family rights. It would appear, one district officer wrote, that these questions were being handled by 'other agencies of society' which avoided imposed decisions.[36] This might suggest to us that legalisation was by no means an inevitable process but that it appealed as a strategy when it was perceived to bring benefits.

Discussion

'When the kinship groups disintegrated', wrote Max Weber, '... the question arose as to how far the legal procedure of the political association would intrude into relations among members of the same kinship group or even the same community.'[37] We might consider the case of *R*. v. *Syamusunya*, a prosecution for larceny heard in Zambia in 1931, which illustrates the way in which new economic behaviour and new judicial ideas and institutions entered into people's lives. In the new economy there was a market for African cattle but in the previous system of economic and legal relations there was no clear definition of who had a right to sell them. In Syamusunya's case a white cattle-dealer bought cattle from a junior member of a family who had removed them from the Kraal of his family head. The latter claimed the return of the cattle on the ground that they could not be taken and sold without his consent. The Boma was drawn into the affair, as it was a dispute between a white setttler and an African, and was confronted with the problem of deciding whose the cattle really were, and whether, if they had been taken without permission, they had been stolen. In terms of the Boma's legal system two things were needed: a clear answer to the question of title; and a consequent clarity in defining a wrongful act of infringement of title, which would enable a prosecution to proceed. But establishing title was not easy. It appeared from the witnesses that all the kin 'owned' the cattle in question. Nonetheless, the evidence extracted as to the customary law appeared to establish that no one could sell family-owned cattle without the permission of the senior member. So far, so good: a wrongful act of appropriation appeared to have been made. But what were to be the consequences? One witness on customary law told the court that 'no one will take his brother to be tried.' As another witness put it, if a kinsman took a beast in your absence, 'you can be very angry but you will be ashamed to prosecute it as no one does it.' This made things difficult for R.O. Ingram, the presiding magistrate. Was a theft a theft if it would not have been prosecuted? A third witness insisted that only a 'hard-hearted' person would take the case to a chief, who would not order compensation. Ingram had to consider whether the customary law, so established, with its apparent amalgam of communality of rights in goods, the prerogative powers of senior kinsmen, and lack of punitive enforcement, fell within the definition of repugnancy. If not, it should stand. Like so many of the colonial magistrates he turned to Maine's *Ancient Law*, as the authority on primitive life of all kinds. Maine showed, said a confused Ingram, that the law of 'primitive humanity' was simply a series of precedents and that, this being so, the custom of people in 'helping themselves to their relatives' cattle' was legal, and was not theft. His unwillingness to define the limits of property rights, and the proper attendant relationships and behaviour, brought forth a scandalised response from the prosecutor in the case. Natural justice and morality, he wrote, meant neither English law nor the African view of things but 'the ordinary common sense point of view of a European'. He would not accept that Africans should have 'only the instincts of their relatives for fair

234

play to prevent their being robbed'. There was 'no reason to believe that a native's sense of honour is superior to that of a white man and if such a custom existed among Europeans I have little doubt of the result.'[38] Yet as the case itself shows, the increasing commercialisation of rural life was creating situations in which the prosecutor's faith in a universal human greed was being justified. There were more and more situations in which the 'honour' of a system of kin property was crumbling in the face of new opportunities for individual appropriation, and the new legal order could not be long satisfied with a situation in which people were not individual bearers of rights in property and protected as such.

We have seen many indications of the ways in which the penetration of the money economy could be experienced. Iliffe quotes a moving Nyakyusa lament expressed in 1937:

> The tribal law which God gave us is being destroyed completely . . . . those who have been chosen and salaried are happy, thus they despise their unfortunate friends in the same rank. In the old days when there was no money, there was no killing each other, no jealousy or falsehoods; while in these present days all these have happened simply because the new customs have upset the old ones, in nothing save in money alone.[39]

This disintegration of community, out of which, Marx remarked, law emerged, was widely experienced. It appears to me to be broadly true to say that while much of recent African literature has been dominated by the theme of Things Falling Apart, much of recent historical writing has been about Things Being Brought Together. Yet the literary insights appear to have more to tell us about the ways in which living through these years was experienced. I have drawn attention to Epstein's recent account of this experience in the urban areas but I cannot emphasise too strongly that this was also a rural phenomenon. With the development of migrant labour, and of agriculture for the market, settlements and families fragmented and conflict and injury were experienced as the circle within which obligations were acknowledged narrowed. In the new economy management of money rather than of people was becoming important. This is most neatly encapsulated in Long's observations regarding the changing role of the *nkhoswe*, that most important figure in the affairs of the matrilineal group, the negotiator, guardian and guarantor of marriages. The term was extended, by 1963/4, when Long did his fieldwork, to cover any member of a group of matrikin who acted as a banker for the family. 'The role of the modern *nkhoswe* is to safeguard the money, property and interests of all those close relatives who are away working in town.'[40]

The development of the market was pushing people towards contractual relationships, the struggle for control of things – money, land, crops, cattle – rather than of people. Yet there was often insufficient profit to hire labour, and farmers had to squeeze kin labour for market purposes, leading to an emphasis on traditional obligations for one purpose, at precisely the time when they were being increasingly ignored for other purposes. In these contradictory circumstances, in which the money economy led people to break some ties while strengthening other claims, conflicts about what was and what was not customary were intense. An emerging class conflict, conflict between generations and between genders are all apparent, and claims about custom were a way of legitimating positions in all three. Depression in the rural areas, and the scarcity of money, as well as the availability of land, slowed the emergence of paid agricultural labour, which meant that unpaid labour continued to be important. Thus while larger kin groups were fragmenting under the impact of the market economy, which was also breaking elders' control over adult male labour, the emphasis on rights over the younger generation, and in particular over women, intensified. The mass 'escape' of women to the towns, in spite of the difficulties that they had faced there, is one manifestation of these pressures. On the political front the potential for resistance by women to their position was building up, and was later to be channelled into their role in the nationalist parties. Heisler[41] has drawn attention to the part played by women, 'sometimes violent, in undermining the continuity of the peasant systems'. All aspects of the web of relationships which secured women were to be strained by the struggle for political emancipation: 'if women showed disrespect to a Native Court or headman who sought to enforce regulations about contour ridging or smallpox', as they did in the course of political campaigns against the colonial government's rural programmes, 'why should they heed Native Authority orders which would bottle them up in their villages?' We might think of all of these circumstances as the hidden agenda when discussions regarding moral breakdown raged.

The literature of legal anthropology has demonstrated most effectively that law and politics are not isolatable but permeable, and that while normative institutions are shot through with political behaviour, politics manipulates normative resources. It is an advance to have secured the understanding that legal and political behaviour are not easily separable and that the pretence that they are serves a particular political purpose. But it is not the end of the road. As I have suggested it does not reach an understanding of the specificity of legal behaviour. British officials manning the colonial state cast some of their acts in a special form which they conceived of as legal and in this sense it is correct to associate the coming of the state with 'legal form'. But it was by no means inevitable that Africans would adopt and use these forms and many remained largely uninfluenced by this mode of conceptualising power and order. Many were to choose to use it, however, as a way of ordering their social and economic relations with others, and their relations with the colonial state, because in the circumstances they found it to be the most advantageous instrument for translating their values and interests into power over others, of redefining, limiting and enforcing obligations. It is in this sense that law comes with the state to colonial Central Africa, both as an imposed form and as one logically adopted for use by many Africans. To use the terminology of an earlier era of African

236

historiography, Africans were the active users, not the passive recipients, of the new form, creating a customary law to deal with their new situation.

Both the colonial state and many Africans chose what sort of obligations and relationships were to be conceived of as legal ones. British colonial policies sought to support a particular rural power structure and economic base and therefore gave the state's legal imprimatur to it, legitimising these policies in the name of tradition. As Fitzpatrick has observed in the context of New Guinea, the colonial government abstracted 'something called "native custom" from the operative dynamic of traditional dispute settlement . . . this stance was basically fiction.'[42] It appears from my account that government was neither alone nor unaided in this process, that it had African partners. Yet the ways open to Africans pursuing legalisation were curiously fashioned, affected by the determination of British legal administrators not to commit customary law to writing for fear that this would freeze it and arrest its development.[43] At the bottom of this was the British lawyers' misunderstanding of their own legal processes. They thought of judges as essentially applying rules and precedents rather than as adapting them to fit new situations. They thought therefore that the absence of definition and precedent would make change in Africa easier. But it made it harder, freezing the law in a reactionary stance rather than allowing it flexibility. For writing and precedent do not fix legal development, they make it possible. The alternative to an appeal to precedent, which is adaptable, is not fluidity, but an appeal to moral first principles. My interest throughout this account has been in the African agency in making the customary law in interaction with British institutions, rather than in the content of the colonial legal system. From my standpoint, the view of some writers with a law and development perspective that the customary law is a traditional obstacle, a survival which needs to be modernised, seems opaque.[44] Throughout the colonial period, as now, customary law was not the dead hand of tradition, but represented the responses of living interests, though channelled in special ways, to new developments. It has been convenient to depict them as traditional and on the way out because they are often not interests which coincide with those of the developers.

In 1936 R.R. Marrett wrote of the study of early law that 'Any help that can come from the side of the study of primitive peoples must relate wholly to [the] historical branch of Jurisprudence, since we are not likely to want to go back to the savage in order to substitute his values for ours.'[45] At the present time this appears to have been an exact misreading, because the anthropology of law has become respectable in legal studies at large because it reveals usable values in so-called early systems. But Marrett also went on to say, 'what we call civilisation is but the relatively adult stage of an evolutionary process which even in its crude beginnings reveals a fairly uniform tendency . . . . Thus comparative Jurisprudence can well afford to find room for a section devoted to the embryology of law.' Yet whatever may have been the case in the evolutionary development of law in Europe, an

237

historical rather than an evolutionary approach shows, I suggest, the opposite processes at work in Africa. In Central Africa developed law came first, while the elaborated customary law came afterwards, not an embryonic form of, but a product of, the western legal form, the colonial state, and its economy.

If we can fix firmly in our minds that the law of the western state comes first in time, and customary law afterwards, rather than vice versa, a new range of questions regarding contemporary processs is opened to us. For if the customary law comes first it is bound to be seen by modernisers, British and African, as an increasingly irrelevant survival, shrinking, and being made to shrink, as 'real' law expands. Or, as the perceived predecessor of the state's law, it lends itself well to appeals by traditionalists, both British and African nationalist, to whom it is useful as a means of legitimation. If it is seen to come afterwards we might expect that the presence of the state and its legal form could continue to produce a 'customary law' and we will be alive to questions about what kinds of interest and activities seek to, and are able to, express themselves in this form, rather than finding a more straightforward political expression. This kind of strategy could be applied to an understanding of the development of the customary land law.

We might understand too the connections between the development of the customary law and that of the new tribes. In the development of ethnicity during the colonial period, as well as in the development of the colonial and post-colonial states, the customary law served most usefully, not as a system of rules, but as a method of legitimation. The new 'tribes' had recourse to an ideology of traditionalism of which the customary law was a part. It defined practices that were special to groups, and also carried along with it the important symbolism of a traditional world of tribal ways and practices, which helped people both to make identifications and to legitimate new demands.

Not only did the colonial state and the new tribes need the new law to be customary, but so does modern cultural nationalism, and the interests of the new legal professional elite. For the colonisation of Africa by western legal forms and institutions continues under the aegis of the growing legal profession, which, in other circumstances, has been among the most verbally ardent of the opponents of colonialism.[46] This process, however, is partly being legitimated by its presentation as a development of a customary law which is essentially African, a recapturing of a pre-colonial dynamic. Yet if it is rules that the legal systems of the successor states require in the areas in which the customary law now operates, it would be possible to formulate far more equitable ones than those deriving from the inequities of the colonial situation which currently find acceptance on the basis that they are essentially and traditionally African. If it is 'custom' that is wanted, in the sense of a system which uses living principles in flexible and popular disputing processes, one could have this without the oppressive and authoritarian legalism of the neo-traditional customary law. In either case the customary law appears to offer the worst of both worlds: masquerading as stemming from African communities, it pre-empts their more fruitful participation in this area of national life. In this context we may recall Ihering's dictum that illuminates much of this book 'the progress of law consists in the destruction of every natural tie, in a continued process of separation and isolation.'[47] There is some sadness in looking to law as an instrument of cultural nationalism and symbolic of the restoration of the African community. The logic of the legal form was adapted to the process of individuation that I have described. It is inappropriate as a means of restoring a lost and lamented social solidarity.

Notes

1. Social and legal history in Central Africa

1 I will use the word 'custom' for norms and practices existing in the pre-colonial period and for those used in dispute-settlement, not involving governmental agencies, under colonial rule. Customary law refers to the norms and practices recognised by the courts in the colonial period. Custom changes: the customary law is what Hobsbawm has called an 'invented tradition'. See E. Hobsbawm and T. Ranger (eds), *The Invention of Tradition* (Cambridge, 1983) 1–3.

2 See e.g. J. G. A. Pocock, 'Time, Institutions and Actions, an Essay on Traditions and Their Understanding', in *Politics, Language and Time* (New York, 1971) esp. at 235.

3 See F. S. Maitland, 'Why the History of English Law was Not Written'. Inaugural Lecture, Cambridge, 1888.

4 R. W. Gordon, 'Historicism in Legal Scholarship', *Yale Law Journal* 90 (1981).

5 Address on opening the Ghana Law School, *Journal of African Law* 6, (1962).

6 See Baron Hailey, *An African Survey* (London, 1938) ch. 7.

7 E. Stokes, *The English Utilitarians and India* (Oxford, 1959).

8 See H. Macmillan, *The Tides of Fortune* (London, 1969), 273. Cf. B. N. Pandey, *The Introduction of British Law into India* (London, 1967), foreword by C. H. Philips.

9 'The Adaptation of Imported Law in Africa', *Journal of African Law* 4, (1960).

10 J. Maquet, *Africanity* (New York, 1972) 76; B. Davidson, *The Africans* (London, 1973) 206–7; and A. Nekam, *Experiences in African Customary Law* (Edinburgh, 1966).

11 See e.g. J. B. Ojwang, 'Rural Dispute Settlement in Kenya', *Zambia Law Journal* 7–9 (1975–7) 64, 66.

12 We might recall John Austin's remarks on the customary origins of European serfdom and slavery: 'Let us turn our eyes in what direction we may, we shall find that there is no connection between customary law and the well-being of the many.' See Gordon, 'Historicism', 1033–4.

13 M. G. Marwick, *Sorcery in its Social Setting* (Manchester, 1965) 226, 196–7, 529.

14 D. A. Strickland, 'Kingship and Slavery in African Thought', *Comparative Studies in Society and History* 18 (1976) 373, 375.

15 R. Canter, 'Dispute Settlement and Dispute Processing in Zambia: Individual Choice vs Societal Constraints', in L. Nader and H. Todd (eds), *This Disputing Process – Law in Ten Societies* (New York, 1978) 261.

16 See J. Starr and B. Yngvesson, 'Scarcity and Disputing: Zeroing in on Compromise Decisions', *American Ethnologist* 2 (1975); and M. Chanock, 'Signposts or Tombstones?', *Law in Context* 1 (1983).

17 H. Franklin, *The Flag Wagger* (London, 1974) 38. See also below Chapters 4 and 6.

18 This has been a fairly common phenonemon in Africa. See L. Rosen, 'Law and Social Change in the New Nations', *Comparative Studies in Society and History* 20 (1978). See also M. L. Chanock, 'Neo-traditionalism and the Customary Law in Malawi', *African Law Studies* 16 (1978). See also E. Maliwa, 'Customary Law and the Administration of Justice in Malawi' (London, M.Phil., 1969) 48–9; L. Chimango-Lefani, 'The Traditional Courts in Malawi', East African Social Science Conference (Makerere, 1971).

19 M. Bloch, *Feudal Society*, vol. 1 (London edn, 1965) 113. Cf. J. G. A. Pocock, 'The Common Law Mind: Custom and the Immemorial', in *The Ancient Constitution and the Feudal Law* (Cambridge, 1957; New York edn, 1967) 36, where he discusses the ambiguities in the idea of custom. It implies that law is in a 'constant change and adaptation . . . and it might seem that there was no theory more likely to lead to a historical conception of the nature of law.' Yet the English common lawyers also held custom to be immemorial and immutable.

20 F. Kern, *Kingship and Law in the Middle Ages* (London, 1939), quoted in M. T. Clanchy, *From Memory to Written Record, England 1066–1307* (London, 1979) 233.

21 M. Bloch, *Feudal Society* 14; and M. T. Clanchy, 'Remembering the Past and the Good Old Law', *History* 55 (1970) 165 and 171.

22 Clanchy, 'Remembering the Past', 172.

23 H. Morris and J. S. Read, *Indirect Rule and the Search for Justice* (London, 1972) 186–7.

24 See J. Goody and I. Watt, 'The Consequences of Literacy', in J. Goody (ed.), *Literacy in Traditional Societies* (Cambridge, 1968).

25 See M. L. Chanock, 'Political Economy of Independent Agriculture in Colonial Malawi', *Journal of Social Science* 1 (1972), and 'Ambiguities in the Malawian Political Tradition', *African Affairs* 74 (1975).

26 For figures see J. M. Davis, *Modern Industry and the African* (1933, London edn, 1967); E. Berger, *Race, Labour and Colonial Rule* (Oxford, 1974); and A. Roberts, *History of Zambia* (London, 1976).

27 As Collier has written of Fallers' analysis of Soga law, he confined his analysis to the logical and systematic realm of ideas without sufficient attention to the vested interests which were being justified by the conceptual system. Litigants in adultery cases and marital disputes were, she observed, 'really fighting about money . . . not over rights to a woman's presence', J. Collier, review of L. A. Fallers, *Law Without Precedent* in *American Anthropologist* 74 (1972) 857.

28 See in general R. Palmer and N. Parsons (eds), *The Roots of Rural Poverty* (London, 1977); and H. L. Vail, 'The Political Economy of East-Central Africa', in D. Birmingham and P. Martin (eds), *History of Central Africa*, vol. 2 (London, 1983).

29 See G. Wilson, *The Economics of Detribalisation in Northern Rhodesia* (Livingstone, 1941–2); and Davis, *Modern Industry*. 'The mine', Davis chided, 'is not primarily interested in native morals' (77).

30 H. J. Stanley to Secretary of State for Colonies, 19 Sept. 1924, quoted in C. Perrings, *Black Mineworkers in Central Africa* (New York, 1979) at 147–8. My italics.

31 See e.g. C. Murray, 'Migrant Labour and Changing Family Structure in the Rural Peripheries of Southern Africa', *Journal of Southern African Studies* 2 (1980) 155–6, 140–2; and see C. Murray, *Families Divided* (Cambridge, 1981); and D. Parkin, 'Kind Bridewealth and Hard Cash', in J. Comaroff (ed.), *The Meaning of Marriage Payments* (London, 1980) 198.

32 See Chanock, 'The Political Economy of Independent Agriculture'.

33 J. Iliffe, *A Modern History of Tanganyika* (Cambridge, 1979) 163.

34 See in particular F. S. Snyder, *Capitalism and Legal Change* (London, 1981).

35 N. Long, *Social Change and the Individual* (Manchester, 1968) 222.

36 K. O. Poewe, 'Matriliny in the Throes of Change', *Africa* 48 (1978) 353.

37 Long, *Social Change*, 64–5 and 22–3; and Poewe, *Matriliny*, 206–8.

Notes

38 C. Lancaster, 'Gwembwe Valley Marriage Prestations in Historical Perspective: A Rejoinder to Colson and Scudder', *American Anthropologist* 83 (1981) 372–3.

39 E. Colson, quoted in Lancaster, ibid., 374.

40 See also G. Chauncey, 'The Locus of Reproduction: Women's Labour on the Zambian Copperbelt 1927–1953', *Journal of Southern African Studies* 7 (1981).

41 A. Richards, *Land, Labour and Diet in Northern Rhodesia* (London, 1939) 142, 211, 214, 172.

42 C. Lancaster, 'Brideservice, Residence and Authority among the Goba (N. Shona) of the Zambesi Valley', *Africa* 44 (1974) 47, 49.

43 See in particular C. H. Bledsoe, *Women and Marriage in Kpelle Society* (Stanford, 1980); J. Comaroff and S. Roberts, *Rules and Processes* (Chicago, 1980); J. Guyer, 'Household and Community in African Studies', *African Studies Review* 24 (1981); W. MacGaffey, 'Lineage Structure, Marriage and the Family Amongst the Central Bantu', *Journal of African History* 24 (1983); S. Marks and R. Rathbone, 'The History of the Family in Africa: Introduction', *Journal of African History* 24 (1983).

44 T. C. McCaskie, 'State and Society, Marriage and Adultery: Some Considerations Towards a Social History of Pre-Colonial Asante', *Journal of African History* 22 (1981) 481, 492.

45 J. L. Comaroff, 'Bridewealth and the Control of Ambiguity in a Tswana Chiefdom', in J. L. Comaroff (ed.) *The Meaning of Marriage Payments* (London, 1980) 192–3.

46 Lancaster, 'Brideservice', 47, 46.

47 R. Canter, 'Dispute Settlement', 253.

48 R. Frankenburg, Introduction to Long, *Social Change*.

49 J. Lonsdale, 'States and Social Processes in Africa: A Historiographical Survey', *African Studies Review* 24 (1981) 195.

50 W. M. J. Van Binsbergen, 'The Unit of Study and the Interpretation of Ethnicity. Studying the Nkoya of Western Zambia', *Journal of Southern African Studies* 8 (1981) 71, 74, 79.

51 Canter, 'Dispute Settlement', 255.

52 D. Birmingham, 'The Forest and Savannah of Central Africa', in J. Flint (ed.), *The Cambridge History of Africa*, vol. 5 (Cambridge, 1976) 300: 'the overpowering of the weak by the strong in society became a feature of social relations.'

53 A. Roberts, *A History of Zambia* (London, 1976) 80, 90, 141, and *A History of the Bemba* (London, 1973) xxix, 295.

54 Long, *Social Change*, 132.

55 Iliffe, *Tanganyika*, 323.

56 G. Prins, *The Hidden Hippopotamus* (Cambridge, 1980) 28, 32, 97, 102. See also E. Colson, 'African Society at the Time of the Scramble', in L. Gann and P. Duignan (eds), *Colonialism in Africa*, vol. 1: *The History and Politics of Colonialism* (Cambridge, 1969) 29.

57 *The Handbook of Nyasaland* (London, 1932) 142.

58 Ibid., 128, quoting Protectorate Annual Report 1904.

59 Quoted in Long, *Social Change*, 81.

60 H. L. Vail, 'Ecology and History: The Example of Eastern Zambia', *Journal of Southern African Studies* 3 (1977) 136.

61 'The Story of Bwembya of the Bemba Tribe', told to Audrey Richards in M. Perham (ed.), *Ten Africans* (London, 1936).

62 *Ten Africans*, 19, 17, 23–4, 39–40.

63 See J. Hooker, 'Tradition and "Traditional Courts": Malawi's Experiment in Law', *American University Fieldstaff Reports: Africa* 15 (3) (March, 1971).

64 M. Chona, *Zambia Hansard* 1966, 10 March 1966, 174. See generally on this subject, 'One Nation, One Judiciary: the Lower Courts of Zambia', *Zambia Law Journal* 2 (1970).

65 *Zambia Hansard* 1966, 10 March and 16 August 1966.

Notes

2. African law and anthropologists

1 For surveys of the literature on the anthropology of law see M. L. Chanock, 'Signposts or Tombstones? Some Reflections on Recent Works on the Anthropology of Law', *Law in Context* 1 (1983); F. Snyder, 'Anthropology, Dispute Processes and Law: A Critical Introduction', *British Journal of Law and Society* 8 (2) (1981); S. Roberts, *Order and Dispute* (Harmondsworth, 1979); S. F. Moore, *Law as Process* (London, 1978); J. Collier, 'Legal Processes', *Annual Review of Anthropology* 4 (1975); B. Yngvesson, 'Law in Pre-industrial Societies', in H. M. Johnson (ed.), *Social System and Legal Process* (London, 1978).

2 R. S. Rattray, *Ashanti Law and Constitution* (Oxford, 1929) 1–6. Rattray trained as an English barrister. Cf. also S. Hartland, *Primitive Law* (London, 1924).

3 C. K. Meek, *Law and Authority in a Nigerian Tribe* (London, 1937; New York edn, 1970).

4 *Law and Authority* xiii, 251, 124, 20, 87, 320, 251.

5 Ibid., 326, 333, 348.

6 See J. H. Driberg, 'The African Conception of Law', *Journal of Comparative and International Law* 16 (1934).

7 Prominent amongst these were I. Schapera, *Handbook of Tswana Law and Custom* (London, 1938); H. Cory and M. Hartnell, *Customary Law of the Haya Tribe* (London, 1945); and H. Cory, *Sukuma Law and Custom* (London, 1953).

8 K. Llewellyn and E. A. Hoebel, *The Cheyenne Way* (Norman, 1941).

9 P. G. Sack, *Land Between the Laws* (Canberra, 1973) 5, 18.

10 A. Nekam, *Experiences in African Customary Law* (Edinburgh, 1966); cf M. Galanter, 'The Aborted Restoration of Indigenous Law in India', *Comparative Studies in Society and History* 14 (1972), for the idealisation of the harmonious nature of village justice and the desire to revive its essence.

11 This was based on fieldwork done between 1940 and 1947 and published in Manchester in 1955. For further comment on it see P. Gulliver, *Cross-examinations*, *Essays in Memory of Max Gluckman* (Leiden, 1978) and the Conclusion below.

12 *Judicial Process*, 23. H. Rider Haggard's *King Solomon's Mines* (London, 1887) helped to distil an image of African justice in which the process is one of random terror, dominated by witchdoctors who 'smell out' victims. Reform is finally imposed by whites who extract an undertaking from the new king they have installed that in the future no man would be put to death without a fair trial. This image is one which some white South African writers on African law have taken great pains to correct: see I. S. Schapera (ed.) *The Bantu-Speaking Tribes of South Africa* (London, 1937) ch. 9. He takes pains to stress that African law recognised the idea of 'the King's Peace' and that there was neither random justice nor a vendetta system of self help. A. Sachs in *Justice in South Africa* (London, 1973) puts a similar stress on the similarity between African and European law.

13 M. Gluckman, *African Traditional Law in Historical Perspective* (London, 1974) 6, 21.

14 *Judicial Process*, 20–1, 77–8.

15 *Justice and Judgement Among the Tiv* (London, 1957). See also L. Nader (ed.), *Law in Culture and Society* (Chicago, 1969) 337–401, for discussions by Gluckman and Bohannan and others on the question of comparability.

16 P. H. Gulliver, *Social Control in an African Society* (London, 1963) 241.

17 *Judicial Process*, 38, 93–5, 215, 236, 241.

18 J. A. Barnes, *Marriage in a Changing Society* (Livingstone, 1951) xl.

19 London, 1969. The fieldwork was done in 1950.

20 *Law Without Precedent*, 3, 36, 66, 39–40, 56.

21 J. van Velsen, *The Politics of Kinship* (Manchester, 1964) x, where Mitchell is quoted.

22 Gluckman is quoted by V. Turner, *Schism and Continuity* (Manchester, 1957).

23 van Velsen, *Politics*, 83, 2.

Notes

24 Ibid., 49. For MacGaffey see pp. 44–7.
25 E. Evans-Pritchard and M. Fortes, *African Political Systems* (London, 1940).
26 W. Watson, *Tribal Cohesion in a Money Economy* (Manchester, 1958) 159.
27 Ibid., 161.
28 van Velsen, *Politics*, 220–1. Boma was the term used to describe government in both its physical location and its *persona*. It refers to the concentration together of all the officers and officials of the district government, the district officer and the administrative offices, the courthouse, police, gaol, etc. The physical lay-out of government, as well as the multiple roles of officials, represented the unity of powers rather than their separation.
29 I. Cunnison, *The Luapula Peoples of Northern Rhodesia* (Manchester, 1959) 191–3, 194. This can be illustrated by Cunnison's description of the state of the Lunda of Kazembe, where the discussion of who heard what kind of cases is based on words like 'presumably' and 'probably' which derive not from his evidence but from the model.
30 Turner, *Schism and Continuity*, 14–16.
31 van Velsen, *Politics*, 311.
32 Marwick, *Sorcery*, 175.
33 E. Colson, *Marriage and Family Among the Plateau Tonga of Northern Rhodesia* (Manchester, 1958) 12.
34 A. Epstein, 'Divorce Law and the Stability of Marriage Among the Lunda of Kazembe', *Human Problems in British Central Africa* 14 (1954) 3.
35 Marwick, *Sorcery*, 196–7, 198–9.
36 Colson, *Marriage and Family*, 111.
37 J. A. Barnes, *Politics in a Changing Society* (Manchester, 1967).
38 M. Wilson, *Good Company* (Oxford, 1951; Boston edn, 1963) 136–48, esp. 140.
39 Colson, *Marriage and Family*, 127.
40 van Velsen, *Politics*, 261.
41 Marwick, *Sorcery*, 95, 199.
42 Turner, *Schism and Continuity*, 229.
43 Colson, *Marriage and Family*, 127.
44 Watson, *Tribal Cohesion*, 19, 178–9.
45 Marwick, *Sorcery*, 51, 43.
46 Colson, *Marriage and Family*, 127.
47 Turner, *Schism and Continuity*, 43, 125.
48 Colson, *Marriage and Family*, 211.
49 Ibid., 117, 235.
50 Maine, *Ancient Law*, 271, quoted by Gluckman, *Judicial Process*, 28.
51 Gluckman, *Judicial Process*, 29.
52 Colson, *Marriage and Family*, 160–1.
53 Colson, *The Plateau Tonga* (Manchester, 1962) 122.
54 Ibid., 113.
55 C. Mitchell, *The Yao Village* (Manchester, 1956).
56 Colson, *Plateau Tonga*, 281.
57 Gluckman, *Judicial Process*, 217.
58 Marwick, *Sorcery*, 223.
59 Barnes, *Politics*, 159.
60 Colson, *Marriage and Family*, 170.
61 Gluckman, *Judicial Process*, 217. My italics.
62 Colson, *Marriage and Family*, 183.
63 Epstein, *Divorce Law*, 15–17.
64 van Velsen, *Politics*, 242.
65 A. Epstein, *Politics in an Urban African Community* (Manchester, 1958).
66 Barnes, *Politics*, 164.

67 Epstein, *Politics*, 2, 24, 5.
68 See below Chapter 11.
69 See F. Snyder, *Capitalism and Legal Change* (New York, 1981), and also 'Colonialism and Legal Form', *Journal of Legal Pluralism* 19 (1981).
70 *Capitalism* 134, 139 *et seq.*, 161–2, 168.
71 P. P. Howell, *A Manual of Nuer Law* (London, 1954) vii.
72 Ibid., 61.
73 Ibid., 28.
74 Ibid., 231, 236. Howell noted with approval that the Nuer over the past twenty years 'are rapidly becoming conscious of the value of punishment as a deterrent' (235).
75 See *Manual*, 144 *et seq*. It is worth pointing out, in the light of the heavy emphasis on it in the Central African literature, that the disintegration of which Howell speaks was not associated with labour migrancy, the prolonged absence of young males, or urbanisation.
76 MacGaffey, *Custom and Government*, 206, 230–1, 232, 242.
77 Ibid., 271, 260–1.
78 Ibid., 259, viii–ix, 133 *et seq.*, 136.
79 Ibid., 215, 34. My italics.
80 Ibid., 107, 302, 189 *et seq*.
81 Ibid., 290, 303.
82 Ibid., 103. My italics. See also 305.

3. African law and lawyers

1   See H. Morris and J. Read, *Indirect Rule and the Search for Justice* (London, 1972); and F. Lugard, *The Dual Mandate in British Tropical Africa* (London, 1922; 5th edn, 1965) 553 and 539. For the repugnancy test see below Chapter 4.
2   Cmd 4623 of 1934, 8–9; 17–19; 57–9.
3   Ibid., 131, Gov. Uganda/Sec. of State, 18/11/33; and 155, Gov. Tanganyika/Sec. of State, 28/2/34.
4   L. Barnes, *Empire and Democracy* (London, 1939) 168–9.
5   F. Melland and C. Young, *African Dilemma* (London, 1937) 101ff.
6   Baron Hailey, *African Survey* (London, 1938) 265. My italics. Cf. A. S. Diamond's evolutionist *Primitive Law* published in 1935.
7   *African Survey*, 261, 264, 5, 6, 295–7, 303–5.
8   Colony and protectorate of Kenya, 1944.
9   Phillips Report, 156, 161, 274.
10 But there was also a partial retention of the view that codification of any sort would rigidify development. With regard to the towns, for example, Phillips quoted with approval a report saying 'There is as yet no fixed or known body of native law and custom in Nairobi, and it is the tribunals' function to create it.' Phillips Report, 297.
11 Pim is quoted in J. Lewin, *Studies in African Law* (Philadelphia, 1971; 1st edn, 1947) 4–5. Pim's report is printed as Cmd 4368. And see J. Lewin, 'British Courts and British Justice in Africa', *Africa* 14 (1943–4) 448.
12 African Conference on Local Courts and Customary Law, September 1963, Report, Section 1. The conference was under the chairmanship of the Tanganyika minister of justice.
13 Quoted in G. Carter and A. Paden (eds), *Expanding Horizons in African Studies* (Evanston, 1969) 170.
14 See the introduction to N. Rubin and E. Cotran, *Readings in African Law* (New York, 1970); and T. O. Elias, *The Nature of African Law* (Manchester, 1956), discussed further below.
15 Elias, *Nature*, Introduction.

Notes

16 A. Schiller, 'African Law', in R. A. Lystad, *The African World: A Survey of Social Research* (New York, 1965).

17 F. O. Spalding, with E. L. Hoover and J. C. Piper, 'One Nation, One Judiciary: The Lower Courts of Zambia', *Zambia Law Journal* 2 (1970) esp. 5, 10–11.

18 *Readings*, xxi.

19 'One Nation, One Judiciary', 5, 8, 10, 17–18, 54, n. 268. See too Hailey's *African Survey* at 308–9, where change in the customary law is recognised but seen as something novel.

20 'One Nation, One Judiciary', 26. Writing in another context Smith has also noted the assumption in the legal scholarship that real customary law was rural and had little place in the urban sector and that developments like urbanisation and modernisation produced something different in the place of customary law. Part of the reason for this was the inability of the legal literature to take account of the processes of change as opposed to the 'facts' of change. As Smith writes of theories of modernisation in general, process is given scant attention. 'Rather, one is struck by the domination of concepts of polarity: primitive and modern: village and metropolis; status and contract.' D. N. Smith, 'Man and Law in Urban Africa: A Role for Customary Courts in the Urbanisation Process', *American Journal of Comparative Law* 20 (1972) 227. The dominating conceptual polarisations of customary law and modern law, like those of African law and foreign law, have tended to overshadow the processes of change where the boundaries are blurred.

21 Lloyd Fallers, quoted in 'One Nation, One Judiciary', 39, and Report on Native Tribunals.

22 Elias, *Nature*, ch. 13, quoted in 'One Nation, One Judiciary', 90.

23 'One Nation, One Judiciary', 89.

24 In their minds anthropology of law became the repository of interesting but unpractical knowledge about the past; 'the manner in which customary law once functioned', *Readings*, xvii.

25 Smith, 'Man and Law', 238–40, quoting A. N. Allott, *New Essays in African Law* (London, 1970) and Epstein, *Politics*. Conflict-of-laws problems are those related to the question of which body of law should govern a dispute when the parties are from different legal systems.

26 Smith, 'Man and Law', 77n., 240; and see also Elias, *Nature*.

27 'The Development of East African Legal Systems During the Colonial Period', in D. A. Low and A. Smith (eds), *History of East Africa*, vol. 3 (London, 1976) 348, 368–73, 380–1. My italics. It is notable that this is the first general history, or collection, to contain an account of legal developments of any kind. There is an odd nod in the direction of relativism: 'Some of the European visitors, administrators and the like were so struck by the barbarity of the punishments, the arbitrary character of accusation and convictions, and the prevalence of slavery in some of the indigenous legal systems that they found it difficult to appreciate the merits of rationality of these systems generally' (366).

28 Read is also an academic lawyer. *Indirect Rule and the Search for Justice* (Oxford, 1972) chs 6, 8, 9, esp. ch. 6.

29 See Read, *Indirect Rule*, 191–5.

30 Ibid., 169.

31 Ibid., 74.

32 Ibid., 183.

33 Ibid., 201–3.

34 Ibid., 175; and T. O. Beidelman, 'Inter-Tribal Tensions in Some Local Government Courts in Colonial Tanganyika', *Journal of African Law* 10 (1966).

35 Hooker is also an academic lawyer. See *Adat Law in Modern Indonesia* (Oxford, 1979).

36 See 'The Study of Indonesian Customary Law' and 'Families of Language and Families of Law', *Illinois Law Review* 13 (1919) and 15 (1921).

37 See Hooker, *Adat Law*, 33, 34, 41, 57–62, 80, 144.

38 Adewoye, *The Judicial System in Southern Nigeria* (London, 1977) 69.

39 Ibid., 11–14. In contrast to his political view of English law in the colonial context he appears

246

to be heavily committed to the mythological view of pre-colonial African law, the aim of which he sees as 'peace keeping', maintaining the social equilibrium, and 'interpersonal reconciliation', though later he writes, 'It is difficult to escape the conclusion that the judicial system in Southern Nigeria was rooted in fear: fear of the supernatural, fear of ordeals, fear of ancestors, and even fear of the elders, especially in chiefly communities.' On what part fear played in the acceptance of 'interpersonal reconciliation' and the maintenance of equilibrium he does not speculate (1–3, 10).

40　C. Bohmer, 'Community Values, Domestic Tranquility, and Customary Law in Upper Volta', *Journal of Modern African Studies* 16 (1978) 296, 301, 306–7.

41　W. Van Binsbergen, 'Law in the Context of Nkoya Society', in S. Roberts (ed.), *Law and the Family in Africa* (The Hague, 1977) esp. 44–9.

42　These questions are also grappled with by a Zambian academic lawyer. See M. P. Mvunga, 'Law and Social Change: A Case Study in the Customary Law of Inheritance in Zambia', *African Social Research* 28 (1979): 'A restatement of the rules of inheritance among the Tonga appears a futile exercise. This is so because the Tonga inheritance is not automatic' (647).

43　See R. Abel, *Customary Law of Wrongs in Kenya: An Essay in Research Method*, Yale Law School Studies in Law and Modernisation No. 2 (New Haven, n.d.) 7.

44　F. Snyder, 'Colonialism and Legal Form: The Creation of "Customary Law" in Senegal', *Journal of Legal Pluralism* 19 (1981) 49, 52, 74, 76.

45　D. A. Washbrook, 'Law, State and Agrarian Society in Colonial India', *Modern Asian Studies* 15 (3) (1981) 675.

4. The lawgivers in Central Africa: social control

1　Malawi Archives Index. Short Administrative History of the Judicial Department.

2　ZNA KST 2/1/1, 31/3/00.

3　On protectorates see C. Palley, *The Constitutional Law and History of Southern Rhodesia* (Oxford, 1966) ch. 4.

4　A. J. Swann, *Fighting the Slave Hunters in Central Africa* (London, 1910, 1969 edn) 328–9. Italics in original. Swann was district officer at Nkhota-Kota.

5　ZNA IN/1/1/1, 1906.

6　ZNA US/3/1, Feb. 1916.

7　The East Luangwa Annual Report for 1913 was dubious about how much judicial power chiefs could be left with because 'their idea of damages due varies so much in relation to the contending parties.' Macdonnell, though, saw nothing wrong in this. While the law of assault, for example, applied to everyone, he pointed out in *R. v. Tomo*, different penalties would be given for assault on an 'Englishman of good standing' and a 'mean white'. ZNA 7/1/4 and *R. v. Tomo*.

8　ZNA Sec. 2/406, D. C. Mumbwa to P. C. Lusaka, 22/2/33.

9　MNA J1/1/1, Livingstone Duff to Nunan, 29/11/00.

10　E.g. MNA J1/2/6 Commissioner to Griffin, June 1906.

11　H. Duff, *Nyasaland Under the Foreign Office* (London, 1903) 238, 326, 330. This was written in 1903. Duff was later to pass his own verdict on the district officers' legal performance. Reconsidering the experience thirty years later he wrote that it was a 'manifest scandal' when one remembered how wide the jurisdiction of magistrates had been and how intimately and in what ignorance they had affected lives and liberties. See *African Small Chop* (London, 1932). R. Gordon has commented aptly that the law administered by the district officers 'more closely resembled their own concepts of equity than the common law . . . of England': 'African Law and the Historian', *Journal of African History* 8 (1967).

12　ZNA NR G2.

13　Jurisprudential fashions change. The clear distinction which civilised law made in Macdon-

247

nell's view between crime and tort was becoming blurred in British legal thinking seventy years later when the victims of crime in Britain were finally provided with compensation.

14 MNA S1/572/20; NCK 2/2/1, 20/11/20. Also NC1/21/3 where district commissioners were advised that defendants should always be made to pay compensation for not attending the funeral of a dead spouse or 'it may lead to further quarrelling and end in one of the parties having to resort to trial by ordeal.'

15 MNA Fort Manning District Book, 2/4/30.

16 MNA NC1/21/3, 11/7/28.

17 A. T. and G. M. Culwick, *Ubena of the Rivers* (London, 1935) 299.

18 'Native Customs in Nyasaland', published in *NADA* 16 (1939).

19 As Barnes noted, 'The imputed rules of the past have become the "customs" of the present, and the adjective Ngoni is applied not to what the Ngoni people do today but what they like to think they did in the virtuous past.' J. A. Barnes, *Marriage in a Changing Society* (London, 1951) 124. So too Culwick and Culwick, *Ubena of the Rivers*, 66–7: 'Law and Custom is elastic ... depending on circumstances, popular feeling, the balance of power among the most influential factions .... Its elasticity is not admitted: is not, indeed apprehended.'

20 *Nkhoswe* were the representatives of the families of those marrying through whom negotiations and arrangements took place and they continued to be generally responsible for the marriage relationship. As one description puts it, *nkhowse* 'are not merely casual witnesses to a ceremony, but may be described as trustees for the two parties .... They meet before the actual marriage and discuss all the necessary arrangements, they are always charged with the preservation of the marriage and with the settlement of any disputes which may arise in connection with it.' Stannus wrote: 'in any matter relating to them as married people, the girl will consult the husband's sponsor and *vice versa*. Everything is referred to them and they become the repository of all the events of the couple's married life. Theirs is the accredited testimony on family matters, and their consent has to be asked in all questions.' H. G. Stannus, *The Wayao of Nyasaland* (Cambridge, Mass., 1922); and I. D. Thomson, Rhodes House *Mss Afr*.

21 *Customary Law and the Status of Women*, ch. 3, 119.

22 E. Colson, 'Possible Repercussions of the Right to Make Wills Upon the Plateau Tonga of Northern Rhodesia', *Journal of African Administration* 11 (1950).

23 MNA NCK 5/1/2 Annual Report Marimba, 1919.

24 L. Fallers, *Law Without Precedent* (Chicago, 1969) 188–9.

25 F. Melland, *In Witchbound Africa* (London, 1923; New York edn, 1967) 107–8.

26 Ibid., 299–304.

27 Ibid., 305–7.

28 ZNA ZA 1/9/79/1, Secretary for Native Affairs to Chief Secretary. My italics.

29 For one settler who held court see W. Beresford, 'Harrison Clark: King of Northern Rhodesia', *Northern Rhodesian Journal* 2 (1954).

30 See N. R. Bennett and M. Ylvisaker (eds), *The Central African Journal of Lovell J. Proctor, 1860–64* (Boston, 1971).

31 Ibid., 150–1.

32 H. Rowley, *The Story of the Universities Mission to Central Africa* (London, 1867; New York edn, 1965) 220.

33 E. Maples, *Chauncey Maples* (London, 1897) 117.

34 See A. Chirnside, *The Blantyre Missionaries – Discreditable Disclosures* (London, 1880); A. J. Hanna, *The Beginnings of Nyasaland and North Eastern Rhodesia 1859–95* (London, 1969) 26–34; J. McCracken, *Christianity and Politics in Malawi 1875–1940* (Cambridge, 1977), 50, 62–9, 141, 164.

35 D. J. Rankin, *The Zambesi Basin and Nyasaland* (Edinburgh and London, 1893) 273.

36 D. C. Scott, *Cyclopaedic Dictionary of the Mang'anja Language Spoken in British Central Africa* (Edinburgh, 1892).

37 See McCracken, *Christianity and Politics*, 141.
38 A. J. Hanna, *Beginnings*, 41–2.
39 Hine was a bishop of the U.M.C.A. See J. E. Hine, *Days Gone By* (London, 1924) 159; and N. Maclean, *Africa in Transformation* (London, 1914) 109–10.
40 Rowley, *Story*, 228, 231.
41 F. S. Arnot, *Garenganze* (1889; London edn, 1969) 70, 73, 91.
42 E. Maples (ed.), *Journals and Papers of Chauncey Maples* (London, 1889) 120–1, 156.
43 *Central African Mission Report*, 1889, 29.
44 See J. Schoffeleers, 'The Interaction of the Mbona Cult and Christianity, 1859–1963', in T. O. Ranger and J. Weller (eds), *Themes in the Christian History of Central Africa* (London, 1975); and G. Prins, *The Hidden Hippopotamus* (Cambridge, 1980) 197.
45 R. Laws, *Reminiscences of Livingstonia* (London, 1934) 115–16; and Maples in *Central African Mission Report*, 1885, 36.
46 A. Hetherwick, *The Gospel and the African* (Edinburgh, 1932) 110–12. Cf. Donald Fraser in *The Future of Africa* (London, 1912) 194, on the 'moral hindrances' to progress. 'The greatest obstacle of all is the lack of any sense of sin. Evil as offence against God is unknown. The only fear of evil is the fear of the social consequences.'
47 See B. W. Randolph (ed.), *Arthur Douglas, Missionary on Lake Nyasa* (London, 1902) 156–7.
48 F. L. M. Moir, *After Livingstone, An African Trade Romance* (London, n.d.) 50–1.
49 Ibid., 22.
50 See e.g. Randolph, *Arthur Douglas*, 147–9.
51 *Life and Letters of A. F. Sim* (London, 1896) 178.
52 G. E. Butt, *My Travels in North Western Rhodesia* (London, 1910) 23.

5. Witches and ordeals

1 See e.g. T. O. Elias, *The Nature of African Customary Law* (Manchester, 1954), 28 and n.
2 A. L. Epstein, *Juridical Techniques and the Judicial Process*, Rhodes–Livingstone Paper no. 23 (1954), 2. Cf. A. Sachs, *Justice in South Africa* (London, 1973) 116. European and African legal systems were comparable in that both 'investigated the problems of veracity in a context of probability, and . . . in both the element of the supernatural existed on the fringes.'
3 M. Gluckman (ed.), *Ideas and Procedures in African Customary Law* (London, 1969) 35–7.
4 M. Douglas, *The Lele of Kasai* (London, 1963); J. Vansina, 'The Bushong Poison Ordeal', in M. Douglas and P. Kaberry (eds), *Man in Africa* (London, 1969) 256.
5 R. B. Burton (trans.), *Lacerda's Journey to Kazembe's in 1798* (London, 1873) 76 and 117.
6 A. C. P. Gammitto, *King Kazambe*, trans. I. Cunnison (Lisbon, 1960) 69, 89, 104.
7 See N. R. Bennett and M. Ylvisaker (eds), *The Central African Journal of Lovell J. Proctor* (Boston, 1971) 145, 150–1, 162, 208, 253, 252; H. Rowley, *The Story of the Universities Mission to Central Africa* (London, 1867; New York edn, 1965) 95, 215–28; D. Livingstone, *Last Journals* (London, 1874) 134, 163; J. MacDonald, 'East Central African Customs', *Journal of the Royal Anthropological Institute* 22 (1895); D. MacDonald, *Africana or the Heart of Heathen Africa* (London 1882) 44–5, 158–61; H. E. O'Neill, 'A Three Month Journey in the Makua and Lomwe Countries', *Proceedings of the Royal Geographical Society* 4 (1889); R. Codrington, 'The Central Angoni Land District of the British Central Africa Protectorate', *Geographical Journal* (May, 1895); H.E. Angus, 'A Year in Azimba and Chipataland' (1895), *Journal of the Royal Anthropological Institute* 27 (1898); L. T. Moggeridge, 'The Nyasaland Tribes, Their Customs and Their Poison Ordeal', *Journal of the Royal Anthropological Institute* 32 (1902).
8 Especially J. Johnston, *Reality vs. Romance in South Central Africa* (London, 1882; 2nd

edn, 1969) 317–19; A. Werner, *The Natives of British Central Africa* (London, 1906) 90; R. S. Rattray, *Some Folklore, Stories and Songs in Chinyanja* (London, 1907) 85, 125.

9 See Bennet and Ylvisaker, *Central African Journal*; and H. Rowley, *Story*.

10 D. Malekebu, 'A Plea for Africa', MNA library collection. Cf. Stephen Bwalya, 'Customs and Habits of the Bemba', Rhodes House *Mss Afr.* 1213. He tells us, 'In a word the Bemba had three possible ways of settling cases: by trial, an ordeal, or charms.'

11 Y. Abdullah, *The Yao* (Zomba, 1919) 3.

12 Mwashitete, *Ways I Have Trodden* (London, 1932) 17.

13 S. Nyirenda, 'History of the Tumbuka/Henga People', trans. T. C. Young, *Bantu Studies* 5 (1931) 74. The passage was written prior to 1909. See also D. Fraser, *Winning a Primitive People* (London, 1914; 1970 edn) 214–15. To Fraser the use of the ordeal in this way was a sign of lack of political development, and he credited the Ngoni, whom he thought to be a cut above the Chewa and Tumbuka, with having destroyed the ordeal in the North. Its later revival he attributed to the diminution of Ngoni power following white conquest and the subsequent opportunity given to Chewa and Tumbuka to fall into old ways.

14 F. L. M. Moir, *After Livingstone, An African Trade Romance* (London, n.d.) 54ff.

15 See *Livingstonia News* (June 1913), for Robertson's account of mass ordealing after Chikusi's death. The mission's predicament in Bandawe was also seen as a case for diagnosis by ordeal. 'Again and again the trial by *mwavi* has been proposed to discover why my colleagues one after another had to be laid to rest in the little graveyard.'

16 See I. Linden (ed.), 'Mponda Mission Diary', successive parts published in the *International Journal of African Historical Studies* 7 (1974). The account gains in value as it is part of continuing close observation recorded at the time and has little trace of exaggeration caused by moral outrage.

17 'Mponda Diary', part 4, *International Journal of African Historical Studies* (1975) 121.

18 E. W. Smith and A. M. Dale, *The Ila-Speaking Peoples of Northern Rhodesia* (London, 1920; New York edn, 1968) 123.

19 Linden says few survived. From Moir's account of the mass administration at Chikusi's it seems that the pecentage death rate was under 5 per cent. Moir, *After Livingstone*, 56 *et seq.* But these figures are too vague to constitute knowledge, as are the conjectures of Linden and the White Fathers. Perhaps the important thing is that virtually all white observers *suspected* manipulation of the dose. This approach has certainly dominated white writing on African ordeals. See, for example, on West Africa, J. L. Wilson, *Western Africa* (London, 1856). She writes of the ordeal prepared – 'a good deal of ceremony is used' – for administration to women suspected of adultery. 'There is seldom any fairness in the administration of the ordeal. No particular quantity of the red water is prescribed, and the amount administered always depends on the state of feeling in the community towards the accused' (51). See too H. L. Ward Price, *Dark Subjects* (London, 1939); and E. Warner, *Trial by Sasswood* (London, 1959). Philip Mitchell, as a young district officer in Nyasaland, was also certain that the dose was varied, and his was the predominant administrative view. See *African Afterthoughts* (London, 1954) 25–31. For boiling-pot ordeals, see F. S. Arnot, *Garenganze* (1889; London edn, 1969) 66, 70, 75–6, 94–5.

20 F. Coillard, *On the Threshold of Central Africa* (London, 1897; 1969 edn) 66, 70, 75–6, 94–5.

21 MNA, 'Notes on Native Law and Custom', Y. Mwase.

22 The *mwavi* ordeal, it has been suggested, picked out troublesome personalities rather than evidence of particular acts.

23 Cf. the note on Mahenge in 1930 in the Tanganyika District Book, vol. 4, 60: 'Trials by ordeal among the Waporogo are generally aimed at establishing the guilt or otherwise of a woman of adultery'.

24 5 Geo. IV, c. 83, s. 4, ZNA GF2.

25 MNA J2/1/7 1909.

26 See D. Fraser, *African Idylls* (London, 1923) 104. See too Ngalande's case MNA NCI/13/2,

in which the difficulties caused by the presence of the Boma were made clear by several witnesses, all accused by Ngalande, the witchfinder, of being *mfiti*. They testified that they were unable to clear themselves by drinking *mwavi* as they would have done before the white man came and that there was now no way of establishing their innocence.

27 The villages taking the ordeal were in the Dedza and Lilongwe districts. See MNA L2/15/1 and MNA L2/8/1 1928. See too CO 626/17, 1937, for comments on witchcraft cases in the Dedza district of Nyasaland and tensions between Chewa and Ngoni.

28 MNA Judicial circular no. 32 S1/250/21 and S1/60/F/32, MNA 22/1/7, 1909.

29 ZNA KDG 2/2/1, 13/10/04 Nagunda's case, and KST 2/1/2, Fort Jameson, 21/12/04.

30 ZNA ZA 4/1, 'Native Laws and Customs'. It was noted some forty years later in North Eastern Zambia that there was strong social pressure preventing a person accused of sorcery from taking his accuser to court. This seems to have been the case earlier. M. Marwick, *Sorcery In Its Social Setting* (Manchester, 1965) 72.

31 ZNA KST 2/1/2, 13/8/04. Cf. the reports of Catholic priests in the 1930s of the Yao chief Kachindamoto's 'deep-rooted preoccupation' with 'poisoning' in circumstances in which the mass *mwavi* ordeal was no longer available to protect him against Chewa subjects. See I. Linden, 'Chewa Initiation', in T. Ranger and J. Weller (eds), *Themes in the Christian History of Central Africa* (London, 1975) 36.

32 ZNA 1/9/1881, 5/9/31.

33 CO 626/18 1938, 27. For the cases see CO 626/11, Police Report 1932, 16, and CO 626/15, Police Report 1936, 13.

34 Marwick, *Sorcery*, 93, 92.

35 C. Mitchell, 'The Political Organisation of the Yao of Southern Nyasaland', *African Studies* 8 (1949).

36 Marwick, *Sorcery*, 18, 68, 71–2; E. Colson, *Marriage and Family Among the Plateau Tonga of Northern Rhodesia* (Manchester, 1958) 256; and V. W. Turner, *Schism and Continuity in an African Society* (Manchester, 1957) 127.

37 CO 626/14, 1935, Provincial Commissioner Annual Report.

38 ZNA 1/9/181.

39 Secretary for Native Affairs to Chief Secretary ZNA 1/9/181, 30/10/33.

40 ZNA 1/9/181.

41 G. Orde-Brown, 'Witchcraft and British Colonial Law', *Africa* 8 (1935) 484.

42 F. Melland, 'Ethical and Political Aspects of Witchcraft', *Africa* 8 (1935).

43 CO 525/157 44023. Sir Charles Ross, *Memoirs* (unpublished Ms in Rhodes House Library, Oxford) 71, Sir Charles Belcher, *Reminiscences* (unpublished Ms in Rhodes House Library, Oxford) 244. Ross and Belcher both dealt with the problem of intent by accepting that the poison varied and that the giver decided whether the receiver was to die. There was not much real insight into actual murder cases. Ross wrote that real murder, which was comparatively rare, often 'had no apparent motive'.

44 See M. Wilson, *Good Company* (London, 1951, 1963 edn) 198–221, for the most valuable collection of *mwavi* cases published.

45 Ibid., 229–30; cases 25 and 32; 251 and case 31.

46 Rowlands suggests that this was the function of ordeals in Kenyan judicial procedure, and Moore makes the same suggestion for the Chagga in Tanzania. J. S. S. Rowlands, 'Notes on Native Law and Custom in Kenya', *Journal of African Law* 6 (1962); and S. F. Moore, 'Politics, Procedures and Norms in Changing Chagga Law', *Africa* 40 (1970) 329.

47 T. C. Young (trans.), 'Habits and Customs of the Olden Days Among the Tumbuka-Damanga People', *Bantu Studies* 10 (1936).

6. The courts and the people: law in action I

1 Johnston to Anderson, March 1893, quoted by J. Hanna, *The Beginnings of Nyasaland and North Eastern Rhodesia 1859–95* (London, 1969) 209.

Notes

2 Nunan to Sharpe, MNA J1/2/2, 26/8/02.

3 ZNA G.I. 27/1/10. One is reminded of the state of affairs in the South African Republic where the government had to make it a criminal offence for magistrates not to acquaint themselves with the law. See A. Sachs, *Justice in South Africa* (London, 1973) 69–70. As late as 1918 the Colonial Office review for Nyasaland found 'a hopeless state of affairs'. No regard was paid to the laws of evidence; essential facts in cases were unproved; and district officers were resentful of judicial supervision. CO 525/87 61085. Review for year ending 31/3/18 and Bushe Minute.

4 Henry Maine had observed that 'when a province hitherto especially ill-governed is annexed to British India, the first effect ordinarily is neither satisfaction nor discontent, neither the peaceful continuance of old usages nor the sudden adoption of new, but an extraordinary influx of litigation into the British courts, which are always at once established.' Maine put this down to the 'immense ascendancy' which courts of justice hold over men's minds. H.S. Maine, *Dissertations on Early Law and Custom* (London,1883) 384–5. I will be suggesting other reasons.

5 See the remarks of the deputy commissioner in MNA J1/2/3, 24/9/04.

6 Reminiscences of H.T. Harrington, 'The Taming of North Eastern Rhodesia', *Northern Rhodesia Journal* 3, (1955) 17.

7 Harrington, ibid.

8 See MNA J2/6/3 Mzimba district report of 1910 and J2/6/2 26/4/11.

9 The central African experience from high expectations to double disillusion was parallel to the South African one. As Dudley Kidd, *Kafir Socialism* (London, 1908) 65, had written of the empire, 'The love of justice is the god of our idolatry.' There was nothing of which Britain was 'so proud as their impartial administration of justice to all the races they govern'. But it was already evident from his South African observations that magistrates went out of their way to give the inestimable boon of substantial British justice only to see Africans leaving the courts 'in a grumbling and discontented spirit'. This was because, according to Kidd, Kafir justice was based on collective and not individual responsibility and they therefore failed entirely to understand British courts' standards of proof and notions of punishment. But it may have been that they understood all too well what the colonial courts had to offer.

10 MNA J1/2/5, 16/10/05.

11 Cf. C. Dundas, *African Crossroads* (London, 1955) 36–7. Dundas joined the East African Service in 1908, was secretary of native affairs in Tanganyika, chief secretary of Northern Rhodesia and later governor of Uganda. He wrote of the Kamba in early Kenya that they peddled their suits from one court to another 'seeking the most favourable verdict'.

12 The Dowa district report of 1921 complains of the few criminal cases being brought to the Native District Court. It was found that one of the principal headmen was settling cases in the village and that the sergeant of police, the headman's brother, had been preventing people from bringing cases to the Boma. MNA S1/489/20, March 1921. But not many cases of so open an assertion of a rival jurisdiction are recorded. In a report for the Tanganyika Territory for 1932 quoted by Read, the process in which official courts were used as a stage in the process of settlement, rather than as the main instrument, is again apparent. White courts were, for the Masai, 'in practice appeal courts, as only those cases in which arbitration has failed to come to them'. *Indirect Rule and the Search for Justice*, 184n.

13 J.A. Chastell, Rhodes House *Mss Afr.* S 606, 8.

14 For Malawi see J2/1 and J2/1/1, Correspondence – Judicial.

15 See M. Wright, *German Missions in Tanganyika* (Oxford, 1971) 57.

16 H. Duff, *African Small Chop* (London, 1932) 77–8. Meebelo is of the opinion that a 'Boma messenger's duties, even more than those of an obliging chief, always earned him the implacable suspicion and hatred of the village people.' H.S. Meebelo, *Reaction to Colonialism* (Manchester, 1971).

252

17 Gann writes that district officers had 'been advised that it would not contribute to the dignity of proceedings if the Magistrates spoke the native tongue'. H. Gann, *The Birth of Northern Rhodesia* (Manchester, 1958) 96.
18 See e.g. ZNA F3/1/9, 8/11/02; F3/1/8, 21/10/02.
19 ZNA F3/1, *R. v. Mupalanga and Mandala*, 19/8/09. ZNA NE/1N1H/3/1, Abercorn no. 22.
20 E. Berger, *Labour, Race and Colonial Rule* (Oxford, 1974) 37.
21 ZNA F3/1/10, H. Croad to Beaufort, 24/9/10.
22 MNA Index, Judicial Dept, Short Administrative History.
23 ZNA G2 Law Dept Circular no. 2, 1917.
24 E.W. Smith and A. Dale, *The Ila-Speaking Peoples of Northern Rhodesia* (London, 1920; New York edn, 1968) 351 *et seq*. They show how the white courts could be used by the village courts as a back-up to their own authority, and describe a case where a man was sentenced in the village to pay compensation with the accompanying threat that if he did not he would be taken to the white court where another sentence would be passed on him.
25 ZNA IN/1/12, Instructions to Native Commissioners, December 1903.
26 The courts were also intolerant of aberrant behaviour among white settlers. In Fort Jameson, James Highfield was fined for firing at the bottles in the Royal Hotel with a revolver and in another case from the Royal Hotel a man was fined for being drunk and disorderly and delivering 'a tirade against natives and bar-boys generally'. ZNA INA 2/1/1902 and ZNA KDG 6/1.
27 ZNA G2.
28 ZNA NE/INH/31.
29 See ZNA KSJ 2/1/2, 1904–5.
30 See C. Gouldsbury and H. Sheane, *The Great Plateau of Northern Rhodesia* (London, 1911) 53.
31 MNA J2/6/2, 31/1/12.
32 E.H. Chomeley, 'The Very Early Days', *Northern Rhodesia Journal* 5 (1957) 61–2.
33 *Northern Rhodesia Journal* 3 (1955) 49.
34 ZNA KST 2/1/2.
35 ZNA LDG 6/1.
36 ZNA F3/1/10, Serenje, 1908. A window into the spirit in which justice could be administered is provided in the reminiscences of Sir Charles Belcher, a former Nyasaland judge, who records the case of a man hung for murdering an Indian, although he as judge had recommended mercy, because Indians might have protested about commutation. 'After all', Belcher wrote with some bitterness, 'Nyasaland natives are very plentiful and not very vocal. One of those responsible for the advice to exact the capital penalty said when it was being discussed, "I don't think it would hurt to hang a few of them."' *Reminiscences* (unpublished Ms in Rhodes House Library, Oxford) 234.
37 MNA J2/6/5 and S1/1107/19.
38 S1/1114/23.
39 See MNA S1/2372/22 and S1/1093/28.
40 Berger, *Labour, Race and Colonial Rule*, 74; and G. St J. Orde Brown, *The African Labourer* (London, 1933). These legal principles established their acceptability to African employers, who were to seek to use the Native Courts to impose their discipline. In May of 1950, for example, demands were made in the Nyasaland northern provincial council that Native Courts be given the power to fine labourers who broke their contracts.
41 Berger, *Labour, Race and Colonial Rule*, 26–8.
42 ZNA law dept circular no. 8, 1917 S3/498.
43 MNA S1/5572/20, 13/5/21.
44 MNA S1/486/20, 11/6/20.
45 MNA S1/1107/39; S1/1194/20.
46 MNA S1/1042/25.

47 ZNA N. Rhodesia District circular no. 16 1923, 10/10/23.

48 MNA S1/1093/28.

49 MNA S1/572/20, Amery/Bowring, 24/1/29.

50 MNA S1/572/20; 7/1/28 and 1/4/30.

51 K.R. Bradley, *Once a District Officer* (London, 1966) 65.

52 K.R. Bradley, *Handbook on Native Courts in Northern Rhodesia* (London, 1947) 83.

53 ZNA ZA 1/9, Secretary for Native Affairs to P.C. Fort Jameson, 17/6/29; Conference of 22–4 April 1929.

54 Ordinance no. 33 of 1929. It came into force on 1 April 1930.

55 Their separation from any sphere of white authority was such that no summons was to be sent to an African in European employment except through the district officer, who could then transfer the case to his own court. Guidance as regards the apportionment of crimes between Native Courts and Bomas was of this sort: 'For instance a rap on the head with a stick a yard long and as thick as a broom handle resulting in a bruise with an abrasion is a case for a Native Court, 10/- or one month. If the complaint shows the accused has paid compensation say 7/6 – then 2/6 or 7 days. If however the assault . . . [was] caused by a glancing blow from a warded asseggai thrust; then the case must go to the Boma.' Note the amalgamation of the system of compensation and punishment. ZNA ZA 1/9, 15/4/29.

56 ZNA U2/3/1, 18/3/14 and 17/18/14. They are reproduced as typical of a large number of similar claims. Occasionally outside factors interfered with the government's determination to support traditional authority. Before 1930 the N. Rhodesian courts had supported the continuation of tribute labour, ruling that a chief's order requiring it was a 'reasonable order' in terms of Proclamation 8 of 1916. But the controversy over forced labour in the East African colonies forced the N. Rhodesian government to set its face against all forms of compulsory labour. See ZNA Judicial circular Feb. 1927 and *R* v. *Shambalama & others*.

57 ZNA ZA 1/9.

58 ZNA KDE 2/2/1, 1914 and 1921. See below Part III for the *Khotla* and slavery cases.

59 ZNA ZA 1/9 Annexure. Annual Report Sesheke sub-district 1929. KDI 2/2/1 Ngambela NC 17/2/21.

60 ZNA KDC 2/18/3.

61 ZNA ZA 1/9/1929. There was also a fear that intervention would simply lead the Native Authority Courts not to record their decisions, as they did in witchcraft cases. See Rhodes House, *Mss Afr.* 961.

62 ZNA KDC 2/18/3, 1930.

63 ZNA KDC 2/18/5, Namwala, 1922.

64 A.H. Kirk-Green (ed.), *Native Administration and Political Development in British Tropical Africa*, Confidential Reports for the British Government by Lord Hailey 1940–2 (Liechtenstein, 1979) 256.

65 CO 626/14, Nyasaland. Provincial Commissioner for Northern Province, Report for 1935 65.

66 CO 626/12, Nyasaland 1933 7.

67 CO 626/9, Nyasaland. Provincial Commissioner for Southern Province, Report for 1936 22.

68 CO 626/17, Nyasaland. Provincial Commissioner for Northern Province, Report for 1937.

69 CO 626/18, Nyasaland, 1938.

70 CO 626/15, Nyasaland 1936.

71 CO 626/24, Nyasaland. Provincial Commissioner for Northern Province, Reports for 1947 and 1948.

72 E. Colson, 'Modern Political Organisation in the Plateau Tonga', *African Studies* 7 (1948) 75.

73 M.C. Hoole, 'Report on Recommendations for the Re-organisation of the Native Administrations of the Lilongwe District', 23/11/37, Rhodes House, *Mss Afr.* S. 997.

74 See Hailey, *Native Administration and Political Development in Tropical Africa*, Northern Rhodesia, 285.

75 CO 626/22, Nyasaland. Provincial Commissioner for Northern Province, Report for 1945.
76 CO 626/24, Nyasaland. Provincial Commissioner for Northern Province, Report for 1947.
77 Colson, 'Modern Political Organisation', 94–5.
78 CO 626/13, Nyasaland. Northern Province Native Administration Report 1934.
79 CO 626/14, Nyasaland. Provincial Commissioner for Southern Province and Northern Province, Reports for 1935.
80 CO 626/17, Nyasaland. Provincial Commissioner for South Province, Report for 1937 24.
81 J.A. Barnes, 'Some Aspect of Political Development Among the Fort Jameson Ngoni', *African Studies* 7 (1948).
82 Lord Hailey, *Native Administration in British African Territories* (London, 1950; 1979 edn).
83 CO 626/12, Nyasaland Native Affairs Report 1933, and CO 626/13 and 14. Hoole, of the Native Administrations'.
84 Hailey, *Native Administration and Political Development in Tropical Africa*, 28.
85 See CO 626/15, Nyasaland 1936.
86 CO 626/14, Nyasaland. Provincial Commissioner for Northern Province, Report for 1935 63.
87 CO 626/15, Nyasaland. Provincial Commissioner for Northern Province, Report for 1936 62, and CO 626/16, 1936.
88 Hailey, *Native Administration and Political Development in Tropical Africa*, 30.
89 *Malawi*

1931	Charged	5,715	
	Convicted	5,297	
'Common law'	crimes	Statutory offences	(major categories only)
Larceny	630	Hut tax	1,881
Assault	484	Forest Laws	597
Arson	31	Employer,	
Total	1,145	Liquor and	
		Licensing,	
		and Township	
		Regulations	297
		Total for all statutory offences	3,471

90 The relatively high proportion of Penal Code offences, roughly one-third, is accounted for by the disturbed conditions in the tea-plantation areas, where a combination of white settlement, extreme land shortage and an influx of immigrant labour produced a mini-wave of larceny, burglary and housebreaking. There was also a higher crime-rate in the urban areas of Blantyre and Limbe. These conditions were not characteristic of the protectorate as a whole where the relative absence of serious crime continued to be remarked upon.
91 R. Stokes, Rhodes House, *Mss Afr.* 971, Annual Reports Chinsali District, Northern Rhodesia, 1948–51, and 'Some Notes on Native Law and Procedure and its Development Under Modern Social Conditions'.
92 CO 626/18, Nyasaland. Provincial Commissioner for Southern Province, Report for 1938.
93 CO 626/22, Nyasaland. Provincial Commissioner for Southern Province, Report for 1945.
94 CO 626/24, Nyasaland. Provincial Commissioner for Northern Province, Report for 1947. The tendency to standardise compensation and punishment is also noted in Zambia – see *Annual Reports*, Native Affairs 1932 and 1933.
95 A.L. Epstein, *Politics in an Urban African Community* (Manchester, 1958) 58–9, 77.

Notes

7. Africans and the law

1 *Lacerda's Journey to Kazembe in 1798*, trans. R. F. Burton (London, 1873) 40.
2 H. Duff, *Nyasaland Under the Foreign Office* (London, 1903) 238.
3 D. MacDonald, *Africana or the Heart of Heathen Africa* (London, 1882); E. W. Smith and A. M. Dale, *The Ila-Speaking Peoples of Northern Rhodesia* (London, 1920; New York edn, 1968) vol. 2, 16–17; A. Hetherwick, *The Gospel and the African* (Edinburgh, 1932) 19; G. F. Hugo, 'Aanknopingspunte vir die Evangelie by die Achewa' (unpublished M.Th. Stellenbosch, 1953) 57–8; J. P. Murray, York Archive File, 1, 24.
4 H. Rowley, *Africa Unveiled* (London, 1876) 119.
5 A relative exception is Dundas' observation of the Kamba and Kikuyu in Kenya. 'Punishment', he wrote, 'is almost unknown and therefore the fear of injustice in the form of cruelty is a mere spectre.' It was, he thought, as a result of their contact with Europeans that Africans were losing their respect for human life. C. Dundas, 'Native Laws of Some Bantu Tribes of East Africa', *Journal of the Royal Anthropological Institute* 51 (1921).
6 MNA J2/6/2, 1912.
7 Duff, *Nyasaland Under the Foreign Office*, 239, 317. See too B. Campbell, *In the Heart of Bantuland* (London, 1922), who stresses heavy pre-colonial punishments and the problems of colonial mildness: 'the transition to European law has brought about a laxity of application in the more stern and rigorous native laws and their code of morals' (158).
8 Y. B. Abdullah, *The Yaos*, trans. M. Sanderson (Zomba, 1919; 2nd edn, London, 1973) 5, 10–11, 20, 33–6, 48, 52, 54, 58.
9 'Habits and Customs of the Olden Days Among the Tumbuka-Kamanga People', texts translated by T. Cullen Young, *Bantu Studies* 10 (1936) 317, 333.
10 D. Fraser, *African Idylls* (London, 1923) 157.
11 *The Ideas in Barotse Jurisprudence* (Manchester, 1972).
12 In losing control over the definition of deviance, in Erikson's terms, people lost a sense of the definition of their own society. They need to reformulate their 'boundaries' and regain control over their own stability. African communities were going through a period of stressful change. The things that they feared most in the present were the ones that they projected back into the past, to legitimate the claim to control them. Erikson writes:

> wherever a community is confronted with a significant relocation of boundaries, a shift in its territorial position, it is likely to experience a change in the kinds of behaviour handled by its various agencies of control . . . . the crisis itself will be reflected in altered patterns of deviation and perceived by the people of the groups as something akin to what we now call a crime wave. These waves dramatise the issues at stake when a given boundary becomes blurred in the drift of passing events, and the encounters which follow between new deviants and the older agents of control provided a forum, as it were, in which the issue can be articulated more clearly, a state in which it can be portrayed in sharper relief.

See K. T. Erikson, *Wayward Puritans* (New York, 1966) ch. 1 and 68–9.
13 D. R. Mackenzie, *The Spirit-Ridden Konde* (London, 1925) 83; MNA L 2/15/1, 10/3/19, and NCI/21/3, 1923.
14 MNA S1/2065/19, 17/5/23, and Dedza District Book, vol. 3.
15 See M. L. Chanock, 'Ambiguities in the Malawian Political Tradition', *African Affairs* 74 (1975) 337–8.
16 A comparable example of the way in which anxiety about a decine in morality, combined with an overlay of biblical influence, could turn into ideas about pre-colonial law can be found in Uganda. In 1935 the Kabaka wrote that the Baganda had 'observed most strictly the doctrine of the ten commandments'. Theft was always punished severely (by mutilation); murder was followed by a 'very severe vendetta'; 'there was filial obedience and no giving of false evidence.' See 'Education, Civilisation and Foreignisation in Buganda', by H. H. Daudi Chwa, in D. Low (ed.), *The Mind of Buganda* (London, 1971) 105–6. The Bible is still a major source of justification of the death penalty in the traditional courts.

Hooker J., 'Malawi's Experiment in Law', *American Universities Fieldstaff Reports*, vol. 15, no. 3 (March, 1971). The question as to whether the laws of the Bible were applicable in the Nyasaland protectorate was actually ruled upon judicially. After the founding of his breakaway church the Reverend Y. S. Mwase and the Presbyterian Church went to court over who had control over local church property. Mwase claimed that the law applicable should be customary law or 'the law to be found in the scriptures'. But Johnston J. ruled that 'the law of the Scriptures is chiefly to be found in the Old Testament and it forms no part of Native Law. It is the product of a semitic civilisation foreign to Africa. It has not been applied to Nyasaland, and can only operate insofar as it has influenced English law.' *Ysaye Mwase and the Blackman's Church of God which is in Tongaland v. C.C.A.P. Sanga Division, Nyasaland Reports*, 4, 1935.

17 D. Fraser, *Winning a Primitive People* (London, 1914; New York edn, 1970) 10 and 195.
18 H. Rowley, *20 Years in Central Africa* (London, 1889) 66.
19 J. H. Morrison, *Streams in the Desert* (New York, 1919; 1969 edn) 47–8.
20 D. J. Rothman, *The Discovery of Asylum* (Boston, 1971) 15.
21 J. Iliffe, *A Modern History of Tanganyika* (Cambridge, 1979) 227.
22 G. S. Mwase, *Strike a Blow and Die*, ed. R. Rotberg (Cambridge, Mass., 1967) 114–15.
23 W. P. Johnson, *Nyasa. The Great Water* (London, 1922) 25.
24 Mwase, *Strike a Blow*, 32; J. McCracken, *Christianity and Politics in Malawi 1875–1940* (Cambridge, 1977) 207 and 217. A *chikoti* was a hide whip.
25 MNA NC 1/3/2, Petition of Native Civil Servants, 1923; and ZNA Livingstone native welfare association, 1932.
26 Morrison, *Streams in the Desert*, 108.
27 Mwase, *Strike a Blow*, 81–3; MNA NC 1/3/2, Petition of Native Civil Servants, 1923.
28 Mwase, *Strike a Blow*, 81–3; MNA NC 1/3/2, Petition of Native Civil Servants, 1923.
29 MNA NC 1/3/2.
30 MNA S 3263/23, 1928.
31 L. S. Mumba, *The Administration of Justice in Nyasaland*, MNA n.d.
32 Morrison, *Streams in the Desert*, 112–13.
33 Mwase, *Strike a Blow*, 60–2.
34 'Alonda' were watchmen. It is instructive to compare Mumba's analysis with that of Norman Leys, which he wrote in 1918 after his period as medical officer in Nyasaland. People were being turned into a 'vagrant proletariat . . . . the cement that binds individuals in a common ethic and belief . . . is being dissolved . . . . Society becomes atomic, a mere aggregation of individuals . . . and the social virtues . . . disappear. That is why crimes and vagrancy are rapidly increasing in British East Africa.' Leys to Secretary of State for the Colonies 7/2/18, in J. W. Cell (ed.), *By Kenya Possessed: The Correspondence of N. Leys and J. H. Oldham 1918–26* (Chicago, 1976) 98.
35 See ZNA 1/9. Memo 1927. Sec. Native Affairs/Chief Secretary. For the period January to October 1927 the following figures on voluntary court use by people are given:

District	Population	No. of actions
Fort Jameson	108,000	19
Petauke	55,000	80
Namwala	23,500	320
Mumbwa	31,700	370
Kalomo	41,400	35
Mazabuka	64,700	16
Kafue	16,000	0
Chilanga	19,900	37

Most of these were matrimonial cases.

Notes

36 PRO DO 35/826, R8/282.
37 ZNA ZA 7/6/3.
38 MNA S1/2065/10.
39 S. W. Speck, 'African Local Government in Malawi: Its Development and Politics under British Rule', Ph.D. thesis (Harvard, 1969) 149–50.
40 MNA S1/2859/23, 14/9/23.
41 MNA NC1/3/2, 19/11/27.
42 ZNA AZ 1/15/1 2, Memorandum by Maxwell, 9/8/32.
43 *Zoona* 3/1/36. Translation in MNA. Meebelo's account reflects the 'new men's' version. Chiefs, he writes, administered justice with an 'iron hand' under indirect rule, and Native Courts 'assumed something of the importunate image of the notorious 17th century Star Chamber'. He quotes Chief Chikwanda's admission that chiefs 'tended to over-exert themselves by punishing'. But, Meebelo assures us, this was because the chiefs had lost their 'traditional sense of justice' and had undergone 'moral decay'. H. S. Meebelo, *Reaction to Colonialism* (Manchester, 1971) 205–6. One might note, however, that the chiefs' own version of their 'traditional sense of justice' was even more ferocious than that which they practised under indirect rule.
44 Leys to Secretary of State Colonies, 7/2/18, in Cell, *By Kenya Possessed* 126; and L. Barnes, *Empire and Democracy* (London, 1939) 158–9.
45 A report of the debate is to be found in ZNA Nat K/9, 19/7/47. One must note here (see also above pp.40–1) that Epstein's writings on the Urban Courts on the Copperbelt emphasise that complex conflict-of-laws problems were easily resolved because people were not law- or rule-minded: that they dealt with facts, social relationships and values of right- and wrongdoing rather than rules of law. Because for example, the urban courts dealt in marriage cases with 'supreme values' it was 'possible for the majority of disputes to be settled by methods which are traditional, yet involve no reference to any particular system of tribal law'. See A. L. Epstein, *Politics in an Urban African Community* (Manchester, 1958) and *Juridicial Techniques and the Judicial Process* (Manchester, 1954); D. N. Smith, 'Man and Law in Urban Africa: a Role for Customary Courts in the Urbanisation Process', *American Journal of Comparative Law* 21 (1972) 237–40. But all urban Africans were clearly not happy without legalism. What must be looked for are the reasons which drove some people towards a demand for legalism.
46 ZNA Sec. 2/448, African Welfare Association Abercorn, Minutes of Meeting 5/10/48.

8. The lawgivers in Central Africa: marriage and morality

1 H. Duff, *Nyasaland Under the Foreign Office* (London, 1903) 340–1. C. Gouldsbury and H. Sheane, *The Great Plateau of Northern Rhodesia* (London, 1911) 75. Nine-tenths of cases brought before the Boma courts, Dundas wrote, were matrimonial, concerning the recovery of wives, dowries and children. C. Dundas, *African Crossroads* (London, 1955) 46. This was to remain a dominant feature of the 'law' throughout the colonial period. Gluckman noted that 80 per cent of the Lozi cases were matrimonial; Bohannan that 'a large proportion of cases concerned women and marriage'; Barnes that 'adultery suits are the commonest heard in court.' *The Judicial Process Among the Barotse* (Manchester, 1965) 64; *Justice and Judgement among the Tiv* (London, 1957), 72; *Marriage in a Changing Society* (London, 1951) 37. The predominance was not confined to the Boma courts alone. In the 1930s, for example, four out of five cases in Nyakyusa courts were matrimonial: 'All cases are about women', said one chief. See M. Wilson, *For Men and Elders* (London, 1977), 51–2.
2 Cf. Godfrey Wilson, *The Constitution of Ngonde* (Livingstone, 1939) 36.

3 Correspondence in MNA J2/4/1, 1903.
4 E.W. Smith and A.M. Dale, *The Ila-Speaking Peoples of Northern Rhodesia* (London, 1920; New York, 1968) vol. 2, 54; Guillaime, *Mss Afr.* 1213, translated 1902.
5 F. Coillard, *On the Threshold of Central Africa* (London, 1897) 284, 398.
6 E.D. Young, *Nyassa: A Journal of Adventures* (London, 1877) 47–8.
7 D. Fraser, *Winning* (London, 1914; reprinted New York, 1970) 185.
8 T.M. Thomas, *Eleven Years in Central Africa* (London, 1872) 259; Duff, *Nyasaland Under the Foreign Office*, 235.
9 Gouldsbury and Sheane, *The Great Plateau*, 107–8; and see below, pp. 182–6.
10 Griffin, J. in MNA J2/6/6.
11 *The Great Plateau*, 108.
12 ZNA 4/1. *Native Laws and Customs* 1907–10.
13 J. Coxhead, 'The Native Tribes of North Eastern Rhodesia: Their Laws and Customs', *Journal of the Royal Anthropological Institute* Occasional Paper no. 5 (London, 1914) 4, 14, 26.
14 Melland also wrote, some years later, in reference to the registering of African marriages before the native commissioner: 'an important matter, as the slight ceremony necessary for a native marriage is apt to grow less and less: which might result in marriage degenerating into concubinage were there no registration.' In *Witchbound Africa* (London, 1923; New York edn, 1967) 61.
15 Griffin, C. J. in CO 525/18/04890, Nyasaland, 1907.
16 ZNA law dept circular no. 9, 1914.
17 C. Dundas, 'The Organisation and Laws of Some Bantu Tribes of East Africa', *Journal of the Anthropological Institute* 45 (1915) 305.
18 C. Dundas, 'Native Laws of Some Bantu Tribes of East Africa', *Journal of the Royal Anthropological Institute* 51 (1921) 263–6.
19 ZNA B33/498, Judicial circular, Jan. 1922.
20 ZNA U2/3/1, Namwala, 23/10/16.
21 A. Hastings, *Christian Marriage in Africa* (London, 1973) 15.
22 A. Glossop, *Central African Mission Report* (1898) 15; and A.G. Blood, *The History of the Universities Mission to Central Africa*, vol. 11, 1907–1932 (London, 1957) 47.
23 J.E. Hine, *Days Gone By* (London, 1924) 159.
24 N.R. Bennett and M. Ylvisaker (eds), *The Central African Journal of L.J. Proctor* (Boston, 1971), 288, 18/7/62. The complainant was a Makololo, the women presumably captives.
25 W.P. Johnson, *My African Reminiscences 1875–95* (London, n.d.)
26 D. Fraser, *Autobiography of an African* (London, 1925) 104–5.
27 Glossop, *Central African Mission Report*, (1898), 15.
28 York Archive ZAM 1, File 3 Notes written in 1975 by Sir Kenneth Bradley.
29 I. Linden with J. Linden, *Catholics, Peasants and Chewa Resistance in Nyasaland* (London, 1974) 172–3.
30 *Livingstonia News*, October 1910, 85–6.
31 A. Hetherwick, *The Romance of Blantyre* (London, 1931) 126 and 226 *et seq.*
32 Lyttelton/Sharp, 18/5/04. All correspondence on this topic is in MNA J1/2/5.
33 Hetherwick, *Romance of Blantyre*, 126 and 226 *et seq.*
34 It may have been that the penalties for bigamy under the Christian Native Marriage Ordinance caused the alarm. The *Livingstonia News* noted in 1915 that the penalties brought to light a 'latent sympathy with polygamy', and that people feared them more than the consequences of breaking God's law and 'shirked marriage under the Ordinance'.
35 ZNA BS 3/82, 12/2 17, D.R.C. Petition to Lord Buxton. An Anglican address of 1918

which accompanied the Christian ratification of marriage invoked the prestige of the imperial state, advising couples that 'King George is a Christian and he says "divorce is bad".' Couples were told that 'The marriage of heathens is a small matter' as they had many wives and could be divorced, while 'the marriage of Christians is a very great matter . . . they cannot be divorced.'

36 ZNA High Court of N.E. Rhodesia, Civil case book, January 1910. Significantly, a district officer argued the case before the High Court for the woman, a missionary for the husband.

37 A. Richards, *Bemba Marriage and Present Economic Conditions* (Livingstone, 1940) 26.

38 As the Lindens wrote, Catholic villagers 'now found themselves subjected to the laws of medieval Rome. The extraordinary complexities of canon law were brought to bear on the marriage of uncomprehending peasants.' *Catholics*, 172.

39 Under the *privilegium Paulinium* in canon law, where one of two pagan spouses were converted to Christianity, a 'divorce' was in certain circumstances possible. See 1 Corinthians 7, verses 12 to 15: 'If any brother hath a wife that believeth not and she be pleased to dwell with him, let him not put her away . . . . But if the unbelieving depart, let him depart. A brother or a sister is not under bondage in such cases.'

40 Hine, *Days Gone By*, 168.

41 Case no. 6, p. 14, U.M.C.A., *Marriage Cases* 1922. We might also note case no. 46: N.L., the husband (a Christian), married B. and then went away to work. When he returned in 1922 B.'s mother had come and taken her away to her own village and B. refused to return. N.L. asked for nullity on the grounds that his mother-in-law and wife, not being Christians, did not understand the conditions of a Christian marriage and therefore had not consented to it. He was refused. One assessor said: 'The fact that she afterwards changed her mind or was overruled by her mother does not imply that at the time she made the promises she did not fully understand and mean what she consented to. I cannot accept . . . the ground . . . that a broken promise implies that the promise was never meant or understood. It would open the door far too wide.'

42 This case is reported in the *Nyasaland Diocesan Chronicle* for July 1928. See also I. Schapera, *Married Life in an African Tribe* (1940; Evanston edn, 1966) for a parallel process among the Tswana where the Church's attack on *lobola* marriage waned, and stability of marriage became the mission's major interest.

43 Cf. W.P. Johnson, *Nyasa: The Great Water* (London, 1922) 71–5, for the U.M.C.A.'s fostering of the development of 'customary' marriage payments.

44 The Church Court would not free the first husband: 'I feel sorry for this man but I can see no grounds . . . . What he is really asking for here is a divorce on the grounds of his wife's adultery, and this cannot be granted.' *Marriage Cases* 72. See also 77 and 114.

45 *Central African Mission Report* (1893), 24.

46 See Bennett and Ylvisaker, *Central African Journal*; and W.P. Johnson, *Nyasa* and *My African Reminiscences*.

47 This 'retreat' was not peculiar, of course, to the U.M.C.A. See J. McCracken, *Politics and Christianity in Malawi 1875–1940* (Cambridge, 1977) 253, for the declining interest of the Presbyterian missions in the liberation of women.

48 G.E. Butt, *My Travels in Northern Rhodesia* (London, n.d.) 260. Cf. the 'Pitiful Story' which was 'so common' related by E. Price of the South African General Mission on the Lower Shire. Price found a man beating and kicking his wife for selling grain. In addition her mother-in-law was accusing her of witchcraft. The husband, a far older man, had 'bought' his wife when she was a young girl. Price described her life as one of perpetual misery. But she was not perceived as a candidate for uplifting or liberation. Price counselled her on the necessity of marital obedience. *South African Pioneer* xxvi (1) (Jan. 1913) 10.

49 It has been suggested that becoming a nun was 'one of the few channels for female

independence in colonial Malawi – liberation from the constraints of a male-dominated world'. Linden, *Catholics*, 175–6.

9. Slaves and masters

1 S. Miers and A. Kopytoff (eds), *Slavery in Africa: Historical and Anthropological Perspectives* (Madison, 1977) 5–6.
2 J. M. Sarbah, *Fanti Customary Law* (2nd edn, London, 1904).
3 See J. F. Munro, *Colonial Rule and the Kamba* (Oxford, 1975) 39.
4 V. W. Turner, *Schism and Continuity in an African Society* (Manchester, 1957) 189.
5 H. Maine, *Ancient Law* (London, 1930 edn) 176.
6 *Slavery in Africa*, 23 *et seq*. See also W. MacGaffey, 'Lineage Structure, Marriage and Family Amongst the Central Bantu', *Journal of African History* 24 (1983) at 175: ' "Slavery" . . . is to be seen as an arrangement of the same kind as "marriage".'
7 See e.g. M. Klein, 'The Study of Slavery in Africa', *Journal of African History* 19 (1978); F. Cooper, 'The Problem of Slavery in African Historical Studies', *Journal of African History* 20 (1979); P. Lovejoy, 'Indigenous African Slavery', in M. Craton, *Roots and Branches: Current Directions in Slave Studies* (Toronto, 1979); G. Prins, *Hidden Hippopotamus* (Cambridge, 1980).
8 W. G. Clarence-Smith, 'Slaves, Commoners and Landlords in Bulozi', *Journal of African History* 20 (1979) esp. 226–31. All forms of slavery were not, of course, the same: what is being remarked on is the willingness to write in condemnatory terms.
9 Lovejoy, 'Indigenous African Slavery', 23–4.
10 Ibid., 42, n. 45.
11 G. Balandier, *Daily Life in the Kingdom of the Kongo*, 185, quoted in J. A. K. Kandawire, 'Village and Class in Southern Malawi', *Africa* 50 (1980) 139.
12 Miers and Kopytoff, *Slavery in Africa*, 64, 74, 76.
13 On p. 8 they give a case to illustrate the complexity and precision of transactions concerning rights in persons. That the case is complex is obvious, but the 'precision' appears to be the end result of a negotiation in which each held out for as much of the power and advantage related to a particular woman as they could get. The rights were not legally 'existent' in a general sense outside of the particular negotiation. Miers and Kopytoff are quite capable of seeing the difference between legality and reality when they discuss the rights of redress of slaves recited by informants (51–2) but fail to make this distinction when discussing the 'ordinary law' of kinship.
14 See E. A. Alpers, *Ivory and Slaves* (London, 1975).
15 S. Ntara, *Headman's Enterprise* (London, 1945) 40, 63, and *The History of the Chewa*, trans. W. S. K. Jere (Wiesbaden, 1973).
16 See Alpers, *Ivory and Slaves*, 230.
17 K. M. Phiri, 'Chewa History in Central Malawi and the Use of the Oral Tradition', Ph.D. thesis (Wisconsin, 1975) 126–7. Cf. the remarks about the Yao in the Tanganyika District Book for Mahenge, vol. 4, 196: 'The prevalence of the traffic in slaves played an important part in the law (if law it can be called) of the tribe; a man unable to pay a debt could be enslaved, if his relatives could not pay it. But if the transgressor was of sufficient stature, the price for the crime or debt would be paid by someone else in the clan, usually a young girl.' E. W. Smith and A. M. Dale observed of the Ila that people became slaves either by purchase, or by their own fault, or through the fault of others. Stealing, and even trivial and unintentional acts of damage to property 'are thought sufficient to doom a person to loss of liberty'. *The Ila-Speaking Peoples of Northern Rhodesia* (London, 1920; New York edn, 1968) 402–3. See Alpers, *Ivory and Slaves*, 240, for the case of a Makua boy, pawned in compensation for his brother's adultery, and later sold. According to MacDonald, 'When a man is sorely pressed by some legal action and has to pay heavy fines, he begins by

Notes

selling off his junior wives.' *Africana or the Heart of Heathen Africa* (1882, 1969 edn, London) 135.

18 Mwashitete, *Ways I Have Trodden* (London, 1932) 17–18; and Narwimba, in *Stories of the Old Times* (London, 1932) 29. See also the case of *R.* v. *Manunka* below.

19 N. R. Bennett and M. Ylvisaker, *The Central African Journal of Lovell J. Proctor 1860–64* (Boston, 1971) 374–5; and H. Rowley, *Africa Unveiled* (London, 1876) 175.

20 W. P. Johnson, *Nyasa: The Great Water* (London, 1922) 22–3.

21 F. Melland, *In Witchbound Africa* (London, 1923; New York edn, 1967) 200. The context of his remark concerns the payment of diviners, but its force remains applicable.

22 J. McCracken, *Christianity and Politics in Malawi 1875–1940* (Cambridge, 1977) 46, based on MacDonald, *Africana*; see also P. Redmond, 'Some Results of Military Contacts Between the Ngoni and Their Neighbours in 19th Century Southern East Africa'. *Transafrican Journal of History* 5 (1976), re the use by the Ngoni of captives to till the fields; and F. S. Arnot, *Garenganze* (1889; London edn, 1969) 212–14.

23 *Africana*, 134. MacDonald claimed that among the Yao a man 'normally' had one 'free' and three to four 'slave' wives.

24 F. Coillard, *On the Threshold of Central Africa*, 468 *et seq*. The Ngoni were, it seems, usually incorporators rather than traders. See Redmond, 'Some Results', 86; Alpers, *Ivory and Slaves*; and W. Rau, 'Mpeseni's Ngoni of Eastern Zambia 1870–1920' (unpublished Ph.D. thesis, U.C.L.A., 1976) 173. On distribution of captives and political power see e.g. M. Wilson, *For Men and Elders* (London, 1977) 72.

25 The Yao chief, Mponda, for example, is estimated by McCracken to have had seventy to eighty slave wives. See also Wilson, *For Men and Elders*, 66, and Miers and Kopytoff, *Slavery in Africa*, 33–4.

26 K. M. Phiri, 'Some Changes in the Matrilineal Family System Among the Chewa of Malawi Since the 19th Century', *Journal of African History* 24 (1983) 264–5.

27 The Northern Rhodesian administration noted that appeals to the Boma by relatives of slaves for their freedom were common, while appeals by slaves themselves were rare. ZNA ZA 4/1, 1907–10.

28 P. Kilekwa, *From Slave Boy to Priest* (London, 1937) esp. 11–15. For similar life stories see M. Wright, 'Women in Peril', *African Social Research* 20 (1975) and *Ways I Have Trodden* and *Tales of the Old Times*.

29 R. G. Stuart, 'Christianity and the Chewa: The Anglican Case 1885–1950', Ph.D. thesis (London, 1974) 32, quoting B. H. Barnes.

30 A. J. Swann, *Fighting the Slave Hunters* (London, 1910; New York edn, 1969) 321. His methods were not those of a new and technical legal order. 'In the case of young children', he recorded, 'the ruse of Solomon frequently needed to be put into practice.'

31 ZNA KST 5/1. Nawalia Native Commissioner's Case Book, 15/1/08. ZNA U2/3/1, 30/3/16. Godfrey Wilson records an informant telling him that in the old days a man who had been wronged 'would catch and keep the child' of a person who might be able to put pressure on the wrongdoer or pay him. *The Constitution of Ngonde* (Livingstone, 1939) 58–9.

32 ZNA KSR 1/1/1, Hall to Rennie, 3/1/07.

33 J. C. C. Coxhead, 'The Native Tribes of North-Eastern Rhodesia: Their Laws and Customs', *Journal of the Royal Anthropological Institute* Occasional Paper no. 5 (London, 1914).

34 ZNA BS3/498, circular no. 6, 1916. The claim in this circular that slavery had never been recognised by the North Eastern Rhodesian courts is clearly incorrect.

35 MNA NCK 2/1/1, 13/7/17.

36 MNA S1/924/24, S2/28/23. In 1939 on the Upper Shire the daughter of two former slaves actually applied to the Boma court for a declaration that she was free to move in spite of her servile descent. She must have been forced into this application because her claim had been denied in the village. Upper Shire Annual Report 1939, Rhodes House *Mss Afr*. The shift in

262

administrative attitudes is neatly encapsulated in the memoirs of a former Northern Rhodesian district officer. Writing in the 1970s about the late 1920s he was 'astonished to find that [slavery] still existed . . . when two old men came to the Boma and complained that they were slaves of the local chief . . . I was furious.' The chief was sent for, the slaves freed in his presence, and 'I told the Chief that any other slaves in his or any other chiefdom must be sent into the Boma, with their owners, and freed. He or any other chief who disobeyed this order would be removed from office . . . lose his . . . subsidy and see the inside of the . . . gaol.' 'I need not have got so angry about it anyway. I do not think they really minded being slaves . . . . They probably carried on much as before.' H. Franklin, *The Flag Wagger* (London, 1974) 106.

37 ZNA U2/3/1, *Konalo* v. *Milika*, Civil no. 46, 10/3/15, Fort Jameson. Turner gives an account of a 1928 case in which the issue was not the autonomy of the 'slaves' but whether the rights over their children still existed. *Schism and Continuity*, 181.

38 See ZNA BS3/498, circular no. 6, 1916; and Clarence-Smith, 'Slaves, Commoners and Landlords', 233.

39 Smith and Dale, *Ila-Speaking Peoples*, 412 and n.; and ZNA BS3/498. Certain problems were anticipated in the case of female slaves as it was accepted that in customary law a woman had to have a guardian as there was no *femme sole*. To admit that the former owner was her guardian 'would be too much like an admission of the existence of slavery'. It was thought that, failing finding her relatives, the native commissioner could assume the position of guardian. It seems more than likely, however, that women without kin would have remained where they were.

40 ZNA KDE 2/22/1, 26/9/21, Ngambela/Native Commissioner, 17/2/21. Prins records a case twenty years after abolition, of a murder trial of a master who killed a slave for disobedience saying, according to the evidence, 'What right have you to go where you like? . . . you are only a slave.' Prins stresses that there were many more cases of this kind than ever surfaced in the government's records. Prins, *Hidden Hippopotamus*, 75–6.

41 ZNA U2/3/1, Ndola, 1915.

42 Turner, *Schism and Continuity*, 188, 192–3. Turner had written of the first period of colonial rule that it was a time in which 'Traditional ties became more brittle; traditional social machinery for reintegrating a disturbed group became replaced in several situations by the legal machinery of the superordinate alien authority . . . . the first effect of these innovations tended to be the loosening of traditional ties rather than their replacement by new ones. The first of these ties to snap was the owner–slave link.' Ibid., 196.

43 See B. W. Randolph, *Arthur Douglas: Missionary on Lake Nyasa* (London, 1912) 147–9. Also 88–9 for a 'serious' case where pupils referred to their teacher's former slave status.

44 C. Mitchell, quoted by Kandawire, 'Village and Class', 137, and *Yao Village*, 77.

45 J. van Velsen, *The Politics of Kinship* (Manchester, 1957) 175.

46 Ibid., 254. Turner, *Schism and Continuity*, 64 n., 180–3. See Miers and Kopytoff, *Slavery in Africa*, 34, where they point out that even among the 'absorptive' Sena status differences linger on 'in such things as discrimination in the assignment of land and a certain disdain in . . . treatment'. Generally they show that ' "who is" and "who isn't" a slave are even now sensitive questions.'

47 Kandawire, 'Village and Class', 140–1.

48 van Velsen, *Politics*, 254.

49 *African Slavery*, 64, 74, 76. My italics.

50 For a suggestive account of how criminal penalties, formerly applied to slaves, came to be applied to the lower orders of freemen as the status of slavery disappeared in Europe see T. Sellin, 'Slavery and the Punishment of Crime', in R. Hood (ed.) *Crime, Criminology and Public Policy* (London, 1974).

Notes

10. The courts and the people: law in action II

1 T. Baker, 'Tax Collection in Malawi: An Administrative History, 1891–1972', *International Journal of African Historical Studies* 8 (1975); Zambia National Archives Calendars vol. 1; ZNA law dept circular no. 7, 1924; ZNA Box 66, Registration of Native Marriages, 1927; ZNA ZA 4/1, 1907–10. The plural tax was particularly resented, it appears, in the patrilineal areas, and the system was eventually abolished, in Zambia in 1929 and in Malawi in 1940, leaving only the male polltax. It is noteworthy that in British India, where the taxation system was based upon land, British courts were choked with land litigation and neither they, nor the populace, involved the government with the laws of marriage. In Central Africa, where tax depended upon relations between persons, British courts were forced into the area of personal litigation and law.

2 The French colonial authorities perceived a similar connection between traditional familial authority and the stability of the colonial order. The governor-general of French West Africa wrote in 1920, 'The right of a father to dispose of his daughters ... [is] a custom incompatible with the principles of our civilisation ... [but] the emancipation of the individual ... risks a profound disturbance of the indigenous order .... I do not need to remind you that it is this paternal authority, and by extension, the authority of the village and canton chiefs which we recently drew upon to recruit military contingents destined for European battlefields.' Quoted in J.I. Guyer, 'Household and Community in African Studies', *African Studies Review* 24 (1981). See too J.R. Hooker, 'Witnesses and Watchtower in Rhodesia and Nyasaland', *Journal of African History* 5 (1963) at 100–4. Both African tribal authorities and the Northern Rhodesian government specifically objected to the Watchtower adherents' ignoring of traditional sexual laws and practices, identifying this aspect of the movement as particularly subversive. The governor picked out for objection 'the practice of free love'. All sides made the connection between existing sexual ethics and existing power relationships.

3 C. Dundas, *African Crossroads* (London, 1955) 46.

4 ZNA KDG 5/11, 1906; ZNA INA 1/1/2, 3/3/06; KDG 5/11, 1915; and MNA J 2/1/4, 1903.

5 Cf. I. Schapera, *Married Life in an African Tribe* (1940; Evanston edn, 1966) 103, 336–40, where he discusses how women, who could not resort to village courts in marital disputes as they had no jural status in them, went instead independently to the Boma court.

6 J. Barnes, *Marriage in a Changing Society* (London, 1951) 4; cf. H. Duff, *Nyasaland Under the Foreign Office* (London, 1903) 342, where he writes of Zomba district that it was only women who sought divorce in the Boma court.

7 T. Cullen-Young, 'Tribal Intermixture in Northern Nyasaland', *Journal of the Royal Anthropological Institute* 63 (1933).

8 *Nkhoswe*: the representatives of the families who negotiated the marriage. See above Chapter 4.

9 MNA Mzimba District Book; MNA L1/4/1, 12/4/18, and NC 1/21/3, Notes by the Provincial Commissioner, Central Province. A. Hodgson, 'Notes on the Achewa and Ngoni of Dowa District in the Nyasaland Protectorate', *Journal of the Royal Anthropological Institute* 63 (1926) 135. Cf. J.O. Ibik, 'The Laws of Marriage in Nyasaland', Ph.D. Thesis (London 1966) 444, n. 1, and 451. Lucy Mair observed the 'inextricable intermingling' of Ngoni and Chewa marriage in Dedza. See 'Marriage and Family in the Dedza District of Nyasaland', *Journal of the Royal Anthropological Institute* 81 (1951).

10 MNA NS 1/23/6, 8/11/26; NS1/23/6, 16/10/27.

11 Cullen-Young, 'Tribal Intermixture', 12.

12 ZNA, Fort Rosenberry, 27/8/10.

13 Cf. the remarks of one of M. Wilson's Nyakyusa informants: 'With us if you do not give marriage cattle for a woman she will be proud. She has too much freedom. She goes about anywhere. If she goes to sleep across the river she says "I do no wrong because you did not

give marriage cattle for me". We give marriage cattle to bind women that they may not be proud; they are like prostitutes if the husbands do not give cattle.' *For Men and Elders* (London, 1977) 148.

14 E. Colson, *Marriage and Family Among the Plateau Tonga of Northern Rhodesia* (Manchester, 1958) 183. The fieldwork for this was done between 1946 and 1950.

15 Wilson, *Men and Elders*, 112 and 162–3.

16 ZNA Box 66, 1927. This was in an area where bridewealth was already the 'norm'. He referred to a Southern Rhodesian rule limiting bridewealth paid by commoners to four head of cattle.

17 A.S. Chapman, Asst Native Commissioner Fort Roseberry, 26/9/22, Rhodes House *Mss Afr*. 1355, 19.

18 The Nyasaland Census Report for 1945 observes, 'Any study of tribal distribution in Nyasaland is confused by the tendency to intermarry. This is especially true in the Shire Highlands where the Anyanja, Yao, Angoni, Alomwe and Achikunda live side by side in the same villages. Patriarchal and matriarchal tribes in this area mix and intermarry in a way that is probably unique in East Central Africa.' I think that the evidence suggests that such intermixture was far from unique, and that the chief reason for suggesting that it was so was the model in the official mind of separate tribes with discrete marriage systems. At the very least these observations help to underline the point that the 'detribalisation' of marriage in Central Africa was not simply a phenomenon of urbanisation of the Northern Rhodesian Copperbelt. The census is quoted by Hailey in *Native Administration in British African Territories* (1950; London, 1979) 25.

19 Wilson, *Men and Elders*, 6–7, 17, 24, 59, 63, 147, 175, 182. Gouldsbury and Sheane are quoted at 59. An elder told Wilson 'Cattle bind the girl so that she becomes like a slave. If her husband beats her she thinks "I am caught by the cattle; if there were no cattle I would leave"' (149). In these circumstances only prostitutes and nuns could escape the dominance of husbands. The Nyasaland authorities noted the steady increase in the size of bridewealth being demanded, the long delays in payment which were necessary, and the consequent increase in litigation. It was not simply women whose interests were adversely affected by this development, but those of young men as well. CO 626/25 Nyasaland Northern Province.

20 A.I. Richards, *Bemba Marriage and Present Economic Conditions* (Livingstone, 1940) 38, 91 *et seq*.

21 Barnes, *Marriage*, 37.

22 ZNA U2/3/1, Evidence in *Zamiwa* v. *Malalo* Civil Suit 106–15, Fort Jameson, 25/8/15.

23 MNA NS 1/23/6.

24 G. Wilson, *An Essay on the Economics of Detribalisation in Northern Rhodesia* II (Livingstone, 1942) 47; and Richards, *Bemba Marriage*, 58. See also C. Lancaster, in Chapter 1 above.

25 ZNA ZAI/9, East Luangwa Native Authorities.

26 Colson, *Marriage and Family*, 334. Turner gives a clear indication of the tensions involved in the area in his remark that there is a tendency in societies with extended kinship systems for members of the matricentric family to gravitate together. It was a 'tacit recognition of the strength of this bond' that had given rise in patrilineal societies to 'institutions directed against divorce since the patrilineage of the father has a powerful interest in retaining his children to replenish its local membership, and there is a danger that where the mother goes her children will go also.' V.W Turner, *Schism and Continuity in an African Society* (Manchester, 1957) 223.

27 ZNA Sec. 2/406/4. See below for a discussion of Urban Courts and marriage.

28 ZNA Sec. 2/407, Provincial Council Western Province, 1/2 May 1945, and Sec. 2/40, *Mufula* v. *Simfukwe*, 21/7/44.

29 Barnes, *Marriage*, 110.

Notes

30 Ibid, 'Laws of Marriage', Appendix 3.
31 Colson, *Marriage and Family*, 320.
32 ZNA KSF 1/1/1, 1920.
33 This applied also to the parents of women where no bridewealth had passed. They had an interest in a continuing first marriage, as subsequent marriage was often virilocal. Consequently, as a Bemba parent told Godfrey Wilson, 'If my daughter leaves the man she first marries, the son-in-law whom I know, I refuse to have anything more to do with her.' *Economics*, 46–7, n.47. Cf. the magistrate's questions and remarks in *Kanbuje* v. *Kasoka* ZNA KDE 2/28/3, 5/2/27. J.S. Horne bombarded his witness on customary law with hypothetical cases, saying, 'I ask you these questions because it is well that the law should be the same all over Barotseland but the local chiefs do not know the Barotse law well, and usually settle cases according to their own local customs . . . . If I know what the Barotse law is I can always follow it in cases of dispute.'
34 ZNA U2/3/1, 9/8/15, Evidence on the customs of the Alamba. In this case a 10/- redemption payment was agreed to, equivalent to about a year's tax. Return of bridewealth on refusal of inheritance was also enforced in Malawi. See MNA NSI/23/6.
35 'The Legal Status of Women in Malawi from the Colonial Period to Independence', Ph.D. thesis (London, 1970) 26 and 173.
36 For Malawi see MNA NS 1/23/5, 19/2/31.
37 Cmd 5784, *Correspondence Relating to the Welfare of Women in Tropical Africa*, 1935–7.
38 Official Memorandum published in *NADA*, vol. 14 (1939).
39 Malawi Government Department of Antiquities Interview with the Reverend Hanoch Phiri (Nov. 1969); MNA NS1/23/6, Hodgson/P.C. Lilongwe 15/4/27.
40 Richards, *Bemba Marriage*, 47.
41 Barnes, *Marriage*, 101–2.
42 G. Wilson, *The Constitution of Ngonde* (Livingstone, 1939) 56, 76; *Economics*, 39.
43 Richards, *Bemba Marriage*, 86.
44 Ibid., 101–10.
45 Wilson, *Men and Elders*, 130, 173.

11. Africans, law and marriage

1 ZNA Sec/Lab/71, 25/1/44, referred to in H. Heisler, *Urbanisation and the Government of Migration* (London, 1974); see also Heisler, *Urbanisation*, 98–9.
2 MNA S1/3263/23.
3 MNA S1/2065/19, 17/5/23.
4 G. S. Mwase, *Strike a Blow and Die*, ed. R. Rotberg (Cambridge, Mass., 1967).
5 ZNA U2/3/1, Mpeseni's evidence in *Fani* v. *Daviti*, Fort Jameson, 23/3/15.
6 ZNA U2/3/1, 27/4/15, and *R* v. *Maliki*, Fort Jameson, 26/8/15, Evidence of Chinunda and Nyongo. 14/9/17 Evidence of Mafuta *et al.*
7 ZNA U2/3/1, Kawamba Annual Report 2/3/14; 30/10/14.
8 ZNA U2/3/1, *R* v. *Yoram*, Ndola, 9/6/16.
9 ZNA BS1/44, Actg Administrator to High Cmnr S. Africa, 11/11/10.
10 ZNA BS3/81, 16/9/16, and BS1/44.
11 ZNA U2/3/1.
12 ZNA BS3/81, 16/9/16; ZNA BS3/498.
13 ZNA BS3/498.
14 ZNA KSF 1/1/16, Tagart to Magistrate Namwala, 20/2/18.
15 MNA S1/23/6, 15/5/27 and 13/2/28.
16 ZNA U2/3/1.
17 ZNA Sec. 2/406 vol. 2, Actg Cmnr to Chief Secretary, 19/9/39, Encl. Minutes Nkana Advisory Council.

18 ZNA Sec. 2/419/2, Judicial circular no. 7, 1933.
19 Ibid.
20 MNA S1/210/29, Fort Manning District Notebook.
21 The assertion that Africans were unable to comprehend the civil/criminal distinction has produced an indignant counter insistence on the existence of a customary criminal law by a Malawian lawyer. See 'Traditional Criminal Law in Malawi', by L. J. Chimango, *Society of Malawi Journal* 28 (1975). See too CO 626/22, Nyasaland Central Province, 1945, and CO626/24, 1946/7.
22 CO 626/24, Nyasaland Northern Province, 1948.
23 ZNA Sec. 2/407, Central Province African Provincial Council, 30/7/45. Gerard Chipepo, Member for Broken Hill Rural.
24 ZNA Sec. 2/419/2.
25 J. A. Barnes, *Marriage in a Changing Society* (London, 1951) 19, 124. The Christian element is evident in the letter of Charles Chinula, the Association's secretary, to the mission council in 1927, assuring the missionaries that 'as Christians, one of our strongest beliefs is that Christianity condemns polygamy ... as it ... makes family life impossible.' MNA Dutch Reformed Church Archive, 18/1/27.
26 MNA NS1/3/26, 'Native Customs General'. He also notes that many spouses were slaves who did not have the capacity to divorce.
27 MNA S1/3263/23.
28 L. Mumba, 'The Administration of Justice', Malawi National Archives.
29 H. Duff, *Nyasaland Under the Foreign Office* (London, 1903) 346; K. Bradley, *Once a District Officer* (London, 1966) 49.
30 A. T. Culwick, *Good Out of Africa. A Study in the Relativity of Morals*, Rhodes–Livingstone Paper No. 8 (1942).
31 Mwase, *Strike a Blow*, 115–17.
32 CO 525/710, 44178, Blantyre Native Association to Provincial Cmnr Southern Province, 15/10/36.
33 ZNA Sec. 2/422, Livingstone Native Welfare Association, 14/12/30. The chief secretary reacted vituperatively, threatening the dismissal of Association members for attacking the integrity of the judiciary, but the governor observed, 'I should not threaten; a little ridicule is often more effective than a threat.' One should not go too deeply into the substance of the complaint but 'take up very much the attitude of a school master towards a stupid boy in the third form'.
34 ZNA Sec. 2/442, Livingstone Native Welfare Association, 14/12/30.
35 ZNA Sec. 2/406, vol. 1, D.C. Ndola to P.C. Ndola, 9/3/36.
36 ZNA Sec. 2/406, vol. 1, P.C. Lusaka to Secretary Native Affairs, 30/3/33, containing resolution of Lusaka African Welfare Association.
37 ZNA Sec. 2/406, vol. 1, D.C. Ndola to P.C. Ndola, 9/3/36; ZNA Sec. 2/406/4, African Representative Council, Nov. 1946, 1st Meeting. People had disregarded the registration system when there was no further advantage in it. As a senior white official recalled 'men and women omit to report to the District Commissioner the dissolution of a marriage when it takes place.' P.C. Eastern province to Chief Secretary, 2/11/45, ZNA Sec. 2/406/4.
38 ZNA Sec. 2/406, vol. 2, Actg P.C. to Chief Secretary, 19/9/39, Encl. Minutes of Native Advisory Council. My italics.
39 ZNA Sec. 2/406, vol. 2, 9/10/39, incl. Resolutions of the 8th General Missionary Conference and the African Christian Conference.
40 ZNA Sec. 2/406, vol. 3, 1943.
41 ZNA Sec. 2/406/3, D.C. Kitwe to P.C. Ndola, 20/11/40; D.C. Mufulwa to P.C. Ndola, 10/1/40. G. Wilson, *The Economics of Detribalisation in Northern Rhodesia* (Livingstone, 1941–2) 65, 51.

42 ZNA Sec. 2/406/3, P.C. Kasama to Chief Secretary, 20/2/42; Prov. Commr report W. Prov. 1943.
43 ZNA Sec. 2/407, Conference of Provincial Commissioners and Heads of Social Services.
44 ZNA Sec. 2/406/4, D.C. Mufulwa, 21/2/45; D.C. Ndola, 7/2/45; D.C. Chingola, 7/2/45.
45 ZNA Sec. 2/406/3, Circular Minute Chief Secretary, All Provincial Commissioners, 28/7/43. T. Cullen-Young and H. Banda (eds), *Our African Way of Life* (London, 1946) 18.
46 ZNA Provincial Annual Reports 1934/5, and Report on Emigrant Labour from the Luapula Valley, 1936.
47 CO 626/14, Nyasaland, Northern Province Annual Report, 1935, 54; CO 626/22 Nyasaland, Northern Province, 1945; T.D. Thomson, Draft Report Upper Shire District, 1939, Rhodes House *Mss Afr*. The compulsory rules were enacted in the Southern Province of Malawi in 1947 as a result of a resolution by the province's African provincial council.
48 ZNA Sec. 2/406/3, July 1942. Report on Native Courts from Superintendent of Native Affairs.
49 ZNA Sec. 2/406/4, Minutes Nat./A/6, Encl. Views of Matego Kakumbi and Silas Kubili.
50 ZNA Sec. 2/419, 4th meeting Central Province African Provincial Council, July 1946.
51 Barnes, *Marriage*, 101.
52 Cullen-Young and Banda, *Our African Way of Life*, 17. Cf. C. M. W. White, *An Outline of Luvale Social and Political Organisation*, Rhodes-Livingstone Papers no. 30 (Manchester, 1960) 22; 'Matrilineal kinship was the main level at which rural control operated among the Luvale and the idea of Native Authority Courts to deal with litigation which the administration introduced was a complete innovation.' Over most of the area I am writing about this would have been the case.
53 ZNA Sec. 2/406/3, Proceedings of 1st Session of African Representative Council, November 1946.
54 ZNA Sec. 2/407, 3rd meeting of Northern Province African Provincial Council, 1–3/546.
55 See ZNA Sec. 2/407, 1945.
56 See A. L. Epstein, 'Divorce Law and the Stability of Marriage Among the Lunda of Kazembe', *Rhodes–Livingstone Journal* 14 (1954); and C. Mitchell, 'Social Change and the Stability of African Marriage in Northern Rhodesia', in A. Southall (ed.), *Social Change in Modern Africa* (London, 1961) 327.
57 See e.g. E. Colson, 'Possible Repercussions of the Right to Make Wills upon the Plateau Tonga of Northern Rhodesia', *Journal of African Administration* 11 (1950).
58 ZNA Sec. 2/442, Livingstone Native Welfare Association, 1st Annual Report 1931. See too Sec. 2/406/2. Labour Officer Ndola/P.C. Ndola, 19/10/40, re the difficulties caused by marriages with local women of Lozi and Ila men whose 'tribes are patrilineal and particularly jealous of a father's rights'.
59 See D. L. Keet, 'The African Representative Council 1946–58', M.A. thesis (University of Zambia, 1975).

12. Writing African legal history

1 B. Malinowski, Introduction to L. Hogbin, *Law and Order in Polynesia* (London, 1934) xii.
2 J. Starr and B. Yngvesson, 'Scarcity and Disputing: Zeroing in on Compromise Decisions', *American Ethnologist* 2 (3) (1975); and E. Colson, in P. H. Gulliver (ed.), *Cross-Examinations: Essays in Memory of Max Gluckman* (Leiden, 1978) 21.
3 For a critical summary of the literature, see F. Snyder, 'Law and Development in the Light of Dependency Theory', *Law and Society Review* 14 (1980).
4 See D. Dwyer, 'Substance and Process: Re-appraising the Premises of the Anthropology of Law', *Dialectical Anthropology* 4 (1979).
5 On the anthropology of medicine see H. Fabrega, 'Medical Anthropology', in B. J. Siegal (ed.), *Annual Review of Anthropology* 1972; B. J. Loudon (ed.), *Social Anthropology and*

Medicine (London, 1976); G. M. Foster and G. B. Anderson, *Medical Anthropology* (New York, 1978); J. M. Janzen, *The Quest for Therapy in Lower Zaire* (Los Angeles, 1978).

6 I use the words radical and conservative in their broadest everyday political sense.

7 See M. Chanock, 'The Political Economy of Independent Agriculture in Colonial Malawi', *Journal of Social Science* 1 (1972), and 'Ambiguities in the Malawian Political Tradition', *African Affairs* 74, (1975).

8 We might recall here Chinua Achebe's *leitmotif* novel *Things Fall Apart* (London, 1958) and the lines following the words of Achebe's title in Yeats' 'Second Coming': 'Mere anarchy is loosed upon the world . . . everywhere. The ceremony of innocence is drowned.'

9 M. Douglas, *The Lele of Kasai* (London, 1963) 223. M. Wilson's *For Men and Elders* (London, 1977), the most significant work yet of Central African social history, deals extensively with this problem.

10 A. L. Epstein, *Urbanisation and Kinship: The Domestic Domain on the Copperbelt of Zambia 1950–56* (London, 1981) 81, 100.

11 Ibid., 351, 158.

12 Ibid., 107–8.

13 Ibid., 243, 166–7.

14 Ibid., 188. He does tend to take for granted, however, the existence of the customary law in a traditional rural society. While this may be of use for the purposes of contrast when writing about urbanisation and change, it tends to obscure the conflicts about change and norm-formation present in rural societies both in the earlier period of colonial rule and at the time Epstein is writing about the urban areas.

15 Lewis Bandawe. See Chanock, 'Ambiguities', 345.

16 Chanock, 'Political Economy', 15. In the 1950s in Zambia the following ordinances were administered by the Native Courts:
The African Education Ordinance
The African Migrant Workers Ordinance
The Alien Natives Registration Ordinance
The Arms and Ammunition Ordinance
The Control of Bush Fires and Trespass Ordinance
The Control of Dogs Ordinance
The Cotton Ordinance
The Employment of Natives Ordinance
The Fauna Conservation Ordinance
The Fish Conservation Ordinance
The Forests Ordinance
The Game Ordinance
The Markets Ordinance
The Mine Townships Ordinance
The Municipal Corporations Ordinance
The Native Authority Ordinance
The Native Beer Ordinance
The Native Courts Ordinance
The Native Foodstuffs (Control of Acquisition) Ordinance
The Native Registration Ordinance
The Natural Resources Ordinance
The Native Tax Ordinance
The Notification of the Births of the Children of Africans Ordinance
The Prevention of Cruelty to Animals Ordinance
The Public Order Ordinance (Sections 4B, 4C, 5, 6 and 10(2))
The Stock Diseases Ordinance
The Townships Ordinance

Notes

The Tsetse Control Ordinance

17 Northern Rhodesia, Annual Reports Chinsali District 1948–1951, Rhodes House, *Mss Afr.* 971.

18 W. Clifford, *Criminal Cases in the Urban Native Courts of Northern Rhodesia* (Lusaka, 1960).

19 Nyasaland Protectorate Annual Reports, Judicial Department, 1953, 1959, 1963, 1964.

20 Clifford, *Criminal Cases*, 23, 16. The statutory definition of contempt included failing to pay an award of compensation ordered by a court, an attempt to deal with the tendency of people to ignore the orders of native courts which was alluded to in an earlier chapter.

21 T. O. Beidelman, 'Inter-Tribal Tensions in Some Local Government Courts in Colonial Tanganyika', *Journal of African Law* 10 (1966) 40. Under the native authority system the courts' officers were also local administrators and tax collectors and had therefore a wide range of extra-judicial sanctions available to enforce obedience.

22 Nyasaland, African Provincial Council, Central Province. Debates 5–7 May 1947. To overcome the increasing disadvantage they felt in the struggle to control the judicial machinery, they demanded a translation of the laws of the protectorate into Chinyanja, a demand which draws our attention to the neglect of any real attempt by the colonial government to publish the laws of the territory among those to whom they were applied.

23 E. Colson, 'The Impact of the Colonial Period on the Definition of Land Rights', in V. Turner (ed.), *Colonialism in Africa*, vol. 3: *Profiles of Change* (Cambridge, 1971). See too G. Kitching, *Class and Economic Change in Kenya* (New Haven, 1980) 204–6, on the 'effective absence' of customary rules on land tenure in pre-colonial Kenya.

24 Lord Hailey, *Native Administration in British African Territories: Nyasaland* (1950; London edn, 1979), 285–8.

25 Lord Hailey, *Confidential Report* (Nyasaland, 1942) 242.

26 Hailey, *Native Administration in British African Territories*, 30.

27 J. Iliffe, *A Modern History of Tanganyika* (Cambridge, 1979) 245.

28 Kitching, *Class and Economic Change*, 284–6, 282.

29 P. Mayer and I. Mayer, 'Land Law in the Making', in H. Kuper and L. Kuper (eds), *African Law Adaptation and Development* (Berkeley and Los Angeles, 1965) 67–9.

30 Hailey, *Native Administration in British African Territories*, 30–1.

31 Colson, 'Impact', 196–7.

32 Kitching, *Class and Economic Change*, 283, 285–6. The Mayers write, 'The content of traditional Kikuyu land law was much disputed; the copious literature on the subject reveals a notable failure to recognise the ideological basis of many versions put forward by Kikuyu informants.' 'Land Law in the Making', 76.

33 Colson, 'Impact', 196–7.

34 Colson, 'The Modern Political Organisation of the Tonga', 93.

35 E. Colson has discussed testamentary legislation and the effects of the introduction of written wills. For recent developments in Zambia see M. P. Mvunga, 'Law and Social Change: A Case Study in the Customary Law of Inheritance in Zambia', *African Social Research* 28 (1979).

36 R. Stokes, Annual Report Chinsali District 1952.

37 See M. Weber, *Economy and Society: An Outline of Interpretative Sociology*, ed. G. Roth and C. Wittich (New York, 1968) 677.

38 ZNA U2/3/2, 1931.

39 Iliffe, *History of Tanganyika*, 297.

40 N. Long, *Social Change and the Individual* (Manchester, 1968) 145.

41 H. Heisler, *Urbanisation and the Government of Migration* (London, 1974).

42 P. Fitzpatrick, *Law and State in Papua New Guinea* (London, 1980) 68.

43 This view is shared by some recent writers who fear that customary law, which they appreciate is still being formed around them, will become less adaptable to the development

270

process if it is written down. See B. O. Bryde, *The Politics and Sociology of African Legal Development* (Frankfurt am Main 1976) 108–9.

44 See e.g. R. Seidman, *The State, Law and Development* (London, 1978).

45 R. R. Marrett, quoted by L. Adams in L. H. Buxton (ed.), *Custom is King* (London, 1936) 120.

46 See O. Adewoye, *The Judicial System in Southern Nigeria* (London, 1971), for an account of African lawyers as a class in opposition to colonialism.

47 Quoted by S. Diamond, 'The Rule of Law as the Order of Custom', *Social Research* 38 (1971).

Bibliography

Abdullah Y.B. *The Yao*. Zomba, 1919. London edition ed. E. Alpers, 1973.

Abel, R. *Customary Law of Wrongs in Kenya: An Essay in Research Method*. Yale Law School Studies in Law and Modernisation No. 2. New Haven, n.d.

Achebe C. *Things Fall Apart*. London, 1958.

Adewoye O. *The Judicial System in Southern Nigeria*. London, 1971.

Allott A.N. *New Essays in African Law*. London, 1970.

Allott A.N. 'The Development of East African Legal Systems during the Colonial Period' in *History of East Africa*, vol. 3, ed. D.A. Low and A. Smith. London, 1976.

Alpers E. *Ivory and Slaves*. London, 1975.

Angus H.C. 'A Year in Azimba and Chipataland, 1895'. *Journal of the Royal Anthropological Institute* 27 (1898).

Arnot F.S. *Garenganze*. 1889. London edition, 1969.

Auerbach J.S. *Justice Without Law*. New York, 1983.

Baker T. 'Tax Collection in Malawi: An Administrative History'. *International Journal of African Historical Studies* 8 (1975).

Barnes J.A. 'Some Aspects of Political Development Among the Fort Jameson Ngoni'. *African Studies* 7 (1948).

Barnes J.A. *Marriage in a Changing Society*. London, 1951.

Barnes J.A. *Politics in a Changing Society*. Manchester, 1967.

Barnes L. *Empire and Democracy*. London, 1939.

Beidelman T.O. 'Inter-Tribal Tensions in Some Local Government Courts in Colonial Tanganyika'. *Journal of African Law* 10 (1966).

Bennett N.R. and Ylvisaker M. (eds) *The Central African Journal of Lovell J. Proctor, 1860–64*. Boston, 1971.

Berger E. *Labour, Race and Colonial Rule*. Oxford, 1974.

Bernstein H. and Depelchin J. 'The Object of African History: A Materialist Perspective (2)'. *History in Africa* 6 (1979).

Bhila H.H.K. 'The Role of Ngoni and Lomwe Labour in the Growth of the Plantation Economy in the Shire Highlands 1890–1912'. *Journal of Social Science* 5 (1976).

Birmingham D. 'The Forest and the Savannah'. *Cambridge History of Africa*, vol. 5, ed. J. Flint. Cambridge, 1979.

Bloch M. *Feudal Society*. London edition, 1965.

Bohannan P. *Justice and Judgement Among the Tiv*. London, 1957.

Bohmer C. 'Community Values, Domestic Tranquility and Customary Law in Upper Volta'. *Journal of Modern African Studies* 16 (1978).

Bradley K.R. *Handbook on Native Courts in Northern Rhodesia*. London, 1947.

Bradley K.R. *Native Courts and Authorities in Northern Rhodesia*. London, 1948.

272

Bradley K.R. *Diary of a District Officer*. London, 1966.
Bradley K.R. *Once a District Officer*. London, 1966.
Bryde B.O. *The Politics and Society of African Legal Development*. Frankfurt am Main, 1976.
Burton R.F. (trans.) *Lacerda's Journey to Kazembe in 1798*. London, 1873.
Butt G.E. *My Travels in North Western Rhodesia*. London, 1910.
Buxton L.H. (ed.) *Custom is King*. London, 1936.
Cameron Sir D. *My Tanganyika Service and Some Nigeria*. London, 1939.
Campbell B. *In the Heart of Bantuland*. London, 1922.
Canter R. 'Dispute Settlement and Dispute Processing in Zambia: Individual Choice versus Societal Constraints', in *The Disputing Process – Law in Ten Societies*, ed. L. Nader and H.F. Todd. New York, 1978.
Carter G. and Paden A. (eds) *Expanding Horizons in African Studies*. Evanston, 1969.
Cell J.W. (ed.) *By Kenya Possessed: The Correspondence of N. Leys and J.H. Oldham 1918–1916*. Chicago, 1976.
Chanock M.L. 'The Political Economy of Independent Agriculture in Colonial Malawi: The Great War to the Great Depression'. *Journal of Social Science* (1972).
Chanock M.L. 'Ambiguities in the Malawian Political Tradition'. *African Affairs* 74, (1975).
Chanock M.L. 'Neo-traditionalism and the Customary Law in Malawi'. *African Law Studies* 16 (1978).
Chanock M.L. 'Agricultural Change and Continuity in Malawi', in *The Roots of Rural Poverty*, ed. R. Palmer and N. Parsons. London, 1979.
Chanock M.L. 'Making Customary Law: Men, Women and Courts in Colonial Northern Rhodesia', in *African Women and the Law: Historical Perspectives*, ed. M. Hay and M. Wright. Boston, 1982.
Chanock M.L. 'Signposts or Tombstones? Some Reflections on Recent Works in the Anthropology of Law'. *Law in Context* 1 (1983).
Chauncey G. 'The Locus of Reproduction: Women's Labour in the Zambian Copperbelt 1927–53'. *Journal of Southern African Studies* 7 (1981).
Chirnside A. *The Blantyre Missionaries – Discreditable Disclosures*. London, 1880.
Clanchy M.T. 'Remembering the Past and the Good Old Law'. *History* 55 (1970).
Clanchy M.T. *From Memory to Written Record, England 1066–1307*. London, 1979.
Clarence-Smith W.G. 'Slaves, Commoners and Landlords.' *Journal of African History* 20 (1979).
Clifford W. *Criminal Cases in the Urban Native Courts of Northern Rhodesia*. Lusaka, 1960.
Codrington R. 'The Central Angoniland District of the British Central Africa 1893'. *Geographical Journal* (1898).
Coillard F. *On the Threshold of Central Africa*. London, 1897.
Collier J. Review of L. Fallers, *Law Without Precedent* in *American Anthropologist* 74 (1972).
Collier J. 'Legal Processes'. *Annual Review of Anthropology* 4 (1975).
Colson E. 'Modern Political Organisation of the Plateau Tonga'. *African Studies* 7 (1948).
Colson E. 'Possible Repercussions of the Right to Make Wills upon the Plateau Tonga of Northern Rhodesia'. *Journal of African Administration* 11 (1950).
Colson E. *Marriage and Family Among the Plateau Tonga of Northern Rhodesia*. Manchester, 1958.
Colson E. *The Plateau Tonga*. Manchester, 1962.
Colson E. 'African Society at the Time of the Scramble', in *Colonialism in Africa*, vol. 1, ed. L. Gann and P. Duignan. Cambridge, 1969.
Colson E. 'The Impact of the Colonial Period on the Definition of Land Rights', in *Colonialism in Africa*, vol. 3, ed. V. Turner. Cambridge, 1971.
Comaroff J.L. 'Bridewealth and the Control of Ambiguity in a Tswana Chiefdom', in *The Meaning of Marriage Payments*, ed. J. Comaroff. London, 1980.
Cooper F. 'The Problem of Slavery in African Studies', *Journal of African History* 20 (1979).

Bibliography

Cooper F. 'Peasants, Capitalists and Historians: Review Article'. *Journal of Southern African Studies* 7 (1981).

Cory, H. *Sukuma Law and Custom*. London, 1953.

Cory H. and Hartnoll M. *Customary Law of the Haya Tribe*. London, 1945.

Coxhead J.C.C. 'The Native Tribes of North Eastern Rhodesia: Their Laws and Customs'. *Journal of the Royal Anthropological Institute*, Occasional Paper no. 5. London, 1914.

Cullen-Young T. 'Tribal Intermixture in Northern Nyasaland'. *Journal of the Royal Anthropological Institute* 63 (1933).

Cullen-Young T. 'Habits and Customs of the Olden Days Among the Tumbuka-Kamanga People'. *Bantu Studies* 10 (1936).

Cullen-Young T. and Banda H.K. *Our African Way of Life*. London, 1946.

Cullen-Young T. and Melland F. *African Dilemmas*. London, 1937.

Culwick A.T. *Good out of Africa*. Rhodes–Livingstone Paper 8. Livingstone, 1942.

Culwick A.T. and Culwick G.M. *Ubena of the Rivers*. London, 1935.

Davidson B. *The Africans*. London, 1973.

Davies S.G. 'The Growth of Law in the Gold Coast'. *Journal of African Administration* 9 (1957).

Davis J.M. *Modern Industry and the African*. 1933; London edn, 1967.

Decle L. *Three Years in Savage Africa*. 1900; Bulawayo edn, 1974.

Diamond A.S. *Primitive Law*. London, 1935.

Diamond S. 'The Rule of Law versus the Order of Custom'. *Social Research* 38 (1971).

Doke C.M. *The Lambas*. London, 1931.

Douglas M. *The Lele of Kasai*. London, 1963.

Douglas M. 'Matriliny and Pawnship in Central Africa'. *Africa* 34 (1964).

Douglas M. 'Witch Beliefs in Central Africa'. *Africa* 37 (1967).

Driberg J.H. 'The African Conception of Law'. *Journal of Comparative and International Law* 16 (1934).

Drummond H. *Tropical Africa*. London, 1888.

Duff H. *Nyasaland Under the Foreign Office*. London, 1903.

Duff H. *African Small Chop*. London, 1932.

Dundas C. 'The Organisation and Laws of Some Bantu Tribes in East Africa'. *Journal of the Royal Anthropological Institute* 45 (1915).

Dundas C. 'Native Laws of Some Bantu Tribes of East Africa'. *Journal of the Royal Anthropological Institute* 51 (1921).

Dundas C. *African Crossroads*. London, 1935.

Elias T.O. *The Nature of African Customary Law*. Manchester, 1956.

Epstein A.L. 'Divorce Law and the Stability of Marriage Among the Lunda of Kazembe'. *Rhodes–Livingstone Journal* 14 (1954).

Epstein A.L. *Politics in an Urban African Community*. Manchester, 1958.

Epstein A.L. *Juridical Techniques and the Judicial Process*. Rhodes–Livingstone Paper no. 23 (1954). Manchester, 1964.

Epstein A.L. *Urbanisation and Kinship, The Domestic Domain on the Copperbelt of Zambia 1950–1956*. London, 1981.

Erikson K.T. *Wayward Puritans*. New York, 1966.

Fabrega H. 'Medical Anthropology'. *Annual Review of Anthropology* 1 (1972).

Fallers L. *Law Without Precedent*. Chicago, 1969.

Fitzpatrick P. *Law and State in Papua New Guinea*. London, 1980.

Foster G.M. and Anderson G.B. (eds) *Medical Anthropology*. New York, 1978.

Franklin H. *The Flagwagger*. London, 1974.

Fraser D. *The Future of Africa*. London, 1912.

Fraser D. *Winning a Primitive People*. London, 1914; New York edn, 1970.

Fraser D. *African Idylls*. London, 1923.

Fraser D. *The Autobiography of an African*. London, 1925.

Galanter M. 'The Aborted Restoration of Indigenous Law in India'. *Comparative Studies in Society and History* 14 (1972).

Gammitto A.P.C. *King Kazembe*, trans. I. Cunnison. Lisbon, 1969.

Gann L. *The Birth of a Plural Society*. Manchester, 1958.

Gluckman M. *The Judicial Process Among the Barotse*. Manchester, 1965.

Gluckman M. (ed.) *Ideas and Procedures in African Customary Law*. London, 1969.

Gluckman M. *The Ideas in Barotse Jurisprudence*. Manchester, 1972.

Gordon J. 'Law and the African Historian'. *Journal of African History* 8 (1967).

Gordon R.W. 'Historicism in Legal Scholarship'. *Yale Law Journal* 90 (1981).

Gouldsbury C. and Sheane H. *The Great Plateau of Northern Rhodesia*. London, 1911.

Gulliver P.H. *Labour Migration in a Dual Economy*. Kampala, 1955.

Gulliver P.H. *Social Control in an African Society*. London, 1963.

Gulliver P.H. (ed.) *Cross-examinations, Essays in Memory of Max Gluckman*. Leiden, 1978.

Guyer, J.I. 'Household and Community in African Studies'. *African Studies Review* 24 (1981).

Hailey, Lord *African Survey*. London, 1938.

Hailey, Lord *Native Administration in British African Territories: Nyasaland*. 1950; London edn, 1979.

Hailey, Lord *Native Administration and Political Development in British Tropical Africa 1940–42*, ed. A. Kirk Greene, Nendeln, 1979.

Hanna A.J. *The Beginnings of Nyasaland and North Eastern Rhodesia 1859–95*. London, 1969.

Hannigan A. St J. 'The Impact of English Law upon the Existing Gold Coast Custom'. *Journal of African Administration* 8 (1956).

Hannigan A. St J. 'The Imposition of Western Law Forms on Primitive Societies'. *Comparative Studies in Society and History* 3 (1961).

Harrington H.T. 'The Taming of North Eastern Rhodesia'. *Northern Rhodesia Journal* 3 (1955).

Hartland E.S. *Primitive Law*. London, 1924.

Heisler H. *Urbanisation and the Government of Migration: The Interaction of Urban and Rural Life in Zambia*. London, 1974.

Hetherwick A. 'Some Animistic Beliefs Among the Yao of British Central Africa'. *Journal of the Royal Anthropological Institute* 32 (1902).

Hetherwick A. (ed.) *Robert Hellier Napier in Nyasaland*. Edinburgh, 1925.

Hetherwick A. *The Romance of Blantyre*. London, 1931.

Hetherwick A. *The Gospel and the African*. Edinburgh, 1932.

Hine J.E. *Days Gone By*. London, 1924.

Hobsbawm E. and Ranger T. (eds)*The Invention of Tradition*. Cambridge, 1983.

Hodgson A. 'Notes on the Achewa and Ngoni District in the Nyasaland Protectorate'. *Journal of the Royal Anthropological Institute* 63 (1926).

Hogbin L. *Law and Order in Polynesia*. London, 1934.

Hooker J. 'Witnesses and Watchtower in Rhodesia and Nyasaland'. *Journal of African History* 5 (1963).

Hooker J. 'Tradition and "Traditional Courts". Malawi's Experiment in Law'. *American University Fieldstaff Reports*, vol. 15, no. 3 (March 1971).

Hooker M. *Legal Pluralism*. Oxford, 1975.

Hooker M. *Adat Law in Modern Indonesia*. Oxford, 1979.

Hopkins E. 'The Politics of Crime: Aggression and Control in a Colonial Context'. *American Anthropologist* 75 (1975).

Howell P.P. *A Manual of Nuer Law*. London, 1954.

Ibik J.O. *Malawi 1. The Law of Marriage and Divorce. Re-statement of African Law* (3). London, 1970.

Iliffe J. *A Modern History of Tanganyika*. Cambridge, 1979.

Janzen J. M. *The Quest for Therapy in Lower Zaire*. Los Angeles, 1978.

Bibliography

Johnson W.P. *Nyasa: The Great Water*. London, 1922.
Johnson W.P. *My African Reminiscences 1875–1895*. London, 1926.
Johnston J. *Reality vs Romance in South-Central Africa*. 1893; London edn, 1969.
Jordan E.K. 'Namwalia in 1906'. *Northern Rhodesia Journal* 2 (1954).
Kadzamira Z. 'Local Politics and Administration During the Colonial Period in Malawi'. *Journal of Social Science* 3 (1974).
Kandawire J.A.K. 'Village and Class in Southern Malawi'. *Africa* 50 (1980).
Kern F. *Kingship and Law in the Middle Ages*. London, 1939.
Kidd D. *Kafir Socialism*. London, 1908.
Kilekwa P. *From Slave Boy to Priest*. London, 1937.
Kitching G. *Class and Economic Change in Kenya*. New Haven, 1980.
Klein M.A. 'The Study of Slavery in Africa'. *Journal of African History* 19 (1978).
Krader L. *The Ethnological Notebooks of Karl Marx*. Assen, 1979.
Kuper H. and Kuper L. (ed.) *African Law. Adaptation and Development*. Berkeley, 1965.
Lancaster C. 'Brideservice, Residence and Authority among the Goba (N. Shona) of the Zambesi Valley'. *Africa* 44 (1974).
Lancaster C. 'Gwembwe Valley Marriage Prestations in Historical Perspective; A Rejoinder to Colson and Scudder'. *American Anthropologist* 82 (1981).
Laws R. *Reminiscences of Livingstonia*. London, 1934.
Lewin J. 'Native Courts and British Justice in Africa'. *Africa* 14 (1943–4).
Lewin J. *Studies in African Law*. 1947; Philadelphia edn, 1971.
Linden I. (ed.) 'Mponda Mission Diary'. *International Journal of African Historical Studies* 7 (1974).
Linden I. with Linden J. *Catholics, Peasants and Chewa Resistance in Nyasaland*. London, 1974.
Livingstone D. *The Last Journals*. London, 1974.
Llewellyn K. and Hoebel E. *The Cheyenne Way*. Norman, 1941.
Long N. *Social Change and the Individual*. Manchester, 1968.
Lonsdale J. 'States and Social Processes in Africa: A Historiographical Survey'. *African Studies Review* 24 1981.
Lovejoy P. 'Indigenous African Slavery', in *Roots and Branches: Current Directions in Slave Studies*, ed. M. Craton. Toronto, 1979.
Low D.A. (ed.) *The Mind of Buganda*. London, 1971.
Lugard F. *The Dual Mandate in British Tropical Africa*. 5th edn, London, 1922.
McCaskie T.C. 'State and Society, Marriage and Adultery: Some Considerations Towards a Social History of Pre-colonial Asante'. *Journal of African History* 22 (1981).
McCracken J. *Politics and Christianity in Malawi 1875–1940: The Impact of the Livingstonia Mission in the Northern Province*. Cambridge 1977.
MacDonald D. *Africana or the Heart of Heathen Africa*. London, 1882.
MacDonald J. 'East Central African Customs'. *Journal of the Royal Anthropological Institute* 22 (1895).
MacGaffey W. *Custom and Government in the Lower Congo*. Berkeley, 1970.
MacGaffey W. 'Lineage Structure, Marriage and the Family Amongst the Central Bantu'. *Journal of African History* 24 (1983).
Mackenzie D. *The Spirit-Ridden Konde*. London, 1925.
Maclean N. *Africa in Transformation*. London, 1914
Macmillan H. *The Tides of Fortune*. London, 1969.
Maine H. *Ancient Law*. London, 1861.
Maine H. *Dissertations on Early Law and Custom*. London, 1883.
Mair L. 'Marriage and Family in the Dedza District of Nyasaland'. *Journal of the Royal Anthropological Institute* 81 (1951).
Mair L. *African Marriage and Social Change*. London, 1969.

Maitland F.S. 'Why the History of English Law Was Not Written'. Cambridge, 1888 (in *Frederick William Maitland Historian*, ed. R.L. Schuyler. Cambridge, 1980).

Malinowski B. *Crime and Custom in Savage Society*. London, 1926.

Maples E. *Chauncey Maples*. London, 1897.

Maples E. (ed.) *The Journals and Papers of Chauncey Maples*. London, 1899.

Maquet J. *Africanity*. New York, 1972.

Marks S. and Rathbone R. 'The History of the Family in Africa: Introduction'. *Journal of African History* 24 (1983).

Marwick M. *Sorcery in its Social Setting*. Manchester, 1965.

Matthews T.I. 'Portuguese, Chikunda and Peoples of the Gwembwe Valley: The Impact of the "Lower Zambesi Complex" on Southern Zambia'. *Journal of African History* 23 (1981).

Maugham R.C.F. *Portuguese Africa*. London, 1906.

Meebelo H.S. *Reaction to Colonialism*. Manchester, 1971.

Meek C.K. *Law and Authority in a Nigerian Tribe*. London, 1937; New York edn, 1970.

Melland F. 'Ethical and Political Aspects of Witchcraft'. *Africa* 8 (1935).

Melland F. *In Witchbound Africa*. London, 1923; New York edn, 1967.

Miers S. and Kopytoff P. (eds) *Slavery in Africa: Historical and Anthropological Perspectives*. Madison, 1977.

Mitchell P. *African Afterthoughts*. London, 1954.

Moggeridge L.T. 'The Nyasaland Tribes, their Customs, and their Poison Ordeal'. *Journal of the Royal Anthropological Institute* 32 (1902).

Moir F.L.M. *After Livingstone: An African Trade Romance*. London, n.d.

Moore S.F. 'Politics, Procedures and Norms in Changing Chagga Law'. *Africa* 40 (1970).

Moore S.F. *Law as Process*. London, 1978.

Morris H.F. and Read J.S. *Indirect Rule and the Search for Justice*. London, 1972.

Morrison J. *Streams in the Desert*. New York, 1919.

Munro J.F. *Colonial Rule and the Kamba*. Oxford, 1975.

Murray C. 'Migrant Labour and Changing Family Structure in the Rural Peripheries of Southern Africa'. *Journal of Southern African Studies* 2 (1980).

Mvunga M.P. 'Law and Social Change: A Case Study in the Customary Law of Inheritance in Zambia'. *African Social Research* 28 (1979).

Mwase G.S. *Strike a Blow and Die*, ed. R. Rotberg. Cambridge, Mass., 1967.

Mwashitete *Ways I Have Trodden*. London, 1932.

Nader L. and Todd H. (eds) *The Disputing Process: Law in Ten Societies*. New York, 1978.

Nekam A. *Experiences in African Customary Law*. Edinburgh, 1966.

Nkrumah K. 'Address on Opening the Ghana Law School 1962'. *Journal of African Law* 6 (1962).

Ntara S. *Headman's Enterprise*. London, 1949.

Ntara S. *The History of the Chewa*, trans. W.S.K. Jere. Wiesbaden, 1973.

Nyirenda S. 'History of the Tumbuka-Henga People'. trans. T.C. Young. *Bantu Studies* 5 (1931).

Ojwang J.B. 'Rural Dispute Settlement in Kenya'. *Zambia Law Journal* 7–9 (1975–7).

O'Neill H.E. 'A Three Month Journey in the Makua and Lomwe Countries'. *Proceedings of the Royal Geographical Society* 4 (1889).

Orde-Browne G. St J. 'Witchcraft and British Colonial Law'. *Africa* 8 (1935).

Palley C. *The Constitutional Law and History of Southern Rhodesia*. Oxford, 1966.

Pandey B.N. *The Introduction of British Law into India*. London, 1967.

Parkin D.J. 'Medicines and Men of Influence'. *Man* 3 (1968).

Parkin D.J. 'Kind Bridewealth and Hard Cash', in *The Meaning of Marriage Payments*, ed. J. Comaroff. London, 1980.

Penwill D.J. *Kamba Customary Law*. London, 1951.

Perham M. (ed.) *Ten Africans*. London, 1936.

277

Bibliography

Perrings C. *Black Mineworkers in Central Africa*. New York, 1979.

Philips A. *Survey of African Marriage and Family Life*. London, 1953.

Phiri K.M. 'Some Changes in the Matrilineal Family System Among the Chewa of Malawi Since the 19th Century'. *Journal of African History* 24 (1983).

Poewe K.O. 'Matriliny in the Throes of Change'. *Africa* 48 (1978).

Prins G. *The Hidden Hippopotamus*. Cambridge, 1980.

Randolph B.W. *Arthur Douglas: Missionary on Lake Nyasa*. London, 1912.

Ranger T. 'Reflections on Peasant Research in Central and Southern Africa'. *Journal of Southern African Studies* 5 (1978).

Ranger T. and Weller J. (eds) *Themes in the Christian History of Central Africa*. London, 1975.

Rankin D.J. *The Zambian Basin and Nyasaland*. Edinburgh and London, 1893.

Rattray R.S. *Some Folklore, Stories and Songs in Chinyanja*. London, 1907.

Rattray R.S. *Ashanti Law and Constitution*. Oxford, 1929.

Read M. 'Tradition and Prestige Among the Ngoni'. *Africa* 9 (1936).

Read M. 'The Moral Code of the Ngoni and their Former Military State'. *Africa* 11 (1938).

Read M. 'The Ngoni and Western Education', in *Colonialism in Africa*, vol. 3, ed. V. Turner. Cambridge, 1971.

Redfield R. 'Primitive Law', in *Law and Warfare*, ed. P. Bohannan. New York, 1967.

Redmond P. 'Some Results of Military Contacts between the Ngoni and their Neighbours in 19th Century Southern East Africa'. *Trans African Journal of History* 5 (1976).

Richards A.I. 'A Modern Movement of Witchfinders'. *Africa* 8 (1935).

Richards A.I. 'The Story of Bwembya of the Bemba Tribe', in *Ten Africans*, ed. M. Perham. London, 1936.

Richards A.I. *Land, Labour and Diet in Northern Rhodesia*. London, 1939.

Richards A.I. *Bemba Marriage and Present Economic Conditions*. Rhodes–Livingstone Paper no. 4. Livingstone, 1940.

Roberts A.D. *A History of the Bemba*. London, 1973.

Roberts A.D. *A History of Zambia*. London, 1976.

Roberts C.C. 'Witchcraft and Colonial Legislation'. *Africa* 8 (1935).

Roberts C.C. *Tangled Justice: Some Reasons for a Change of Policy in Africa*. London, 1937.

Roberts S. 'Matrilineal Family Law and Custom in Malawi'. *Journal of African Law* 8 (1964).

Roberts S. (ed.) *Law and the Family in Africa*. The Hague, 1977.

Roberts S. *Order and Dispute*. Harmondsworth, 1979.

Roberts-Wray, Sir Kenneth 'The Adaptation of Imported Law in Africa'. *Journal of African Law* 4 (1960).

Rosen L. 'Law and Social Change in the New Nations'. *Comparative Studies in Society and History* 20 (1978).

Rothman D.J. *The Discovery of Asylum*. Boston, 1971.

Rowlands J.S. 'Notes on Native Law and Custom in Kenya'. *Journal of African Law* 6 (1962).

Rowley H. *The Story of the Universities Mission to Central Africa*. London, 1867; New York edn, 1965.

Rowley H. *Africa Unveiled*. London, 1876.

Rowley H. *20 Years in Central Africa*. London, 1889.

Rubin N. and Cotran E. (eds) *Readings in African Law 1*. New York, 1970.

Rudolph S.I. and Rudolph L.H. *The Modernity of Tradition*. Chicago, 1967.

Sachs A. *Justice in South Africa*. London, 1973.

Sack P. *Land Between the Laws*. Canberra, 1973.

Sarbah J.M. *Fanti Customary Law*. 2nd edn, London, 1904.

Schapera I. *A Handbook of Tswana Law and Custom*. London, 1938.

Schapera I. *Married Life in an African Tribe*. 1940; Evanston edition, 1966.

Schiller A. 'African Law', in *The African World: A Survey of Social Research*, ed. R.A. Lystad. New York, 1965.

278

Schoffeleers J. 'The Interaction of the Mbona Cult and Christianity 1859–1963', in *Themes in the Christian History of Central Africa*, ed T. Ranger and J. Weller. London, 1975.

Seidman R.B. *The State, Law and Development*. London, 1978.

Sellin T. 'Slavery and the Punishment of Crime'. *Crime, Criminology and Public Policy*, ed. R. Hood. London, 1974.

Simm A.F. *Life and Letters*. London, 1896.

Simon H.J. *African Women: Their Legal Status in South Africa*. London, 1968.

Smith D.M. 'Man and Law in Urban Africa: A Role for Customary Courts in the Urbanisation Process'. *American Journal of Comparative Law* 20 (1972).

Smith E.W. and Dale A.M. *The Ila-Speaking Peoples of Northern Rhodesia*. London, 1920; New York edn, 1968.

Snell G.S. *Nandi Customary Law*. London, 1981.

Snyder F. 'Law and Development in the Light of Dependency Theory'. *Law and Society Review* 14 (1980).

Snyder F. *Capitalism and Legal Change*. London, 1981.

Snyder F. 'Colonialism and Legal Form: The Creation of "Customary Law" in Senegal'. *Journal of Legal Pluralism* 19 (1981).

Southall A. (ed.) *Social Change in Modern Africa*. London, 1961.

Spalding F.O. with Hoover E.C. and Piper J.C. 'One Nation One Judiciary: The Lower Courts of Zambia'. *Zambia Law Journal* 2 (1970).

Stannus H.G. *The WaYao of Nyasaland*, Harvard African Studies, vol. 3. Cambridge, Mass., 1922.

Starke D.W. *Barotseland: Eight Years Among the Barotse*. London, 1922; New York edn, 1969.

Starr J. and Yngvesson B. 'Scarcity and Disputing: Zeroing in on Compromise Decisions'. *American Ethnologist* 2 (1975).

Stokes E. *Stories of Old Times*. London, 1932.

Stokes E. *The English Utilitarians and India*. Oxford, 1959.

Strickland D.A. 'Kingship and Slavery in African Thought'. *Comparative Studies in Society and History* 18 (1976).

Swann A.J. *Fighting the Slave Hunters*. London, 1910; New York edn, 1969.

Tew M. *Peoples of the Lake Nyasa Region*. London, 1950.

Thomas T.M. *Eleven Years in Central Africa*. London, 1872.

Thompson E.P. *Whigs and Hunters*. London, 1975.

Turner V.W. *Schism and Continuity in an African Society*. Manchester, 1957.

Vail H.L. 'Ecology and History: The Example of Eastern Zambia'. *Journal of Southern African Studies* 3 (1977).

Vail H.L. 'The Political Economy of East Central Africa', in *History of Central Africa*, vol. 2, ed. D. Birmingham and P. Martin. London, 1983.

van Binsbergen W.M.J. 'The Dynamics of Religious Change in Western Zambia'. *Ufahamu* 6 (1976).

van Binsbergen W.M.J. 'Law in the Context of Nkoya Society'. *Law and the Family in Africa*, ed. S. Roberts. The Hague, 1977.

van Binsbergen W.M.J. 'The Unit of Study and the Interpretation of Ethnicity'. *Journal of Southern African Studies* 8 (1981).

Vansina J. 'A Traditional Legal System, The Kuba', in *African Law: Adaptation and Development*, ed. H. Kuper and L. Kuper. Berkeley and Los Angeles, 1965.

Vansina J. 'The Bushong Poison Ordeal', in *Man in Africa*, ed. M. Douglas and P. Kaberry. London, 1969.

van Velsen J. *The Politics of Kinship*. Manchester, 1957.

van Velsen J. 'Procedural Informality, Reconciliation and False Comparisons', in *Ideas and Procedures in African Customary Law*, ed. M. Gluckman. London, 1969.

Bibliography

Ward-Price H.L. *Dark Subjects*. London, 1939.
Warner E. *Trial by Sasswood*. London, 1959.
Watson W. *Tribal Cohesion in a Money Economy*. Manchester 1958.
Washbrook D.A. 'Law, State and Agrarian Society in Colonial India'. *Modern Asian Studies* 15 (1981).
Weber M. *Economy and Society: An Outline of Interpretative Sociology*, ed. G. Roth and C. Wittich. New York, 1968.
Welsh D. *The Roots of Segregation*. Cape Town, 1971.
Werner A. *The Natives of British Central Africa*. London, 1906.
Willis R.G. 'Kamcape: An Anti-Sorcery Movement in South-West Tanzania'. *Africa* 38 (1968).
Wilson G. 'An African Morality'. *Africa* 9 (1936).
Wilson G. 'An Introduction to Nyakyusa Law'. *Africa* 10 (1937).
Wilson G. *The Constitution of Ngonde*. Livingstone, 1939.
Wilson G. *The Economics of Detribalisation in Northern Rhodesia*, 2 parts. Livingstone, 1941–2.
Wilson J.L. *Western Africa*. London, 1856.
Wilson M. *Good Company*. London, 1951.
Wilson M. *For Men and Elders*. London, 1977.
Winspear F. 'Some Reminiscences of Nyasaland'. *Nyasaland Journal* 13 (1960).
Wissman H.V. *My Second Journey Through Equatorial Africa from the Congo to the Zambesi 1886–7* (English translation). London, 1911.
Wright M. *German Missions in Tanganyika*. Oxford, 1971.
Wright M. 'Women in Peril'. *African Social Research* 20 (1975).
Young E.D. *Nyassa: A Journal of Adventures*. London, 1877.
Young R., Paden J.M. and Soja C.W. (eds) *The African Experience*, vol. 1, Evanston, 1970.

Archival sources

Malawi National Archives (MNA) to 1931.
Zambia National Archives (ZNA) to 1945.
Colonial Office files (CO). Nyasaland 1931 to 1945.

Official publications

Nyasaland Annual Reports
Nyasaland Handbook (1932)
Nyasaland Law Reports
Nyasaland Provincial Council Debates
Nyasaland Legislative Council Debates
Malawi Parliamentary Debates
Northern Rhodesia Annual Reports
Northern Rhodesia African Representative Council Debates
Northern Rhodesia Legislative Council Debates
Zambia Parliamentary Debates
Cape Colony 1883. *Report on Native Law and Custom*
Kenya 1944. *Report on Native Tribunals*
East Africa. 1906–9 *Law Reports*
Tanganyika 1963. *African Conference on Local Courts and Customary Law*
Great Britain 1934. *Report on the Royal Commission of Enquiry into the Administration of Justice in Kenya, Uganda and Tanganyika in Criminal Matters* (Cmd 4623)
Great Britain 1935–7. *Correspondence Relating to the Welfare of Women in Tropical Africa* (Cmd 5784)
Great Britain 1942. Hailey, Lord. *Confidential Report*, Nyasaland.

Newspapers

South African Pioneer
Central African Mission Report

Unpublished

Belcher, Sir Charles *Reminiscences*. Manuscript in Rhodes House Library, Oxford.

Bwalya S. 'Customs and Habits of the Bemba'. Rhodes House *Mss Afr*.

Hoole M.C. 'Report on the Recommendations for the Organisation of the Native Administrations of the Lilongwe District 23/11/37'. Rhodes House *Mss Afr*. s. 997.

Hugo G.F. 'Aanknopingspunte vir die Evangelie by die Achewa met spesiaale betreking tot die voorbereiding van die jeug vir hul plek in die stamlewe'. M. Th. Stellenbosch, 1953.

Ibik J.O. 'The Laws of Marriage in Nyasaland'. Ph. D. Thesis. London, 1966.

Keet D.L. 'The African Representative Council, 1946–58'. M.A. Thesis. University of Zambia, 1975.

Malekebu D. 'A Plea for Africa'. Malawi National Archive.

Maliwa E. 'Customary Law and the Administration of Justice in Malawi'. M. Phil. Thesis. London, 1967.

Maliwa E. 'The Legal Status of Women in Malawi from the Colonial Period to Independence'. Ph. D. Thesis. London, 1970.

Mumba L. 'The Administration of Justice in Nyasaland'. Malawi National Archive.

Phiri K.M. 'Chewa History in Central Malawi and the Use of Oral Tradition'. Ph.D. Thesis. Wisconsin, 1975.

Rau W. 'Mpeseni's Ngoni of Eastern Zambia 1870–1920'. Ph.D. Thesis. U.C.L.A., 1974.

Roberts S. 'The Growth of an Integrated Legal System in Malawi'. Ph.D. Thesis. London, 1967.

Ross, Sir Charles *Memoirs*. Manuscript in Rhodes House Library, Oxford.

Speck S.W. 'African Local Government in Malawi: Its Development and Politics Under British Rule'. Ph.D. Thesis. Harvard, 1969.

Stokes R. Annual Reports Chinsali District, Northern Rhodesia, 1948–1951, and 'Some Notes on Native Law and Procedure and its Development Under Modern Social Conditions'. Rhodes House, *Mss Afr*. 971.

Stuart R.G. 'Christianity and the Chewa: The Anglican Case 1885–1950'. Ph.D. Thesis. London, 1970.

Universities Mission to Central Africa. *Marriage Cases*. 1922.

University of York. Centre for Southern African Studies. Archive. Papers of J.P. Murray and Sir Kenneth Bradley.

Wanda B. 'Colonialism, Nationalism and Tradition. The Evolution and Development of the Legal System of Malawi'. Ph.D. Thesis. London, 1979.

Index

Abdullah, Y. B., 88, 126–7
adat, in Indonesia, 63–4
adultery, 78, 116, 147–8, 179, 192–201
African Methodist Episcopal Church, 207
African Representative Council (Zambia), 139–40, 213
agriculture, market, 4, 11–14, 38–9, 42, 235
  regulation of, 120, 122, 229, 236
Allott, A. N., 59, 60, 65
anthropology, 25–47, 219–24
  of disputing, 220–1
  feminist, 221
  functionalist, 3, 19, 25–32, 219–20
  and indirect rule, 25–7
  legal, 25–47, 219–24, 236–7
  of medicine, 223–4
Arnot, F. S., 81, 92
askaris, 105, 130
Austin, John, 25, 30

Banda, H. K., 211, 214
Barnes, J. A., 35, 119, 178–9, 182, 188–90, 214
Beaufort J., 108, 154–5
  R v. *Uliakawa*, 196–7
Bemba, 125, 163, 250 n. 10
  adultery, 194
  chieftaincy, 22–3
  marriage, 188–9
Bible, 79, 81–2, 128, 256–7 n. 16
Blantyre mission, 79, 80, 82
Bohannan, P., 30
Boma, definition of, 244 n. 28
Booth, J., 82
Botswana (Bechuanaland Protectorate), 53
bridewealth, 37, *172–85*, 197–8, 202, 204–5, 214–15
Bushe, H. G., 50

Cameron, Sir Donald, 60
Catholics

and divorce, 152, 155, 260 n. 38
Chewa
  adultery, 195, 197, 202
  chieftaincy, 90
  judicial institutions, 6, 34
  marriage and Ngoni, 90, 96, 149, 173–5, 179
  slavery, 163–8
  women, 38, 78, 90, 96
chiefs
  administration of justice, 137–8
  adultery, 195–6
  judicial powers of, 18–20, 22–3, 33–5, 45, 112
  marriage 188–9
Chikulamayembe, 238
Chikusi, 89–90
children
  custody 215–16
  discipline, 126
  labour, 14, 38
  slavery, 168
Chilembwe, John, 82, 130
Christians, 130, 135, 202
  crime and sin, 128–30
  and customs, 76, 80
  law, 81–2
  marriage, 82, *150–9*
Church courts, 132, *150–9*
Church of Central Africa Presbyterian (C.C.A.P.), 79, 80, 82
Civil cases, 111
  non-enforcement of judgement in, 116–17
class, 13, 66, 235–6
codification, 41, 53, 56, 63, 136, 139–40, 188
Codrington, R. E., 108
Coillard, F., 82, 92, 146
Colson, E., 15, 34, 38–9, 77, 98, 117–18, 176, 181, 231–3
conflict of laws, 59, 62, 64
contempt of court, 117–18, 230
contract, 14, 224

282

Index

Index

Scott, D. C., 80
settlers, 79
Sim, Arthur, 83–4
sin, 80–2, 128–30
Sitambuli, A., 213
slavery, 15, 21–2, 46, 83, 160–71
  abolition of, 166–71
  and children, 168
  and Christianity, 156–7
  and compensation, 127, 163, 261–2 n. 17
  and marriage, 46, 81, 156–7, 161–71, 186
  and ordealing, 88–9
  slave trade, 57, 163–4
  and witchcraft, 86
Snyder, F. S., 42, 66
sorcery, see witchcraft
state and law, 34–6, 221–3, 236
  pre-colonial, 18–19, 32–4
statute law, 114–15, 120–2, 205, 229–30, 269–70
Swann, A. J., 72, 83, 166

Tanganyika, 20, 50, 60, 77, 100, 129, 252 n. 12
taxation, 106, 108, 230
  and marriage, 172, 206
tenants, labour service, 109
Ten Commandments, 78, 82, 256 n. 16
Tonga
  lakeside, 32–3, 170, 174–5
  plateau, 118, 181–2
traditions, 3, 8, 46
tribe, 9, 18, 20–1
  see also ethnicity
Tumbuka, 82, 102, 127, 138, 147, 166
Turner, V., 32, 34, 36, 38, 160, 170

Universities Mission to Central Africa
  (U.M.C.A.) 79–84, 128–9, 155–9, 204–5
urban, 11

life, 193, 199, 227–8
marriage, 180, 206
workers, control of, 192–3

Vagrancy Act, 94, 108
van Velsen J., 32–3
villages and customary law, 21, 23, 42

war, 1914–18, 11
Watchtower Movement, 114, 264 n. 2
Watson, W., 33
Weber, M., 222, 234
White Fathers, 90–1
Wilson, M., 35, 100, 176, 264 n. 13
witchcraft, 21, 82, 85–101
  proclamations, 94
  and property, 36–7
women
  adultery, 147–8, 192–201
  atitudes towards, 38
  behaviour, 126, 202–3, 236
  bridewealth and status, 175–82
  Christianity, 150–9
  consent to marriage, 186, 193, 205–6, 208
  control of movement of, 113, 207, 212
  and courts, 39, 104, 145–50
  deportation from urban areas, 192–3
  inheritance of, 147, 167, 182–6
  labour of, 14, 38–9
  marriage registration, 207–8, 211–12
  Native Authority Courts and, 115, 186–91
  and property, 37
  revolt of, 236
  and slavery, 165–70
  and urban areas, 192–3, 227–8
Writing, see literacy, law and

Yao, 39, 88, 90–1, 94, 163, 165–6, 170, 187, 251 n. 51

286